Korea

ART AND
ARCHAEOLOGY

Korea

ART AND
ARCHAEOLOGY

Jane Portal

Thames & Hudson

Dedicated to my parents and
parents-in-law, with thanks

First published in paperback in
the United States of America
in 2000 by Thames & Hudson Inc.,
500 Fifth Avenue, New York,
New York 10110

Published by arrangement with
the British Museum Press

Library of Congress Catalog Card Number
99-66554

ISBN 0-500-28202-1

Designed and typeset in Minion
and Meta by Harry Green
Printed in Italy by Imago

PREVIOUS PAGES
A garden in one of the Choson dynasty
royal palaces of Seoul, capital of Korea
from the late 14th century onwards.

RIGHT
Mount Paektu and Heaven Lake. Korea's
holy mountain, site of its creation myth,
is the source of both the Amnok (Yalu)
and Tuman rivers, which form the greater
part of its border with China.

Contents

Preface

This book is intended to inform and enthuse non-specialists about the long-neglected subject of Korean art and archaeology. It precedes and complements the opening at the British Museum of a permanent gallery for Korean art, thanks to the generosity of the Korea Foundation.

Accidents of history have led to a neglect of the study of Korean culture, with the result that most people in the West have very little idea of its long and illustrious history. I have attempted, in this book, to redress the balance a little, with the aim of encouraging readers to explore the subject further. With such a long period of history to cover, I can only hope to introduce and summarize some areas and there are bound to be simplifications and omissions. North Korea for example is not included in the contemporary section, due to lack of available information.

I am indebted to many people who have helped and continue to help my study and developing understanding of Korea. I am very aware that, as a foreigner, my interpretation of some aspects of Korean culture will be different from that of Korean scholars. I trust that there is room for both approaches and for openness and generosity in disagreement.

This project originated with a meeting in Kyongju in 1983 between Han Byong-sam and Sir David Wilson, and I would like to acknowledge their encouragement with thanks. Since then, I have been supported and encouraged by the Director of the National Museum of Korea, Chung Yang-mo, the Director of the British Museum, Robert Anderson, and both Jessica Rawson (now Warden of Merton College, Oxford) and Robert Knox, successive Keepers of Oriental Antiquities, as well as by the Chairman, Graham Greene, and all the Trustees, especially Sir David Attenborough, Sir John Boyd, Sir Matthew Farrer, Sir Joseph Hotung and Sir John Morgan. Successive Presidents and staff of the Korea Foundation have also supported my work and I would like to mention in particular the late Lew Hyuck-in, Sohn Chu-hwan, Yoon Keum-jin and Sohn Hee-jeong. Samsung Foundation of Culture, under its President Madame Hong Na-hee, provided generous support for our *Arts of Korea* exhibition in 1997. Dr Hahn Kwang-ho CBE has made a substantial gift to the British Museum for purchasing Korean art and he and his family have facilitated my work with many acts of kindness and generosity, while Tom and Mei-ling Harris provided support beyond the call of ambassadorial duty. Ambassadors Lee Hong-koo, Roe Jae-hee, Choi Dong-jin, Choi Song-hong, Lawrence Middleton, Sir David Wright and Sir Stephen Brown have also been most supportive, as have Sir John Stanley MP and Lord Camoys, with whom I have a shared interest in contemporary Korean ceramics.

My first taste of Korea resulted from a visit to the British Museum by the late Ye Yong-hae in 1989 and a subsequent scholarship from the International Cultural Society of Korea. Since that date, I have studied both at London University School of Oriental and

African Studies, where I obtained a degree in Korean Studies in 1996, and at Yonsei University Language Institute in Seoul (1994–5). I would like to record my thanks to all my teachers and advisors, both in England and in Korea. These include: Ahn Hwi-jun, Martina Deuchler, the late Hahn Chang-gi, Hong Kyong-pyo, Keith Howard (who has read chapters 5 and 6), Kang Woo-bang, Kim Hong-nam, Kim Jae-yeol, Kim Lena, the late Kim Won-yong, Kim Young-na, Ross King, Pak Youngsook, Shin Young-hoon, Roderick Whitfield, Yeon Jae-hun and Yi Song-mi. I would also like to thank the many volunteers who have worked for me on the Korean collection at the British Museum. These include: Choi Mun-jung, Kim Myung-kyung, Emily and Joan Lee, Ji Lee, Meher McArthur, Song Hye-yong and Yim Yu-bin. Friends and colleagues who have provided support in a variety of ways include: the late Lisa Bailey, Gina Barnes (who has read chapters 1 and 2), David Bellamy, Jehanne de Biolley, Kay Black, Richard Blurton, Sheridan Bowman, Sheila Canby, John and Peggy Carswell, Cho Chung-hyun, Chon Ok-kyong, Robin Crighton, Erik Dege, Anne Farrer, George and Margaret Fergusson, Cyril Frankel, Ha Dong-chul, Jessica Harrison-Hall, Riitta Henshall, Jim Hoare, Hyung-kee Hogarth, Charlotte Horlyck, Mike Hughes, Burglind Jungmann, Sally-Anne Kerridge, Kim Gwon-gu (who has read chapters 1 and 2 and checked the maps), Kim Yik-kyung, Kim-Paik Kumja, Priscilla Kumpe (and all the staff of Seoul Foreign School), Rose Lee, Limb Hee-joo, Keith Matthews, Carol Michaelson, Sheila Middleton, Oliver Moore, Sarah Nelson, Jane Newsom, Pak Un-sun, Ann Paludan, Geoff Pickup, Keith Pratt, Roe Jae-ryung, Stephen Ruscoe, Richard Rutt, Shin Sang-ho, Sophie Sorrondegui, Maureen Theobald, Terry and Young-hae Toney, David Turley, Martin and Fiona Uden, Horace and Nancy Underwood (best of neighbours), Shelagh Vainker, Bie Van Gucht, Helen Wang, Rachel Ward, Tom White, Michael Willis, Keith Wilson and Yi Doo-young. Photography of British Museum objects used in this book has been carried out excellently by John Williams, Kevin Lovelock and Tony Milton, and drawings prepared by Ann Searight. Kirsti Williams, Anne Lumley and Tony Simpson kindly produced the maps, no easy task. My extremely knowledgeable editor Susan Pares has provided stalwart and vigilant support and advice, without which this project could not have been completed. Nina Shandloff, Senior Editor at British Museum Press, has overseen the project and provided helpful advice on many points as well as personal support. My greatest debt of thanks, however, is due to my colleague and friend Beth McKillop of the British Library, who has read and commented on the entire text and helped in numerous ways. Her calm, reliable and reasoned company on my journey down a seldom trodden and sometimes tricky path has been invaluable over a number of years.

Note on romanization

Although basically using the McCune-Reischauer system for Korean, I have, in the interests of simplicity, omitted diacritical marks, since this book is aimed at non-specialists. In the case of living artists and scholars, I have attempted to use the most common romanization of their names, where there are alternatives. These do not always adhere to the rules of any romanization system. The standard pinyin system has been used for the romanization of Chinese names and words. Diacritical marks have been omitted from Japanese terms. Chinese, Korean and Japanese personal names are presented in the customary form of family name first, followed by the given name(s). Any mistakes are entirely my responsibility.

INTRODUCTION
Korea: Land and People

The Korean peninsula occupies a pivotal position in East Asia, geographically, politically and culturally. It is attached to the continent of Asia at the point where China meets Russia, and stretches south for some 1000 km (620 miles), reaching towards the Japanese islands. Perhaps because of its location between these three important powers, its history has been dominated by invasions, from China, Mongolia and Japan. However, Korea has remained a remarkably homogenous nation of people who have continued to live in the same geographical area, remaining relatively unaffected by such invasions or by immigration (map 1, p. 10).

The land of Korea, over 70 per cent of which is formed of mountains, possesses a unique and relatively unknown beauty. The Taebaek mountain range forms a spine down the long eastern coast of the peninsula, rising as high as 1571 m (5152 ft), while the lower west coast is characterized by many bays and small peninsulas. The contrast between the two coastlines is paralleled by that between the mountains and the rice-paddy valleys (fig. 1). Sometimes likened to the outline of a rabbit or a tiger, the Korean peninsula is about the same size as mainland Britain. Its northern frontier with China is formed by the Amnok and Tuman rivers, which rise on the slopes of Mt Paektu, 2744m (9000 ft) high (pp. 4–5), while the distance south across the sea to Japan is only 206 km (128 miles).

The Korean climate consists of a very cold winter and a very hot summer, with relatively short spring and autumn seasons. The extreme cold of Korean winters was remarked upon by the Jesuit priest, Gregorio de Cespedes, who went to Korea with the Japanese invasion in the late sixteenth century. He noted in the winter of 1594–5: 'The cold in Korea is very severe and without comparison with that of Japan. All day long my limbs are half benumbed and in the morning I can hardly move my hands to say mass.'[1] The measurement of rain in Korea began as early as 1442 under King Sejong and precipitation data are available from that date until the present day, interrupted only by the period during and after the Japanese and Manchu invasions. Although reached by monsoons, Korea has no active volcanoes and experiences very few earthquakes.

Part of the Altaic race, the Koreans are of the Tungusic group of Manchuria and Siberia. In common with Mongolian and Turkic, the Korean spoken language belongs to the Tungusic branch of the Altaic language group. Korean also displays some similarities with Japanese, and both languages employ a considerable proportion of loan words from Chinese, the dominant language and script of the area. In fact, Chinese was used as the written word in Korea until Korean songs started to be written down in the sixth century using Chinese characters as sounds only (known as the Idu system). Although a foreign language to the mass of Koreans, written

1. The contrast between mountains and fertile rice-paddy valleys is an enduring feature of the Korean landscape.

CHINA

KOREA

JAPAN

Tuman (Tumen) river

Mt Paektu △

HAMGYONG
PUKDO

Amnok (Yalu) river

HAMGYONG
NAMDO

PYONGAN
PUKDO

Taedong river

PYONGAN
NAMDO

EAST SEA

Pyongyang ●

PRESENT DMZ LINE

△

Kumgang-san
(Diamond mountains)

HWANGHAE
DO

KANGWON
DO

Mt Odae
△

Kanghwa
Island

KYONGGI
DO
Han river

Taebaek mountains

Seoul ●

YELLOW SEA

卍

CHUNGCHONG
PUKDO
Pusok-sa △

CHUNGCHONG
NAMDO

Andong ●

Kum river

△
Mt Kyeryong

KYONGSANG
PUKDO

CHOLLA
PUKDO

△ Mt Kaya

Sokkuram

Kyongju ● 卍

卍
Hae'in-sa

Naktong river

Pulguk-sa

Mt Chiri

Yongsan river

Hwaom-sa △
卍

KYONGSANG
NAMDO

Kwangju ●

Somjin river

Pusan ●

Songwang-sa
卍

CHOLLA
NAMDO

Mountain range △
Buddhist temple 卍

Map 1. Position of
the Korean peninsula
within Asia.

Chinese was employed in all official, educational and literary spheres up to the modern period. The Korean script, invented in the fifteenth century, was originally intended as a way of helping ordinary people to read Chinese.[2] A remarkably logical and scientific system of twenty-eight (now twenty-four) graphic signs representing consonants and vowels, *han'gul* was at first resisted by Confucian scholars and not until the eighteenth century did it begin to flourish in the form of vernacular literature. Opinions are divided currently about the virtues of using a han'gul-only script or a mixed Chinese-han'gul script where the more complicated concepts are written with Chinese characters (fig. 2).

The Altaic origins of the Korean people are reflected in their native religion, which was a kind of shamanism similar to that practised in Siberia. It shared as well some animistic features with Japanese Shinto, such as worshipping gods of natural phenomena such as the sun, moon and mountains. The antler-like gold crowns of the Three Kingdoms period (*c*. fifth–sixth centuries) in Korea (see fig. 33) recall Siberian antler head-dresses and suggest that the Korean kings of that time may have been identified as a type of state shaman.

With the adoption of Buddhism from China by the sixth century and later Confucianism, shamanism became more associated with women and the lower classes.[3] Buddhism reached a highpoint in Korea from the seventh to the fourteenth centuries, while strict Confucianism prevailed from the fifteenth century. Modern Korea's Confucian heritage can still be seen in many aspects of life, despite the rapid pace of modernization since the end of the Korean war in 1953, while shamanism and Buddhism are still practised (see fig. 78).[4]

Western knowledge of Korea

Western knowledge of Korea was extremely limited and the accounts that reached the West were sometimes of dubious accuracy. The first inklings arrived through Arab traders in the ninth century. Ibn Khordhbeh, who was employed at the Court of the Caliph Motamid from 870 to 892, wrote:

What lies on the other side of China is unknown land. But high mountains rise up densely across from Kantu. These lie over in the land of Sila, which is rich in gold. Mohammedans who visit this country are often persuaded by its fine qualities to settle down there. Ghorraib [probably ginseng], kino resin [probably lacquer], aloe, camphor, nails, saddles, porcelain, atlas, cinnamon and galanga are exported from there.[5]

Marco Polo, who may have visited China between 1271 and 1295, also mentions Korea in the context of the annexation of four provinces by

2. The Korean script, *han'gul*, invented in the 15th century, is a source of great national pride. Here the original text of the *Hunmin Chong'um* is copied by the modern master calligrapher Soh Hwi-hwan, 1995. Ht: 1 m.

China under Kublai Khan. But it was not until Hideyoshi's invasion of Korea in 1592 that news of Korea reached the West, through Jesuit missionaries to Japan and China, such as Matteo Ricci. On European maps of this period, Korea is sometimes shown as an island and sometimes as a peninsula. It appears correctly on the atlas of the Jesuit M. Martini, published in 1653, together with a written geographical outline.[6] However, it is the account of the Dutchman Hendrik Hamel, whose ship *Sparrow Hawk* was stranded on the island of Cheju, south of the Korean peninsula, in the same year and who lived for thirteen years in captivity in Korea, that constitutes the first Western eye-witness report of Korea. The next one was not to appear for another 250 years, because until 1880 foreigners were forbidden, on pain of death, to set foot in the country. It was this exclusion policy that led to Korea's being known in the West as the 'Hermit Kingdom'.

Hamel's *Description of the Kingdom of Corea* (1668) (fig. 3) was a fairly objective account of Korea at a time when it was nearing the cultural highpoint of the eighteenth century. Hamel was impressed at the Korean respect for education: 'The Nobility, and all Free-men in general, take great care of the Education of their children, and put them very young to learn to read and write, to which that Nation is much addicted.'[7] This could be true today and is an accurate reflection of the Confucian literati preoccupation with the written word. Hamel described the difference between the houses of the nobility and those of the poor and the fact that the right to a tiled roof was limited to the nobility, with the majority using thatch. He also said:

> Houses are built with Wooden Posts or Pillars, with the Interval betwixt them fill'd up with Stone up to the first Story, the rest of the Structure is all Wood daubed without and cover'd on the inside with Whitepaper glew'd on. The floors are all vaulted, and in Winter they make a fire underneath, so that they are always as warm as a Stove. The floor is covered with Oil'd Paper.[8]

This is a good observation of a traditional Korean house with *ondol* heating system.

The opening of Korea to the West followed the Treaty of Kanghwa, signed with the Japanese in 1876. This was Korea's first modern treaty, signed under foreign pressure. It was unequal and paved the way for the Korean-American Treaty in 1882 and subsequent treaties with Britain, Germany, Italy, Russia, France and the Austro-Hungarian Empire. The Korean-French Treaty contained a clause permitting the propagation of Christianity in Korea and it was this that led to an influx of Western missionaries, some of whom were to write descriptive books about life in Korea. The opening also led to the establishment of Chemulpo (Inchon), west of the capital Seoul, as a treaty port and to the arrival of consular and customs officials, who also produced accounts of Korea. A large number of travel accounts were written after 1880, many of which were superficial and inaccurate. The volume of writing is borne out by the fact that Horace Underwood, one of the earliest missionaries in Korea, lists in his bibliography 152 publications on Korea in Western languages for the period 1595–1880 as opposed to 2730 for the period 1881–1931.[9]

One of the first comprehensive works on the history and ethnology of Korea, by W.E. Griffis, was written around 1880 while he was working in Tokyo and had never actually set foot in Korea. It was totally based on Japanese sources.[10] The eye-witness accounts can be divided into three categories: those written by missionaries, such as Horace Underwood, James Gale, Horace Allen, Homer Hulbert and Lilias Underwood;[11] those written by

pofant, à peine d'amende, & autres peines y portées, ainſi qu'il eſt plus amplement porté audit Privilege.

Ledit Iolly a fait part de ſondit Privilege à Simon Benard, pour en joüyr ſuivant l'accord fait entr'eux.

Regiſtré ſur le Livre de la Communauté, ſuivant l'Arreſt de Parlement du 8. Octobre 1653. Signé, ANDRY SOUBRON, *Syndic.*

RELA

RELATION

D U

NAUFRAGE

D'UN VAISSEAU HOLANDOIS,

Sur la Coſte de l'Iſle de Quelpaerts:

AVEC LA DESCRIPTION du Royaume de Corée.

Ous partîmes du Texel ſur le ſoir du 10. de Janvier de l'année 1653. avec un fort bon vent, & apres avoir eſſuyé beaucoup de tempeſtes & de mauvais temps, nous moüillâmes le 1. Juin à la rade de Batavie. Comme nous. nous fûmes rafraîchis. là pen-

Ianⁱvier 1653.

Iuin.

A

2

3. Frontispiece of the 1670 French edition of the Dutchman Hendrik Hamel's account of his shipwreck off Korea in 1653. Quelpart was the old Western name for Cheju island. 17.3 × 15.4 cm.

diplomats or officials, such as W.R. Carles and W.G. Aston;[12] and those written by independent travellers. Of the latter category, Isabella Bird Bishop's *Korea and Her Neighbours* (1898) has become a classic of its type and, although she was not a true anthropologist, her book comes nearer to an anthropological study than any other. She made four trips to Korea between 1894 and 1897 and described the political events of this unsettled period as well as discussing shamanism in some depth and describing life amongst the Buddhist monks of Kumgangsan.[13] William Franklin Sands was one of the most 'integrated' of the Westerners in Korea at that time. An American diplomat, he later became an independent advisor to King Kojong and wrote *Undiplomatic Memories*.[14] Unusually for a foreigner, he was right in the thick of events both amongst the diplomats and at Court. He also understood the rules of a highly stratified society, reflected in its language:

> Each grade in Korean society is indicated by the verbal forms used in conversation. You change your verbal endings according to the social position of the person with whom you are speaking, and it is very important to give exactly the right shade. If you miss it, either for a degree too high or a degree too low, you brand yourself as being unused to Court life, a rustic and not a man of the world.[15]

Subjects such as religion and folklore could lead foreigners to misinterpretations of what they saw, especially in long, elaborate rituals. They were also, on the whole, predisposed to disapprove of non-Christian beliefs as superstitions. They tended to be at their most disparaging when talking of religion. Inaccuracies also arose from straightforward ignorance, reflecting the lack of Western scholars of Korea at that time. For instance, Carles accurately described Bronze Age dolmens (see fig. 13), but claimed that 'though it must have cost immense labour to place these stones in position, no legend was current to account for their existence, except one which connected them with the Japanese invasion at the end of the sixteenth century, when invaders were said to have erected them to suppress the influences of the earth.'[16] Happily, Hulbert, writing in 1906, had a more informed approach: 'I incline strongly to the opinion that they are very ancient graves, in spite of the fact that no bones are found.'[17]

4. *The Scholar*, 1921, colour woodcut by the Scottish artist Elizabeth Keith (1887–1956), who visited Korea in 1919.

The Korea described by these travellers and residents was a rapidly changing one. The period from the opening to the West in the 1880s until the Japanese occupation in 1910 saw such innovations as the introduction of railways, a postal system, a customs system, Western-style newspapers, including one in English, and Western medicine practised by missionary doctors. The value of the foreigners' accounts lies in the fact that they chronicled a fixed period of time. After 1910, Korea was not as open to the West and was greatly under the influence of Japan, with the result that the study of Korea in Japan far outstripped that in the West. Although they are circumscribed by the prejudices and ignorance of their authors, the eye-witness accounts, together with the valuable prints and photographs which illustrate them (fig. 4), introduced the West to a country of which it was largely ignorant, despite the earlier account by Hamel. Unfortunately, the West became aware of Korea during one of the low points in its cultural history, at the end of a long-declining dynasty. This inevitably affected the Western view of Korea, which was not a very positive one at that moment, with a general perception of Korea as a backward, unmodernized country.

Growth of Western knowledge and collecting of Korean art

The general ignorance about Korean art in the late nineteenth century in the West is shown in Stephen Bushell's pronouncement in 1899 in a major work on oriental ceramics, that 'Korea has been thoroughly explored during the last few years and it is now known that no artistic pottery is produced there in the present day, and no indisputable evidence of any skill in former times has been discovered'.[18]

There was actually a scattering of scholars who had a considerable knowledge of Korea at that time, although it tended to be as an offshoot of Japanese studies. The British Foreign Office staffed its Korean consulate-general from its Japanese embassy. W.G. Aston, for example, a Japanologist and Britain's first consul-general in Seoul after diplomatic relations were established in 1883, was also quite an expert on Korea and had published a highly praised article in 1879 in the journal of the Royal Asiatic Society, comparing the Japanese and Korean languages.[19] He also built up a fine library of books on Korea and a collection of Korean ceramics, of which the whereabouts is now unknown, although he donated one vase to the British Museum, its first Korean acquisition, in 1888.

Another scholar of Korean ceramics at this time was William Gowland, ARSM, FCS,

5. Original glass slide of Korean and Japanese tomb wares (left: Japanese, right: Korean), made by William Gowland in the 1890s. Gowland was one of the first Westerners to notice the similarity between the tomb wares of the two countries.

a British employee of the Imperial Japanese mint in Osaka. A noted metallurgist, he was also a keen and scholarly amateur archaeologist who carried out many excavations in Japan which led him to suspect (correctly as it turned out) that Japanese tomb pottery may have originated in Korea. He therefore visited Korea in 1884, travelling from Seoul to Pusan and purchasing a group of Three Kingdoms ceramics which were later, in 1889, donated to the British Museum. He also published an article in the journal of the Anthropological Institute in 1895 in which he made some remarkably astute comments: 'In form, inscribed designs, marks of matting and the material of which they were made, many are allied to the sepulchral vessels of the dolmens of Japan, but they are not all identical'(fig. 5).[20]

It is ironic that it was during the Japanese occupation from 1910 to 1945 that people in the West began to see evidence of Korea's rich past in the form of objects excavated from former capitals such as Kyongju and Kaesong as well from the Han Chinese colony of Lelang (Korean: Nangnang) near Pyongyang. Japanese scholars such as Sekino Tadashi and Umehara Sueji in 1921 excavated such important sites as the Gold Crown tomb in Kyongju, Silla's ancient capital, as well as rediscovering the Sokkuram cave temple and excavating some of the Koguryo tomb paintings. They also published a very useful survey of the ceramic industry of Korea in 1926, as one of a series of investigative reports on the peninsula's natural resources.[21] In fact, it has been said that:

> Archaeology in Korea at this time was far more developed and more rationally organised than archaeology in Japan itself … Korean preservation of cultural remains as well as excavation and display were done by a single group which gave a unified approach to the problem of archaeology in Korea. With less than ten personnel and with very limited funds, they were able to achieve a remarkable degree of progress, which far outdistanced similar groups in China and Japan at the same period.[22]

As early as 1911, the British Museum received a gift of a group of thirty-three Koryo

celadons collected by George Eumorfopoulos, which may well have been the results of Japanese excavations of the Koryo capital at present-day Kaesong, although there is no documentation to prove this. Indeed, in 1937–8 George Eumor-fopoulos provided the British Museum with more Korean art than any other connoisseur, having displayed his collection for a long time in his home in Cheyne Walk in Chelsea in London, where he used to encourage interested visitors to go and view it (fig. 6).

The first time that Korean artefacts were exhibited in London was in a Korean Pavilion at the Anglo-Japanese Exhibition at the White City in 1910, at which Korean crafts were displayed (fig. 7). Held in the year that Japan annexed Korea, this exhibition was designed to increase cultural and commercial ties between Britain and Japan. The shared ethos of empire was, at that time, an important part of their relation-ship; thus Korea was included as an example of one of the peoples subdued by an expanding imperial Japan, together with Taiwan (Formosa) and the Ainu. Korean objects from that exhibi-tion were donated to the British Museum. They consist mostly of ceramics and folk crafts, such as sedge mats (see fig. 89), fans, chatelaines (see

6. Choson dynasty painting of a Buddhist monk on display on the staircase at the house of George Eumorfopoulos in Cheyne Walk, Chelsea, London, in 1935, before being acquired by the British Museum. 106 × 74 cm.

Appendix 2, fig. 4) and lacquer sewing equipment.[23]

It was in great part due to the interest of Japanese Folk Crafts scholars such as Yanagi Soetsu, Kawai Kanjiro and Hamada Shoji that appreciation particularly of Korean ceram-ics developed in the West during the first half of the twentieth century. Bernard Leach, who lived and worked in Japan for many years and also travelled to Korea, was part of this group and very influential in educating Western taste. He admired Korean pots for their natural unselfconsciousness, and Yanagi, too, talks of the freedom found in Korean pots, compared to Japanese ones:

> In modern art, as everyone knows, the beauty of deformity is very often emphasised, insisted upon. But how different is Korean deformity. The former is produced deliberately, the latter naturally. Korean work is merely the natural result of the artisan's state of mind, which is free from dualistic man-made rules ... Here lies buried the mystery of the endless beauty of the Korean artisan's work. He simply makes what he wants, without pretension.[24]

Although there was a certain amount of idealization and even condescension in the attitude to Korean art and craft of Yanagi and his group, there is no doubt that, particularly through Bernard Leach, they opened many Western eyes to its beauty. Bernard Leach is

known to have collected Korean ceramics and furniture[25] and one particularly beautiful piece of
white porcelain, which he acquired in Korea in 1935
and gave to the potter Lucie Rie in 1943 and which
was kept by her in her studio until her death, is now
in the collection of the British Museum (fig. 8).[26]

The fact that most Western collections of
Korean art are predominantly of ceramics is probably due partly to the influence of the Japanese
Folk Crafts scholars and partly to the general and
long-standing Japanese appreciation of Korean
ceramics. Such appreciation is seen in the quality
of Japanese collections of Korean ceramics (such
as the Ataka collection in Osaka). Paintings,
screens and sutras remained inaccessible to many
Westerners and were not collected in such numbers. Their fragility added to the difficulty of collecting them. Other notable European collectors of
Korean ceramics were the Fischers, whose collection is now in the Museum of Far Eastern Art in
Cologne. In France, several diplomats built up
Korean collections, from Collin de Plancy in the
late nineteenth century to Landy and Chambard
more recently. However, the size of Western collections of Korean art has always been relatively
small, a result in part of the destruction of so
much during the wars and occupations suffered by
Korea.

The Second World War and the Korean War
(1950–53) resulted in many more Westerners
becoming aware of Korea. Some collections of
Korean art were built up in the postwar period by
military, diplomatic and medical personnel from
the West, resulting, for example, in the Henderson
collection of ceramics at Harvard, the
Poulsen-Hansen collection in the British Museum
and the Kalbak collection in Copenhagen and
Stockholm.[27]

7. Above: Korean pavilion in the Anglo-Japanese Exhibition at the White City,
Shepherd's Bush, London, in 1910, the year Korea was formally colonized by
Japan. The objects exhibited were later donated to the British Museum.

8. Right: The Austrian-born potter Lucie Rie in her studio with the Choson
dynasty white porcelain 'full-moon' jar collected by Bernard Leach in Korea
in 1935 and later given to her by Leach, before being purchased by the
British Museum. Ht: 47 cm. Photograph by Lord Snowdon.

The development of archaeology and art history in Korea since the Korean War has
been rapid and there is a vast and growing literature in Korean on these subjects, although
still relatively little in English.[28] A great amount of Japanese scholarship remains from the
occupation period and there is still a great deal of interest in and study of Korean art and
archaeology in present-day Japan. When compared with the study of Chinese and Japanese
art history and archaeology by Western scholars, which started much earlier, that of Korea
is still in its infancy. The loan exhibitions from Korea which toured the USA in 1980–81

and Europe in 1984 did much to enthuse and inform the West, and there is now an exciting period when new Korean galleries for Korean art are opening in great Western museums such as the British Museum, the Metropolitan Museum, the Musée Guimet (part of the Louvre), the Victoria and Albert Museum and the Asian Art Museum of San Francisco.[29] This is the direct result of sponsorship from the government of South Korea and from large Korean companies, initiated during the economically flourishing period of the early 1990s.

General features of Korean art

Several eminent scholars have attempted to summarize what it is that makes Korean art distinctively Korean and distinguishable from that of neighbouring China and Japan. It is a question that greatly exercises Korean minds in particular. The task is difficult as, especially to Western eyes, there are clear general similarities which arise from a shared heritage of Buddhism and Confucianism and a shared writing system and from geographical proximity and common everyday habits. Korea was a vassal kingdom of China for hundreds of years and latterly a colony of Japan. These are historical facts which cannot be ignored. What has been largely misunderstood in the West, however, are the manifold influences that travelled from Korea to Japan from very early times, perhaps even as early as the Neolithic period. It was the eminent Korean scholar, the late Kim Won-yong, who said: 'The flow of artistic influences and inspiration has always been one-way traffic from China or Korea to Japan ... Korea acted as a cultural bridge between China and Japan, but she was also at times an independent source of inspiration for Japanese art from the bronze age to the 7th century'.[30] The tremendous Korean input into many aspects of Japanese culture has been undervalued. Some would say that this was a deliberate distortion, generally in the form of reference to vague 'continental' influence rather than Korean influence.[31] Other scholars, however, point to amateurish studies by unqualified and ignorant Westerners as a source of misunderstanding in the more recent past about the true nature of Korean art.[32]

9. Japanese woodblock print depicting the procession of the official Korean envoys to Japan in 1711. Such embassies were sent regularly to Japan during the Choson period, accompanied by Korean artists who brought with them the latest trends in painting. 33 × 60 cm.

The general consensus of opinion is that first expressed by Seckel, if somewhat vaguely, that Korean art can be characterized by 'vitality, spontaneity and unconcern for technical perfection'.[33] The latter can be seen in the way that many Korean pots are slightly asymmetrical, so that if they are turned around, the shape seems to change. The scale of the decoration, on ceramics in particular, gives an impression of spontaneity, with very large flowers or fish being placed beside relatively small trees in an unconcerned fashion. The English collector, Godfrey Gompertz, whose works on Korean ceramics played such an important part in the education of the West, said: 'The Korean potters were often careless or inexpert in technique; they were more concerned to achieve an artistic effect and seldom paid attention to detail'.[34] Since his work was largely the result of Japanese scholarship, however, it may be that he is reflecting the Japanese preoccupation with imperfection as a virtue.

The field of Korean painting and sculpture has been much less studied by Western

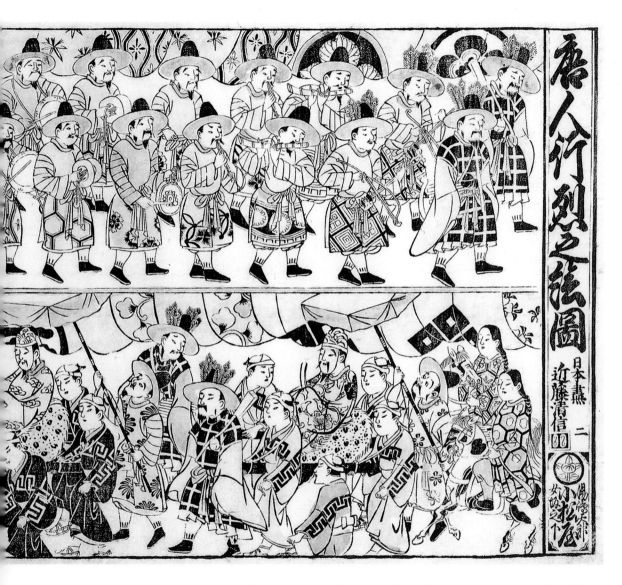

scholars than that of ceramics, partly because of lack of good examples in the West. Where it has been, it seems to contradict these general assumptions. Recent scholarship in the field of early Buddhist painting, for example, has shown that, far from displaying a lack of concern for technical perfection, the Korean painters and monk-scribes were great masters whose works were appreciated and prized in China and Japan.[35] The same surely applies to Buddhist metalwork of the same period, while the eighth-century cave temple at Sokku-ram is as technically perfect and elegant as it is possible to be. The paintings by some of the Korean artists who accompanied the official Korean envoys on their visits to Japan in the late Choson period (fig. 9) were clearly greatly admired and sought after by Japanese cognoscenti, as examples to be followed.[36] Much more objective study of Korean painting and sculpture needs to be carried out in the West before any generalizations can usefully be attempted.

CHAPTER 1
Prehistoric Period

10. Group of Neolithic
bracelets, necklace,
ornaments, mask and
female figure, made from
stone, bone and shell.
c. 5000–4000 BC.
Max. width: 8.8 cm.

The ancient history of that area of land now called the Korean peninsula cannot be divorced from that of the neighbouring areas, which are present-day China and the Japanese islands. In the Palaeolithic period (before 10,000 BC) no such national boundaries would have existed and early man would have wandered freely. The archaeology of this period in Korea has developed dramatically in the last three decades and it is now established that early man inhabited Korea during the Pleistocene period (up to 10,000 years ago). Pioneers in the field, such as Kim Won-yong and Sohn Pow-key, have been followed by a younger generation of archaeologists and scholars and there are now several scores of known Palaeolithic sites.[1]

Homo erectus, known since the discovery of Zhoukoudian near Beijing[2] to have existed in China about 500,000 years ago, may have arrived in Korea at this time. The sea-level in the glacial periods was low enough to expose the floor of the Yellow Sea, thus connecting Korea and China in this area as well as in the north by way of Manchuria. Homo erectus fossils have been discovered in the Liaodong peninsula at Jinniushan, suggesting that early humans could have taken that route from China to Korea,[3] and possible Homo sapiens fossils have also been discovered in Korea.[4] Since the straits between Korea and Japan were also exposed at this time, a land-bridge was provided to the present-day Japanese islands, allowing for free movement. A further land-bridge north connected Japan with Siberia through Sakhalin and Hokkaido.

Dating of the earliest Palaeolithic sites in Korea is problematic. The limestone cave at Hukwuri (Komunmoru), southeast of Pyongyang in what is now North Korea, which was excavated between 1966 and 1970, contained stone tools (choppers and scrapers) as well as bones of rhinocerous, megalocerous, monkey, bison, boar, horse, elephant, tiger and cave bear. Remains of both a rat and a horse type which became extinct after the Middle Pleistocene have led North Korean archaeologists to estimate the earliest date of the cave at 400,000 years ago.[5] Other important early Palaeolithic sites are at Kumgul cave in south-central Korea, Chon'gok-ri in central Korea and Sokchang-ri on the Kum river (map 2, p. 25). The discovery of Acheulian-type hand-axes at Chon'gok-ri between 1979 and 1983 is extremely significant because it disproves Movius's theory, formed in the 1940s, that only choppers and not hand-axes were used in East Asia. (Large, pointed hand-axes have also been found at Dingcun in China.)[6]

Human remains have been found at Middle Palaeolithic (100,000–40,000 BC)[7] sites such as Turubong in South Korea and Daehyundong near Pyongyang in North Korea. Cave 2 at Turubong had a living floor with a hearth containing charcoal made from pine, alder and maple.[8] During this interglacial period the climate was warm, and pollen found at Turubong came from a flowering plant. The presence of carved deer-bones and depictions of deer led Yi Yung-jo to suggest that the inhabitants of Turubong may have engaged in a deer cult.[9] Other mid-Palaeolithic sites are Chommal cave, Myong'ori open-air site on the South Han river and Kulpori on the northeast coast (see map 2).

Sites such as Suyanggae, discovered as a result of the Chungju Dam project, span the Middle-Upper Palaeolithic (40,000–10,000 BC). An open-air site, it contains well-made hand-axes, rectangular knives, scrapers, tanged points and burins using quartzite, shale, rhyolite and obsidian, as well as microblades, of which the cores seem to have been used as tools. Camellia, pine and larch wood has been identified as well as animal fur.[10] The upper layers at Sokchang-ri, the first Palaeolithic site to be excavated in South Korea starting in 1964, belong to the Upper Palaeolithic and include a dwelling outlined by two lines of stones, with a hearth and five post-holes, suggesting a living area for about ten people.[11]

The use of obsidian and quartz for making blade tools, worked antler and bone and smallish dwellings with hearths and post-holes are features of this time. It seems likely that people lived in family groups rather than larger communities, finding their food by hunting and foraging in the deciduous forests. As for the tricky question of Korean Palaeolithic art, it is far from certain whether there are any extant examples, although Sohn Pow-key maintains that the deer pecked out of rock at Sokchang-ri are late Pleistocene because they portray particular grey deer and reindeer which became extinct when the climate grew warmer.[12]

Kim Won-yong writes of a 'cultural hiatus' of several thousand years between the Palaeolithic and the Neolithic and suggests that the Palaeolithic population migrated north. Nelson, however, thinks it unlikely that the Korean peninsula would have remained uninhabited. The question of the existence of a Mesolithic period (10,000–?6000 BC) depends somewhat on terminology, with small stone tools sometimes being described as microliths. Chinese, Korean and Japanese sites containing microcores and microblades have been discovered, those in Korea including Chommal cave and Yokchi-do.[13] Im Hyo-jae suggests that this period may be clarified by excavations at Kosan-ri on Cheju island, as this site belongs to the pre-Neolithic period, which he calls the 'Palaeo-neolithic' period. Finds here in 1994 of small stone arrow-heads shaped like equilateral triangles, made by chipping and flaking, as well as plain brown pot sherds, are quite different from mainland Korean products and show some similarities to finds in Japan at Kamikuroiwa in Ehime Prefecture and at Kita Matsuura in Nagasaki Prefecture, which have radiocarbon dates of 10,085±320 BP (Before Present) and 12,400±300 BP respectively. The similarity is not surprising; close links were facilitated by a lower sea-level at that time, resulting in the two land masses which are now modern Korea and Japan being physically closer together.[14]

Neolithic

Although the culture of the Neolithic period (*c.* 6000–1000 BC) is generally defined by the beginnings of an agricultural way of life, as in China, the Korean Neolithic is, rather, defined by the appearance of pottery among a population that subsisted mainly by hunting, fishing and gathering. It was only in the late Neolithic in Korea that agricultural food production was adopted.[15] As a result of excavations in northeast China during the 1980s and 1990s, it has become apparent that the early Neolithic in Korea has close links with that area, particularly with eastern Liaoning province and the Liaodong peninsula.[16] For example, flat-bottomed pottery decorated with Z-shaped patterns found in North Korea at

Map 2. Principal Palaeolithic and Neolithic sites in Korea.

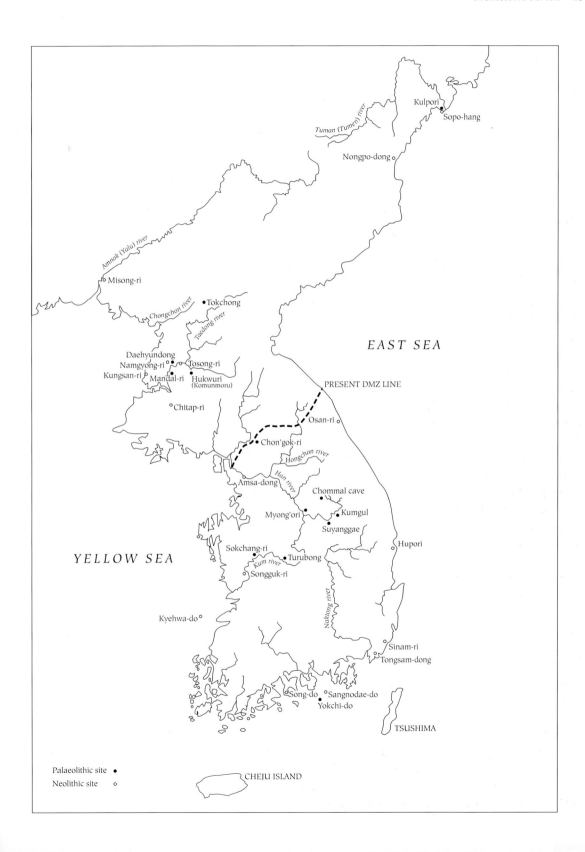

Kulpori
Sopo-hang
Tuman (Tumen) river
Nongpo-dong

Amnok (Yalu) river
Misong-ri

EAST SEA

Chongchon river
Tokchong
Taedong river

Daehyundong
Namgyong-ri
Tosong-ri
Kungsan-ri
Mandal-ri
Hukwuri
(Komunmoru)

PRESENT DMZ LINE

Chitap-ri

Osan-ri

Chon'gok-ri

Hongchon river

Amsa-dong
Han river

Chommal cave

Myong'ori
Kumgul
Suyanggae

YELLOW SEA

Hupori

Sokchang-ri
Kum river
Turubong
Songguk-ri

Naktong river

Kyehwa-do

Sinam-ri
Tongsam-dong

Song-do
Sangnodae-do
Yokchi-do

TSUSHIMA

Palaeolithic site ●
Neolithic site ○

CHEJU ISLAND

Misong-ri is similar to that of the Chinese Lower Xiaozhushan culture (on Donglu island, east of the Liaodong peninsula). Moreover, flat-bottomed North Korean bowls decorated with dotted and slanting lines and herringbone patterns and tempered with steatite, found at Tosong-ri, are very similar to the Chinese Middle Xiaozhushan culture.[17]

Settlements

Hundreds of Neolithic sites have been discovered on the Korean peninsula which, on the basis of pottery types, fall into four regional groups: northwest, northeast, west and south. The earliest Korean Neolithic sites of all have been located at Osan-ri, on the east coast in Kangwon province (see map 2, p. 25). The radiocarbon dates are clustered between 6000 and 4500 BC. Neolithic settlements in Korea generally occur along river valleys or on the coast, the northern groups developing along the Amnok river (for which the Chinese name is the Yalu) and the Tuman (Chinese: Tumen) river, the western group south of the Chongchon river, being concentrated around the Taedong and Han river valleys, and the southern group developing along the Naktong river and on islands off the south coast (see map 2). These village sites are characterized by hand-made pottery and chipped stone tools which were usually found in or around semi-subterranean dwellings with central hearths. Each village contained only a few houses but the villages tended to be clustered. Coastal sites are generally sited just above the present high-tide line, but some sites may have disappeared under the rising sea-level. The Neolithic period in Korea is sometimes called the Chulmun period, because of the comb-patterned pottery by which it was originally characterized. However, since other types of pottery have been discovered in Neolithic Korea, this is now rather a confusing term, as the comb-patterned pottery is limited to the Mid-Late Neolithic and to certain areas. The name Chulmun can therefore only be used as a very general term for a long and varied period, as is Jomon in Japan, and it will not be used here.[18]

Tools and ornaments

Stone, bone and shell tools and implements excavated from Neolithic sites are evidence of the way of life at this time, one which depended primarily on hunting and fishing. No wooden tools have been preserved and there are many more stone than bone ones, the latter having been preserved only in shell-mounds. Stone arrow-heads and larger spear-points are widespread, made either of slate or of obsidian (particularly in the northeast). Some are polished, with six faces. Stone axes are frequent, large polished nephrite examples being found at Hupori on the east coast and smaller nephrite or agate ones at Kungsan-ri in central Korea and Kyehwa-do island off the southwest coast. Domestic grinding stones and pestles and mortars, cutters and scrapers are also widespread but spindle whorls are more frequent in the north. Agricultural tools found in the very north and at Amsa-dong include large, flat chipped stone implements with large tangs which have been identified as ploughshares and which resemble those found in China.[19] Also, hoes made of antler and stone have been found at Kungsan-ri. Thin hoes or axes made of river pebbles are a feature of central Korea, while reaping tools such as stone sickles have been reported at Chitap-ri and Osan-ri.[20]

   Pointed stone weights found at Osan-ri may be plumb bobs and, together with the large stone fish-hooks found there, suggest that the inhabitants engaged in sea fishing. The stone fish-hooks are mostly made of a thin stone cylinder which was probably tied to a wood or bone point in a V-shape. Similar ones have been found at Tongsam-dong, near Pusan, and in Siberia. At Tongsam-dong, many bones of large fish are evidence of a healthy diet: shark, sea-bream, tuna, cod (as well as sea-lions and whales). All shell-mound sites are of course essentially rubbish dumps, the shells being evidence of the large numbers of shell-fish consumed. The top layer at Tongsam-dong produced harpoons, fish-hooks, spatulas and awls, suggesting a fishing-centred way of life.[21]

11. Comb-patterned pot with pointed base, excavated from Amsa-dong, near Seoul. Neolithic period, *c.* 4000 BC. Ht: 25.9 cm.

The human face and body were already being portrayed in the Neolithic period in Korea, as can be seen from a small shell mask found in the top layer at Tongsam-dong, featuring three holes which resemble a mouth and two eyes (see fig. 10). This mask is similar to one reported to have been found in Japan.[22] Another mask found at Osan-ri is made of clay, with a pinched nose and the eyes and mouth poked in with a finger.[23] The small stone figurine of a nude female excavated near Pusan at Sinam-ri is the only one of its type found so far (see fig. 10, centre bottom), although pinched clay figurines of both humans and animals were found at Nongpo-dong in the northeast.[24]

Pottery

From the Tuman river in the far northeast down the east coast to Kangwon province, as well as in the northwest around the valleys of the Amnok and Chongchon rivers, the pottery produced in the early Neolithic is flat-bottomed, thin-walled and brown. It was generally tempered with sand or sometimes ground shell. Decoration was incised on the middle or upper part of the body and the lower half was undecorated. The lower layers at Osan-ri in Kangwon province and at Sopo-hang in the far northeast (also known as Kulpori when referring to the Palaeolithic) (see map 2) provide the earliest examples, dating to between 6000 and 4500 BC.[25]

Pottery with incised decoration includes a type where the decorative patterns are confined to the rim (*kuyonmun*), such as at Osan-ri. Raised design pottery, called *yunggimun* in Korean, is also characteristic of the northeast during the early Neolithic, having been found first at Osan-ri. Yunggimun includes pinched, raised decoration, plain raised lines and raised and impressed lines. The other main type of pottery from this period and region is that with incised square spiral decoration, which is found in the far northeast along the Tuman river.[26]

Flat-bottomed, yunggimun pottery is also found in the southeast at shell-mound sites, the most famous of which is Tongsam-dong on Yong-do island in Pusan bay. Yunggimun is also dominant in the southwest, as at Song-do in South Cholla province, dated to around 4500 BC. Although it is possible that the yunggimun tradition passed from north to south, this is not yet certain.[27]

Pottery vessels with combed patterns (*chulmun*) and with pointed or conical bottoms are characteristic of the central western area of Korea. In these vessels, the clay body is generally tempered with mica, steatite or asbestos and the surface is decorated with patterns of herringbone or slanted parallel lines, incised with a toothed, comb-like implement. Earlier chulmun pottery tends to be decorated over the whole surface of the vessel but over time decoration gradually becomes restricted to the rim area (fig. 11). Chulmun appears around 5000 BC and seems to have originated in the area between the valleys of the Chong-chon river to the north and the Han river to the south. It then gradually diffused to other parts of Korea between 4500 and 3500 BC.[28]

The best-known site yielding chulmun pottery is at Amsa-dong, on the Han river on the outskirts of present-day Seoul. Amsa-dong is also one of the most important Neolithic dwelling sites (another being at Sopo-hang in North Korea). First discovered in 1925 as the result of a flood, it was systematically excavated from 1967 onwards. Thirty semi-subterranean pit dwellings have been discovered, each about 5–6 m (16–19 ft) long and containing a rectangular hearth outlined with stones. There are post-holes at each corner of the houses, and holes to support pointed-bottomed pottery were found all over the floors of the pit dwellings. It is thought that this and other similar sites nearby may have formed a small community (fig. 12).[29] The Amsa-dong site has been made into a museum with some restored houses and a recreation of the inside of a Neolithic house.

The chronology of Neolithic pottery in Korea is still far from certain and the regional divisions appear clearer than the temporal ones. In general, the north is characterized by flat-bottomed pottery. The appearance of yunggimun pottery in the northeast seems to coincide with the appearance of chulmun pottery in the west, chulmun then spreading to the other parts of Korea from 4500–3500 BC, together with the cultivation of millet. Im Hyo-jae considers the period from 2000 to 1000 BC as the Late Neolithic, but Nelson calls this the Megalithic period, on the basis that the appearance of both megaliths and plain (*mumun*) pottery indicates a profound change in society, although the presence of bronze at this stage is uncertain.[30]

12. Foundations of a semi-subterranean circular house, showing post-holes, at Amsa-dong Neolithic village, on the Han river outside Seoul.

Links with Japan

Korean, Japanese and Western scholars all acknowledge the probability of maritime trade between southern and eastern Korea and Japan during the Neolithic period. Finds of early Jomon potsherds at Tongsam-dong substantiate this, together with obsidian flakes which may have originated in Kyushu. Similar yunggimun pottery, moreover, decorated with plain and zigzag lines, has been found both in Korea at sites such as Tongsam-dong, Sinam-ri and Osan-ri, and in Japan at Fukui cave in Kyushu, on Tsushima island and at several other sites. Since the dates of the Japanese finds, for example those at Fukui cave and Kamikuroiwa, are earlier than 10,000 BC, this could suggest that yunggimun-type pottery may have originated in Japan and spread to eastern Korea. However, it may be that future archaeological work in Korea, such as at Sangnodae island, may prove that Korean pottery is as old as or older than that in Japan.[31]

Kim Won-yong suggests that the emergence of Sobata pottery in northwest Kyushu was influenced by trade with Tongsam-dong.[32] Im Hyo-jae, on the basis of finds on Tsushima island at Myutoishi, claims that comb-patterned, pointed-bottomed chulmun pottery was introduced to Japan from Korea in the Neolithic. His argument is that although Japanese-style, mid-Jomon pottery was found in the third layer of excavations at Myutoishi, earlier comb-patterned pottery found in the sixth and seventh layers may be Korean, on attribution of its typically Korean herringbone-patterned decoration.[33] Im also posits the introduction of comb-patterned chulmun pottery from southeast Korea to sites in northeastern Japan, such as Aomori and Uriba, facilitated by the northeasterly flow of the Tsushima current.[34] The whole area of early contacts between the Korean peninsula and the Japanese islands is an exciting subject which awaits elucidation by future archaeologists.

Bronze Age

The period between 2000 and 1000 BC, characterized by the introduction of megaliths, stone cist graves and undecorated mumun pottery, is variously called the Late Neolithic or the Megalithic period, as opposed to the Bronze Age proper (1000 BC–*c*. 300 BC), which is generally thought to have begun around 1000 BC with the appearance of Korean-made bronzes. Most Bronze Age dwelling sites were situated on hillsides, as opposed to the Neolithic riverside villages, and the Bronze Age is sometimes called an age of chiefdoms, which would turn into states in the following Iron Age or Proto-Three Kingdoms period.[35]

The great change in the way of life which brought about practices such as the use of stone cist tombs, dolmens, mumun pottery, bronzes and agricultural production, including rice cultivation, has been ascribed to immigration into the Korean peninsula from the north of a Tungusic people, sometimes identified as the Yemaek or the Dong-yi ('eastern barbarians'), or linked with the Rong or the Di barbarians referred to in Chinese sources. Several legendary figures are thought to have lived at this time. Of these, the most important is Tan'gun, said to have founded Korea in 2333 BC, who was half-man half-bear and who became a spirit after his one-thousand-year life, at Heavenly Lake on Mt Paektu in present-day North Korea (pp. 4–5). Another story is that the nephew of the last Shang dynasty king, called Qizi in Chinese or Kija in Korean, went into exile in Korea around 1100 BC, founding the state of Choson.

The question of immigration has always fascinated Korean scholars, who regard the ethnic origins of the Korean people as one of the most important questions which archaeological excavations may be able to answer. It is probable that the Manchurian Lower Xiajiadian culture, with carbon-14 dates in the range of the mid-third to the mid-second millennium BC, may be in some way a transitional 'Chinese-Korean' culture.[36] And it is the

so-called 'Liaoning dagger' (see p. 34), with its characteristic mandolin shape, that seems to provide a link between bronze production in China and its subsequent development in Korea.[37]

13. Northern 'table'-type dolmen situated on Kanghwa island, west of Seoul. Early Bronze Age, *c*. 1000 BC.

Tombs

Dolmens (Korean: *ko'indol* or *chisongmyo*) are usually found near villages and, judging from the sorts of burial goods found in them, are thought to have been tombs for people of higher rank, such as clan chiefs. There is no direct connection with dolmens in other parts of northern Asia or Europe, although they seem similar in appearance. Around 200,000 dolmens have been found on the Korean peninsula and 90 per cent of them are located in what is now South Korea. Korean dolmens can be divided into three types: the northern or 'table' type (fig. 13), the 'southern' type which has one large flat boulder covering a pile of stones, and the 'capstone' type, which is a large stone lying flat on the ground on top of a cist burial. Although the northern type is predominantly found in the north of the peninsula and the southern type in the south, this pattern of distribution is not uniform. Southern-type dolmens usually occur in rows, while northern ones often stand in isolation, although sometimes they also occur in rows and groups. Capstone types seem to be later and usually cover a stone cist grave, while southern types sometimes cover jar burials and sometimes stone cists. Dolmens are found on Cheju island and other small southern islands, and single standing stones (menhirs) also occur all over the peninsula. At Hwangsong-ri, a pair of standing stones has been interpreted as a male and female, similar to the later Korean folk custom of wooden pairs of *changsung* village guardians.[38]

Cists are tombs lined with stone slabs, the most common form of burial in Korea at that time. They are usually about 2 m (6.5 ft) long and 30 cm (1 ft) wide, that is, long enough for adult burials; occasionally small jar-coffins, presumably child burials, are found together with stone cists. The practice of using cist tombs probably came from Manchuria, as it is characteristic of the Tuanjie culture of eastern Manchuria and the earliest Korean examples are in the northeast, close to the Tuman river. Some of these contain unusual spoon-like objects carved with human heads. It may be that the alignment of the cist tombs, which differed from region to region, pointed to different ethnic groups. The fact that curved beads (*kogok*) and tubular beads made of amazonite, bronze daggers and burnished pottery have been found in cist tombs has led to the theory that they represent high-class burials. A particularly long stone cist at Namsong-ri contained over a hundred bronze objects, including mirrors, daggers, a socketed axe, a chisel, a kogok, 106 tubular jade beads and fragments of a lacquered birch-bark scabbard. It has been suggested that some of the unusual bronzes found there were a shaman's ritual paraphernalia.[39]

The relationship between stone cists and dolmens is not clear. Although many stone cists are covered by southern-type dolmens in southern Korea, possibly as a kind of marker, it is thought by some scholars that the distribution of cist burials and dolmens are not connected. Kim Won-yong is reported to have favoured the theory that dolmens were originally more numerous than stone cists but that cists were later adopted for their convenience and relative ease of construction. It has also been suggested that differences in size of dolmen capstones reflected the incumbent's status. The burial goods excavated from cists are greater in number and elaborateness than those from dolmens, suggesting higher social rank.[40] However, Kim Byung-mo maintains that the difference lies in the fact that cist burials were a northern practice, while dolmens probably originated in South Asia, being related to rice cultivation.

Settlements

Bronze Age villages consisted in general of semi-subterranean dwellings, both round and square, with several hearths, the numbers of houses in each village ranging from tens to hundreds. The villages were almost always situated on hillsides and the inhabitants cultivated the lower slopes. Some scholars call these villages 'walled towns'.[41] Sometimes longhouses are found, such as at Yoksam-dong on the Han river and Oksong-ri in Kyonggi province (see map 3, p. 32). The small village of Hunam-ri, excavated in the 1970s by Seoul National University, is a very early Bronze Age site (about 1200 BC) on a hill slope near the Han river, where fourteen houses were excavated on both sides of the hill. The houses were of different sizes, some with hardened clay floors and some with a lime plaster. The interiors also differed, and objects excavated attest to the village's way of life: chipped stone axes, stone daggers, semi-lunar reaping knives, pottery, net-sinkers and spindle whorls, whetstones, small triangular stone projectile points and grains of rice.

A later and larger village at Songguk-ri, near Puyo, dates to the early Bronze Age (fifth

Tuman (Tumen) river

Amnok (Yalu) river

• Misong-ri

Chongchon river

Taedong river

EAST SEA

PYONGYANG ■
▲ Tosong-ri
• Simchol-ri
PRESENT DMZ LINE
• Soktal-ri
Shinhung-dong •

• Sinmae-ri

• Oksong-ri
Han river
SEOUL ■ • Karak-dong
Yoksam-dong • • Hunam-ri
• Sangjapo-ri

• Hwangsong-ri

YELLOW SEA

Namsong-ri •

Kum river

• Koejong-dong
Songguk-ri •
• Choyang-dong ▲

Naktong river

KYONGJU ■
Koryong • • Chonjon-ri
Pan'gudae •
KIMHAE ■
Tahori ▲
Taepyong-ri • ▲
PUSAN ■

Yongsan river

▲ Taegok-ri

TSUSHIMA

Iron Age site ▲
Bronze Age site •
Modern towns ■

CHEJU ISLAND

Map 3. Principal Bronze
and Iron Age sites in
Korea.

century BC) and was excavated several times from 1974 onwards. Here dolmens, a cist burial, a jar burial and a kiln site have been found, as well as burnished pottery and grains of rice of the *japonica* variety, suitable for a northern climate. Twenty-two semi-subterranean houses were found, both circular and rectangular. There are unusual oval pits in the centre and rows of post-holes down the long sides and burned remains of beams, as well as a ditch and post-holes for a palisade around the edge of the village. Recent excavations in the 1990s have revealed more dwelling sites with wooden fences. The cist burial found here contained a 'Liaoning' bronze dagger (see p. 34), a polished stone dagger, stone arrow-heads, tubular jades, ornamental beads and curved jades or kogok. It was the first time that a 'Liaoning' dagger and a polished stone dagger had been found together in Korea.[42] Other village sites are at Soktal-ri and Simchol-ri in Hwanghae province, Sinmae-ri on the north Han river and Taepyong-ri near the south coast (see map 3).

It is thought that rice was imported to Korea from China via Manchuria, because semi-lunar stone reaping knives, characteristic of the Chinese Longshan culture in Shandong, have been found in Korea. The shape of these reaping knives is thought to be peculiar to rice cultivation, in contrast to the rectangular knives common in the Chinese Yangshao culture, which are linked to millet cultivation. However, this is by no means certain. In Manchuria it seems that the cutting edge was the straight rather than the convex side. Hunting and fishing are indicated by the presence of the projectile points and net-sinkers, while pig bones at dwelling sites are evidence of their domestication.[43]

14. Above: Detail of rock engravings at Pan'gudae, southeast Korea, showing animals and fish. Late Bronze Age, *c.* 4th–3rd century BC.

Rock art

At up to nine sites in southern Korea, around the Naktong river valley, large panels of rock art have been found, usually on the banks of rivers. The dating of these sites is difficult but the consensus of present opinion is that they date to the late Bronze Age or early Iron Age, that is, to the late first millennium BC or early first millennium AD. Some scholars date them to the Neolithic.[44] The best known are at Pan'gudae and Chonjon-ri near Kyongju. Unfortunately a man-made dam has caused the panel at Pan'gudae to be submerged for a large part of each year. Motifs vary from animals, fish (fig. 14), boats, hunting, fishing, human figures, abstract lozenges and spirals to mask-like figures. The techniques used are pecking, grinding and engraving and there are two styles of depiction of animals and humans: the 'silhouette' style and the 'x-ray' style – the latter showing the bones as if in an x-ray. Sasse suggests the possibility of a link between Korean 'x-ray'-style rock art and that of prehistoric Eurasia and the Arctic circle and compares the depictions of animals at Pan'gudae with contemporary Inuit drawings.

Although much more research is needed to create any sort of chronology for Korean rock art, it seems that the engraved drawings which have V-shaped incisions must have necessitated a metal tool. Identification of the different animals and fish depicted is contentious, with a turtle-like creature also being interpreted as a human. Whales and other fish are depicted in silhouette style and it is difficult to tell, at present, whether both styles of drawing were used at once or whether they represent a chronological development. It is possible that the large numbers of fish and animals depicted at Pan'gudae represent some sort of creation story, while the geometric motifs at Chonjon-ri and Kaejin-myon near Koryong may represent gods, suns or faces and are comparable to motifs found on dolmens in France.[45]

Bronzes

The date of the beginning of bronze production in Korea is disputed. The earliest bronzes are the so-called 'Liaoning daggers', found both in Liaoning in northeast China and in Korea. North Korean archaeologists put the date of the earliest of these daggers, found at Shuangfang, eastern Liaoning, at the thirteenth–eleventh century BC, but the general consensus is that they started to be produced in the eighth–seventh century BC. The 'Liaoning dagger' has bracket-shaped projections and is therefore likened to a mandolin or violin (see fig. 15:1). It is found in the Liaodong peninsula, in the Bohai bay area and in Korea, but nowhere in China south of the Great Wall. Unlike mainstream Chinese bronzes of this period, it was made using a stone mould, as opposed to ceramic piece moulds.

Lee Chung-kyu divides the period of 'Liaoning daggers' into three, spanning the eighth to fourth centuries BC, and thinks that the development of 'Korean-style' slender daggers occurred sometime in the fourth century BC, probably being connected with the expansion of the northern Chinese state of Yan into

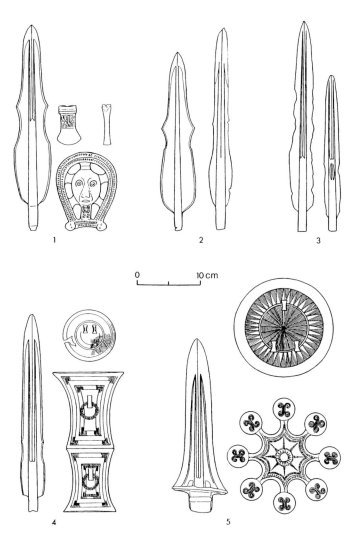

15. Drawing showing the development of bronze types during the Bronze Age through five phases from Phase 1 (8th–7th century BC) to Phase 5 (2nd century BC).

the Liaodong peninsula at the end of the fourth to the beginning of the third century BC. He then divides the slender-dagger period into two, finishing in the second century BC (fig. 15).[46] Although the early type of 'Liaoning dagger' has been found at several Korean sites, the absence of moulds suggests that they were not made in Korea. Late 'Liaoning daggers' have been found mostly in northwest Korea, south of the Chongchon river, while daggers with the early 'Liaoning' blade shape but with a notch in a part of the hilt have been found in the southwest, as at Songguk-ri. This suggests the latter type were locally produced in the south, although no moulds have been discovered yet. Also produced in the south at this time were bronze spear-heads and fan-shaped axes, as evidenced by the discovery of stone moulds.

In the transitional period (fourth century BC), when slender daggers were being introduced, the type produced in Liaoning differed from that produced in Korea, as can be seen by comparing a dagger found at Yujiacun in eastern Liaoning with that found in Sangjapo-ri in southern Korea, the latter having a pronounced constriction in the middle. Korean-style slender daggers proliferated during the third century BC, particularly in the Kum river valley in southwest Korea. Spear-heads and fan-shaped axes also increased in number and other bronze artefacts, in the shape of a shield, bamboo sections or a trumpet, were also produced. These original shapes could be seen as evidence of the development of an indigenous Korean bronze culture in the southwest of the peninsula. The last phase, in the second century BC, is one of a great increase in bronze production, especially in the southwest, and many moulds have been discovered, particularly in the Yongsan river valley. Not only daggers, but also taller spear-heads, Korean-style *ge*-halberds (with narrower blades than the Chinese type), mirrors with fine-lined geometric designs, axes with distinct shoulders, sword-sheaths decorated with twisted rope-like rings, horse- and tiger-shaped bronze belt hooks (fig. 16) and ritual paraphernalia such as several types of jingle bells and pommel rattles are characteristic of a distinctly Koreanized bronze culture. The assemblage of bronzes discovered at the Koejong-dong cist burial in the west of Korea bears evidence of this distinctiveness. It was at this time, too, that Korean-style bronze weapons and mirrors were taken to Kyushu in Japan.[47]

Korean bronze mirrors differ from those made in China in that they are decorated with geometric patterns and have two handles which are off-centre. Kim Won-yong first pointed out the similarity between the geometric patterns on early Korean mirrors and those found, accompanied by 'Liaoning' daggers, at Shi-er-tai yingzi in Liaoning; these are decorated with a kind of geometric Z-pattern. He suggests that the Shi-er-tai yingzi mirrors, with their multiple loops and sometimes decorated on the front, were probably designed to be fastened to a garment and used for ritual purposes, possibly a kind of shamanistic ritual.[48] The decoration on Korean bronze mirrors developed from Z-patterns to hatched triangles and they became finer and more delicate during the period of the Korean Bronze Age (fig. 17). By the third–second century BC mirrors with concentric patterns were being produced, decorated with fine lines, swirls and triangles. Barnes

16. Above: Horse-shaped bronze belt buckle. Late Bronze–Early Iron Age, *c.* 2nd–1st century BC. Length: 8 cm.

17. Right: Bronze mirror with geometric patterns and two off-centre loop handles; possibly for use in shaman rituals. Late Bronze Age, *c.* 300 BC. Diameter: 19.6 cm.

suggests that the later, finer bronze mirrors may have been produced using clay moulds; such intricate designs would have been difficult to carve in stone, and there is moreover an absence of any excavated stone moulds for the finer mirrors.[49]

Raw materials for making bronzes were available in Korea: copper can be found in several mountainous regions, Korea is in one of the world's tin belts and zinc can be found both in North Korea and in the Taebaek mountains in the south. According to Jeon, the zinc content of Korean bronzes varies from 7 per cent to 13 per cent, which is higher than is normal in Chinese bronzes; while Kim has found that 'Liaoning'-type daggers contain a significant amount of lead – 5 per cent to 9 per cent.[50]

Unusual and technically difficult decorative motifs have been found, such as the figures

ploughing and the birds perched on branches (fig. 18), cast on to a fragment of a bronze implement dating to the late first millennium BC. Bronze bells, particularly the star-shaped variety, are examples of shamanistic ritual practices at this time (see fig. 15:5). They are all the more interesting as they are similar to those still in use today by Korean shamans.

18. Detail of part of a bronze implement with decoration of birds on branches. Late Bronze Age, *c.* 4th–3rd century BC. 7.3 × 12.8 cm.

Pottery

More than bronzes do, pottery of the Bronze Age appears to reflect different cultural groups, so the distribution of different types of pottery can be used to identify different cultural regions.[51] Bronze Age pottery is generally called mumun or undecorated pottery, although in Korea it is also called Plain Coarse Pottery. In fact, since incised and painted designs sometimes appear, neither of these terms is strictly accurate, although they represent the general trend towards less or no decoration. Other differences from Neolithic pottery are thicker walls, resulting from the addition of a coarse temper, giving a somewhat crude appearance; the vessel shapes differ, and there is a much wider range of shapes, which include handled jars, steamers and pedestal bowls. The regional variations depend on the vessel shape, decoration and differences in rims.[52]

According to Lee Chung-kyu, northwestern Korea and western Liaoning can be seen as one cultural region in the early Bronze Age, on the basis of the appearance of Misong-ri-style pottery (fig. 19), named after a site on the Amnok river (see map 3, p. 32). This type of pottery has horizontal handles, a gourd-shaped body and trumpet-shaped neck and is decorated sparsely with incised parallel lines. Sometimes, when it is decorated with incised or painted squared spiral designs (similar to those found in the Upper Xiajiadian culture in Manchuria), it is called *pon'gae*, meaning 'lightning'. The Misong-ri type extends south to the Chongchon river and its derivatives as far as the Taedong river. A second type, sometimes called *paengi* after its shape, which resembles a Korean toy spinning-top, is the Shinhung-dong style of pottery. This is prevalent in the Taedong river valley and extends as far north as the Chongchon river and as far south as the Han river. Paengi pots are usually undecorated, have double rims and narrow, flat bases. A variation of the paengi pots is found to the south of the Han river and is called the Karak-dong type, after a site in Seoul. These pots sometimes have a much wider mouth than paengi pots. A third major group, found south of the Han river and extending right down to Cheju island, is the Yoksam-dong type, characterized by a line of holes just below the rim. A fourth regional group, confined to southwest Korea, is the Songguk-ri type, named after the dwelling site near Puyo; these have an everted mouth and a bulging body which narrows towards the bottom. The fifth group, called the Koejong-dong type, after the site in southwest Korea near the Kum river, occurs in the later Bronze Age, during the period when Korean-style bronze daggers were made (third–second century BC); these pots are either burnished or have an applied clay band around the rim, although there are also regional variations (see fig. 19:5).[53] Burnished pottery appears in two types: either small globular jars, burnished a bright orange-red using iron oxide, or rarer black jars with long narrow necks, which appear very late in the Bronze Age and early in the Iron Age. The red variety is found more often in burials than in dwellings, suggesting that it was a mark of high status.[54] It is interesting to note that both burnished pots and pedestal bowls (Chinese: *dou*) are characteristic of the Chinese Longshan culture of Shandong province. Although they were produced much earlier in China (*c.* 2000 BC onwards), the proximity of the Shandong peninsula to northwest Korea suggests that the techniques may have been introduced through that route. In the final stage of the Korean Bronze Age, grey paddled pots appear in the northwest, while pots with applied clay bands continued in southern Korea.

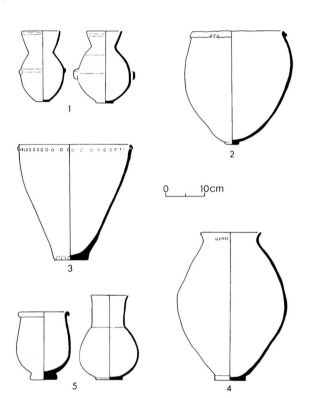

19. Drawing of the five main types of Bronze Age pots: (1) Misong-ri; (2) Shinhung-dong; (3) Yoksam-dong; (4) Songguk-ri; (5) Koejong-dong.

0   10cm

Iron Age and Proto-Three Kingdoms period

This period is sometimes divided into the Early Iron Age (300 BC–0) and the Later Iron Age or Proto-Three Kingdoms period (0–AD 300).[55] Choi Sung-rak divides it rather into four phases and also divides the Iron Age archaeological sites in southern Korea into three regional groups. The first, located around the Naktong river valley, comprises earthen pit burials, containing either a wooden coffin or a wooden chamber tomb, accompanied by bronze daggers and mirrors as well as iron artefacts. The second group, located in the south coastal and island areas, includes shell-mounds and jar burials, which are usually connected. The jar burials of the Iron Age consisted of two large jars placed mouth to mouth, in contrast to those of the Bronze Age which consisted of a single pottery vessel set vertically in a pit with a stone slab cover. Large jar-coffin burials appeared after the third century AD in the Yongsan river valley.[56] The third group of Iron Age sites include stone cists and some dwelling sites, most of which are located in central inland areas.[57]

Archaeological evidence shows a direct relationship with China at this time. For example, Chinese mirrors, coins and oracle bones have been found along the coastal areas of southern Korea. In addition, the practice of using earth pit burials is thought to have come from China through north Korea, probably via the Taedong river valley. Pit burials in the Taedong river area contained horse trappings and carriage fittings, suggesting that the élite of that area had close contacts with northern China. This is corroborated by historical evidence in the Chinese histories. The *Shi ji*, for instance, records that in 195 BC an official of the Chinese state of Yan, called Weiman (Korean: Wiman), fled to Korea (called Chaoxian in Chinese or Choson in the Korean reading of the same characters), where he founded a 'state' called Choson, with its capital near present-day Pyongyang. Wiman Choson was ruled by Weiman's grandson until Han Chinese troops destroyed it in 109–108 BC. It is difficult to be sure whether the Chinese historical record, which would have been written from a particular viewpoint, can be regarded as entirely accurate. It is therefore not certain whether Choson extended over a large area of territory or just the capital city. Korean historians tend to call Wiman Choson an early Korean state, although in fact it was connected with and derived from the Chinese state of Yan. Choi argues that the presence of knife-shaped Yan coins implies long-distance trade and that Wiman Choson was a true state. Barnes suggests that Choson was probably only one of several élite groups in the northern half of the Korean peninsula at that time.[58]

Lelang and the Chinese commanderies

The Han Chinese attack on Choson was part of its expanionist policy and connected with its search for alternative sources of salt and iron, both of which were government monopolies. Chinese commanderies or colonies were then established, which covered the northern half of the Korean peninsula. The southern half of the peninsula, called Chin (Chinese: Chen) in the Chinese *Wei ji* (part of the *Sanguo ji*), was much less influenced by China. It split into three groups, which are recorded in the *Hou Han shu*, called Pyonhan, Mahan and Chinhan or the Three Han (but having no connection with the Chinese Han dynasty).

Although five commanderies were set up in the north, only three – Liaodong, Xuantu and Lelang – lasted any time. A fourth commandery, Taebang (Chinese: Taifang), established in the third century AD, lasted until AD 313, when Koguryo attacked from the north and the Chinese withdrew. The most important commandery was Lelang (Korean: Nangnang), which had its capital near Pyongyang on the site of the old Wiman Choson capital. Excavations by Japanese archaeologists in 1934–5 revealed the walled enclosure at Tosong-ri, on the south bank of the Taedong river near Pyongyang, which is thought to have been the principal town of the commandery. It featured brick-paved lanes, covered drainage culverts and roof-tiles inscribed 'Lelang ceremonial palace'. Many Han bronze coins and clay seals show that this town played an important economic and administrative role. Many tombs of the élite were also excavated at that time in the area to the southeast of the town, where around 1500 earth-mound tombs are scattered. Both the earlier wood-chamber tombs and the later brick or stone chamber tombs, often containing outer and inner coffins, are in Han style, with arches and vaulted ceilings. Luxury goods such as bronze vessels, lacquered baskets and vessels, ceramics, bronze mirrors, silks, jewellery, iron weapons, bronze horse-trappings and chariot-fittings, wood and pottery tomb figures and even wall-paintings found in some of these tombs are evidence of large-scale imports from China, some coming from as far away as Sichuan.[59] Even the wood for the coffins was imported from south of the Yangzi river. The Tomb of the Painted Basket, dating to *c.* AD 100, is perhaps the best known, the basket in question being of lacquered wicker with painted lacquer panels depicting figures. The tomb consists of two chambers with three lacquered coffins and an ante-room containing the burial goods. A wall-painting shows figures mounted on horses. The occupants were a male, a female and a child, the male probably being an important official, as there was also an inscribed wooden tablet stating that Tiangong sent an underling to make a sacrifice with three rolls of yellow silk. Although such inscriptions or official seals can identify some of the occupants of these tombs, the question of whether they were Korean or Chinese is more difficult. It is likely that some of the occupants were Chinese immigrants and some were native Koreans who had adopted Chinese ways and who were employed by the ruling Chinese. Some of the more unusual grave goods show specifically Korean characteristics, however, such as a pair of table legs in the form of bears and a drinking cup of lacquered birch bark.[60]

The Samhan or Three Han in the south

The three areas in the south corresponding to Mahan (southwest), Pyonhan (Naktong river valley) and Chinhan (southeast) are those areas which were to develop in the Three Kingdoms period into Paekche, Kaya and Silla. The northern area, covered by the Chinese commanderies and the Puyo people in the far north, would eventually become Koguryo. It is for this reason that the first three centuries AD are increasingly referred to in modern scholarship as the Proto-Three Kingdoms period. In reality the three Han were each divided at that time into many small polities or chiefdoms, seventy-eight in all. Some of the local chiefs were in contact with the Chinese commanderies, but the south was far behind the north in administrative organization. Evidence of contact with China and beyond comes from tombs such as the pit burials of the first–second centuries AD at Choyang-dong near Kyongju, which contained Han mirrors, iron weapons and lacquer sheaths, as well as imported glass. In the Pyonhan area, however, at Taho-ri Tomb no. 1, plain lacquer stem-cups of circular and rectangular shape (containing persimmons) and a lacquer writing-brush handle and sword-sheath are evidence of possible local Korean

20. Black lacquered
square stem-cup
excavated from Taho-ri.
Iron Age, *c.* 1st century BC.
Ht: 12.5 cm.

production of lacquer during the first century BC (fig. 20). They are mixed with Chinese imports such as mirrors and *wushu* coins, as well as glass beads. The writing-brush in particular shows a sophisticated cultural level.

Technology and trade

Iron technology in the south is recorded in the Chinese histories, such as the *Sanguo ji*, which states that 'Pyonhan produces iron. Han, Ye and Ancient Japan [Wa or Wae] all come to buy it. Iron is used for buying and selling and Pyonhan also supplies iron to the two Chinese commanderies of Lelang and Daifang.' Choi suggests that, despite the undoubted introduction of iron technology from China through the Chinese commanderies in the north, there is strong evidence for an indigenous development of iron technology in the south predating the commanderies and arising around the time of the founding of Wiman Choson (194–108 BC). Many iron objects, both weapons and tools, are found in tombs from this period but it is sometimes difficult to be certain whether they are Chinese or Korean products. Taylor concludes that although iron artefacts were present on the peninsula from *c.* 500 BC, local production probably began in small pit furnaces in the early Iron Age–Proto-Three Kingdoms period. It is uncertain what the proportions of Korean products were to imported Chinese ones.[61]

Stoneware technology also developed in Korea during this period, under Chinese influence. The precise date of this development is somewhat unclear and is the subject of controversy amongst Korean scholars. On the basis of kiln excavations at Taegok-ri and Chinchon in the southwest of the peninsula, Barnes argues that the long sloping kiln technology of south China was probably carried by sea from southeast China to southwest Korea. Although the earliest kiln remains in south Korea so far date to the late third to early fourth centuries AD, it is likely that stoneware production in the north started considerably earlier than this and was introduced via Lelang. Korean terms for pottery of this period have been revised and now the traditional but rather imprecise term of Kimhae ware (named after the site near Pusan where paddled and incised grey Iron Age pottery, accompanied by iron slag and a Chinese Wang Mang coin dated AD 14, was first excavated in 1921 by Umehara and Hamada) has been replaced by *yonjil* (earthenware), *wajil* (literally 'tile-ware', meaning a sort of high-fired earthenware) and *kyongjil* or true high-fired stoneware made of stoneware clay. A typical yonjil shape is a round-bottomed jar with horn-shaped handles (fig. 21). There is clear similarity between the so-called Kimhae paddled pottery and Late Zhou and Han Chinese vessels, while the cross-hatched designs on the shoulders of some Korean wajil jars reflect southern Chinese stoneware of the second–third centuries AD.[62]

Apart from the references in the Chinese historical records to the Wa or Wae, archaeological evidence in the form of excavated Yayoi pottery attests to trade with ancient Japan during the Iron Age. In the far north, the Puyo people, living in the area of present-day Changchun and Jilin in northeast China, exported horses, sable furs and red gemstones to China. Puyo (Chinese: Fuyu), located between the Xianbei and Koguryo, maintained a mutually beneficial relationship with China. Puyo reached a peak of power in the first century AD, but eventually surrendered to Koguryo in AD 493.[63] Its capital was at Jilin, where excavations at the cemeteries of Mao'ershan and Laoheshan have revealed gold earrings as well as bronze cauldrons with pierced stands, both of which are interesting precursors of Korean metalwork and ceramics of the Three Kingdoms period.

21. *Yonjil* (earthenware) jar with horn-shaped handles. Proto-Three Kingdoms period, *c.* 1st century AD. Ht: 43 cm.

CHAPTER 2
Three Kingdoms and Unified Silla Period

Although the first part of this period is usually called the Three Kingdoms period (*c.* AD 300–668), Korea was in fact at first divided into four. Koguryo controlled the largest area, in the north; Paekche controlled the southwest. Kaya or Karak was the name given to a confederation of political powers in south-central Korea around the Naktong river basin and present-day Pusan, but it could not be called a kingdom and in AD 532 was conquered by and absorbed into Silla, which occupied the southeast (map 4, p. 44). Silla went on to unify the majority of the Korean peninsula in 668 and from 668 to 935 ruled as Unified Silla.

Specific dates, established partly on ancient histories, have been traditionally assigned to the foundation of each of the Three Kingdoms: Koguryo in 37 BC, Paekche in 18 BC and Silla in 57 BC. The corresponding date for Kaya is AD 42. Modern scholarship, basing itself on archaeological and documentary evidence, is moving towards a re-assessment of these dates. In place of a long undifferentiated stretch of around six hundred years, it suggests two broad divisions into a Proto-Three Kingdoms period, covering the first three centuries of the modern era and overlapping with the later part of the Iron Age (0–*c.* AD 300), and a Three Kingdoms period from *c.* AD 300 which ended in AD 668 in the unification of the peninsula under Silla. These issues remain controversial.

Historical sources for this period include Chinese, Japanese and Korean records. The latter comprise the *Samguk sagi (History of the Three Kingdoms)* by Kim Pusik and the *Samguk yusa (Memorabilia of the Three Kingdoms)* by Ilyon, a Buddhist monk.[1] Both were written much later, in the twelfth and thirteenth centuries. Their reliability and usefulness is therefore limited as they are not objective records, although they are thought to be based on lost contemporary histories. Chinese records such as the *Wei ji* are also useful as they make frequent references to Korea, and the Chinese histories, in general, provide reliable and organized information stemming from a long historiographical tradition. The Japanese *Nihon shoki* and *Kojiki* are informative on Japan's early links with Korea, but the dating is not entirely consistent. The Japanese histories, furthermore, have been used in the twentieth century to justify Japan's colonial ambitions towards Korea. Partly because of the unhappy history between the two countries during this century, scholars from Korea and Japan have quite different interpretations of the references in the Japanese histories to contacts between their countries in the early period. There is little doubt that Koguryo, Paekche and Kaya all had close contacts with Japan, which they called 'Wa' or 'Wae'. Trade between Kaya and Wae was motivated by the Japanese need for iron, to be used in farming and warfare. Korea was a source of high culture, technology and luxury items for the

22. Interior of King Muryong's tomb showing the moulded bricks lining the vaulted chamber, based on Liang Chinese tomb design. Paekche, AD 525.

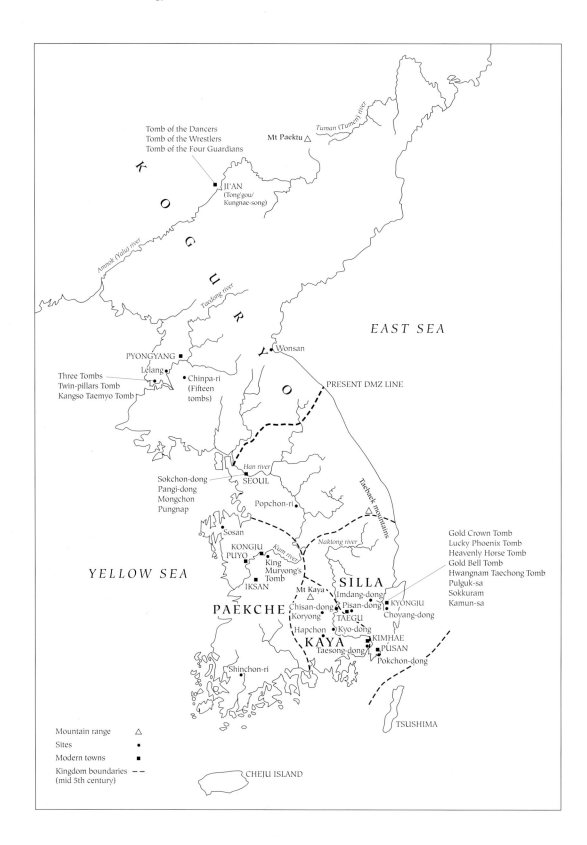

Tomb of the Dancers
Tomb of the Wrestlers
Tomb of the Four Guardians

Tuman (Tumen) river

Mt Paektu △

K
O
G
U
R
Y
O

JI'AN
(Tong'gou/
Kungnae-song)

Amnok (Yalu) river

Taedong river

EAST SEA

PYONGYANG ■

Wonsan

PRESENT DMZ LINE

Three Tombs
Twin-pillars Tomb
Kangso Taemyo Tomb

Lelang

Chinpa-ri
(Fifteen
tombs)

Han river

Sokchon-dong
Pangi-dong
Mongchon
Pungnap

SEOUL ■

Popchon-ri

Taebaek mountains

YELLOW SEA

Sosan

KONGJU
PUYO

Kum river

King
Muryong's
Tomb

IKSAN

Naktong river

Gold Crown Tomb
Lucky Phoenix Tomb
Heavenly Horse Tomb
Gold Bell Tomb
Hwangnam Taechong Tomb
Pulguk-sa
Sokkuram
Kamun-sa

Mt Kaya △

SILLA

Imdang-dong

PAEKCHE

Chisan-dong

Pisan-dong

KYONGJU

Koryong

TAEGU

Choyang-dong

Hapchon

Kyo-dong

KAYA

KIMHAE

Taesong-dong

PUSAN

Pokchon-dong

Shinchon-ri

TSUSHIMA

Mountain range   △

Sites   •

Modern towns   ■

Kingdom boundaries – –
(mid 5th century)

CHEJU ISLAND

Map 4. Principal
archaeological sites
in the Three Kingdoms
period.

Japanese, who were definitely less developed at that time. However, the *Nihon shoki* portrays the Kaya states as a colony of Japan's Yamato court. Korean sources do not substantiate this view and therein lies the basis of the controversy. It is a scholarly dispute charged with emotions that flow from Japan's use, when it colonized Korea by force in 1910, of the argument that it was reclaiming its historical foothold on the peninsula. Ironically, evidence of much of Korea's early history then came to light during the Japanese occupation thanks to the work of Japanese archaeologists such as Umehara Sueji. However, many exciting new discoveries have been made by Korean archaeologists in the Kaya area from the 1980s onwards, which challenge the Japanese colonial interpretation.[2] Much more objective research is still needed to clarify the relationship between the two countries during the Three Kingdoms/Kofun period.[3]

Koguryo

The kingdom of Koguryo grew up sometime in the first century BC. Koguryo people were horse-riders and warriors who, according to the Chinese *Han shu,* were the previous Puyo people from the Songhua river area. Alternative suggestions are that they came from Liaoning or that the Weimo (Korean: Yemaek) were their ancestors.[4] Although they posed a threat to the Chinese and there were constant skirmishes between the two, peaceful trade was also carried on between China and Koguryo: Koguryo exported raw materials such as gold, silver, pearls, furs, ginseng, fabric and slaves, while it imported from China manufactured goods such as weapons, silk clothes, head-dresses, books and stationery.[5]

The earliest archaeological sites belonging to Koguryo also illustrate, by their location, the great territory which Koguryo controlled. These sites are at Tong'gou, near present-day Ji'an, a Chinese city on the northern bank of the Amnok river (map 4). Koguryo managed to advance towards the Chinese Liao river basin to the west and the Taedong river to the south, eventually capturing the area of the old Chinese commandery at Lelang in AD 313 and coming into confrontation with Paekche. It was, however, under the famous King Kwanggaeto (reigned AD 391–413) that Koguryo reached its height of expansion. His name means 'broad expander of domain' and his military campaigns are recorded on a large stone stele at his tomb at Kungnae-song, then the Koguryo capital. Kwanggaeto managed to occupy Liaodong to the west, subdue a Tungusic tribe called the Sushen in Manchuria to the northeast, attack Paekche to the south, expanding to the area between the Imjin and Han rivers, and repel a Japanese Wa force attacking Silla in the southeast. His successor, King Changsu (the 'long-lived'), reigned from 413 to 491 and presided over a flourishing Koguryo, moving the capital south to Pyongyang and cleverly maintaining diplomatic relations with both China's northern and southern dynasties. In 475, Koguryo seized the Paekche capital of Hansong (near Seoul) and beheaded the Paekche king, Kaero. By this time, Koguryo had become a centralized, aristocratic state with a statutory law code and a National Confucian Academy and had officially adopted Buddhism as the state cult.[6]

Tombs

Early Koguryo tombs were cairns consisting of a bed of river cobbles underneath the burial and a mound of more cobbles on top. In the fourth century AD enormous stepped pyramids started to be made of cut stone blocks, containing elevated burial chambers. The square shape of these tombs is thought to be related to those of Liaoning, which date back to the Neolithic period. The largest stone pyramid is at Tong'gou, the site of Kungnae-song, the first Koguryo capital, which was used until 427, when the capital moved to Pyongyang. Almost 75 m (246 ft) long, this tomb is called the Tomb of the General and is thought to be that of King Kwanggaeto, whose power would have been sufficient to mobilize and organize the massive labour force needed to construct it. The lowest level uses enormous stones, up to 3 m by 5 m (10 ft by 16 ft), while smaller tombs resembling

dolmens were placed at the four corners. Enormous tombs such as this were in a minority and were, no doubt, for people of high status. More numerous are hemispherical earth mounds on a square base, covering an inner structure of stone.[7]

23. Dancers from the Tomb of the Dancers, Tong'gou, near Ji'an, northeast China. Koguryo, 4th–6th century AD.

There are two Koguryo tombs of which the date is certain, because of inscriptions found in them. The first, Anak Tomb no. 3, although situated near the mouth of the Tae-dong river near Pyongyang, can in fact be dated to AD 357, before the move to Pyongyang, on the basis of an inscription it contains. It is laid out like a palace, with a central chamber containing eighteen limestone columns surrouded by four other chambers. Paintings show the tomb incumbent riding in a carriage with hundreds of attendants, some of them knights on horseback. The inscription identifies the incumbent as Tong Shou, the last ruler of the Chinese commandery of Taebang. The question of whether this tomb should be regarded as Chinese (commandery period) or Korean (Koguryo) is controversial. It is generally in Koguryo style and may be the oldest Koguryo-type tomb with wall-paintings.

The other dated tomb is at Tokhung-ri, Tae'an, northwest of Pyongyang. Dated by an inscription written in ink on the wall, it is the tomb of a political refugee from China who died in Pyongyang in AD 408. He can be seen painted on the wall of the ante-chamber of his tomb, receiving subordinates who are lined up in two rows.[8]

Of the known Koguryo tombs, around ten thousand in number, seventy-six are decorated with mural paintings in the inner chambers. Many of them were built using sophisticated architectural features such as pillars, corridors and corbelled ceilings. Some of the

24. Female attendants with long pleated skirts from Takamatsu tomb, Nara Prefecture, Japan. Late 7th–8th century AD.

paintings were applied directly on to the bare stone walls and some on to walls first plastered with lime. These paintings are invaluable sources of information about the lives of the occupants as well as about early Korean painting styles and techniques. Details of Koguryo architecture, dress, entertainments and religion are depicted. The most famous includes the fifth-century Tomb of the Dancers (Ji'an Tomb no. 1), which is decorated with paintings of dancers wearing long-sleeved jackets and trousers tied at the ankles (fig. 23), and armoured soldiers on horseback. Tomb no. 12 has portraits of the noble occupant of the tomb and his wife in each of the two interior chambers, which each have an ante-room and corbelled ceilings. This tomb is perhaps one of the richest in details of daily life. In the southern of the two chambers are paintings of a procession of nobles and noblewomen in pleated skirts behind a carriage. Two dogs guard the entrance and also painted on the walls are a stable, a granary, male and female servants pounding grain, a storage jar and a dancing scene. In the corridor are a tiger hunt and deer hunt. The northern chamber depicts a bear hunt and an armoured battle.

The subjects of some of the later tombs show strong influence from Han dynasty China. For example, Ji'an Tomb no. 17 includes animals of the four directions on the walls, together with a ceiling painting of a white tiger and green dragon decorated with gilt metal and jewels. Ji'an Tomb no. 4, dating to the end of the sixth century AD, includes Buddhist guardian figures, evidence of the acceptance of Buddhism.

After Ji'an the other main area of Koguryo tombs is in the vicinity of Pyongyang, where there are thirty-seven tombs grouped in clusters. Since the capital of Koguryo was re-located to Pyongyang in AD 427, these tombs mostly date to that period. Mounded tombs with stone-built chambers sometimes with mural paintings developed here, in the former territory of Lelang, a region where Koguryo permitted many political refugees from China to settle. The Twin-Pillars tomb has two octagonal pillars between the main chamber and the ante-room and many fine paintings that include an ox-drawn two-wheeled chariot with a canopy. Twenty km (12.5 miles) southeast of Pyongyang, at Chinpa-ri, is a group of fifteen tombs which have pivoted stone doors at the entrance to the chambers. Chinese

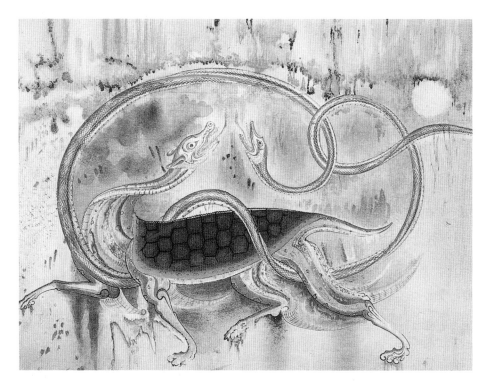

25. Tortoise and snake, symbolizing the north, from the Great Tomb at Kangso, near Pyongyang. Koguryo, early 7th century AD.

26. Tortoise and snake from the north wall of Takamatsu tomb, Nara Prefecture, Japan. Late 7th–8th century AD.

influence can be seen here too in the paintings of constellations on the ceiling and the animals of the four directions on the walls of Tomb no. 4.

The paintings in Koguryo tombs have been divided into three thematic groups by Kim Won-yong: those portraying the occupant; those illustrating events in the occupant's life; and those depicting the Chinese animals of the four directions, as a sort of microcosm. A technical progression can be seen, with the Three Tombs located to the southwest of Pyongyang showing the most developed technique, using dynamic, fluid lines and bright colours (see fig. 25). As well as providing invaluable information about the lifestyle, costumes, architecture and beliefs of the Koguryo people, Koguryo tomb paintings also provide evidence of the beginnings of portrait, landscape and genre painting on the Korean peninsula.[9]

It is apparent that both the Koguryo-type stone chamber tomb and the practice of painting murals inside tombs spread from Koguryo to Japan, possibly taken there by emigrants who may have taken refuge in Japan around the fall of Koguryo in 668. Evidence of this can be seen in the late sixth-century Fujinoki tomb in Ikaruga, excavated in 1985, and the Takamatsu tomb in Nara, excavated in 1972, which can be dated to *c.* AD 700. In the latter, paintings of animals of the four directions are very similar to those in Koguryo tombs (fig. 26), while female attendants on the west wall wear long jackets over pleated skirts, showing great similarity to the fashions displayed in Koguryo tombs (see fig. 24). However, it is not known whether the painters of these tomb murals were from Koguryo or from Tang China.[10]

Apart from those in the regions of the two Koguryo capitals (Kungnae-song, then Pyongyang), Koguryo tombs have also been found in Wonsan, on the Korean northeast coast, and on the upper reaches of the North Han river. Very few grave goods have been found in Koguryo tombs because the method of their construction, incorporating horizontal tunnels, meant that they were easily looted. Two Koguryo gilt-bronze crowns and several earrings are evidence of sophisticated metalworking techniques. An inscribed bronze lidded bowl dating to AD 415 and including the name of King Kwanggaeto was excavated from a Silla tomb, while glazed pottery was found in the Tomb of the Dancers. Little information is available about Koguryo pottery and, until recently, only a few unprovenanced examples of vessels existed, including a white stamped jar and a grey jar with a painted grid pattern in the National Museum of Korea. However, recent excavations have unearthed more Koguryo pots at Pungnap and at Acha fortress, both in Seoul.

Architecture

Remains of Koguryo towns have been discovered at Ji'an (Tong'gou), at Fushun in Liaoning and at Pyongyang. The city wall at Ji'an is rectangular, after the Chinese model, but is constructed of stone as opposed to stamped earth and is 8 km (5 miles) in circumference. The site of a palace has been located by the discovery of decorated ceramic tiles. In the Fushun area in Liaoning, where nineteen Koguryo tombs have also been discovered, there are ruins of a walled city with a wall circumference of 2300 m (7544 ft) and four gates. Bricks, tiles and iron artefacts have also been found. The archaeological remains of the Koguryo capital at Pyongyang include a fortress and a palace. Buildings up to 80 m by 30 m (262 ft by 98 ft) in size were built along streets, and gardens included artificial hills and lotus ponds. A new walled town was constructed after AD 552 on Taesongsan with a fortified wall 7 km (4.3 miles) long. There were twenty gates and towers in the city wall, with wells, storehouses and armouries.[11]

Earthenware roof-tiles and tile-ends are evidence that the Koguryo decorated their palaces and temples in Chinese style with tiles bearing impressed decoration. Koguryo tiles are decorated with lotus flowers and demon masks, the latter to ward off evil spirits. The decoration is generally in higher relief and more vigorous than that on Paekche or Silla roof-tiles.

Evidence of the adoption of Buddhism by Koguryo in the fourth century AD is provided by the remains of temples and some extant sculptures (see section on Buddhist sculpture in the Three Kingdoms, below). A ceramic Buddhist figure and clay models for bronze figures were found near Pyongyang; and three fifth-century Buddhist temple sites have been excavated near the city, one of which had a large octagonal pagoda in the centre.[12]

Paekche

The date of the founding of the kingdom of Paekche is not certain, although the *Samguk sagi* puts it at 18 BC. It developed out of one of the walled-town states in Mahan territory and by AD 246 was strong enough to repel the Chinese commandery of Taebang. By that time, the eighth Paekche king, Koi (reigned 234–86), was on the throne. This King Koi is probably the same person as Kui, whom Paekche later regarded as its founding figure and honoured in ceremonies four times a year. It is recorded that under King Koi sixteen grades of official rank were created, together with an official dress code, and that anti-corruption measures were introduced. Later, under the warrior king Kun Chogo (reigned 346–75), Paekche destroyed Mahan in the south and attacked Koguryo in the north, opening relations with the Eastern Jin in south China and with the Wa in Japan. It was also under King Kun Chogo that the history of Paekche, the *Sogi* (later destroyed), was completed and that queens began to be chosen exclusively from the Chin family. Very soon after this, under King Chimnyu (reigned 384–5), Paekche adopted the Buddhist faith. In 433 Paekche allied with Silla in order to counter the Koguryo threat, and in 475, after Koguryo expansion forced it to move its capital south to Ungjin (present-day Kongju, on the Kum river), the Paekche king, Tongsong, married into the Silla royal family. Paekche then experienced a period of strong rule under kings Tongsong (reigned 479–501), Muryong (reigned 501–23) and Song (reigned 523–54). Song moved the capital yet further south, to the more favourable location of Sabi (present-day Puyo), as well as encouraging the spread of Buddhism and strengthening Paekche's ties with the Chinese Southern Dynasties. Paekche's alliance with Silla was, however, to come to an abrupt end when Silla seized the territories around the Han river which Paekche had won back from Koguryo. King Song was killed in battle and Paekche then allied with Koguryo, its former enemy.[13]

Tombs

Of the Three Kingdoms, Paekche is generally regarded as embodying the greatest artistic refinement and sophistication. Unfortunately, relatively little remains of its buildings or tomb goods, the result of destruction and plunder in the many battles with Koguryo, Silla and ultimately Tang China, which eventually aided Silla in its unification of the peninsula. The construction of Paekche horizontal chamber tombs, moreover, facilitated tomb robbery. However, the burial customs were not uniform over the whole of Paekche and several different types of tomb were employed. Jar-coffins were still used in some areas in the south, some being concentrated in cemeteries with square or keyhole-shaped mounds.

(Keyhole-shaped mounds were common in Kofun-period Japan and may possibly have originated in Korea.) Usually a large and small jar were placed mouth to mouth and contained the whole body of the deceased. Occasionally burial goods are found in these jar-coffins, such as one at Shinchon-ri in Naju, which contained a gilt-bronze crown and bronze shoes. Horizontal chamber tombs were mostly made of stone and sometimes of brick. Stepped-pyramid chamber tombs found in the northern Paekche area at Sokchon-dong are evidence of contacts between Koguryo and Paekche. One of these tombs, which had been looted, still contained two gold earrings and three gold crown ornaments, suggesting that it was the tomb of a ruler and that the Paekche and Koguryo royal families intermarried. Earth-mound tombs were also used in Paekche, a group near Pangi-dong in Seoul revealing underground stone chambers. A small tomb in Pobchon-ri consisting of a stone-lined rectangular pit contained a Chinese Yue-ware sheep dating to the mid-fourth century AD.[14]

The most exciting archaeological find from the Paekche period is undoubtedly the intact brick chamber tomb of King Muryong, discovered in 1971 and excavated under the directorship of the late Kim Won-yong (fig. 22, p. 42). Situated on a hill on the outskirts of Kongju, it contained epitaph plaques identifying the king and the date of his burial (AD 525). Chinese influence is shown in the practice described on one of the plaques of making a contract with the earth spirits for the purchase of the land for the tomb. A string of Chinese coins of the Liang dynasty was placed on the plaque as payment. On the reverse side of this plaque was the epitaph of the Queen, who was buried in 529. The south-facing entrance, the vaulted corridor and the rectangular chamber with a semi-circular vault are all similar to Chinese Liang tombs. The bricks used in its construction have moulded decoration of geometric patterns and Buddhist lotus flowers, and flame-shaped niches in the walls contained bowl-lamps made of green-glazed stoneware (celadon). Although the ceramics in King Muryong's tomb were undoubtedly Chinese, the gold and silver were all of Korean manufacture. The *Jiu Tang shu* records that Paekche kings wore silk caps decorated with gold flowers and that their officials wore caps with silver flowers. Gold floral ornaments excavated in King Muryong's tomb, for decorating the head-dresses of the king and queen, substantiate the historical record. In fact these gold floral decorations are like a flame, similar to those on flaming mandorlas of early Chinese and Korean Buddhist sculptures. Two silver bracelets found beside the queen were dated to AD 520 and inscribed with the name of the silversmith, Dari, and the weight of silver. They were decorated with scaled dragons. According to the excavation report, the 'ri' of the maker's name is a Paekche name and uses the same character as that in the name of the Korean craftsman who made the Sakyamuni triad in the Horyu-ji at Nara in Japan, who therefore also came from Paekche.[15]

Architecture

Paekche architecture can be seen in the present day only through archaeological remains of temple sites and in the wooden buildings in Japan which were constructed by Paekche technicians. The Miruk temple site at Iksan shows that it was larger in size than the renowned Hwangnyong-sa in Silla Kyongju. It had a stone pagoda to the east and west and a wooden pagoda in the centre. Remains of stone lanterns and foundation stones for terraces and columns have also been found. The only remaining pagoda at this site has six of the estimated original seven or nine storeys left. This and a five-storey stone pagoda at the site of Chongnim temple in Puyo are the only Paekche stone pagodas to survive. The temple site at Chongnim has been excavated to reveal the gate, pagoda, golden hall, lecture hall and surrounding corridors.[16]

During the reign of King Song, Paekche doctors, astrological and calendrical experts, monks and artisans were sent to Japan to found Buddhist temples, which in layout resemble those of Paekche.[17] The bracket system of the seventh-century wooden pagoda at the Horyu-ji temple in Nara can be compared with Paekche work and its silhouette shows great similarity to that of the Chongnim-sa pagoda in Puyo, suggesting that it was the work of Paekche craftsmen.[18]

Sculpture

In addition to the architectural similarities between temples in Paekche and Japan, sculptures (see section on Buddhist sculpture in the Three Kingdoms, below) such as the wooden statue of Avalokitesvara (Japanese: Kannon; Korean: Kwanum) in the Horyu-ji (fig. 27) show Paekche features, acknowledged in the popular name of Kudara Kannon given to it in more recent times (Kudara signifies Paekche in Japanese). Paekche features include the gently smiling face, the flowing lines of the drapery, the flaming mandorla, the openwork crown and the double-veined lotus petals at the base. The openwork flowers and coiled vines on the crown are very close to those seen on artefacts from King Muryong's tomb and the hanging pendants at the sides suggest the pendants on Korean pre-Buddhist royal gold crowns. Although there are no extant Paekche wooden sculptures in Korea, the Kudara Kannon is most probably the work of a craftsman of Paekche origin.[19]

Metalware

Evidence of the high quality of sixth-century Paekche metalwork is provided in King Muryong's tomb by a bronze wine-cup with a silver lid, decorated with lotus petals and dragons. The lotus petal decoration is Buddhist in inspiration, while the landscape incised on the lid is more Daoist in tone.[20] This combination of Buddhism and Daoism can also be seen on a spectacular recent find of Paekche metalwork, a gilt-bronze incense-burner in the shape of a mountain, with a dragon stand and phoenix lid (fig. 28), excavated from Nungsan-ri near Puyo. Mountain-shaped incense-burners (Chinese: boshanlu) were common in China from the Han dynasty, when they were associated with Daoist ideas of the afterlife. Decorated with heavenly beings and immortals flying amongst cloudy landscapes, the incense wafting out of the holes in the lid added to the other-worldly atmosphere. These incense-

28 Right: Mountain-shaped Pongnaesan incense-burner in gilt-bronze excavated from Nungsan-ri, near the Paekche capital of Puyo, in 1993. This is so far the only such incense-burner found in Korea and shows Paekche's close links with the Chinese Liang dynasty. Ht: 1.35 m.

27 Left: Wooden sculpture of Avalokitesvara (called Kudara Kannon). A 1920s copy of the original 7th-century sculpture in the Horyu-ji, Nara, this sculpture shows how Paekche wooden sculpture would have looked had it survived. Ht: 3.1 m.

burners were also thought to portray the blessed mountain island of the immortals, Penglai (Korean: Pongnae), which rose out of the waves usually decorating the base. With the introduction of Buddhism to China in the post-Han period, these incense-burners began to acquire Buddhist motifs as well, such as lotus flowers, while retaining their mountain shape and decoration of immortals. The recently excavated incense-burner is one of the most splendid in existence and the only known Korean example. Although similar to such burners produced by the Liang Chinese, it suggests how Paekche master craftsmen may have adapted Chinese ideas and amalgamated them with their own traditions and techniques. The lotus flowers adorning the incense-burner, for example, are similar to that on the knob of the bronze wine-cup from King Muryong's tomb, while the applied figures adorning the mountain recall those on Silla tomb pottery of the fifth–sixth centuries. (These figures in turn in some ways resemble those applied on Yue funerary jars of the Jin period in China.) The overlapping mountains portrayed on the upper part of the burner are also similar to the mountainous landscapes on Paekche moulded bricks.[21]

A seven-branched iron sword was, according to the *Nihon gi*, given by Paekche to Yamato Japan in AD 372; this sword is thought to be the one now preserved in the Isonokami shrine. The sword is evidence of the high level of Paekche iron-manufacture and its incised inscription is taken as evidence that Wae (or the western Japanese islands) was a vassal state of Paekche at the time. (The inscription has, however, also been translated to mean that Paekche was a vassal state of Wae.) The *Nihon gi* also records that a mirror, described as a 'seven-little-one-mirror', was sent together with the sword. A bronze mirror decorated with human figures and now preserved at the Suda Hachiman shrine in Wakayama is thought to be this mirror, although its date is uncertain and could vary between AD 383, 443 or 503. A comparable bronze mirror decorated with a human figure aiming a spear and four galloping animals was also found in the tomb of King Muryong (who died in 523 and was entombed in 525).[22]

Pottery

Two main kinds of pottery have been found in Paekche, a high-fired stoneware and a lower-fired eggshell-coloured pottery. Shapes include tripods on short, fat legs, footed vessels and globular jars. Mongchon fortress on the south bank of the Han river, dating to AD 230, yielded early grey stoneware, while jars with narrow necks and four strap-handles, called Kuidong type, are thought to date from after the capture of the site by Koguryo. Large globular jars covered with check-stamping are a common Paekche type and jar-coffins are characteristic of the southwest area. Pottery inkstones, found in large numbers in the Puyo area, attest to Paekche links with southern China and to its high level of scholarship. An unusual stoneware vessel excavated from Sochon in South Chungchong province has a handle in the shape of an animal with an enormous tail.[23] A low-fired grey cylindrical pottery stand found at Mongchon fortress has been compared by Kim Won-yong with cylindrical *haniwa* of early Kofun-period Japan, which were placed on top of a tomb mound. The similarity of the horizontal ridges, circular holes and flaring mouth on the Mongchon stand with fifth-century Japanese haniwa seems more than coincidental and it may be that there is a direct relationship between the two. [24]

Earthenware tiles have been excavated from various temple sites in the vicinity of Puyo, decorated with moulded designs which show the elegance characteristic of Paekche. Some show Koguryo influence, such as those decorated with a bird motif within a circle or a winged full-face monster, while others, such as those decorated with swirling flames or mountainous landscapes, are influenced by southern China. Roof-tiles are usually decorated with six- or eight-petalled lotus blossoms, the petals being broad and fleshy and the tips upturned. Some fragments with a yellowish-green glaze have been found at the Miruk temple site.[25]

Kaya

Kaya or Karak emerged along the lower reaches of the Naktong river, the original area of Pyonhan's twelve states. These developed into the six states which made up Kaya, the largest being Taekaya or Great Kaya, in the region of Koryong in northwest Kyongsang province. Ponkaya or Original Kaya occupied the Kimhae area at the mouth of the Naktong river. Ponkaya carried out much maritime trade with the Wa in Japan, trading particularly in iron, which was produced in Kaya and not in Japan. Although many Japanese historians claim, on the basis of the *Nihon shoki*, that Kaya was a Japanese colony, Egami's horse-rider theory also has some adherents. This theory was originally propounded by Kita Teikichi and suggests that the earliest Japanese state, Yamato, was founded by horse-riding invaders from the Eurasian steppe, who swept through the Korean peninsula to Japan in the fourth century, conquering the lands they passed through.[26] It has been opposed on various grounds, including that of the absence of archaeological evidence in southern Korea for horse-riders, but recent excavations have produced considerable amounts of iron armour, for both men and horses, at Kaya sites such as Chisan-dong, Imdang-dong, Choyong-dong, Pan'gyeje, Pokchon-dong (fig. 29), Taesong-dong, Wolsan-ri and Yangdong-ri. The armour found at these sites shows similarities to that depicted in Koguryo wall-paintings, featuring, for example, the Mongolian-type helmet, which suggests that Kaya armour developed from a Koguryo prototype. It may be that the horse- riders who crossed over to Japan and brought about a great change in burial customs by introducing tumulus building, will in the future be proved to have come from Kaya.[27]

Kaya was always caught between Paekche and Silla and suffered persistent harrassment until it was eventually conquered by Silla, first Ponkaya in 532 and then Taekaya in 562. All the other smaller states in the Kaya federation endured the same fate. Silla culture was very much affected by the absorption of Kaya and in some aspects, such as tomb pottery, it is not easy to differentiate between the two.

29. Iron horse-armour excavated from Tomb 10.11 at Pokchon-dong, Pusan. Kaya, 5th century AD. Length: 51.6 cm.

Tombs

Kaya burials consisted of rectangular or oval pit graves excavated into hillsides, mounded tombs with rectangular stone-lined pits, usually found on hill slopes (starting from around AD 300) and later stone chamber tombs (450–570). Many large chamber tombs with sacrificial burials have been found. After the beginning of the sixth century, tombs were constructed with horizontal entrances. Some, of higher status, had separate chambers for burial goods. These comprise large amounts of tomb pottery (figs 30 and 31), armour, horse-trappings, gold and gilt-bronze jewellery and bronze vessels. Four tombs at Chisan-dong revealed horse-trappings which included saddle-parts, stirrups, buckles, bits and bells as well as a suit of iron armour and a helmet, iron swords and arrow-heads. Also buried were a gilt-bronze crown with a very wide central upright, similar to Paekche crowns, necklaces of round beads and curved kogok, tomb pottery and food offerings of fish, bird and crab. Finds at Pokchon-dong in Pusan from tombs dated from around AD 300 onwards also include iron armour – cuirasses, helmets, horse-masks (see fig. 29) and iron weapons. The presence of the earliest riveted cuirass among these finds, as opposed to thonged armour, makes them significant. It is conjectured that riveting therefore spread from fourth-century Korea to fifth-century Japan.[28] Numerous examples of iron armour have been excavated recently from other Kaya tombs, suggesting a society to which horse-riding warfare was central.[29] Excavation of two of the five large tomb mounds

30. Group of *kobae* or stem-cups buried in rows at Sungsan-dong, near Koryong, evidence of the large numbers of the most commonly shaped tomb vessels buried in one tomb, often containing food or drink for the after-life. Kaya, 5th–6th century AD.

31. Stoneware spouted funerary cup in the shape of a duck, with combed and incised decoration of wings and feathers. Kaya, 5th–6th century AD. Ht: 16.5 cm.

belonging to the royal family of Taekaya situated at Koryong provided evidence of the family's wealth and power, despite the relatively small size of a Kaya state. This wealth was probably based on the rich iron ore deposits and the fertile soil. Tomb no. 44 contained thirty-five burial pits, with three large pits arranged in a T-shape and surrounded by all the other subsidiary pits. Since they were all constructed and covered at the same time, this tomb is thought to provide evidence that the over thirty people interred in the subsidiary pits were forcibly buried with the king as human sacrifices.[30]

Tomb pottery was placed in large quantities in Kaya tombs, for example at Taesong-dong, in a group of graves dating from the mid-fourth to early fifth centuries. Here 241 ceramic vessels were found in Tomb no. 39, stacked in rows at the head and foot of the body. (Sixteen suits of armour were also found at this site.) It is thought that these vessels were used in shamanistic burial rites, where they would have contained ritual food and wine. Sometimes the remains of the offerings have been found. The most common type of pottery vessel found in Kaya tombs is the stem-cup, with rectangular pierced decoration on the stand and incised and combed decoration on the lid (see fig. 30). This type of vessel was also common in Silla. Other types include large jars with round bases, tall stands also with pierced decoration and long-necked jars on small pierced stands. Impressed mat- or lattice-patterned jars of an earlier type are also sometimes found. The most elaborate Kaya tomb pots were made in shapes such as ducks (see fig. 31), shoes, boats, houses and mounted armed warriors, as well as horn-shaped rhyton cups which suggest contact with Western Asia, an assumption which is strengthened by the discovery at Taesong-dong of a Scythian or Northern-type bronze jar, 25 cm (10 in) high. Nelson suggests that this contact may have been the result of sea trade.[31]

Although it is difficult to differentiate between some Kaya and Silla tomb wares, in general Kaya pieces are characterized by a more rounded profile and an inward-curving stand, as opposed to the straighter Silla profile. The technology of Three Kingdoms pottery has been researched by Tite, Barnes and others. Scientific analysis of sherds shows that the clay of which they were made can be classed as stoneware clay.[32] Already sloping kilns had been introduced, and there is no doubt that the development of stoneware technology was the result of contacts with China, probably through the Han commanderies in the north. The development of the high temperatures associated with the production of stoneware is also linked with the production of iron at this time.[33]

Kaya stoneware with characteristic shapes and incised, pierced and combed decoration, found in a Yamato tomb of the early fifth century, provides evidence that it was exported to Japan at this time, before the technique for producing high-fired stoneware had been introduced there by Korean potters (a development which was to result in the production of Japanese *sueki* ware in the fourth–fifth century).[34]

Other interesting examples of Kaya tomb art and artefacts include a mural painting discovered in a tomb at Koa-dong in Koryong, consisting of lotus flowers and cloud designs in red, green and brown. The date of this tomb is uncertain but the motifs would suggest a Buddhist connection. Two gilt-bronze crowns with shamanistic upright tree and antler-shaped projections have been found at Pisan-dong near Taegu, similar to early Silla gold crowns (see section on Silla metalware, below).

Silla

The Silla kingdom evolved out of Saro, one of the seventy-eight walled-town states of Samhan. Saro consisted of six villages or clan communities, according to the *Samguk yusa*, and its leaders all came from the Pak, Sok and Kim families. The Korean terms used to describe the rulers of Saro (early Silla) varied, but one, 'chachaung', meant shaman or priest, showing that rulers at this time probably also acted as shamans. The title 'Maripkan', a native Korean word meaning 'ridge' or 'elevation', was adopted by King Naemul (reigned 356–402) and from that time his Kim family dominated the succession. The Chinese title 'wang', meaning 'king', was not adopted until the sixth century. In the latter part of the fifth century the six clan communities were organized into administrative districts, as part of the development of a centralized authority. Post stations were set up and markets established in the capital. Although Silla was harrassed by Koguryo and concluded an alliance with Paekche in 433, its relatively isolated position meant it was largely left alone, separated from the rest of the peninsula by mountains. Under King Chijung (reigned 500–514), ploughing by oxen and irrigation works were introduced, bringing about a great increase in agricultural production. A law code was promulgated in 520, instituting the 'bone-rank' system, and Buddhism was officially adopted by 535, considerably later than in the other kingdoms.

The 'bone-rank' system (*kolpum*) was a kind of caste system, whereby every member of society was graded according to their hereditary blood line or 'bone-rank'. The top rank (*songgol* or 'sacred bone') was occupied by the monarch, the second rank (*chin'gol* or 'true bone') was occupied by ministers and high aristocrats. Below this were six grades of 'head-rank'. One's rank determined one's position and function in society as well as the size and decoration of one's house or the kinds of clothes one could wear and the utensils one might use. For example, male chin'gol were not allowed to wear embroidered trousers made of fur, brocade or silk and female chin'gol were forbidden to wear hairpins engraved and inlaid with gems and jade. Saddles were also graded into specific types for certain ranks, including women.[35] The authority of Silla kings was somewhat tempered by the *hwabaek* assembly, a council of aristocrats that decided the most important matters of government and governed by consensus. The third distinctive feature of Silla society, in addition to the kolpum and hwabaek, was the *hwarang* cult of aristocratic youths, who were educated and trained as military heroes. Hwarang has been translated as 'Flower Boys' and some scholars have attributed shamanistic elements to this group. However, their tenets were based on five commandments of the learned Buddhist priest, Won'gwang, although, in contrast to traditional Buddhist pacifism, they elevated the importance of war, and death in battle was highly prized. To a certain extent, the imported Buddhist church justified and supported Silla's aristocratic system, the monks being drawn primarily from the noble class. However, Buddhism also appealed to the common people through ritual healing and wish-granting teaching, which partly replaced native shamanistic practices. That shamanism continued to be practised after the introduction of Buddhism is evidenced by the gold crowns found in Silla royal tombs which are dated to the fifth–sixth centuries (see section on Silla metalware, below).

Gold mines and iron mines were exploited by Silla and fourteen state-run departments existed specifically for the production of silk, cotton, hemp and ramie fabrics, wool blankets, leather products, tables, wooden containers, willow and bamboo products, ceramics and tiles, clothes and embroideries, tents, lacquer and metal weapons and tools. Trade with Tang China is recorded and can be seen in the form of a Silla envoy painted on the wall of the tomb of Zhang Huai near Xi'an, complete with a hat with wing-like projections similar to those found in Silla gold (see fig. 40). From China, Silla imported threads, silks, gold and silver ornaments, tea and books. Tang *sancai* ware has also been found in one Silla tomb. Silla exported to China gold, silver, copper or bronze needles, horses, ginseng, dogs, skins, ornaments and slaves. King Chinhung established boundary stones to mark the extent of his rule from 540 to 576, the northernmost of which was at Pibong on Pukhan mountain, north of Seoul, thereby showing the extent to which Silla had expanded its territory. Unusually, Silla was ruled by two successive queens in the seventh century, the result of a lack of male successors in the songgol royal line. These were Queen Sondok (reigned 634–47) and Queen Chindok (reigned 647–54). Queen Sondok introduced Chinese court dress and customs, established temples and schools and sent Korean students to study in China. It was also under her rule that the Chomsongdae astronomical observatory was set up, which still stands in Kyongju (see fig. 36). At the time of Queen Chindok's death, Silla was threatened by Koguryo, Paekche and Tang China and so the powerful Silla general Kim Yu-sin succeeded in placing his brother-in-law on the throne as King Taejong Muyol, the first non-songgol king. He instituted a policy of strengthening the bureaucracy and of increasing military, political and cultural ties with Tang China. The outcome was Silla's unification of the Korean peninsula in 668.[36]

Tombs

Silla tombs, known as 'stone-surround wooden chamber tombs', consisted of a pit filled with a wooden chamber covered with a huge pile of stones and a mound of earth. Layers of clay over the pile of stones ensured that there was no water seepage and, when the wooden chamber collapsed through decay, the stones and earth would fall into the chamber, making it virtually impossible to rob. Silla tombs were therefore quite different from those of Koguryo and Paekche, both of which were more easily looted because of their horizontal entrances. Although the most famous Silla tombs are in the vicinity of Kyongju, there are also some in groups along the Naktong river, the Han river, the east coast and on the island of Ullung. Sometimes up to ten burials are found under a single mound, and occasionally jar-coffins are used. Following Buddhist practice, cremations were introduced in the Unified Silla period. The chronology of the excavated tombs is in dispute amongst Japanese and Korean scholars and several sequences have been proposed.[37]

Japanese archaeologists such as Umehara Sueji first carried out excavations of Silla tombs in the early twentieth century, during the Japanese occupation. He excavated the Gold Crown tomb and, since then, further Silla tombs such as the Gold Bell tomb, the Hwangnam Taechong tomb, the Lucky Phoenix tomb and the Heavenly Horse tomb have been unearthed around Kyongju.

One of the most famous of these is the Hwangnam Taechong tomb, also known as Tomb no. 98 and excavated between 1973 and 1975. Controversy surrounds its date. The tomb encloses a double burial. The northern of the two mounds contained a gold crown, which must have been for a woman because it was accompanied by a belt inscribed 'girdle for the lady'. The southern of the two mounds contained large numbers of weapons and a gilt-bronze, not a gold, crown. Since the two known Silla queens ruled in the seventh century, it is curious that fifth-century pottery types have been found in this tomb. This anomaly has led to the suggestion that this is possibly a double tomb of a couple who reigned jointly in the fifth century, the man as military head and the woman as religious and ceremonial leader, who would therefore have worn the gold crown.[38] The tomb site is large, 80 m by 120 m (262 ft by 393 ft), and the twin mounds are respectively 22 and 23 m (72 and 75 ft) high. Some Korean archaeologists believe that it may be the tomb of King Soji (reigned 478–500) and his queen. The inclusion of foreign glass vessels, however, suggests direct contact with China, which only became possible after the reign of King Chinhung (reigned 540–76). If it is assumed that it was the burial of one of the two recorded Silla queens, then it is more likely to be that of Queen Chindok, as the tomb of her predecessor, Queen Sondok, is known and recorded in the *Samguk sagi*. Queen Chindok died in 654 and, according to the *Samguk sagi*, the Tang emperor Gaozong sent envoys with three hundred bolts of silk to her funeral. If this is the case, then the burial goods from Hwangnam Taechong should be dated to the mid-seventh century. The dating of this tomb and its contents are still in dispute, but the generally accepted date is fifth–sixth century.[39]

The Heavenly Horse tomb, excavated in 1973, contained 140 funerary objects including a Syrian blue glass cup, and is named after the white winged horses painted on the birch-bark saddles and saddle-flaps found in a chest in the tomb (fig. 32). These constitute some of the very few examples of Silla painting and can be compared with the early seventh-century Koguryo winged horse painted in the Kangso Taemyo tomb near Pyongyang. The

32. Painting on a birch-bark saddle-flap of a winged horse. Excavated in 1973 from the Heavenly Horse tomb in Kyongju, this is one of Korea's earliest paintings and shows the importance placed upon horses in the Silla. 5th–6th century AD. 53 × 75 cm.

Heavenly Horse motif can also be seen as a reflection of influence from the Silk Route, having similarities to the famous Chinese Flying Horse of Gansu or the 'sacred horse' in the Dingjia Tomb no. 5 at Jiuquan in northwest China. The crescent-shaped forms on its body, however, show similarities to inlaid jades from Scythia. It is moreover thought that Silla people had an indigenous belief in horses, as shown in the foundation myth of Silla recorded in the *Samguk yusa*.[40] Other scholars interpret the horse as a unicorn (*kirin*) and trace it back to Han China. In the Heavenly Horse tomb, the coffin was placed on a stone platform and contained a sword and gold ornaments worn by the king: a crown, earrings, rings, bracelets and a girdle. A pair of gilt-bronze openwork shoes were probably originally lined with silk. The chest containing the riding gear also contained pottery, metal vessels and lacquer. Since there was no epitaph tablet, it is not known to which Silla king this tomb belonged.[41]

Metalware

Magnificent regalia have been excavated from the tombs of the Silla kings and queens, justifying the name of Kumsong, or 'city of gold', given to Kyongju during the Silla. Crowns, belts, shoes, earrings, caps and vessels were made of thin sheet-gold and twisted gold wire and decorated with dangling leaf-shaped gold and curved jade ornaments, evidence of the elegant and sophisticated lifestyle of the rulers of the period. Some scholars contend that these regalia were not for use, but were made especially for the tomb, for use in the after-life, pointing out, for example, the impracticality of wearing gold shoes. Others point to evidence of wear and tear, showing that the crowns were used by the rulers. There is no doubt that, if worn, the shimmering crowns would have made a splendid and impressive sight, the upright projections swaying and the dangling pendants tinkling as the king or queen walked in procession (fig. 33).

In tracing the route through which the motifs found on Silla crowns and the sheet-gold working technique may have arrived in Korea, comparisons have been made between Silla gold crowns and one found at Novercherkassk on the northeastern shore of the Black Sea, from a Sarmatian royal burial of the first to second century BC. Both the tree projections on top of the crown (interspersed with stags) and the gold pendants dangling from the lower edge are similar to those on Silla crowns. The thin sheet-gold construction of Silla crowns is, however, closer to that of one found in the former kingdom of Bactria at Tillya Tepe (present-day Shibarghan in northern Afghanistan), dating to the first century AD. It may have been that this type of gold-working entered Korea through northeast China, as gold head-dress ornaments, one pair of which is tree-shaped, have been excavated from a tomb at Fangshen in Liaoning province dating to the Northern Jin period (AD 265–316).[42] It seems likely that the shamanistic rituals practised in Silla were influenced by Scytho-Siberian shamanism and that the transfer of the outward symbols of these rituals and beliefs was facilitated by the nomadic lifestyle of the peoples of the steppe region. However, the gold crowns were not only full of religious symbolism, they were also indications of rank, worn only by the songgol or later chin'gol rulers, in the strictly hierarchical Silla society.

Ten gold crowns have been excavated so far in Korea, although only six are of the spectacular kind with elaborate appendages. Some simpler ones are closer to one said to have come from a late Kaya tomb at Koryong. The crown from the Gold Crown tomb also had an inner cap with wing-like projections and the crown from the Lucky Phoenix tomb ends in a phoenix-like finial. Another crown from Uisong, north of Kyongju, has feathery-looking uprights. These all suggest association of burial with birds, which is borne out by the record in the Chinese *Sanguo ji* that the predecessors of the Silla people included birds' wings in their graves.[43]

Gold belts with pendant objects, found together with most of the crowns, show some influence from China, and possibly came to Silla via Paekche. The openwork plaques forming the belts would probably have been sewn on to a backing of leather or fabric. A series of pendants are attached on a chain of ovoid and small square plaques. Usually one particular pendant on each belt is longer and larger than all of the others. The pendant objects include fish, a small knife in a gold sheath, curved jades and a gold wire tassle. They stem from a long tradition of official belts originating in Han dynasty China or earlier.[44]

Gold earrings with leaf-shaped gold and curved jade pendants were also found in all the excavated royal tombs, worn by both males and females. The British Museum is fortunate to have in its collection some fine examples of Silla gold earrings. The granulation technique of decoration, which occurs on some of these earrings, also has its origins in Han China. The fact that Paekche tombs also featured gold earrings suggests that the technique travelled through Paekche to Silla. The earrings decorated with granulation

33. Royal crown in sheet-gold excavated from the Gold Crown tomb, Kyongju, in 1922. The antler- and tree-shaped uprights show links with Siberian shamanism, and the curved jade pendants are similar to those found in Japan. Silla, 5th–6th century AD. Ht: 27.5 cm.

are often the more elaborate ones, with a thick, hollow main ring. Hexagon patterns often occur in the granulation and some of the very small hanging leaf-shaped pendants are serrated around the edge to imitate granulation. Some earrings contain a rattle and are set with glass beads.

Pottery

The most comprehensive study of Silla pottery, which was buried in large quantities in Silla tombs, has been the work of the late Kim Won-yong, whose lifelong studies of the subject started with his PhD thesis in New York in 1960 and continued until his death in 1993. Other important work has been done by Han Byong-sam.[45] One of the difficult questions in the study of Silla and Kaya pottery is differentiating Silla from Kaya pieces. Kim Won-yong divides Silla pottery into four periods which he calls Former (250–350), Early (350–450), Middle (450–550) and Late (550–650) Silla. This does not include the Unified Silla period. His chronology differs from those of the Korean scholar Choi Pyonghyon and the Japanese Fujii Kazuo. His Former Silla and Early Silla periods overlap with Kaya. Some wares that he calls Early Silla other scholars call Kaya.[46]

Although Silla pottery is famous for its dramatic, sculptural forms, which are associated with pre-Buddhist shamanistic burial rituals, many Silla pottery shapes are utilitarian ones and the vessels were probably placed in tombs for their contents. They contained food-stuffs and other items needed in the after-life. By far the most numerous are the mounted cup (*kobae*) and the long-necked jar (*changgyong ho*). It is believed that the kobae (see fig. 30) were used not just for storing food in burials, but also for serving food on special occasions or during rituals. The kobae shape shows clear influence from the ancient Chinese *dou* form of a cup on a high foot. Its lid could be inverted and used as a separate dish. The long-necked jar can also be compared with the curved profile of the ancient Chinese *hu*. Other cups had wheels attached and some were horn-shaped, similar to Kaya ones. Bell cups were so called because the hollowed-out lower section contained clay pellets which rattled when shaken. Very large globular jars with short necks also appear frequently, as do cups with no stand and with one handle.[47]

Ewers fashioned in the shape of horse-riders are amongst the most spectacular of Silla ceramics. The most famous examples came from the Gold Bell tomb, excavated in 1924. Two riders of different ranks were depicted on pouring vessels placed next to the head of the deceased man, probably a king or prince. One, a servant, has a bag slung across his shoulders and wears a jacket and trousers. The other wears pointed shoes resting in stirrups and a high, narrow cap with broad ornamented rim. Mounted-warrior cups from the Kaya period have also been found, the most famous being a figure of a rider wearing scale-armour, who is shaped into a twin-horn cup. Twin-horn cups usually have a tube joining the two horns, so that the liquid can reach the same level in both sides.

The most dramatic of all Silla pottery forms is the stand. Stands were produced in both the Paekche and Kaya kingdoms, but they reached their height of development in fifth-and sixth-century Silla. The stands come in two types: one is purely a support and has a dish-shaped rim at the top, designed to hold a round-bottomed vessel; the other has an integral bowl at the top of the stand. Stands, called *kurut pachim*, usually have horizontal divisions into bands and triangular or rectangular holes in rows. It has been suggested that the largest, monumental stands would have been used for outdoor rituals, perhaps state rituals. Silla stands have more triangular and less rounded profiles than the Kaya-Paekche type.[48]

Pottery lamps may have copied the form of metal ones. In these lamps several small cups are arranged around the rim of a larger mounted cup and the bottom ends of all the smaller cups are connected, to allow a free flow of oil. Perhaps the most elaborate sculptural vessel known from this period is a small ritual spouted ewer in the form of a fabulous bird or a dragon, with flame-like projections along the neck and back, excavated from a grave near the tomb of King Michu. It recalls the flying horse painted on birch bark in the tomb of the Heavenly Horse (see fig. 32).[49]

Silla pottery is mostly grey stoneware, fired at 800°–1000° C in a climbing kiln, which, as already noted, was probably introduced from China, either through Lelang or from southeast China. Accidental glazing sometimes occurred when ash fell from the kiln roof on to the pot. Deliberate glazing seems not to have been attempted until the Unified Silla period. Surface decoration was at first incised and the shapes include parallel lines, wavy lines, triangles, V-shapes, circles and half-circles. Sometimes human and animal forms were incised on the pots and sometimes three-dimensional figures were applied to the outsides. These display many aspects of Silla life, including a figure playing a stringed *kayagum* or zither, and figures engaged in sexual activities. The latter may have been associated with shamanistic fertility rituals. A figure carrying a *chige* (A-frame) has also been found. Snakes also appear applied on some pieces and it has been suggested that they may have been associated with the coming of crops from under the ground. Dangling, leaf-shaped ornaments suspended from rings attached to applied loops also exist, comparable to the dangling ornaments on gold earrings, crowns and belts found in the royal Silla tombs. 'Swollen bands' or convex grooves which divide the vessel into broad horizontal registers are also common decorative features of Silla pottery.

Apart from vessels, small pottery figurines have also been found in Silla tombs, such as those excavated in 1920 during the construction of Kyongju railway station. They are hand modelled and depict people and animals in a simplified form, the male figures frequently with an erect penis, suggesting that they were symbols of fertility. These figures are similar to those found decorating some vessel lids and sides. The bodies are long and cylindrical, some with folded hands and some with open arms and mouth, as if singing. The costumes are baggy skirts or trousers. More elaborately modelled human figures were also made in the following Unified Silla period, some depicting long-sleeved dancers, officials and bearded foreigners, undoubtedly evidence of contact with Western Asia through Tang China.[50]

Buddhist sculpture in the Three Kingdoms

With the introduction of Buddhism in the late fourth century AD from China into Koguryo and Paekche and its gradual adoption throughout the three states by the court and ruling aristocracy, temples were constructed on a large scale, state-protecting Buddhist ceremonies were held and many images, both large and small, were made for worship. Extant Buddhist sculpture from the Three Kingdoms period mainly consists of triads portraying a Buddha with two attendant *bodhisattva*s or single bodhisattva figures. Most of these sculptures are small portable icons made of bronze or gilt-bronze. The destruction of the majority of stone and wood pieces means that it is difficult to gain a complete picture of early Korean Buddhist sculpture. Koguryo Buddhist images tended to reflect the northern Chinese style of the Northern Wei (AD 386–534), which was of non-Chinese origin, while Paekche Buddhist art came under the influence of the southern Chinese Liang dynasty (502–57). In the case of Silla, Buddhism probably entered from both adjacent kingdoms and it is also clear that Koguryo exerted considerable influence on the two southern kingdoms of Paekche and Silla.

The earliest example of Koguryo sculpture is a gilt-bronze standing Buddha dated 539, showing clear evidence of the sixth-century Northern Wei style, particularly in the flaming mandorla and the stiff drapery folds projecting out on either side. It was discovered at Uiryong in South Kyongsang province. The workmanship is quite rough when compared to similar Chinese examples. Triads dating to 563 and 571 show a more sculptural style, with rounder modelling of face and bodies and more order in the flame patterns on the mandorlas. The triad dated to 563, which is in the Kansong Museum in Seoul, also shows a feature which was to become popular – a dot design around the edge of the lotus petals of the pedestal and the inner area of the mandorla.

That Buddhism experienced great growth in Paekche under King Song (reigned 523–54) is known through documentary evidence of Paekche's diplomatic relations with both Liang China and Japan. The early seventh-century triad at Sosan in South Chungchong province is a rare example of Paekche stone sculpture, being carved out of a cliff face (fig. 34). The central Buddha figure has his right hand raised in the *abhaya mudra*, symbolizing freedom from fear, and the left hand lowered in the gesture of wish-granting. The gentle smiles of the figures and their lotus-petal pedestals and haloes are particularly beautiful. A peculiar feature of this triad is that the figure on the left of the Buddha is a standing bodhisattva holding a jewel in both hands, while that on the right is a half-seated figure in the meditation posture, depicting a Bodhisattva contemplating his role in the rescue of people from suffering. The standing figure in the Sosan triad may be Avalokitesvara (Kwanum). It is a type which was very popular in Paekche and which may have been taken by Paekche artists to Japan when they introduced Buddhism there in 552, as this depiction of a standing bodhisattva holding a jewel in both hands became popular in Japan in the seventh century.

34. Buddha and two bodhisattvas carved out of stone at Sosan. The seated bodhisattva on the right is in the half-seated posture of meditation. Paekche, 7th century AD.

Sui Chinese sculptural style can be seen in small seventh-century Paekche figures of Avalokitesvara, as is evidenced by gently swaying bodies and strings of jewellery crossing in front. By the late seventh century, technical expertise was growing as can be seen in the small details on sculptures from this period, which often wear a crown and carry a Buddhist jewel in one hand.

Many Silla stone sculptures dating to the seventh century can be seen in the region of

Kyongju, especially in the Mt Namsan area, which was a centre of Buddhist activities. They tend to show a stocky form with a comparatively large head, a feature of old Silla sculptural style in stone. A growing interest in modelling the head and body out from the surface of the rock and in more deeply carved garment folds can be seen, a development which was to lead to the great sculptures of the Unified Silla period, such as at Sokkuram (see fig. 39).[51]

Meditating bodhisattvas, usually identified as the future Buddha, Maitreya, were also produced in gilt-bronze in the Three Kingdoms period. In two famous Silla examples dating to around 600 the flowing drapery and finely modelled facial features are masterpieces of bronze Buddhist sculpture. The gentle facial expression is of supreme beauty, the naked torso contrasts with the flowing drapery over the seat and the meditative pose (*panga sayusang*) emanates a feeling of calm benevolence (fig. 35). This pose is very similar to that of a wooden example in the Horyu-ji in Kyoto, which was clearly produced under the artistic influence of Korea.

Korea and Japan during the Three Kingdoms

It is clear that there was a close relationship between the Korean peninsula and the Japanese islands during the Three Kingdoms period. Evidence for such contact is not only recorded in the Chinese, Korean and Japanese historical annals,[52] it can also be seen from archaeological finds in Japan and in Japanese art in various media from this period. Although both Koguryo style wall-paintings and Kaya stoneware have been found in Japanese tombs, it seems likely that it was Paekche

35. Gilt-bronze seated Maitreya in meditative pose. Silla, 7th century AD. Ht: 93.5 cm.

people, by origin the old Puyo warriors from the north, who emigrated by boat to Japan in the latter half of the fourth century and created Yamato Wa in Japan.[53] If this is the case, then the dramatic changes that came about in the Kofun period (AD 300–710) in Japan might be attributed to this influx of a more advanced, horse-riding group who brought with them iron, horses, stoneware technology and corridor-type painted chamber tombs for their élite, in which were buried Korean-style gold crowns and shoes, stoneware ritual vessels and curved jades, amongst other objects. Without further archaeological evidence from Japan it is difficult to fully substantiate this theory, but it would seem likely that the Japanese ruling élite originated in Paekche Korea. Early Buddhist architecture and sculpture in Japan also shows their Korean origins in many ways. There is no doubt that these influences are the result of an influx of monks, craftsmen and artists from the Korean peninsula, despite the persistent tendency amongst Japanese historians to point to a more general 'continental' influence.[54]

Unified Silla

Silla, under Kim Chun-chu (later King Muyol), made an alliance with Emperor Gaozong of Tang China, with the strategy of first defeating Paekche and then attacking Koguryo simultaneously from both north and south in order to unify the Korean peninsula. Paekche was defeated in 660 by a combination of Chinese forces under Su Dingfang and Silla forces under Kim Yu-sin, despite strong last-minute resistance by Paekche Prince Pung, who returned from Japan. Then, in 667, a successful invasion of Koguryo was launched under Li Ji of Tang, supported by Silla. However, Tang China's ultimate aim was to subdue the whole of the peninsula as part of the Chinese empire, while Silla wanted power for itself. Silla therefore met the Chinese army in a series of battles in the region of the Han river basin and eventually drove it back in 676. This successful resistance of Chinese aggression by Silla allowed the independent development of the Korean people and has always been seen as an event of great significance and a cause of national pride by Korean historians.[55]

Both Unified Silla and Parhae (a state in south-central Manchuria, which included some former Koguryo people and a large group of semi-nomadic Malgal tribesmen of Tungusic origins) eventually established peaceful diplomatic relations with the Tang, a major change in Korea's relationship with China, which had to a large extent been one of armed conflict throughout the Three Kingdoms period. During the eighth and ninth centuries many luxury goods, books and works of art were imported from China and many monks and students travelled to Tang China to study Buddhism or Confucian scholarship. As a result, Tang influence was widespread and contributed to Korean cultural development. Silla and Parhae also had maritime contacts with Japan and with Arab merchants. Silla, indeed, appears in several Arab publications from the ninth century onwards, portrayed as a kind of paradise (see Introduction, section on Western knowledge of Korea).

After unification, monarchs displayed increasing authoritarianism. They were now not always from the 'sacred-bone' lineage but from the lower 'true-bone' rank. The ruling Kim house came to exercise almost exclusive political power, at the expense of other aristocratic families. The stipend village system, whereby officials were paid a salary in the form of villages and had the use of both the grain tax allocation of that village and the labour of the village peasants, led to the accumulation of great wealth by aristocrats. The New Tang History records: 'Emoluments flow unceasingly into the houses of the highest officials, who possess as many as 3000 slaves, with corresponding numbers of weapons, cattle, horses and pigs.' Conquered aristocrats from Paekche and Koguryo were sometimes given a bone-rank status and forcibly resettled in secondary capitals in order to control them. Representatives of the most powerful families had to be present in Kyongju on a rotating basis, as virtual hostages. Slavery was prevalent and many of the large-scale building projects in the capital were carried out with slave labour. Numerous communities of slaves also existed all over Unified Silla territory.

By the time of Unified Silla, Buddhism was the dominant religion and practised by monarchs, aristocrats and the common people. Monks such as Wonchuk travelled to China and translated sutras and scriptures, while Hyecho went to India on a pilgimage to Buddhist holy places and wrote *Record of a Journey to the Five Indian Kingdoms*. The most popular sect amongst aristocrats at this time was the Chinese Huayan or Korean Hwa'om sect, brought to Korea by the monk Uisang, who founded Pusok temple. It preached a doctrine of all-encompassing harmony within the single Buddha mind. The common people, however, preferred the Pure Land sect, which needed no book-learning but only the invocation of the name of the Amitabha Buddha to ensure rebirth in the Western Paradise where Amitabha dwelled.

Confucianism began to rival Buddhism after unification, with the establishment of a National Confucian Academy in 682 and a state examination for officials in 788. Most officials were of head-rank six and opposed the traditional privileges of the 'true-bone' aristocrats. Scholarship in many fields, such as historiography, mathematics and astronomy, flourished during this period and the technology of woodblock printing developed greatly. In fact, the world's oldest extant example of woodblock printing is a copy of the Dharani sutra excavated from the Sokka-tap pagoda at Pulguk temple in Kyongju, dating to before its construction in 751.[56]

Tombs

After unification, the style of Silla tombs changed from the vertical shaft tombs covered in boulders and mounds of earth to stone burial chambers approached by a horizontal shaft. These chambers were covered by a much smaller mound of earth faced with upright slabs of stone with carved decoration of the twelve animals of the oriental zodiac, all carrying weapons to guard the soul of the deceased. The use of the twelve animals of the zodiac in tombs is a uniquely Korean development, although their origin is in China. The tombs of Kim Yu-sin and of King Wonsong at Kwaerung are the best examples of Unified Silla tomb architecture, the latter tomb also including stone statues of a civil and military official and of two lions. This style of tomb was to be continued and enlarged in the following Koryo dynasty.

Architecture

The magnificent Silla capital, the layout of which was based on Tang Chang'an, grew in splendour after unification. New temples were built as well as pleasure grounds for the amusement of court and aristocrats. It is recorded in the *Samguk yusa* that:

When Silla reached the height of her prosperity the capital, Kyongju, consisted of 178,936 houses, 1360 sections, fifty-five streets and thirty-five mansions. There was a villa and pleasure ground for each of the four seasons, to which the aristocrats resorted ... During the reign of King Hongang (874–85), houses with tiled roofs stood in rows in the capital and not a thatched roof was to be seen. Gentle sweet rain came with harmonious blessings and all the harvests were plentiful.

Already in the early seventh century, under Queen Sondok, the bottle-shaped astronomical observatory, 9 m (29 ft) high, called Chomsongdae had been constructed out of 364 stone blocks in 27 courses (fig. 36). This is now thought to be the oldest existing observatory in East Asia and was probably the centre of astronomy in Silla. It is assumed from its shape that the observatory was built in accordance with the Chinese 'round-heaven, square-earth' theory. Although it is uncertain exactly how it was used, the tower allowed measurement of the sun's shadow, in the same way as a gnomon, to ascertain the season. The window facing south, moreover, opens in such a way that sunlight is fully shed upon the bottom level inside at noon on the spring and autumn equinoxes. It is thought that an armillary sphere was probably mounted on the top for observation purposes at times of unusual phenomena. There is some controversy about whether or not it was used as an open-dome-type observation platform. In any case, it is concrete evidence of the Silla people's preoccupation with the stars and their belief that the heavenly bodies determined the course of men's lives.[57]

The original Wolsong palace complex was complemented soon after unification by a second series of buildings built along the shore of an artificial lake called Anap-chi (Lake of wild geese and ducks). According to the *Samguk sagi*, in 674 King Munmu 'dug a pond and built a mountain in the palace grounds. Flowers and plants were planted and rare birds and strange animals were raised.' Anap-chi and four palace buildings were excavated in 1975–6, yielding many Unified Silla architectural tiles (fig. 37), Buddhist images and ornaments and items for everyday use made of pottery, metal and lacquer. A boat almost 6 m (19 ft) long made of pine planks was discovered in front of the buildings on the western shore. This area, known as a detached palace, was the location of state banquets and the reception of foreign embassies by the king, with feasts including dances performed by palace ladies and boat trips across the lake. Yet another detached palace to the south, called Posok-jong (Abalone stone pavilion), was used by the Silla kings for picnics with court ladies and included a stone-lined water course where they would float wine-cups as part of a drinking-cum-poetry composing game. When the wine-cup stopped, the person nearest to it had to compose the next line of a poem.

Vast sums of money were also spent by the Unified Silla kings on building and restoring Buddhist temples in Kyongju. The *Samguk yusa* records, for example, that 23,000 *sok* of rice was spent on regilding a large Buddhist sculpture at Yongmyo temple in 764. The two greatest temples were Hwangnyong (Temple of the imperial dragon), famous for its great nine-storey wooden pagoda designed by a Paekche architect in 636 (and destroyed in the

36. Left: Chomsongdae Royal Observatory in Kyongju, built under Queen Sondok (reigned 632–47), the period of Silla's greatest activity just before it unified most of the peninsula in AD 668.

37. Above: Ridge-end roof-tile in moulded earthenware, decorated with a monster mask (*kwimyon*) to ward off evil spirits. Kyongju was renowned for its tiled roofs and similar tiles have been excavated from Anap-chi lake. Unified Silla, 8th century AD. Ht: 26.5 cm.

38. Stone pagoda at Hwa'om-sa in south Cholla province, a fine example of Buddhist craftsmanship of the 8th century AD. Decorated in relief around the base with apsaras dancing and playing musical instruments, this three-storey pagoda rests on four crouching lions which surround a Buddhist monk. The lowest storey is carved with doors on all four sides, each flanked by guardian figures. Ht: 5.5 m.

Mongol invasion of the thirteenth century), and Punhwang (Fragrant imperial temple), with a seven-storey stone pagoda built in 634 that included Chinese-style features such as four stone lions seated at the four corners.

Although Pulguk-sa (Temple of the Buddha Land) could not rival either of these great temples, its design is one of great symmetry and beauty. In its present-day restored state, it is one-tenth the size of the original Silla temple, which was founded in 553 and rebuilt after unification by the minister Kim Tae-song (700–774). Kim designed it to rise out of a lotus lake, as did the palaces in Buddhist paradise paintings of the time. Its twin stone pagodas, the Sokka-tap and the Tabo-tap, are in elegant contrast with each other. The former has three storeys, stepped eaves and low sloping roofs, in classic Korean stone pagoda style. The latter is much more complex, featuring four stone stairways up to an open chamber, which may have originally contained a Buddhist image. Above this is an octagonal storey with pillars carved to represent bamboo stalks, covered with an eight-sided flower-shaped roof and the final pillar. A stone lion is seated at the top of the west stairway and it is thought that originally there may have been four, as in the ninth-century stone pagoda at Hwa'om temple (fig. 38). Stone pagodas are one of Korea's unique contributions to Buddhist architecture, in contrast to the brick pagodas of China and the wooden pagodas of Japan.

Kim Tae-song was also responsible for the Buddhist cave temple at Sokkuram on Mount Toham, east of Kyongju, which was built between 751 and 774 and is regarded as one of the masterpieces of all Buddhist art. Based on the plan of ancient Indian cave-temples, it comprises a rectangular ante-chamber leading to a circular domed main chamber that contains a huge seated Sakyamuni Buddha and forty-one figures carved in relief on the walls or in niches (fig. 39). The Sokkuram Buddha watches over the East Sea, protecting the east coast from invasion. Seated Buddha images with the hand in the earth-touching position like the Sokkuram Buddha were widespread in the late Unified Silla. They had their origins in India and were also popular in late seventh-century Tang China. The Sokkuram image is the most refined example of this type.[58] Other impressive figures are the eleven-headed Avalokitesvara, bodhisattvas and arhats on the surrounding wall and the two *inwang* or benevolent kings and four deva kings standing guard.

To the south of Kyongju is the sacred mountain of Namsan, its seventeen valleys reputedly containing over fifty Buddhist temples. Many Buddhist images were also carved there in the stone cliffs, with miniature crevices or overhangs being used to create small cave temples as sanctuaries for Buddhist images, testimony to a country completely dominated by Buddhism.

Architectural remains from Unified Silla include stone lanterns, water basins and support stones for iron pennant poles as well as moulded earthenware tiles for roofs and floors. The most splendid floor tiles, excavated near Anap-chi, are decorated with the *posang* or 'precious visage' flower, which show similarities to motifs found at Dunhuang, on the Silk Route. Lotus flowers are also used to decorate floor and roof tiles, the number of lotus petals increasing in the Unified Silla from six or eight to sixteen or thirty-two. Ridge ends were decorated with elaborate monster masks, to ward off evil spirits. Monster-mask roof tiles originated in China and were used in Korea from the Unified Silla right through the Choson period (see fig. 37).

Painting and calligraphy

The most famous Silla calligrapher, Kim Saeng, was said to have been so accomplished that his work was sometimes confused with that of Wang Xizhi, the renowned fourth-century Chinese calligrapher. Unfortunately none of his work remains, and Unified Silla calligraphy style can now only be judged from inscriptions on stone, such as the Hwa'om sutra passages carved in stone at Hwa'om temple.[59] The only remaining example of painting from this period is on a fragment of an illuminated manuscript of the Hwa'om (Avatamsaka) sutra painted in gold and silver, dated 754–5, now in the Hoam Museum in Seoul.

Metalware

Unified Silla was renowned for its metalworking, which took the principal form of bronze casting, especially of sculpture and temple bells. The oldest remaining Silla Buddhist bronze bell, dated 725, is at Sangwon-sa temple on Mount Odae. The largest and best known is from Pondok-sa and can be seen in Kyongju National Museum. It was cast in 771

as a posthumous honour to King Songdok, is 2.27 m (7.44 ft) in diameter and 3.3 m (10.8 ft) high. The flying heavenly beings and lotus flowers are particularly beautiful examples of the unique beauty of Silla bells, quite different from those of China or Japan. Temple bells, the smaller ones used to sound the time of day and to summon monks to services, and the larger ones struck for services at the beginning and end of the day, developed from ancient Chinese bronze bells. Korean bells are characterized by their suspension loop, which is in the form of a single dragon head beside which is a short hollow post. There are usually bands of floral ornament around the top and bottom of the bell and four panels of nine knobs next to the top border. Although these features hark back to Chinese bronze bells, the low-relief flying heavenly beings are found only in Korea (see fig. 47). The lotus medallions around the lower half mark the striking points, as the bells have no clappers inside. The larger bells are usually housed in a bell pavilion near the entrance to the temple, together with a large wooden pole suspended by a rope, which is swung horizontally to strike the bell. Large amounts of bronze were needed to cast such enormous bells as the one recorded from Hwangnyong-sa, which weighed 500,000 *kun* (equivalent to over 300 tons). Such projects could only have been accomplished with active government support.[60]

Large amounts of bronze and iron were also needed for the Buddhist sculptures which furnished the increasing number of temples. Usually, bronze Buddhist images were gilded with a mixture of gold leaf and a mercury amalgam, heated to 350° C to evaporate the mercury and then polished (the parcel-gilding technique). Large Buddhist sculptures made of cast iron were also popular at this time, moulded in separate parts and joined together after casting, then often covered in brightly coloured paint or plaster. The monumental forms of these eighth-century sculptures are similar to that of the Sokkuram Buddha, with its broad-shouldered body, three characteristic folds in the neck, the round face with elegantly slanting eyes and arched eyebrows and the robe with its naturalistic folds (see fig. 39). In general, Buddhist sculpture of the Unified Silla period was executed with greater refinement than in the Three Kingdoms period. The proportions of the body were realistic and harmonious, facial features were finely modelled, and metal casting and carving in stone were done to a high technical standard. Particularly popular, both in bronze and iron, were depictions of the Buddha of Medicine or Bhaisajyaguru, whose cult enjoyed great popularity at this time. In the ninth century the Vairocana Buddha became popular, identified by the gesture in which the five fingers of the right hand hold the index finger of the left hand. Many images of Vairocana, thought of in esoteric Buddhism as the Supreme Buddhist Deity, were produced in stone and iron at the end of the Unified Silla period.

Perhaps the most exquisite examples of Unified Silla metalwork are the *sarira* excavated from pagodas. Sarira, or reliquaries, usually housed some small remains of the historical Buddha or important Buddhist texts. The innermost containers, often made of glass, were contained in several layers of outer containers, usually of gilt-bronze. Some of these were shaped like houses or pavilions, one seventh–eighth century example excavated from Song-nim temple in 1959 having a finial in the form of a tree, recalling the tree-shaped uprights on Silla gold crowns and Paekche head-dress ornaments. This reliquary finial shows that the sheet-metal technique perfected in the Three Kingdoms period continued to be employed in the Unified Silla, using sheet gilt-bronze; and the tree motif, thought to be associated with the shamanistic religion of the Three Kingdoms, was now employed for Buddhist purposes, perhaps symbolizing the bodhi tree under which the Buddha Sakyamuni achieved enlightenment. Another reliquary casket excavated in 1965 from a pagoda on the site of a now-destroyed temple at Wanggung-ri at Iksan in North Cholla province, in old Paekche territory, was found together with a set of nineteen thin gold sheets bearing a repoussé decoration of the text of the Diamond sutra, and a green glass bottle with a gold lotus bud stopper and gold lotus support. The reliquary casket is decorated with ring-punching and hatched ornaments which are similar to Tang gold and silver. Perhaps the most significant sarira find has been the woodblock-printed copy of the Dharani sutra, noted above, excavated from the Sokka-tap pagoda at Pulguk-sa in Kyongju, dating to before 751.[61]

Glass

Glass excavated from Silla temples and tombs provides evidence of trade with Western Asia. Late Roman, Sasanian and Syrian glass vessels have been found in Korea as well as other objects and vessels thought by Korean scholars to be of Korean manufacture. On the basis of scientific analysis, including lead isotope analysis, which can tell which mine the lead used came from, a basic chronology of Korean glass manufacture has been proposed by Insook Lee. She suggests that in the first of three stages, from 200 BC–AD 300, first lead-barium glass beads and then potash glass beads were made in Korea from Chinese materials. Soda-lime glass, characteristic of Western Asia or Southeast Asia, was first introduced in the early Christian era, possibly by sea. In Lee's second stage, from the fourth to the sixth centuries AD, glass beads and vessels were made in Korea in addition to special products such as horse-harness ornaments, small amulet sculptures and girdle pendants. Of the over forty glass vessels known from this period, the majority are probably of late Roman type but some are Korean, such as a cup with blue dot decoration from Okchon tomb at Hapchon. The vessels are all concentrated in the Kyongju area. Around 400, lead glass without barium began to be made in Korea, the main product developing into high lead-silica glass sarira bottles of the seventh to tenth centuries, Lee's third stage.[62]

Pottery

Pottery of the Unified Silla became smaller and more densely decorated. Many jars were made for burying funerary ashes, as the practice of cremation was introduced with Buddhism. The smaller, regularly incised and stamped motifs began to include Buddhist clouds and lotus flowers, the knobs on the lids often portraying a lotus bud. In general, the decoration reflects that on ring-punched and chased metalwork of the period. Some of the vessels had a rudimentary ash glaze and it was this which was to develop into the beginnings of green-glazed stonewares or celadons sometime during the tenth century. Already in the Three Kingdoms period, temperatures high enough for the production of stoneware had been achieved. Many undecorated everyday pottery wares excavated from Anap-chi show that the decorated wares were in the minority and made for special occasions. Tomb figures of horses, oxen, dancers, officials, foreigners, zodiac figures, soldiers and servants are evidence both of the Unified Silla lifestyle and of contact with Tang China and beyond.[63]

Trade

Further evidence of the extent of trade in Unified Silla, which was perhaps far greater than is generally recognized at present, is provided by the objects stored in the Shoso-in imperial repository at Nara in Japan. This treasury of luxury goods belonged to the Japanese emperor Shomu and, after the principal donation by the empress in AD 756, few other goods were added. Since it is very well recorded, this treasury provides a unique source of information. The country of origin of many of the objects is uncertain. Some Korean scholars believe that some items, presumed to be of Chinese or Japanese provenance, may actually have originated in eighth-century Korea. Some of the objects of Western Asian origin were probably transported to Japan via Korea as sea trade in the East China Sea at that time was undoubtedly dominated by the sailors of Unified Silla Korea.[64] Examples of holdings in the Shoso-in which can be presumed to be of Korean manufacture on the basis of comparison with material excavated in Korea are numerous. However, since many Chinese products also made their way to cosmopolitan Kyongju, it is difficult to be certain whether or not some of the objects excavated in Korea are in fact Korean or Chinese. More research is needed into the area of this contentious subject before any firm conclusions can be drawn.[65]

40. Korean envoy (second from right) with characteristic head-dress, painted on the wall of the tomb of the Chinese Tang dynasty prince Zhang Huai (Li Xian), outside Xi'an, showing the close contacts between the two countries in the 8th century AD.

Many examples of works of art produced in Unified Silla Korea provide evidence of the trade carried out along the Silk Route. These foreign influences no doubt passed through Tang China before reaching Korea. There is material evidence of Korean envoys to Tang China in the form of wall-paintings such as that in the tomb of Prince Zhang Huai (fig. 40) near Xi'an. It seems that such envoys even reached Central Asia, as can be seen in a seventh-century wall-painting in Samarkand. Korean products portraying foreigners include a glass bead inlaid with a Western face excavated from King Michu's tomb, dating to the fifth–sixth century AD, pottery tomb figures and stone sculptures at the eighth-century Kwaerung tomb in Kyongju. Western techniques and designs also abound in Unified Silla works of art. For examples, horn-shaped cups or rhytons have been found from the Kaya period through to the Unified Silla, some with animal heads in Iranian metalwork style. Pearl roundels and pairs of confronting animals are motifs found in Sasanian Iran, Tang China and Unified Silla Korea in a variety of materials, while a silver cup with hexagonal motifs enclosing human figures excavated from the pre-Unification Hwangnam Taechong tomb is very similar to products of Sasanian Iran. [66]

Links between Central Asia and Korea therefore date back at least to the Three Kingdoms period and the cultural impact of Central Asia on the art of the Unified Silla was considerable, much of it being combined with influence from Tang China. The cultural impact of Korea in the Unified Silla period on Japan has yet to be fully recognized.

CHAPTER 3
Koryo Period

The period of the Koryo dynasty (918–1392) was a highpoint in the history and culture of Korea and it is from the name Koryo that Korea's English name derives. Koryo was a long dynasty, beginning at the time of the collapse of the Chinese Tang dynasty, outliving the Song and Yuan, and lasting long enough to witness the rise of the Ming (1368–1644). The founder of Koryo, Wang Kon, had a vision of restoring the glory of the ancient Koguryo kingdom and therefore established a new capital much further north than the Silla capital at Kyongju. The new capital, Songdo, was situated in present-day Kaesong, in North Korea.

Wang Kon (King Taejo) pursued a policy of expansion northwards, which inevitably brought him into conflict with the Khitan (Liao). This eventually resulted in three Khitan invasions of Koryo between 993 and 1018, during which time the Khitan even briefly occupied the Koryo capital. The third invasion resulted in an overwhelming victory for Koryo, following which, between 1033 and 1044, it built a thousand-*li* – a thousand-mile – Long Wall from the mouth of the Amnok river in the west, stretching right across the peninsula to the east coast. This wall was also intended for defence against the northern Jurchen tribesmen who founded the Jin dynasty in 1115, overran the Khitan Liao dynasty in 1125 and eventually captured the Northern Song capital of Kaifeng in 1127. The only reason that the Jin did not invade Koryo was that the latter consented to enter into a relationship of suzerain-subject with the Jin.[1] The early Koryo period was a time of splendour at the capital, a time of peaceful cultural and economic exchange with Song China, which had a great impact on Koryo culture. Within the framework of the tributary system that bound Korea to China, official embassies and private traders exported to China gold, silver, copper, ginseng and pine nuts, as well as paper, brushes, ink and fans. In return, Koryo imported silk, porcelain, books, musical instruments, spices and medicines.[2] However, when the Song requested that Koryo help them resist the Khitan and Jin by allying and attacking from both sides, the Koryo refused, not willing to become part of the conflict between the Jin and Song. Despite this, trade between the Song and Koryo flourished, even resulting in the arrival of Arab ships in Songdo's port, bringing mercury, spices and medicines.[3]

41. The storehouse at Hae'in temple on Mt Kaya in south-central Korea, where the complete Buddhist scriptures, carved on over 80,000 woodblocks in the 13th century, are stored.

Admiration for things Chinese was a feature of Koryo life, especially amongst the upper classes. In fact, Koryo's founder, Wang Kon, said: 'We in the East have long admired Tang ways. In culture, ritual and music, we are entirely following its model.'[4] A Chinese-style civil service examination system was established in 958 and literature in Chinese flourished. Civil officials took pride in their ability to memorize the Chinese classics and students practised writing poems within a stipulated time – this was called 'Notched candle poetics'.[5] However, this emphasis on the literary life led to the downgrading of the status of the military. High-level military commanders were reduced to acting as royal bodyguards in the pleasure-loving royal court at Songdo and ordinary soldiers were looked upon as little more than menial labourers. The reign of King Uijong (reigned 1147–70) is portrayed in the *Koryo sa* as the height of decadence, with the king more interested in building pavilions and digging lily ponds than running the country. Not surprisingly, a military coup erupted in 1170. King Uijong was removed and replaced by his younger brother and power fell to the military, with the authority of the throne rendered powerless, although the monarchy was preserved.[6]

In 1231 the military regime was faced with an invasion by the Mongols and so moved the Koryo capital in 1232 to Kanghwa island, exploiting the Mongols' fear of the sea. Over the next thirty years, the Mongols were to invade Koryo a total of six times, but the court and ruling class remained fairly unaffected on Kanghwa island, continuing their luxurious lifestyle which was supported by tax revenues. The Mongols' intention in invading Korea was to use it as a bridge to invade Japan and thereby reach Southern Song China. Terrible losses were suffered by the Korean peasantry and eventually, in 1258, the last military dictator was assassinated, power reverted to the king and peace was made with the Mongols. As a result, Koryo was forced to take part in two Mongol campaigns against the Japanese in 1274 and 1281, having to take responsibility for the construction of warships and the provision of supplies. Both campaigns failed, largely due to the Mongols' lack of experience of seaborne invasions.[7]

There followed a period of Koryo subservience to the Mongols, who had established the Yuan dynasty in China in 1271. A succession of Koryo kings were married to Mongol princesses, starting with King Chungnyol (reigned 1275–1308) who married a daughter of Kublai Khan and hung sheepskins at the entrance to the palace.[8] Koryo crown princes had to reside in Beijing as hostages until they became king. Mongol dress, hairstyles and language were used at the court in Songdo and the Yuan demanded tribute in the form of gold, silver, cloth, grain, ginseng and falcons for use in hunting. This led to the establishment of many falconries in Korea, the owners of which had special privileges and became very rich.[9]

In China the Yuan faced increasing popular opposition and in 1368 fell to a new leader who established his dynasty as the Ming. Reaction in Korea was divided between pro-Yuan and pro-Ming sentiment. Attempts by the king to impose reform on his nobles added to the confusion within the country, which further faced attacks from Chinese brigands and Japanese pirates. These incursions were fought off, but eventually the Ming threatened to reclaim land in the northeast of the peninsula which they maintained belonged to China. One of the generals sent to repel the Chinese, Yi Song-gye, took advantage of the turmoil, returned south and in 1388 seized control. In 1392 he established the Choson dynasty.

Koryo society was, in general, a very highly stratified one, with descent and kinship of supreme importance. The style was epitomized by the first Koryo king, Taejo, who linked his close kin through marriage. Since he had twenty-nine queens, twenty-five sons and nine daughters, he created a large support group of close kin.[10] Consanguineous marriages were widespread at the beginning of the Koryo, the linking of close relatives by marriage being politically and economically beneficial. The position of women in the Koryo was strong as they shared an equal right of inheritance with their brothers.[11] In fact, bridegrooms commonly moved into the bride's family house after marriage. A man could have several wives, each wife residing with her own family and being visited by her shared husband.[12]

There was, in practice, little scope for social advancement through the examination system, as a result of the *umso* system of protected appointments, whereby one son of an official of the fifth rank or above was entitled to receive an official appointment.[13] The division of Koryo society into aristocrats at the top, commoners in the middle and base people or slaves at the bottom continued throughout the dynasty and it was virtually impossible for the general peasant population of commoners to take the examinations. Commoners tilled the fields while the base people were the artisans who made such products as metal, paper, textiles and ceramics. They lived in village communities isolated from the general population and were forced to intermarry. Because their products were so important to the court and the government, they were exempt from tax and corvée labour.[14]

Religion

Buddhism had an all-pervasive influence during the Koryo (fig. 41). Temples and monasteries were constructed and works of art were produced for the glorification of the church as well as for the accumulation of individual and national merit. Wang Kon (King Taejo) attributed his success in founding the dynasty entirely to the Buddhist church and had ten temples built in Kaesong. He claimed: 'The success of the great enterprise of founding our dynasty is entirely owing to the protective powers of the many Buddhas. We must therefore build temples for both Son and Kyo Schools and appoint abbots to them, that they may perform the proper ceremonies and themselves cultivate the way'.[15]

There was therefore a great proliferation of temples in Koryo and enthusiastic participation in the many Buddhist festivals throughout the year. Some of these festivals represented in fact an amalgamation of Buddhism and native Korean practices. The Yondung-hoe or Festival of Lotus Lanterns was the first major ceremony offered to the Buddha in the New Year; the Chopa-il was the celebration of the birth of the historic Buddha; Paekchung, with shamanist associations, was the feast for the souls of the dead; and Palgwan-hoe was also a feast for the dead, held on the fifteenth day of the eleventh month. Vegetarian feasts for monks fed as many as 100,000 monks at a time and sometimes food was offered to anyone who turned up. Indeed, Buddhist monasteries seem on occasion to have acted as relief agencies, feeding groups of itinerant beggars in mess halls. Sometimes fishing nets were burned and domestic animals freed in ceremonies designed to show faithful adherence to the Buddhist principle of non-killing.[16]

The Buddhist church developed its own economic system to such an extent that it became a kind of state within a state, challenging the functions of the central government. Monasteries were palatial buildings, rivalling the royal palaces. Temple lands produced goods which were sold to provide capital, the labour coming from either worker monks or slaves. Capital was also created from the sale of harvested goods from land owned by the temple and interest on funds was put towards the financing of feasts, relief work or scholarships for monks.[17] The whole system was privileged because it was exempt from tax and because many donations were made by the royal family and the aristocracy, in the hope of gaining merit. Wine-making and high-interest loans of grain increased the wealth of the church. It was even felt necessary to train monks as soldiers in order to protect the church and warrior-monks such as the Subdue Demons Corps were used against the Jurchen invasions.[18]

An examination system for monks was set up, on the lines of that for the civil service examination. The monks' examination had to be divided into two sections in reflection of the division of the Buddhist church into two main sects at that time, the Kyo or textual school and the Son (Zen) or meditational school. In the eleventh century the monk Uichon made an unsuccessful attempt to unite the Korean Buddhist church. He was particularly influential because he was the fourth son of King Munjong (reigned 1046–83), an example of the widespread practice amongst early Koryo aristocrats of sending one of their sons to a monastery. Uichon tried to introduce the Chontae (Chinese: Tiantai) sect from China, attracted by its balance of meditation and doctrine. Although he was unsuccessful, Koryo Buddhism did unite later in the dynasty under the influence of the monk Chinul (1158–1210), with the formation of the Chogye sect. This was a reaction against the secular Buddhism of the early Koryo which catered to the royal family and aristocrats. Chogye was a uniquely Korean sect and developed in remote mountain monasteries.[19]

Confucianism and Buddhism co-existed during the Koryo, with the government supporting Confucian studies as well as Buddhism. During the late Koryo a bureaucratic class of literati grew up, their honesty and integrity in marked contrast to the opulent lifestyle of the early Koryo aristocrats. Under the influence of Chinese Neo-Confucianism, these scholars were to have a profound effect on the development of the relationship between Buddhism and Confucianism during the following Choson period.

Buddhism and the development of printing

It was the desire to propagate the Buddhist scriptures that had led to the development of printing on woodblocks during the Unified Silla period and it is for two great achievements in the field of printing that Koryo is perhaps best remembered. These are the carving of the entire Buddhist scriptures twice on woodblock and the invention of movable metal type.

By the beginning of the eleventh century, woodblock printing had developed in Korea to such a level that it was decided to engrave the entire Buddhist scriptures on woodblocks. This was partly done as a sort of prayer, to protect Korea against the Khitan invasions, and partly to systematize the doctrines taught in the scriptures.[20] When these woodblocks were destroyed in the Mongol invasions, a new edition was begun on Kanghwa island and completed in 1251. This set of 80,000 woodblocks, usually known as the Tripitaka Koreana, is now stored in Hae'in temple in South Korea (see fig. 41). It is generally thought to be the finest of about twenty East Asian versions of the Tripitaka, because of its accuracy, beautiful calligraphy and carving technique.[21] The blocks were made from magnolia wood, soaked and boiled in salt water to extract the gum, and then dried for years in the shade. Each block was 24 cm by 65 cm by 4cm (9.3 in by 25.3 in by 1.5 in), capped with bronze on each corner and supported by two wooden sticks. The surface was painted with lacquer, which was a very good preservative. Each side of each block contained twenty-three vertical lines of characters. Paper was then pressed against the inked surface and volumes of one hundred pages compiled.[22]

Paper-making was also highly developed in the Koryo, to the extent that it was exported to China. Even in the Silla period, Korean 'white hammered paper' had earned the reputation in China of being the best in the world. By that period, Korean paper was made of pith from the paper mulberry shrub (*Broussonetia papyrifera*) as opposed to hemp fibre, which had been used in the Koguryo period.[23] According to records 2000 sheets of white paper and 400 ink sticks were sent from Korea to China in the Koryo. The Yuan were also to demand large quantities of Korean paper for printing the Buddhist scriptures.[24]

Tough paper that could sustain the pressure of metal type was therefore available in Koryo, as was oily, glue-processed ink. Ordinary ink was sufficient for woodblock printing but an oilier ink was necessary for use with metal type. The impetus for the invention of movable metal type in the twelfth century came from the combination of the difficulty of obtaining books from Song China, a result of the war between the Song and the Jin, together with big fires in Korea in 1126 and 1170, in which many books were destroyed and a shortage of wood resulted. Bronze-casting techniques were already well developed in the Silla and the Koryo was experienced in minting good-quality bronze coins. On this foundation, metal type was introduced and by about 1234, twenty-eight copies of the *Sangjong yemun* (*Detailed and Authentic Code of Ritual*) had been printed on Kanghwa island. At first the metal type was cast into sand moulds, which had been made by pressing a wooden version of the character into a bed of sea sand. Molten bronze was then poured into the indentation.[25]

Koryo's use of metal movable type was the earliest in the world. This early experimental period was followed by the establishment, at the end of the Koryo, in 1392, of a National Office for Book Publication. By using movable type, a greater variety of works could be produced, although woodblock printing was useful when a large number of copies of one work was needed.[26]

Tombs

Most of the Koryo royal tombs are located in the vicinity of Kaesong, now in North Korea and therefore difficult to visit. The mausoleum of the thirty-first Koryo king, Kongmin (reigned 1330–74), and his Mongolian wife Noguk is the best preserved. She died in child-birth in 1365, causing great grief to King Kongmin, who never recovered completely from her death. Kongmin was himself a renowned painter and calligrapher and at least one surviving Koryo painting, a hunting scene, is tentatively attributed to him. He has been compared to Emperor Huizong of the Northern Song, as they both excelled in painting birds and flowers.[27] His and his wife's tombs are covered in two round mounds and situated on a wooded hillside outside Kaesong. On the lowest of three terraces stand two pairs of military officers facing each other, dressed in suits of armour and helmets. On the upper terrace are two pairs of civil officials, a pair of stone lanterns and a pair of stone tables or altars. On the third terrace are the tombs, with a pair of hexagonal pillars in front and to either side. Between the pillars and directly in front of each tomb are a pair of stone slabs supported by four drum-shaped legs. The burial mounds are surrounded by carved stone balustrades and alternating statues of seated tigers and standing sheep, representing *yang* and *yin*. The stone-carving is in general sophisticated and detailed. The tombs have been excavated fairly recently, revealing a stone chamber under each mound, decorated with wall- and ceiling-paintings. On the ceilings are star formations such as the Dig Dipper and on the walls are figure paintings of the twelve animal spirits of the oriental zodiac.[28] The

tradition of painting constellations on the ceilings of tombs started in the Han dynasty in China and carried on into the Koguryo kingdom in Korea.

Other Koryo tomb murals remain from the eleventh- or twelfth-century Surakam-dong tomb in Kaesong, the thirteenth-century Poptangbang tomb in Changdan, and Kochang tomb in South Kyongsang province, likewise of the eleventh or twelfth century and discovered in 1971. The latter tomb has musicians and dancers in addition to the twelve zodiac animal spirits. Smooth, flowing lines and bright colours characterize these tomb paintings, as does a residual influence from Koguryo tomb paintings.[29]

Slate coffins were used in Koryo burials, usually filled with precious burial goods such as celadon vessels, placed beside the cremated remains of the tomb occupant. Examples of these slate coffins, which had carved decoration around the outsides depicting the animals of the four directions, can be seen in the Victoria and Albert Museum,[30] the National Museum of Korea and Songgyunggwan University Museum in Seoul.

Temples

No temple buildings survive from the early Koryo, although the establishment of many temples is recorded. As in China and Japan, most of the structures were of wood, which is easily destroyed. The earliest surviving wooden Koryo building is at Pongjong temple in Andong, probably dating to the thirteenth century. The best example is the Hall of Eternal Life (Muryangsu-jon) at Pusok temple in Yongju, also of the thirteenth century. Notable features are tapered columns, three-tiered roof supports, a dual roof edge and ceilingless openwork in the hall giving a sense of grandeur (fig. 42).[31]

Pagoda styles varied in the Koryo, the earlier ones predictably continuing the Silla

42. Above: The Hall of Eternal Life (Muryangsu-jon) at Pusok temple in southeast Korea is one of the earliest surviving wooden buildings in Korea. Koryo period, 13th century AD.

43. Right: Ten-storey stone pagoda from Kyongchon temple, with Mongol Lamaist Buddhist decoration, showing the all-pervading effect of the Mongol defeat of Korea in the late 13th century. Late Koryo period, 14th century AD. Ht: 13.5 m.

straight-lined style. A softer Koryo type then developed, demonstrated in the eleventh-century, seven-storey pagoda at Hyonhwa-sa in Kaepung.[32] Hexagonal or octagonal pago-das such as the nine-storey one at Wolchong-sa on Mount Odae were influenced by Song China, while unconventional, local styles are represented by the curious, mushroom-like thirteenth-century pagoda at Unju temple in South Cholla province. The latter has seven storeys whose flat circular forms may be wheel-shaped, referring to the Buddhist Wheel of the Law.[33] Unju-sa is an example of a temple begun in the Koryo which incorporated shamanistic features, such as seven flat round discs of rock on a hill beside the temple which represent the seven stars of the Dig Dipper, popular in Daoist and shamanist iconography. It is called the 'Temple of one thousand Buddhas and one thousand pagodas', after the numerous pagodas lining the beautiful valley approaching the temple and the Buddha figures dotted all over the temple site. The Lamaist influence of the Mongols can be seen in late Koryo pagodas, such as the ten-storey marble pagoda from Kyongchon temple, now in Kyongbok palace in Seoul. This is dated to 1348 and is 13.5 m (44 ft) high, highly decorated with sculpted figures and buildings in relief (fig. 43).[34]

Stone lanterns of the Koryo were made in many different shapes, with octagonal columns, columns in the shape of a pair of lions, round columns or octagonal plat-forms. One of the best examples of a Koryo stone lantern can be seen at Kwanchok temple in front of the gigantic Miruk statue (fig. 46). It is 5.45 m (17.8 ft) high and was probably made in the late tenth century. It shows influence from the Unified Silla stone lantern at Hwa'om temple, but the juxtaposition of a square top part on a cylindrical column is quite new.[35]

Buddhist illuminated manuscripts

The hand-copying of Buddhist sutras (sermons attributed to the Buddha) was regarded as one of the most meritorious deeds in the Koryo. It required great accuracy and skill in cal-ligraphy. Such hand-written sutra manuscripts (*sagyong*) were therefore commissioned by devotees with the aim of earning merit and thus being reborn in a better state or in par-adise, released from all worldly suffering. Illuminated Buddhist sutras were produced in China and Japan as well as Korea, but in the Koryo dynasty Buddhism reached such a highpoint and artistic creativity was concentrated in such a way that remarkably beautiful works of art were created. Most of the extant Koryo illuminated sutra manuscripts are now in Japan and are little seen. The British Museum is fortunate to have one of the few exam-ples outside Japan or Korea (fig. 44).[36]

The manuscripts were incredibly sumptuous products, commissioned by the palace or aristocrats and written by monk-scribes. They were usually written on high-quality paper, dyed a deep indigo blue and lavishly embellished with the most precious materi-als available – gold and silver. The two most common sutras were the Avatamsaka sutra (*Hwaomgyong*) and the Lotus sutra (*Pophwagyong*). Sometimes white, purple or pale yellow paper was used in either of two formats, a handscroll or a folding, concertina-like booklet, the latter probably influenced by Chinese woodblock-printed sutras of the Song dynasty. It is thought that this folding booklet style originated with the early Indian sutras written on pothi leaves, as opposed to the traditional Chinese handscroll form.[37]

44. Paradise scene on the frontispiece to the Amitabha sutra. Painted and written in silver and gold by a monk-scribe for his mother, this is an example of the large numbers of such magnificent Buddhist manuscripts produced at this time. Koryo period, AD 1341. Ht: 22 cm.

The outer covers of these manuscripts are usually decorated with large flowers known as 'precious visages' (*posang tangcho*), with a rectangular cartouche containing the title of the work in vertical gold or silver characters. Two characters resembling inverted commas are usually placed at the top of the title. These are a mantra, corresponding to the *siddham* seed character *om*. The mantra *om* refers to the 'lion's roar' or the voice of the Buddha, which is present in the sutra because it is the sermon the Buddha preached.[38]

Inside the cover appears a magnificent frontispiece, an illustration of the Buddha preaching to an assembly. This is a painted vision of the words of the scripture and is meticulously drawn entirely in gold, using very thin 'iron wire' lines. Very occasionally tiny touches of colour are used for details of the divinities. The frontispiece presents a dazzling scene on the dark blue background and is usually framed with Buddhist symbols, such as the *vajra* (thunderbolt, symbolizing the indestructibility of the Buddha's teaching) and the *cakra* (wheel, symbolizing the Buddhist Law). Korean sutras can be distinguished from

Chinese and Japanese ones by the border above the painting, which is broader at the top than the bottom.

On the first page of text is written the name of the translator of the original Pali or Sanskrit. The text is written vertically in silver or gold Chinese characters in regular *haeso* (Chinese: *kaishu*), that is, standard script. There are usually seventeen characters to a line, occasionally fourteen or fifteen. At the end of the text is placed a colophon giving the date and the name of the patron who commissioned the manuscript and the reason for doing so. It is interesting that the earlier Koryo sutras were commissioned for the purpose of protecting the nation, whereas the later ones, as revealed by the colophons, were increasingly for the sake of personal happiness or profit.[39]

The quantity and quality of such manuscripts produced in the Koryo is astounding. A Royal Sutra Scriptorium or Sagyongwon was established and appears in the *Koryo sa* in 1181 when the Tripitaka written in silver letters was commissioned by King Myongjong. In addition to monk-scribes, skilled professional calligraphers were employed in the Sagyongwon. It was divided up under King Chungnyol (reigned 1274–1308) into the Scriptorium of Silver Letters (Unjawon) and the Scriptorium of Gold Letters (Kumjawon). Sometimes the king wrote inscriptions on newly finished sutras and in some cases the name of the scribes are recorded, as in the British Museum's example, which is a small Amitabha sutra written by the monk Chonggo in 1341 to earn a meritorious deed for his mother. He must have been a high-ranking monk and was also the scribe of a 1340 copy of the Lotus sutra in gold letters, now in Japan.[40]

Koryo illuminated manuscripts were treasured in China and Japan as much as in Korea. In Muromachi Japan Korean sutras were amongst the most sought-after and in Yuan China they were regular items of tribute. There are references in the *Koryo sa* to Koryo sutra-writers being sent to China: 'In March of the 16th year of King Ch'ungnyol (1290), the Chinese Emperor ordered the writing of gold and silver sutras, and selected excellent monk scribes, therefore 35 Korean monks were dispatched to the Yuan court ... In April of the same year, 65 Koryo monks, sutra-writers, were dispatched to Yuan. ... ' The demand continued and, in 1305, a Mongol envoy took 'one hundred Koryo sutra-writers back with him'.[41]

Both the earliest and the most elaborate Koryo illuminated sutras are now in Japan. The earliest, in the possession of the Bunkacho in Tokyo, is a volume in handscroll format of the *Tae Pojokgyong*, dated to 1006. It has a frontispiece painted in silver of three standing Bodhisattvas and a text in gold on blue paper. The most elaborate is the entire Lotus sutra written in small gold and silver characters on dark blue indigo-dyed silk in the shape of a seven-storey pagoda, mounted as a hanging scroll. It is dated to 1249 and is stored in the To-ji in Kyoto.[42] The latter is an example of a combination of worship of the pagoda and writing of a sutra, the two most meritorious deeds. Writing out the sutra in the form of a pagoda to worship is a supreme instance of pious action.

The fact that so many of these Koryo illuminated manuscripts have been carefully preserved in Japanese Buddhist temples is testimony to the aesthetic and religious values attributed to them. They are beautiful examples of the refined courtly style of Koryo art, as well as important historical documents.

Painting

Buddhist painting

The story of the 'discovery' of Koryo Buddhist painting during the last twenty years is an exciting one. Many astoundingly beautiful Buddhist paintings, stored mainly in Japanese temples since at least the late sixteenth century, were for a long time attributed to China. The beginning of Western knowledge of the process of public re-attribution started with an exhibition in Japan in 1978 at the Yamato Bunkakan. Since then more than one hundred scrolls and murals have been located in Japan, Korea and the West.[43]

Koryo Buddhist paintings can be divided into three formats: those on illuminated manuscripts (see section above); wall-paintings; and hanging scrolls. There are very few extant wall-paintings, although these were the most numerous originally. Six frescoes in the Chosadang shrine at Pusok temple in Yongju are the best known. These depict deva kings and bodhisattvas and are dated to 1377. Fourteenth-century paintings of water-flowers and wild grass also survive on the walls of Sudok temple in Yesan.[44] Hanging scrolls usually depict either Amitabha (the Buddha of the Western Paradise), the bodhisattvas Avalokitesvara and Ksitigarbha or, occasionally, the ten judge-kings of hell. The predominance of Amitabha paintings was due to the growing popularity of Pure Land Buddhism. The paintings are often called 'Descending Amitabha' (Naeyong-do), as it is believed that when a devotee is close to death the Buddha Amitabha will descend with some bodhisattvas to take the person to the Pure Land. Amitabha paintings therefore often include two bodhisattvas (usually Amitabha and Mahasthamaprapta) and are called 'Amitabha triads'.[45] Examples can be seen in the Brooklyn Museum in New York, the Hoam Museum in Korea and the Tokyo National Museum (fig. 45). Paintings of Avalokitesvara (Kwanum posal) usually depict the bodhisattva sitting in a meditative posture, looking over water by moonlight or holding a willow branch and flanked by lotus flowers and a *kundika* or water-sprinkler. Beautiful examples of Kwanum posal paintings can be seen in the Musée Guimet in Paris and the Yamato Bunkakan Museum in Nara. Some examples, such as the ones in the Sumitomo Collection and the Asakusa-dera, both in Japan, are signed by individual artists. The former is by So Ku-bang and is dated to 1323 and the latter is by Hyeho.[46] Paintings of the bodhisattva Ksitigarbha (Chijang posal) are particularly characteristic of the Koryo, when he was very popular. He was generally believed to be able to help those in torment in hell and was closely associated with the ten kings of hell, who weigh all good and bad deeds committed by the dead during their lifetimes and judge them accordingly. The popularity of Ksitigarbha in the Koryo may have been prompted in part by nationalist pride and have arisen from the belief that a Korean prince of the Silla dynasty, who went to Jiuhuashan in China in the eighth century to meditate and whose body remained mysteriously undecayed after death, was an incarnation of Ksitigarbha.[47] The four most important bodhisattvas of Mahayana Buddhism are generally thought to be Avalokitesvara (embodying the virtue of great compassion), Ksitigarbha (showing mercy in delivering sentient beings from hell), Manjusri (displaying knowledge and wisdom) and Samantabhadra (renowned for his teachings and practice of the Buddha). During the Koryo there was a marked preference for paintings of the first two. Fine examples of Ksitigarbha paintings can be seen in the Museum für Ostasiatische Kunst in Berlin and in the Engaku-ji at Kamakura in Japan. It is curious that, by comparison with China and Japan, there are very few paintings of paradise or purgatory during the Koryo.[48]

In general, Koryo Buddhist paintings present the main figure as an overpoweringly large form, with secondary figures, such as attendants and devotees, crowded in the bottom half of the painting below the main subject's knees. A prominent halo usually surrounds the main figure's head. This separation of the main figure from the others has been seen as a reflection of Koryo society, with its unbridgeable gulf between aristocrats and commoners.[49] The paintings were, of course, commissioned by aristocrats or the royal family. An important feature of the paintings is the elaborate and rich jewellery and silks depicted in them. The deities are bedecked in brooches, anklets, bracelets, arm-bands and earrings and the silk costumes with which they are draped are incredibly graceful. The painting of transparent silk is particularly fine and delicate, giving a feeling of lightness. The mineral colours used are predominantly orange-red, olive-green and white, with a fine gold outline. Occasionally bright blue is used for parts of the architecture or the hair of the divinities. The generous use of gold paste gave Koryo painting a characteristic luminous quality (in general Chinese paintings used a more intense red and a brighter green). The painting of the figures in Koryo paintings is characterized by distinctively arc-shaped eyebrows and relatively smaller and sharply drawn facial features. The composition of the figures is often very close together so that the haloes overlap.[50]

Koryo Buddhist paintings are a unique source of information about costumes and silks of the time. Furthermore, the motifs on the silk brocade costumes of many of the deities in the paintings can be compared with those on ceramics and lacquer of the same period to reveal interesting parallels. For example, medallions composed of chrysanthemum florets are common decorative motifs on silk and can also be seen on celadons, such as the British Museum's *kundika* (see fig. 49). Abstract scrolling motifs suggesting leaves, which are the basis of the spiral medallions seen on silk costumes, are reflected in the leaf scrolls on many celadons. Other motifs common to silk and celadons are the busy cloud motif and flying, long-tailed phoenixes.[51]

Secular painting

The lack of surviving examples means that secular painting from the Koryo dynasty is, unfortunately, very little known. The *Koryo sa* relates that a government bureau of painting was established (the Tohwawon) and Chinese records note that Koreans often went to China to buy paintings. A description of Korean fan-paintings of the eleventh century is given by Guo Ruoxu:

> These fans are made of blue-black paper; the paintings on them show persons of quality of the country of their origin, diversified by ladies and saddle horses. There may be streams with banks indicated in gold, or lotus blossoms, trees and waterfowl of various sorts, all most ingeniously worked out with decorative touches. Sometimes they have effects of mist and moonlight, done with silver paint; these can be extremely attractive.[52]

This description highlights several characteristics of Koryo painting: the use of gold and silver paint, indigo-dyed paper and the motifs of trees and waterfowl, which occur very often in Koryo decorative arts such as celadons, lacquer and inlaid bronze. Koryo's greatest professional painter, Yi Nyong, active in the early twelfth century, painted landscapes of actual places in Korea, demonstrating an important development in the history of Korean painting that was to reach a highpoint in the eighteenth century in the 'real

45. Amitabha triad painting in ink, colours and gold paint on silk. The breathtaking beauty of these Buddhist paintings, which are now mostly preserved in Japanese temples and museums, has only recently been recognized in the West. Koryo period, 13th century AD. 123 × 55.8 cm.

landscape' paintings of Chong Son in the following Choson dynasty. Another important trend was for paintings to be produced by scholars and aristocrats as a hobby, not always by professionals. Members of the nobility and ordained monks enjoyed painting for plea-sure.[53] Some idea of Koryo landscape style can sometimes be gleaned from the back-grounds of Buddhist paintings. Strangely shaped rocks and pointed mountain peaks give a tantalizing glimpse of an individual and highly developed landscape painting technique.[54]

Sculpture

Buddhist sculpture in the early Koryo period carried on the styles and traditions of the Unified Silla period, with the production of large iron seated Buddha figures, such as the 'Kwangju Buddha', 2.88 m (9.44 ft) high, now in the National Museum of Korea.[55] There are not a large number of extant early Koryo sculptures, but enough remain to show that sculpture was produced in a variety of materials: iron; marble (such as a plump-faced bodhi-sattva wearing a high, conical headdress from Hansong temple at Kangnung in Kangwon province); clay (for example, a lacquered and gilt-clay seated Buddha of the tenth century at Pusok temple, surrounded by a wooden, flame-like mandorla); and stone (such as an unusual eleventh-century Buddha seated with leg pendant on a lotus flower, cut out of the rock at Popchu temple in North Chungchong province). General characteristics of early Koryo Buddhist sculpture are a flat face with elongated eyes raised at both ends and a rather unfriendly expression. These can be seen in the Popchu-sa image.[56] An interesting development in early Koryo stone sculpture was the appearance of gigantic statues of Bud-dhas, usually Miruk (Maitreya), the Buddha of the future. Sometimes these images were cut out of natural boulders *in situ*, such as the eleventh-century standing Buddhas, 17.4 m (57 ft) high, at Paju in Kyonggi province. The largest of the gigantic Koryo sculptures is the Miruk, 18.1 m (59.3 ft) high, at Kwanchok temple at Nonsan in South Chungchong province. These very large, big-headed figures seem to be meant to overpower the wor-shipper and are characterized by minimal detailing of form and a greater abstraction. Their crudity of form is, however, compensated for by their impressive size. It has been suggested that they were not entirely Buddhist, but also had shamanistic associations.[57] The tall hats worn by these figures are a new and unusual feature (fig. 46). There was also quite a variety of local styles of Buddhist sculpture in the early Koryo[58] and the extent of the influence of local shamanistic religious practices on Buddhist sculpture is evident.

Later Koryo sculpture is marked by a reduction in size. Large-scale stone and iron Buddhas disappeared, to be replaced by small, gilt-bronze figures, often showing in-fluence from the Lamaistic Buddhism of the Mongol Yuan dynasty in China. This was a consequence of the large numbers of Yuan artists who settled in Songdo in the thirteenth century following Koryo's forced capitulation to the Mongols. The gilt-bronze Medicine Buddha at Changgok temple in South Chungchong province is typical of late Koryo sculp-tures, with balanced proportions, flowing garments and a benevolent expression. It can be dated to 1346 on the basis of a votive inscription found inside.[59]

Non-Buddhist sculpture is provided in the figures of military and civil officials at the approach to Koryo tombs, their employment and arrangement in pairs deriving from Chinese burial practice.[60] The wooden masks made for the traditional mask dance in Hahoe village in North Kyongsang province are further intriguing examples of non-Buddhist

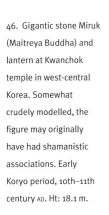

46. Gigantic stone Miruk (Maitreya Buddha) and lantern at Kwanchok temple in west-central Korea. Somewhat crudely modelled, the figure may originally have had shamanistic associations. Early Koryo period, 10th–11th century AD. Ht: 18.1 m.

sculptural style in the Koryo. The deep-set eyes and long, aquiline nose reflect foreign influence, possibly from Central Asia. There may also be influence from the Liao, where gold and silver masks were placed on figures in high-level burials.[61] The link between the Hahoe masks and Japanese No-masks has yet to be fully explored (see fig. 87).[62]

Metalware

Koryo inherited the metal craftsmanship of Silla and combined this with influence from Song and Yuan China to produce some fine metalwork. Much metalware was made for use in Buddhist ritual but there were also many examples of utilitarian secular objects of high quality. Evidence of the importance of metalwork at this time is given in the *Koryo sa*, which states that the golden tower of Hungwang temple was made in 1067 with 427 *kun* (about 256.2 kg or 563.6 lb) of silver and 144 *kun* (about 86.4 kg or 190 lb) of gold. A thirteen-storey tower and several vases are further recorded as having been made in 1223

47. Left: Bronze bell for
use in Buddhist temples,
with cast decoration of
lotus flowers, flying
heavenly beings and a
beautifully modelled
dragon next to the
sounding tube at the
top. Late Koryo period,
13th–14th century AD.
Ht: 45 cm.

with 144 *kun* of gold.[63] Koryo bronzes were either cast or beaten. Cast bronzes were thicker and heavier and often decorated with exquisite inlaid silver and gold. Beaten bronzes were thinner and lighter and almost always plain.[64]

Buddhist metalware

The most important metal objects made for Buddhist use were bronze temple bells. The practice of bell casting was a burden on the people because they had to donate used bronzeware for casting new bells. There are about seventy extant Koryo bronze bells, of which sixteen are dated. In general Koryo bells are smaller than Silla ones. Many Koryo bronze bells are now in Japan, the earliest dating to 963. Of those left in Korea, one example, 1.7 m (5.5 ft) high, dated to 1010 and now in the National Museum of Korea follows the Silla model, in contrast to a smaller bell dated 1222 from Naeso temple in southwest Korea, which has new Koryo features. It is smaller (103 cm or 40 in high), and the outer edge of the crown has a band of lotus petals that project obliquely out of the upper ornamental scroll. Other Koryo features are the replacement of flying devas with a trinity under a flying canopy and the sunflower-like rendering of the lotus medallion striking point. The cylindrical tube-dragon complex on the crown of the bell has four new spherical ornaments on the upper edge. These features became typical of Koryo bells.[65] A particularly fine example of a late Koryo bell is illustrated in fig. 47. Small handbells and vajra bells were also made in the Koryo, the latter influenced by Mongol Lamaist Buddhism. A gilt-bronze cast Koryo hand-bell is preserved in Songgwang temple in southwest Korea.

Bronze incense-burners were an integral part of Buddhist ritual. Although the quality of bronze bells declined in the Koryo by comparison with the Silla, these incense-burners show that Koryo metalworkers could produce new creations of exquisite beauty. Seven dated examples and one undated one exist of silver inlaid Koryo incense-burners in the shape of a pedestal-cup. The British Museum is fortunate to have one undated incense-burner and one dated incense-burner base, both inlaid in silver (fig. 48A). The technique of silver inlay was inherited from the Silla and greatly influenced decoration on celadons and lacquer of the Koryo. Thin silver thread and wider, flat silver strips are both used. The effect of the silver patterns on the dark patinated bronze background is very

48A. Above: Incense-burner base of cast bronze, inlaid with silver. The inscription in Chinese characters incised around the base indicates that this was part of a royal incense-burner produced for King Kongmin in AD 1358 to make a pious offering at the Sojae temple. Ht: 21.3 cm.

48B. Above: Detail of
the incense-burner base
of cast bronze, inlaid
with silver, 1358.

49. Left: Pair of spouted
water-sprinklers
(*kundika* or *chongbyong*)
for purifying the ground
during Buddhist
ceremonies. The shape
originated in India and
was produced in bronze
and celadon in the
Koryo. Left: Bronze
kundika, 11th–12th
century AD. Ht: 29.5 cm.
Right: Stoneware
kundika with inlaid
stylized chrysanthemum
roundels under a
celadon glaze, late 12th
century AD. Ht: 44.5 cm.

beautiful (fig. 48B). The use of siddham-seed characters on some of these bronze vessels shows Mongol influence.

Another important item for use in Buddhist temples was the circular cast bronze gong, for summoning monks to services. There are sixteen known dated Koryo gongs, ranging from 1073 to 1327. They are usually decorated with a central lotus flower to mark the striking point and concentric rings of stylized leaf scrolls or fungus.

Vases and ewers of beaten bronze for use in temples are paralleled in shape by celadon ones. The *kundika* water-sprinkler (fig. 49) was a Buddhist shape originating in India which travelled with Buddhism through China to reach Korea. Chinese Tang dynasty kundikas are difficult to differentiate from Koryo ones, but one of the characteristic features of Koryo metalwork is faceting, which can often be seen on the spouts of Koryo kundikas. Cast examples, such as one in the National Museum of Korea, are also decorated with inlaid silver, portraying a river scene, using motifs of willows, ducks, geese and other such images, common to celadon decoration.

Miniature pagodas were also made for Buddhist worship, copying wooden structures in reduced scale. The details are meticulously reproduced and often provide valuable evidence of the appearance of now-lost Koryo wooden temple buildings.[66] Sarira (reliquary cases) dating from the Koryo have been discovered, although they are not as numerous or as beautiful as Silla examples. One example, dated to 1390, was discovered in the Diamond Mountains, an area where many Buddhist implements are known to have been made and dedicated in the late Koryo, some being produced by Yuan Chinese artists. The outer reliquary is of white porcelain, in contrast to Silla reliquaries. Inside the white porcelain bowl is a bronze one and inside the bronze bowl is an outer casket of beaten silver in the form of an octagonal pavilion. This casket in turn contains a reliquary shaped like an oval stupa, incised with standing Buddhas, supported on a lotus pedestal. This late Koryo reliquary shows Mongol influence.[67]

Secular metalware

Metalwork made for secular use includes tableware for aristocrats, such as rice bowls, spoons and chopsticks, spouted bowls (possibly for ritual use) and cupstands. Women's items such as needlecases and mirrors have often been excavated from tombs together with celadon rouge boxes and hair-oil bottles. Small gilt-bronze appliqué decorations were made for fixing on to costumes and coffins. A great variety of small bronze hairpins, scissors, earpicks and razors are further evidence of the widespread use of bronze in everyday life in the Koryo period. The razors were presumably used by Buddhist monks for shaving their heads.

Koryo mirrors show much influence from Chinese Song and Yuan models. It is in fact very difficult to differentiate between them in many cases, since Chinese motifs were copied in their entirety. Kim Won-yong states that Koryo mirrors contain less tin than Chinese ones, although one example of scientific analysis of the metal content of Korean and Chinese mirrors has revealed that the copper, tin and lead alloy used is similar in both.[68] It is quite possible that some of the mirrors excavated from Koryo tombs are Chinese. However, there are Koryo mirrors which can be dated and provenanced from their inscriptions.[69] Chinese decorative motifs originating in the Han dynasty include dragons, designs resembling the letters T, L and V, commonly known as TLV designs, and the animals of the four directions. Tang style motifs include vine scrolls, 'precious visage' flowers and figures playing the lute. Pairs of fish and a boat scene popular in the Song also appear on Koryo mirrors. Most Chinese-influenced Koryo mirrors are either circular or foliate, whereas more Korean shapes are bell and square shapes. Mirrors with geometric motifs and zodiac figures and completely undecorated mirrors show less Chinese influence.[70]

Of the utilitarian tablewares which survive, spoons and chopsticks are most numerous. Koryo spoons are characterized by their S-shaped curved handles, their 'swallow-tail' handle-ends and oval bowls with a pointed tip. In the following Choson dynasty, spoons were made of brass and were much plainer, with a flat handle and rounder bowl. The use of metal spoons and chopsticks in Korea prevails to the present day, in contrast to China and Japan, where wood or ivory chopsticks are used but spoons are not in common use.[71]

50. Above: Silver bowl and ewer, parcel-gilt with engraved decoration and a lotus-shaped lid surmounted by a phoenix. Celadon vessels were often modelled on the shapes of silver and bronze ones. Koryo period, 11th–12th century AD. Max ht: 38 cm.

The few remaining Koryo vessels made completely of silver are evidence of the extravagant lifestyle of the Koryo aristocracy and show a high quality of workmanship and clear Chinese influence in shape. Both the well-known gilt-silver wine-cup and stand in the National Museum of Korea and the ewer and bowl in the Boston Museum of Fine Arts (fig. 50) are shapes often seen in Chinese Qingbai, Ding and Longquan wares. These shapes were also reproduced in Koryo celadons. The Chinese emissary, Xu Jing, who visited Korea in 1123 (see section on Ceramics, below), refers to the widespread use of silver at table. In his chapter on table customs, he writes: 'Many of the wares and vessels are gilded or made of silver, but green pottery wares were held in esteem'.[72] This passage has been taken to mean that celadons were more highly esteemed than silver vessels, but the meaning is not entirely clear. It does, however, show that Koryo aristocrats made widespread use of silver tableware. A characteristic of small Koryo gilt-silver pieces, such as a bracelet in Chonju Museum and a gourd-shaped bottle in Chongju Museum, is the floral decoration in high relief with blossoms composed of dense circular, stylized florets. The gilt decoration on silver needlecases is often very similar to Tang work, being predominantly chased floral scrolls. These also reflect the decoration on illuminated manuscripts.[73]

Lacquer

There are only about fourteen extant pieces of Koryo lacquer,[74] but their quality is evidence of the high level of skill attained by Koryo lacquer workers. Eight of them are for Buddhist use, being rectangular sutra boxes, such as the one in the British Museum (fig. 51). The suggestion has been made that these boxes may have been used to contain the printed Tripitaka Koreana, but the sizes of all the boxes differ and differ also from the

51. Below: Lacqured wooden box for storing Buddhist sutras. The decoration in mother-of-pearl, tortoise-shell and metal wire of peony scrolls and stylized chrysanthemums is paralleled by that inlaid on celadons of the same period. Koryo period, 13th century AD. Length: 47.2 cm.

size of the woodblocks.[75] It is, however, recorded in the *Koryo sa* that a special government agency was set up in 1272, at the request of the wife of Kublai Khan, to manufacture lacquer cases for a set of the Tripitaka.[76] These eight sutra boxes are distinguished by dense and regular decoration of stylized chrysanthemum scrolls inlaid in mother-of-pearl with twisted silver or copper wire. They also have peony scrolls lining the borders, which are very similar to those on Yuan Chinese inlaid lacquer. Both the use of iridescent haliotis shells and the incising of the shells are also similar to Yuan lacquer inlay.[77] Dating of these boxes to the second half of the thirteenth century has been proposed by Okada Jo.[78] Precise dating of Koryo lacquer is, however, impossible at present. Some of the sutra boxes have applied metal Chinese characters which can be interpreted as numbers, suggesting the numbers of sutra volumes to be stored in that box. One box, in the Tokyo National Museum, has an inlaid inscription on the cover reading 'Avatamska sutra'.[79] A small circular box in the Okura Shukokan Museum in Japan is thought to be for containing Buddhist rosaries. It is undoubtedly for Buddhist use because it has a siddham-seed character inlaid on the lid.

Lacquer was also used in the secular world to make cosmetic boxes for aristocratic ladies. These have the same curved, foliate shape as Koryo celadon cosmetic boxes[80] and are inlaid with both mother-of-pearl and tortoise-shell. The tortoise shell is inlaid over red and yellow pigments and the mother-of-pearl differs from that used in the sutra boxes, being thicker, harder and not iridescent. These features show influence from Tang China, where such painted tortoise-shell was called *fuhong* or *fucai*. Examples of this technique can be seen in the Shoso-in treasury in Nara in Japan.[81] For this reason, these cosmetic boxes are probably earlier than the sutra boxes and date to the twelfth century.[82]

The only example of Koryo lacquer inlaid with a pictorial scene similar to that found on celadons and even, occasionally, on bronzes, is a covered rectangular cosmetic box in the National Museum of Korea. It is not in good condition, but enough remains to show that the outside is covered with lacquer-coated hemp cloth and then black lacquer which is inlaid with a scene of willow trees, ducks and water, very similar to scenes on twelfth-century celadons. The decoration is also partly painted in gold, as were some celadons of the thirteenth century.[83] The scene has been compared to a Liao wall-painting in the East Mausoleum at Qingling in the eastern part of Inner Mongolia, thought to be the tomb of Emperor Shengzong of the Liao dynasty. It can be seen as an example of the effect that refugee or captive Liao craftsmen had on Koryo decorative motifs in the twelfth century.[84]

Ceramics

The most famous of Koryo ceramics are celadons, but unglazed stonewares in the Silla tradition as well as black wares and white porcelains were also produced during this period.

Celadons

Koryo celadons were little known in the West until the early twentieth century when they were excavated from Koryo tombs around Kaesong. However, they have been known and appreciated in both Japan and China for a very long time. The Song writer Taiping Laoren, writing about precious items, said: 'The books of the Academy, the wines of the Palace, the

52. These two celadon vases illustrate the influence of Chinese Ru ware on early Koryo celadons. Right: Chinese Ru ware, late 11th to early 12th century AD. Ht: 19.8 cm. Left: Korean celadon, Koryo period, early 12th century AD. Ht: 19.5 cm.

inkstones of Duan, the peonies of Luoyang, the tea of Jianzhou, the brocade of Shu, the porcelains of Dingzhou ... the secret colour ware of Gaoli [Koryo] ... are all first under heaven.'[85] The fact that they were compared with such high-quality Chinese products shows the high esteem in which Koryo celadons were held in Song China. They have been excavated from the area of the Southern Song capital at Hangzhou, from Yangzhou and from the Yuan dynasty capital site of Dadu (present-day Beijing), evidence of the presence of celadons in trade or tribute from Korea to China in both the Southern Song and the Yuan.[86]

The best literary source of information about Koryo celadons is Xu Jing's account of his trip to Korea in 1123. Xu was a Chinese emissary of the Song dynasty who visited Korea and wrote a forty-chapter summary of Korean affairs, religion, people, customs and products. He notes:

The pottery wares are green in colour and are called kingfisher-coloured by the people of Gaoli. In recent years they have been made more skilfully and their colour and lustre have become finer. There are wine pots of gourd shape with small covers in the form of a duck amidst lotus flowers. They also make bowls and dishes, cups and tea-bowls, flower vases and hot water bowls, all copied from the forms of Ding ware, so that they are not illustrated here, but the wine pots are specially shown because they are different.[87]

Unfortunately, the illustrations made by Xu Jing were lost.

Xu refers to the influence of Ding wares on Koryo celadons, but these were not the only Chinese wares to pattern the development of celadon manufacture during the Koryo. The earliest Chinese influence came in the ninth–tenth century from the Yue kilns in southeast China. It is thought possible that Chinese potters migrated by sea at that time from Five Dynasties China to southwest Korea. Whether or not potters actually travelled to Korea, the technique of making celadons clearly did. Scientific analysis of clays and glazes of both Chinese Yue wares and Koryo celadons has revealed many similarities.[88] Vessel shapes, decorative motifs and the wide-spread use of the wide flat footring all derive from Yue wares. There was also considerable influence from north Chinese wares through the northern land route to Korea. Vessel shapes and carved and moulded decoration show similarities with Ding wares and northern celadons from Yaozhou, while the use of three or six small stones as spurs on which to rest the piece in the kiln during firing derived from Ru wares. The bluish glaze and elegant shapes also show influence from Ru (fig. 52). Chinese Cizhou wares with underglaze iron-painted decoration had an effect on Koryo celadons, which were produced with similar decoration (fig. 53). Liao, whose Khitan people were defeated by Koryo in the eleventh century, also exerted a clear influence. Many Khitans came to Korea and practised their crafts there. Xu Jing refers to them thus: 'I heard that there are many thousands of Khitan captives, of whom one in ten was a craftsman. Those with special skill were selected for the Royal palace.' Their contribution accounts for the similarity in the floral scrolls and openwork decoration between Liao and Koryo ceramics. Koryo vessel shapes, such as the vase with 'dished mouth', also owed a debt to Liao white porcelain, and the Korean practice of making celadon figures recalls Liao green-glazed earthenware figures.[89]

The Koryo craftsmen managed to absorb these many Chinese influences, both technical and stylistic, and yet to produce unique and distinctively Korean creations. The vessels which particularly impressed Xu Jing were the celadon incense-burners, based, no doubt, on Song archaistic bronzes but embellished with animal figures on their lids, through whose mouth the incense would rise: 'A lion emits incense and is likewise kingfisher coloured: the beast crouches on top, supported by a lotus. This is the most distinguished of all their wares: the others resemble the old "secret colour" of Yuezhou and the new kiln wares of Ruzhou.'[90]

Innovations introduced by Koryo potters, which distinguish Korean celadons from Chinese ones, include vessels shaped like vegetables and animals such as gourds, melons

53. Stoneware *maebyong* vase, actually a wine container, with large underglaze iron-brown chrysanthemums under a celadon glaze. The iron-painted decoration shows some links with Chinese Cizhou wares, but such decoration was first used under a celadon glaze in Korea. Koryo period, 12th century AD. Ht: 25 cm.

54. Tea bowl of
stoneware with very rare
underglaze copper-red
decoration of flower
scrolls under a celadon
glaze. Koryo period,
early 12th century AD.
Diameter: 17.8 cm.

(see fig. 56), flowers, ducks, monkeys and turtles or with applied figures of lions, dragons, rabbits and fish. Large areas of openwork or relief-carved lotus petals are also distinctive Korean features. The most important decorative innovation was the use of inlay (*sanggam*), which was probably introduced in the second half of the twelfth century. This was probably inspired both by Silla regularly stamped decoration on pottery and also by inlay on metalwork and lacquer. Designs of clouds, cranes, flowers or grapevines were incised on the leather-hard body of the vessel. Then black or white inlay[91] was painted into the incised designs and the excess wiped off. The vessel was then glazed and fired (see fig. 56).[92] Painting in iron-brown or copper-red under the celadon glaze and in gold over the celadon glaze were also Korean innovations (see fig. 53). Extant vessels painted in red or gold are extremely rare, but the British Museum is fortunate in having one of the best examples of the very difficult underglaze copper-red technique (fig. 54). Although underglaze red was used on Chinese porcelain in the fourteenth century and as early as the Tang dynasty on Changsha wares, it was never very successful because it was difficult to ensure a good colour.[93] Underglaze red was never used on celadons in China, although underglaze iron-brown was used sparingly, particularly in the Yuan.

The chronology of Koryo celadons is the subject of scholarly debate in Korea. Gompertz bases his views on Japanese[94] scholarship and Korean scholars such as Choi Sun-u, Chung Yang-mo, Yun Yong-yi and Kim Jae-yeol all have slightly differing opinions.[95] The general consensus is that celadons began to be produced in Korea in either the ninth or the early tenth century. A jar in the Ewha University Museum, with an inscription dating it to 993, is used as evidence of the production of celadon at that date. However, although the inscription tells us that it was made for royal use at rituals in memory of the first Koryo king, Taejo, this jar is a rather strange one, with a pale greyish-brown glaze. It probably represents a transitional, experimental phase in celadon development. Ninth- to tenth-century kilns producing celadons were located at Kangjin and changhung in South Cholla province, at Shinan and Kochang in North Cholla province and at Wondang and Yangju in Kyonggi province.[96] Excavations in recent years at So-ri in Kyonggi province and at Kangjin have provided interesting new theories about the dating of the earliest Koryo celadons and their relationship to Chinese wares.[97] In the early eleventh century, celadon was still not used commonly because the Chinese *Song shi* records that in the year 1005 all vessels used in private households in Korea were made of bronze.[98] Early Koryo (eleventh- to early twelfth-century) celadons were plain or embellished with incised or carved decoration, as evidenced by those excavated from the tomb of King Injong (reigned 1123–46).[99] The highpoint of celadon manufacture, when exquisite inlaid decoration was produced, is usually said to last from the mid-twelfth to the mid-thirteenth century, up to the Mongol invasion in 1231. The period of court exile in Kanghwa island followed by subordination to the Mongols until the end of the dynasty in 1392 is seen as the period of decline. Nonetheless, many beautiful pieces were produced during this period.[100]

55. White porcelain cupstand with incised decoration of chrysanthemums and squared spirals. White porcelain was made in the same shapes and at some of the same kilns as celadons but in smaller numbers. Ht: 5 cm.

Many Koryo celadons were manufactured for the use of aristocratic ladies in the form of cosmetic sets, including round boxes for rouge or face powder and small bottles for hair-oil. Elegant drinking cups and cupstands (fig. 55), wine ewers, spittoons, tea bowls (see fig. 54) and pillows all demonstrate the refined lifestyle of the court. By the Koryo, tea drinking had become very fashionable, as is evidenced by Xu Jing's description:

> The people of Gaoli have become much addicted to tea drinking and many kinds of tea implements are made: a black tea bowl ornamented with gold, a small tea bowl of kingfisher colour and a silver tripod for heating water are all modelled after Chinese wares. When a party is held, tea is made in the courtyard and covered with a silver lotus [lid]. It is served with a dignified step. Only when it is announced that the tea is ready does everyone drink: thus it is unavoidable that some should drink their tea cold. In the tea room, the tea things are placed in the centre of a red table cloth and covered with red silk gauze. Tea is set out three times daily and is followed with hot water: the people of Gaoli regard hot water as medicinal. It does not fail to please them when guests drink up their tea completely: if some is left it is considered discourteous. For this reason one should always make a point of draining one's tea bowl.[101]

It is apparent from this account that considerable ceremony was attached to the drinking of tea. As in China and Japan, tea drinking was originally associated with Buddhist monks and important Buddhist festivals always involved tea drinking. References to tea drinking are also found in literature and poetry of the Koryo period. As in China, where Yue wares were thought perfect for tea drinking, so Koryo celadons were closely associated with the practice.

By the mid-twelfth century, celadons had become so popular that they were even used for roof-tiles on the summer palace built by the profligate King Uijong. The moralizing *Koryo sa* records that in 1157:

> More than fifty sections of the people's houses were destroyed and the Taep'yong-jong building constructed. The Crown Prince was ordered to inscribe a tablet; famous plants and flowers were installed; rare and precious articles were displayed on all sides. To the south of this building a lake was made and the Kwallan-jong pavilion built. To the north, the Yang-i-jong pavilion was constructed and roofed with celadon tiles.[102]

This represents the highpoint of the flourishing period of Koryo celadons, when the Koryo aristocracy was enjoying an extravagant life in the capital, before it was brought to an end by the Mongol invasions.

Celadons were also made in large numbers for use in Buddhist rituals. Special shapes, often influenced by and paralleled in silver and bronze, were produced in celadon for specific Buddhist purposes. Examples include the *kundika* (see fig. 49), spouted bowls, bowl and ewer sets for hand-washing, alms bowls and many different varieties of incense-burner.

Most Koryo celadons were made in the southwest of the peninsula and transported up the west coast to the Koryo capital at Songdo (present-day Kaesong). A recently excavated shipwreck off the island of Wando in southwest Korea attests to the large numbers of celadons shipped at a time.[103] The kilns were of the sloping 'dragon kiln' type, which had been in use in Korea for high-fired wares since at least the Three Kingdoms period. There were about 270 kilns in existence in the Koryo period, of which about 240 were concentrated in the southwest in the Cholla provinces (see map 5, Appendix 1, p. 222). The two kilns at Sadang-ri in Kangjin district and at Yuchon-ri in Puan district were, to some extent, regarded as official factories. The latter developed much later in the Koryo than the former.[104] Excavations at Kyongso-dong in Inchon revealed a single, sloping tunnel kiln without partitions inside. At Sadang-ri it has been shown that the kiln was on a natural slope, rising at an angle of 5–6°. It has a number of chambers, each with two or three openings. Its length is 7 m (23 ft) and its original width is judged to have been 143–151 cm (56–59 in).[105] The celadons were fired in a reducing atmosphere at a temperature of 1100–1200°C. As with Chinese celadons, it was a small amount of iron oxide in the glaze which, combined with a reducing atmosphere, produced the celadon green colour. It is thought that the bluish tinge to the best Korean celadon glaze is a result of ferrous oxide dissolved in a lime glaze.[106] Some of the very earliest Koryo celadons were sometimes yellow, the result of an inability to control the reducing atmosphere. Towards the end of the Koryo, the celadons again became yellowish or greyish and the designs either schematic or over-elaborate. The fact that the designs became so complicated has been suggested as one of the causes of the decline in the quality of the glaze, which came to assume secondary importance.[107] The greyish, coarser body was a precursor of the *punchong* slip-decorated stonewares, into which Koryo celadons were to develop in the early Choson period.

(See Appendix 1 for an account of the technology and sources of Korean celadons.)

56. Stoneware wine ewer in the shape of a melon or gourd, with inlaid decoration of stylized chrysanthemums under a celadon glaze. Naturalistic fruit and vegetable shapes were favourites with Koryo potters. Koryo period, 12th century AD. Ht: 22 cm.

Other wares

White porcelain was not made in the same quantities as celadons, but finds at kiln sites show that it was produced at some of the same kilns as celadons. High-quality white porcelain was made at Yuchon-ri in Puan district of North Cholla province. Lesser-quality white ware has been found at two other sites, So-ri in Yongin district of Kyonggi province and Sadang-ri in Kangjin district of South Cholla province. They may have been produced from the first half of the tenth century until the fourteenth century, but the chronology is at present unclear. Chung Yang-mo states that the kiln at So-ri, discovered in the 1960s, showed evidence of having produced white porcelain as early as the ninth century.[108] Moulding, incising, carving and inlay were used to decorate white wares (see fig. 55).[109]

Black wares can be seen as a development of underglaze iron-painted celadons. In the case of completely black wares, the underglaze iron was painted over the complete surface of the vessel and then a celadon glaze applied. Sometimes these black wares were decorated with incised, inlaid or slip-painted designs. They were made at Sadang-ri in South Cholla province and at Jinsan-ri in Haenam district of the same province. Bottles, ewers, bowls and *maebyong* vases were made.[110]

Unglazed stonewares were probably in common use by ordinary people during the Koryo and are mentioned by Xu Jing, who says that large ones were used for preserving wine and for storing water on sea voyages, encased in a plaiting of vine or rattan to prevent breakage.[111] Many examples of this unglazed ware exist, in similar shapes to celadons, for example, pear-shaped vases with a pouring hole in the side, *maebyong* vases and spouted ewers. They are usually completely undecorated.

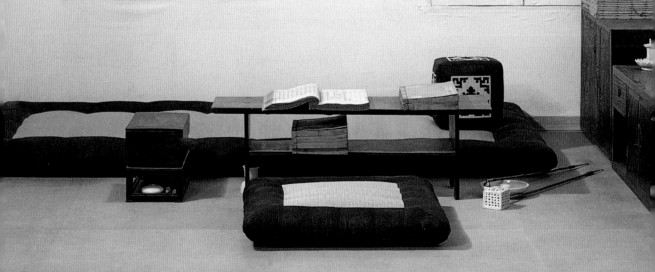

滄碧新甕凜玉茗

硬黃佳帖寫銀鉤

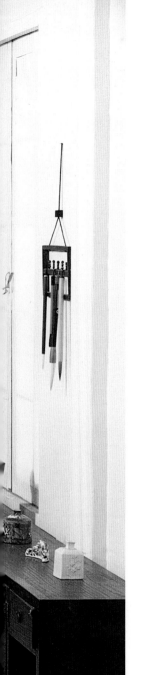

CHAPTER 4
Choson Period

Historians usually divide the five hundred years of the Choson dynasty (1392–1910) into an early and a late period, separated by the Japanese invasions of Korea under Hideyoshi in 1592 and 1597. Choson's founder, Yi Song-gye, who established the capital in Seoul, had a struggle to win the confidence of the old Koryo aristocracy because he came from a non-aristocratic background. He therefore cultivated the support of the Chinese Ming dynasty, using the term *sadae* or 'serving the great' to describe Choson's position. At least three regular embassies were sent annually to Ming China, resulting in much trade between the two countries. Choson exported horses, ginseng, furs, ramie and decorated straw mats and imported silk, medicines, books and porcelain.[1]

The fifteenth century is often regarded as a golden age in Korea's history, largely through the role of King Sejong the Great (reigned 1418–50), the fourth Choson king (see p. 113).[2]

Continuing Koryo's struggles with the people to its north, Choson's relations with its northern neighbours, a Jurchen tribe whom they called Ya'in or 'barbarians', were troublesome in the early years of the dynasty. Six fortresses were established in the northeast, along the Tuman and Amnok rivers. Submission was encouraged with the opening of markets where their furs and horses were traded.[3]

The Japanese on Tsushima island frequently sent forays to Korea in search of food. This led to a Korean attack on Tsushima in 1419 and a subsequent rapprochement, with the Japanese being granted some trading privileges. Following the opening of three southern Korean ports to Japanese vessels there was a huge increase in the export of Korean rice, cotton, beans, hemp, ramie, inlaid lacquer, porcelain, decorated mats, Buddhist and Confucian books, Buddhist sculptures and temple bells. In return the Japanese exported minerals such as copper, tin and sulphur, spices and medicines to Korea. Limits were twice imposed by the Koreans on the amount of exports to Japan and at one point in 1510 trade was stopped altogether.[4]

The Japanese invasion of 1592 was the result partly of the Confucian aristocracy's failure to take the Japanese threat seriously and partly of Toyotomi Hideyoshi's ambition to attack the Ming through Korea, having recently succeeded in unifying Japan's Warring States.

Having attacked the southeast coast at Pusan, the experienced Japanese troops quickly overran nearly the whole country. The king fled north from Seoul, to the disgust of his people, who refused to support his two sons' call to arms. At this point Admiral Yi Sun-sin began to win a series of sea battles, cutting off the Japanese ships from their ground troops. The major factor in these victories was his development of the famous

57. View of the interior of a reconstructed *sarangbang* or gentleman's study, showing the simple furniture and the traditional *ondol* floor and floor cushions for seating.

'turtle ships', which had an iron-clad covering, spikes to prevent the enemy from boarding and cannon around the entire circumference to enable attack in any direction (fig. 58).[5] Together with a combination of guerrilla forces and a Ming relief army, these ships enabled the Japanese to be repulsed, despite some fierce battles, particularly at Chinju on the south coast. A second attack was launched in 1597, but this was much less successful as the Koreans and the Ming were better prepared. The death of Hideyoshi in 1598 led the Japanese to withdraw, killing Admiral Yi Sun-sin with a chance shot on the way.[6]

There was great loss of life and of cultural treasures during the wars with Japan. Many wooden palace and temple buildings were burned, archives were lost and potters abducted. Both the books and the potters seized by Japan had a great influence on Japan's cultural development, particularly in the fields of printing and ceramics, both of which made huge strides in Japan in the seventeenth century. Korea's animosity towards Japan was widely felt and long lasting.

In the seventeenth century, the Choson court supported the Ming during its struggles against the Manchus, and suffered punitive military attacks by the victorious Manchu. King Kwanghaegun (reigned 1608–23) wisely adopted a wait-and-see approach before deciding whom to support. However, he was succeeded by King Injo (reigned 1623–49), whose policy of Ming royalism resulted in the first Manchu invasion of Korea in 1627. When the Manchu ruler, who was to establish his dynasty as the Qing, demanded Korean acknowledgement of his suzerainty, Injo refused and this led to a second Manchu invasion in 1636. Despite Korea's feeling of cultural superiority to the barbarian Manchus, Injo was forced to capitulate.[7] Ming royalism persisted throughout the Choson, and is reflected in the use of Ming reign titles in dates noted on documents and objects.

58. Drawing of one of Admiral Yi Sun-sin's famous iron-clad 'turtle ships', which are thought to have helped the Korean navy to repel the Japanese invasions of 1592–7.

The eighteenth century was a relatively peaceful period of great cultural development, especially under King Yongjo (reigned 1724–76) and his grandson King Chongjo (reigned 1776–1800).[8] Yongjo's son and Chongjo's father, Prince Sado, never became king: Yongjo, disillusioned and alienated by his son's strange behaviour, ordered him to climb into a rice chest and had it closed. Prince Sado died eight days later, still in the rice chest.[9]

Factional conflict was a recurring feature of Choson politics, but in the early nineteenth century in-law families played a particularly important role. Notable among these families, who typically rose to prominence through the marriage of a family member to a prince or crown prince, were the Kims of Andong and the Chos of Pungyang; the latter usurped power so completely that the kings reigned in name only. In 1864 the Taewon'gun, father of the twelve-year-old King Kojong, came to power as Prince Regent. He carried out many reforms designed to reassert the strength of the monarchy and cure the economic decline. He also organized an elaborate and costly renovation of the Kyongbok palace in Seoul, financed by greatly resented taxes. His move against the tax-exempt Confucian private academies or *sowon* provoked great opposition. It is perhaps for his isolationist policy that he is best known, however.

The Taewon'gun resisted the growing pressure of Western demands for trade relations, aware of China's fate in the Opium War of 1839–42 and afraid of contamination by Western ideas and the spread of Catholicism (see following section on Philosophy and religion). His renewed suppression of Catholicism in 1866 resulted in the death of nine French missionaries and retaliatory action by the French under Admiral Roze commanding seven warships. They seized Kanghwa island, west of Seoul, taking away important documents and books from the Royal Library. In 1871 five American warships tried to attack Kanghwa island, in retaliation for the destruction of the American trading ship *General Sherman* on the Taedong river in 1866. This time they were driven back by improved Korean defences. It was, however, not any Western power but the Japanese, after the Meiji imperial restoration and their subsequent rapid modernization, who finally succeeded in opening Korea up to trade and who were eventually forcibly to annex and then colonize Korea in 1910, bringing the Choson dynasty to a close.[10]

Philosophy and religion

Towards the end of the Koryo period, a group of educated scholar-officials, called *sadaebu*, came to the fore. They spread Confucian ideas and encouraged Confucian studies, particularly the Neo-Confucianism that had originated in Song China and which concentrated on a philosophical explanation of the origins of man and the universe. The practices of Neo-Confucianism in Choson Korea were centred on the Jia Li or Family Rites of the Chinese philosopher Zhu Xi.

Under the first Choson king, Taejo, a policy was followed of strictly controlling Buddhism. However, Taejo, as other later Choson kings, was personally close to Buddhist monks and had Buddhist temples and shrines built. This ambivalent attitude to Buddhism by the Choson monarchs continued, with a pattern being set of official government suppression of Buddhism coexisting with the personal piety of some of the monarchs.[11]

It was through a deep commitment to the development of a truly Confucian society that the suppression of Buddhism was intensified during the fifteenth century. Under King Sejong, only thirty-six temples of any significance were allowed to remain open. However, he too built a Buddhist shrine in the palace and wrote Buddhist works. Under King Songjong (reigned 1469–94), Prince Yonsan (reigned 1494–1506) and King Chungjong (reigned 1506–44), the suppression of Buddhism reached its height, with the Buddhist examinations being suspended and the major temples closed. There was a relative revival in the fortunes of the Buddhist church under King Myongjong (reigned 1545–67), when the Buddhist monk Hyujong had a certain amount of influence at court, with his appeal for the essential unity of Buddhism, Confucianism and Daoism. He was also responsible for organizing bands of warrior-monks to assist in the country's defence during the Hideyoshi invasion in 1592.[12]

The climax of the Confucianization of Korea was reached in the seventeenth century. The sixteenth century was characterized by a rising competitiveness amongst the Confucian literati as they fought against each other for office. Factionalism developed, together with purges. However, the power of the literati grew, supported particularly by the private academies or sowon, many of which received royal patronage and ended up by occupying a position in Choson society that was very similar to that of Buddhist temples in the Koryo.[13] Two schools of Neo-Confucianism developed in the seventeenth century, one led by Yi Toe-gye and one by Yi Yul-gok. The latter was also famous for many proposals for practical reform.[14]

Although the principles of Confucianism are basically egalitarian, in practice its teachings were irreconcilable with the traditional Korean social hierarchy. Choson society was divided into three distinct status groups: the *yangban*, who were the élite, the commoners (*yang'in*) and the slaves or base people (*chon'in*). The strict adherence to the Family Rites of Zhu Xi only really applied to the yangban élite and the rituals were in reality status symbols. The examination system, which had originally been adopted from China, was never really intended to introduce egalitarian standards for recruitment of officials in Choson Korea because an impeccable social background was a prerequisite for candidates. If a yangban took a wife from a lower class, the sons produced would be ineligible to take the examinations. Social discrimination was a major factor in Choson society. In Korea, Neo-Confucianism was adapted to the traditional patrilineal lineage system. This unique version of Neo-Confucianism is known as *kuksok* or 'national practice'.[15]

The eighteenth century saw the emergence of a school of thought which aimed to address social problems, such as the growth of wealthy merchants and large-scale farming. It is known as *sirhak* or 'practical learning' and was in general critical of the small number of yangban who held power. Many of the Sirhak scholars came from the southern faction (*Namin*) who had long been excluded from office. Their scholarship was essentially pragmatic and tried to reform agriculture and develop commerce and industry. There was a flourishing of studies of history and geography, law and government at that time, which is seen as a latter-day golden age in Choson history. Although the sending of tribute missions continued under the Qing rule of China, Koreans looked down on the Manchu regime and regarded themselves as the only true adherents to Confucianism, morally superior to the 'barbarian' Manchus. Kings Yongjo and Chongjo were activist rulers who patronized the arts. Court-sponsored encyclopaedias were completed, such as the massive *Tongguk munhon pigo* or *Reference Compilation of Documents on Korea*. Many elaborate paintings and screens of court rituals were completed, as well as regular formal portraits of the kings. There was also a surge of writing in the vernacular Korean script and of genre paintings of scenes of everyday life.[16]

It was during Chongjo's reign that Catholicism or 'Western learning' (*sohak*) started to spread in Korea, particularly among the reform-minded Namin, who were critical of the existing order. Contact with Catholicism came about through Koreans who visited Beijing and encountered Jesuit missionaries. Perhaps the most famous Catholic convert at this time was Chong Yag-yong. King Chongjo proscribed Catholicism in 1785 in response to a papal ruling that ancestor worship and belief in Christianity were incompatible, and in 1801 a severe suppression of Catholicism resulted in many leading figures being put to death or banished.[17]

Shamanism was a continuing popular belief and practice during the Choson period, as it had been in the Koryo. Shamanism was largely practised by the lower classes and particularly by women (see section on folk religion in chapter 5, pp. 144–7).

Inventions, science and technology

The first half of the fifteenth century in Korea was a period of remarkable cultural and scientific creation, largely through the work of the fourth Choson king, Sejong the Great (see figure 2, Appendix 2, p. 234). The country was at peace, and the ruler was wise and surrounded himself with able officials. It is perhaps for his personal involvement in the invention of the vernacular Korean script, now called han'gul, that King Sejong is best remembered. This phonetic syllabary was originally called the 'proper sounds to instruct the people' (*hunmin chong'um*) and its creation was motivated by a desire to further the moral education of the populace as a whole, as opposed to that of the yangban élite alone, who used the difficult Chinese writing system. At that time it is very doubtful that Sejong envisaged that it should completely replace Chinese characters, as some extreme national-ists advocate in present times. Its invention is thought in fact to have had a secondary aim of helping in teaching the common people how to pronounce Chinese characters.[18]

Great developments also took place in printing technology during Sejong's reign. The first bronze type of the Choson dynasty, produced under King Taejong (reigned 1400–1418) and called Kyemi type, was cast in sand moulds and set in beeswax. This caused the type to move sometimes when pressed, thus creating misalignment. Under King Sejong techniques were improved and the Kyongja type produced, which enabled one man to set type for twenty sheets of paper a day. By the time of the development of the fol-lowing Kabin type in 1434, it had become possible to print forty sheets a day. Both small and large type could furthermore be produced. Repeated efforts were made to produce a copper alloy with improved fluidity for moulding durable and clean type. The bronze type made in 1455 included some zinc and lead in addition to copper and tin. No mechaniza-tion of printing had evolved at that time to compare with Gutenberg's press, but type became gradually smaller and books cheaper. This progress was halted by the Japanese invasions in the sixteenth century but recommenced in the seventeenth century. There was much division of labour and the government controlled both casting and printing.[19] The Japanese adoption of movable-type printing in the seventeenth century followed their invasions of Korea and the removal of many important printed books.

Between the thirteenth and fifteenth centuries the population growth rate quadrupled, and there was a change to more intensive, continuous cultivation and a dramatic increase in the size of harvests, a result of advances in farming technology. There was a growth in medical knowledge and the compilation under King Sejong of the *Great Collection of Native Korean Prescriptions* (*Hyang'yak chipsongbang*). Also invented under Sejong were the rain gauge (1441) and the bowl-shaped or scaphe sundial. The rain gauge, the first in the world, was an iron cylinder with a depth of 42.5 cm (16.5 in) and a diameter of 17 cm (6.6 in). It was employed in an effort to alleviate the difficulties caused by seasonal fluctua-tion in rainfall, such as are recorded in the *Sejong sillok* (Veritable Record of King Sejong) around the year 1441. The scaphe sundial, based on Chinese Yuan dynasty ones, served as the first public clock in Korea. Two were ordered by Sejong to be placed in the centre of Seoul for the use of the general public. The originals were lost during the Japanese inva-sions and later versions were installed in the court.[20]

Clepsydras or water clocks were first made in Korea in 718 according to the *Samguk sagi*. A night clepsydra was installed in Seoul in 1398 together with a belfry to ring the standard time throughout the capital. The neighbourhood of the belfry and the clepsydra was called Chongno (i.e. Bell street), the centre of present-day Seoul. A clepsydra with an automatic time-signal apparatus was completed in 1434, under King Sejong, and installed in the Kyongbok palace (see figure 2, Appendix 2, p. 234), and a jade clepsydra is recorded

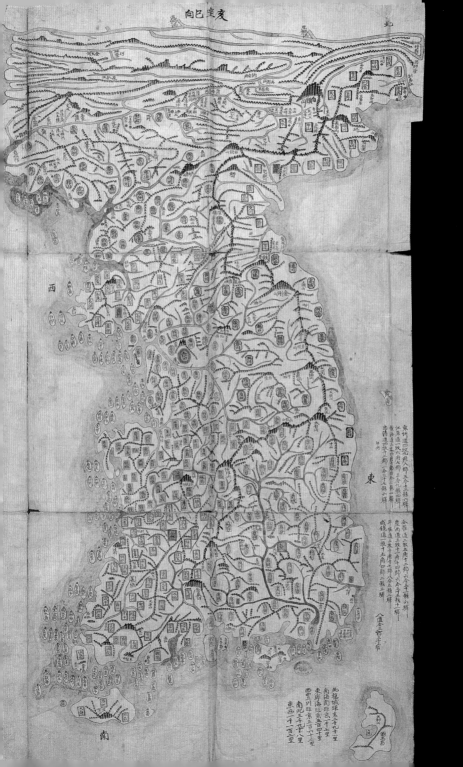

as having been constructed in 1438. The clepsydra now preserved in Toksu palace was the standard clock in use from the reign of King Hyojong (reigned 1649–59) until the end of the Choson. Portable clepsydras, for use in border stations and military camps, were first used in 1437.[21]

Cartography flourished during the early Choson and the world map produced in 1402 has been called the first accurate such map drawn in East Asia. It was based on Yuan Chinese and Arab sources and takes China as the central point. Choson dynasty maps were often collected together in portable atlas form, a practice which was not as common in China or Japan. A typical Choson atlas contained a world map, a map of China, a map of Korea, maps of each of the eight provinces of Korea, a map of Japan and a map of the Ryukyu islands (Okinawa) (fig. 59). The maps were usually folded in half or in six folds and the atlas had a stiff, oiled paper cover. They were either copied by hand or printed from woodblocks. Maps of Korea and the eight provinces were usually based on the 1487 edition of the *Tongguk yoji sungnam*, a geographical encyclopaedia of Korea, the result of King Sejong's encouragement of map-making and the invention in 1467 of a triangular surveying instrument. Efforts were made in the early Choson to produce maps of Korea based on actual survey, and the accuracy of maps gradually increased. Perhaps the best and most famous Choson dynasty map of Korea is that produced on woodblocks in about 1861 by Kim Chong-ho, under the title of *Taedong yoji chondo*, based on his work of thirty years earlier called the *Chonggudo*. They were both made up of rectangular units and Kim introduced the use of a map key. He also concentrated on natural and topographical features in his notes on the map, instead of the earlier emphasis on information about population and administrative centres. Kim's map was also remarkable for the accuracy of coastal lines and mountains.[22]

Western maps of the world were introduced to Choson Korea through Jesuits in China. Matteo Ricci's world map of 1602 was brought back to Korea the very next year by a visiting scholar, Yi Kwang-chong, and in 1631 Chong Tu-won returned from Ming China with a musket, telescope, alarm clock, world map and books on astronomy and Western culture. Later, in 1644, when Crown Prince Sohyon was held hostage by the Manchus in Beijing, he met the Jesuit Adam Schall and also brought back works on Western science to Korea. Chong Yag-yong, one of the best-known early converts to Catholicism, devised pulley mechanisms which were employed in construction of the fortifications at Suwon, using knowledge acquired from Jean Terrenz's *Description of Ingenious Devices*. Advances were also made in calculating the calendar and in astronomy, using Western science.[23]

Tombs

As in China, tombs were constructed at the foot of mountains, facing south between two ridges, in accordance with geomantic theories. The great importance placed on filial piety in Neo-Confucianist teaching led to the tombs of one's ancestors being regarded as sacred places. They played an important part in Confucian ritual and were visited at least twice a year, at lunar new year and at Chusok, the mid-autumn festival. Tombs were also status symbols, as can be seen in the tombs of the last two Korean rulers who were given 'emperor-style' tombs on the Chinese model after King Kojong tried to assert Korea's independence and declared himself emperor in 1899.[24] Up until then, the layout of the Choson

59. Map of Korea from a typical Korean-style portable atlas, which would usually also include a map of each province and a Sinocentric world map. Choson period, 19th century. 92.5 × 50.5 cm.

kings' tombs had followed an established pattern, continuing from that of the Koryo dynasty royal tombs. To a certain extent, this pattern was also based on Chinese imperial tombs; for example, the rows of officials, both civil and military, and the pairs of animals, both real and mythical, derive from China.

Korean royal tombs usually consist of a round tumulus surrounded by stone balustrades and low walls on the north, west and east sides, with, on the south side, a stone table and stone lanterns. The tomb is approached via a shrine (*chongjagak* or T-shaped building, called after its shape). In the kings' tombs, the rows of animals and officials are lined up behind the shrine, whereas in the last two 'emperor-style' tombs, they are in front of it.

Architecture

Korean palaces, shrines, temples, houses and many other structures were built on some of the same basic principles as Chinese ones. For example, they were constructed mainly of wood and had curved, overhanging roofs covered in ceramic tiles. The nail-less bracketing system was also employed in both cultures, enabling the heavy roofs to be supported and also allowing great liberty in roof design. Since the brackets could be seen from both inside and outside the building, they developed into a characteristic decorative feature. The rows of timber columns which formed the basic shape of the building were joined by non-structural walls, allowing a very flexible interior floor plan. Important buildings had coloured roof-tiles and painted wooden beams and brackets. Red, blue, yellow, white and green were the main colours used in the painting of wooden buildings, a technique which developed into an art form called *tanchong* in Korean.[25] Elaborate patterns and pictures covered wooden beams and brackets in important palaces, shrines and temples. Ordinary houses, however, were of plain wood with grey ceramic tiled roofs.

Although Choson dynasty palaces were generally built following the Chinese practice of symmetrical buildings laid out one behind another on a north-south axis facing south, some of them diverged from this strict model and developed asymmetrically in a uniquely Korean way, creating pleasing effects with hills, gardens and adjoining buildings. The Kyongbok palace in Seoul, which was the main and principal official palace, was most like the Chinese model, while the Changdok palace, likewise in the capital and which included the Piwon or Secret Garden, developed in a more independent way. It was originally a detached pleasure palace and only became the royal residence in 1609 after the Japanese invasions and the destruction of the Kyongbok palace. In 1867, when the royal family moved back to the restored Kyongbok palace, the Changdok palace reverted to its original function. It is the best preserved Choson royal palace. Another of the five main Choson royal palaces in Seoul, the Changgyong palace, was built facing east. This departure from the Confucian norm is probably due to the fact that Koryo palaces usually faced east and there had been a palace on the site of the Changgyong palace during the Koryo. The other two royal palaces were the Toksu and the Kyonghui. The former was only twice used as the royal residence, the last time being by King Kojong from 1897 to 1919, following the murder by the Japanese of Queen Min in Kyongbok palace.[26]

Following Confucian practice, the Royal Ancestral Shrine or Chongmyo was built at the beginning of the Choson dynasty to house the ancestral tablets of the kings. Memorial services were held there five times a year from 1392 until 1945. There is now an annual ceremony. The present building dates from 1608, when it was rebuilt after the Japanese invasions. Chongmyo lies to the east of the Kyongbok palace, while the Sajiktan altar, where the king carried out rituals to the earth and the five grains, lies to the west. This arrangement differs from and is much simpler than that in China, where there were originally four altars to heaven, earth, sun and moon located to the south, north, east and west of the capital. Ancestral shrines and portrait halls, where the ancestral spirit tablets and portraits of ancestors were kept, were everywhere regarded as sacred places. Confucian rites centring on the ancestral shrine, which was usually in the family house, took place at designated times throughout the year and involved the whole family.[27]

Buddhist temples during the Choson dynasty tended to be built in remote mountainous areas as they were not officially welcome in the cities. The structure and arrangement of temple buildings therefore came to be determined to a certain extent by their natural surroundings. A traditional pattern of arrangement of temple buildings had, however, evolved in which the southern gate tower, the main hall and the lecture hall ran in a straight line from north to south, with a square corridor surrounding these buildings. This pattern was adapted to fit the mountainous surroundings. The underlying principle was that of the three levels of sanctity of the Mahayana Buddhist pantheon, which governed the layout of the different halls, themselves built to enshrine a particular deity. This principle was also followed in pre-Song China and pre-Kamakura Japan as well as in Korea. Choson Buddhist temples were probably more faithful to early Chinese traditions of Buddhist architecture than were the Chinese, where the residential mansion style developed. Japan, in contrast, developed its own eclectic style of monastic architecture. The destruction of many temples in the Japanese invasions has meant that early Choson Buddhist architecture hardly survives. Late Choson temple architecture and layout can be seen at Songgwang-sa, one of Korea's largest Son (Zen) temples, occupying a beautiful mountainous site in South Cholla province in southwest Korea (fig. 60).[28]

Koreans, like Japanese but unlike Chinese, generally do not sit on chairs but kneel or sit on the floor. This practice has led to the development in Korea of an underfloor heating system called ondol and to the use of waxed paper for covering the warm floors. Shoes are always removed so that the waxed paper floors remain clean and shiny. Plain paper was formerly also used for lining the interior walls of houses and interior decoration was provided mainly in the form of painted screens. There was very little furniture and bedding was rolled up and put away every day in wooden chests. These chests developed into an art form, being decorated with elaborate metal hinges and handles and made in a variety of shapes and sizes according to their particular function. The layout of traditional houses in the Choson dynasty reflected the Confucian principle of separating the sexes and keeping women in the inner rooms, so that they were not seen by visiting men. One of the main rooms of the house (*sarangbang*) was used by the gentleman of the house as a study and for receiving visitors (fig. 57), while the woman's room, called the *anbang* or inner room, was associated with domestic activities such as sewing.

The city walls of Seoul were constructed at the beginning of the Choson dynasty and the surviving South Gate or Namdaemun, originally built between 1395 and 1398, was rebuilt in 1447. It is the oldest wooden structure in Seoul and is now designated National Treasure No. 1. It was originally the main entrance to the capital and a thoroughfare leads from it straight to the Kyongbok palace. The early Choson dynasty style of architecture

OVERLEAF

60. Overview of Songgwang temple in southwest Korea. During the Choson dynasty, Confucianism prevailed and Buddhist temples were mainly hidden deep in the mountains.

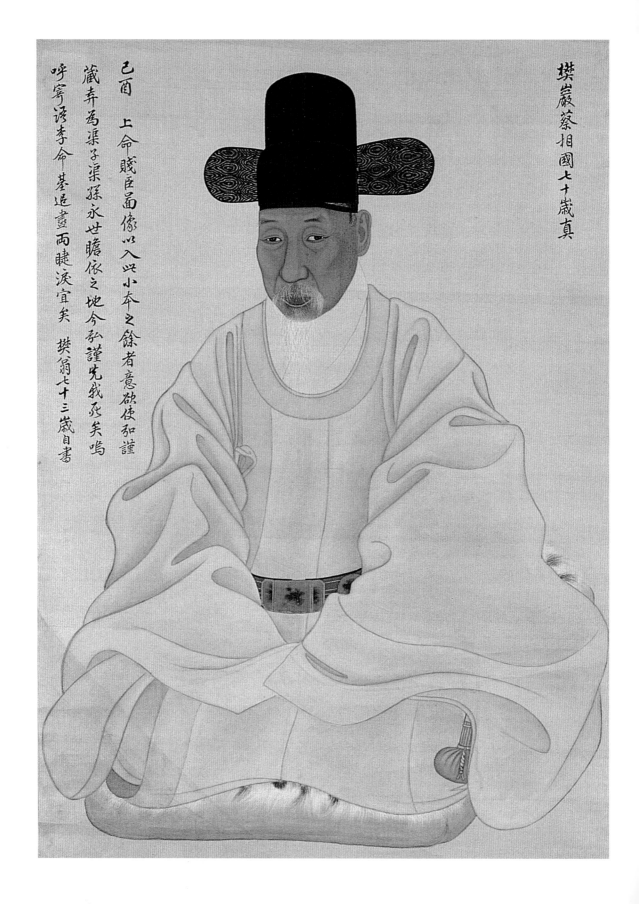

樊巖蔡相國七十歲真

己酉 上命賤臣畵像以入與小本之餘者意欲使弘謹

藏弆爲渠子渠孫永世瞻依之地今弘謹先我死矣嗚

呼寧語李命基造盡兩睫淚宜矣 樊翁七十三歲自書

61. Above: Paldal gate in the city wall of Suwon, built in the late 18th century under the direction of Prime Minister Chae Che-gong and the Sirhak scholar Chong Yag-yong, using Western-style castle-building techniques.

62. Left: Portrait of Chae Che-gong (1720–99), prime minister under King Chongjo in the late 18th century, painted by Yi Myong-ki (1760–1820). Ink and colours on silk, dated 1789. Ht: 69 cm.

which it represents can be compared with the later Choson city wall at Suwon. This was built in the eighteenth century under King Chongjo, when he wanted to build a new royal city adjacent to his father's tomb, as a way of atoning for his father's murder by his grandfather King Yongjo. The south gate at Suwon, called Paldal gate, is a double-roofed structure with baffled walls (that is, protective side walls) (fig. 61). At Suwon, Western-inspired castle-building techniques and labour-saving devices such as cranes were employed by the Sirhak scholar-official Chong Yag-yong, and the whole project came under the supervision of Prime Minister Chae Che-gong (1720–99) (fig. 62).[29]

Painting

Religious painting

Buddhist paintings of the Choson dynasty largely took the form of banners or *taenghwa*. Some extremely large taenghwa were used in outdoor ceremonies, in Tibetan fashion. They often measured as much as 14 m by 8 m (46 ft by 26 ft) and were only brought out for special occasions, such as the Buddha's Birthday, when the temple had to accommodate large numbers of people. These banners, painted on cotton or hemp, were suspended from a set of twin poles, often in front of the main hall of the temple. Their Korean name is *kwaebul taenghwa* and they usually depicted one large Buddha or Bodhisattva. Only late Choson kwaebul taenghwa remain, the earliest dating from 1622. Indoor banner paintings were smaller, ranging in height from 60 cm (23 in) to several metres. They were also painted on cotton or hemp, sometimes on paper. Although banner paintings were produced in the Koryo period, these were usually fairly small, personal paintings for private use. Wall-paintings were more common for temples. It is clear that in Korea, banner paintings increased in popularity from the sixteenth century onwards, much later than in China or Japan. At Dunhuang, for instance, large numbers of banner paintings are evidence of their popularity in China in the Tang period. Banner paintings were also used in Japan from the Heian period onwards. However, the era of popularity of colourful banner paintings in Korea ran parallel with the years when Chinese and Japanese artists were changing to Zen-style ink paintings. It is possible that contact with the Tibetan Buddhist tradition, which was popular in Korea during the Koryo dynasty, led to the development of the taenghwa in Korea in the Choson. The Korean name taenghwa is very similar to the Tibetan word *thangka* and the period of popularity of banner paintings in both countries coincided.[30]

63. Guardian king, one of four Heavenly Kings of the four directions (*Sa chonwang*) who guard the entrance to Korean Buddhist temples, either in painted or sculpted form. Ink and mineral colours on hemp. Choson period, dated 1796–1820. 3 m × 2 m.

Indoor taenghwa depicting the Buddhas Sakyamuni or Amitabha or illustrations of sutras were regarded as the most sacred and would have been placed in the most important halls of a temple. Taenghwa were closely related to the layout of the monastery for which they were painted and each taenghwa was originally intended for the adornment of a particular hall. In the various invasions of Korea in the first half of the Choson period, temples were destroyed and only late Choson taenghwa remain. It is therefore not always possible to match taenghwa with the temple for which they were originally intended. In general taenghwa depicting Buddhas would have been placed behind the altar in a main hall, while paintings of bodhisattvas and arhats, portraits of eminent monks and the ten kings of hell would have been displayed in subsidiary halls appropriate to them, such as the Hall of Patriarchs, the Hall of Ksitigarbha or the Hall of the Underworld Courts. Less sacred were the paintings of the large numbers of tutelary deities or *sinjung*, Indian, Chinese and Korean, such as devas, lokapalas (or the four Heavenly Kings) (fig. 63), the Mountain Spirit and Seven Star Buddhas. Particularly popular in Korea were the banner paintings depicting the Kamro-wang or King of the Immortal Nectar, an incarnation of Amitabha, who delivered souls suffering in hell to the Western Paradise of Amitabha. These paintings depict detailed scenes of hell, a ritual altar in the middle ground and Buddhas and bodhisattvas in the top part.[31]

Although few examples of early Choson Buddhist painting remain, the British Museum has a white-robed Avalokitesvara which can be attributed to the fifteenth to sixteenth century on stylistic grounds. The wall-paintings at Muwi temple are examples of early Choson mural painting and are characterized by new ways of portraying clothes and faces and by the use of ink outlines.[32] There was also a growing use of landscape painting in combination with Son or Zen subjects. This popularity of Son-style painting in the early Choson has been linked to the development of Zen ink landscape in Muromachi Japan.[33]

Representative of the sixteenth century or mid-Choson period is a group of triad paintings from a set of four hundred produced in 1565 under the regency of the Dowager Queen Munjong, who was a fervent Buddhist and patron of Buddhist art.[34] Koryo features still remain, such as the use of gold and deep mineral colours and fine lines. However, the Koryo fine translucent gauze clothes are now replaced by solid colours and ornamentation is more sparse. Medallion patterns become simpler and brushwork is less delicate. There is

therefore a certain flatness and lack of mystery to Choson Buddhist paintings, when compared to Koryo ones.[35]

In the eighteenth century kings Yongjo and Chongjo relaxed the anti-Buddhist policies of their predecessors and a large number of monasteries were rebuilt. The two kings nevertheless had a somewhat ambivalent attitude to Buddhism. Yongjo, for instance, ordered the closing of prayer temples and forbade the entry of monks into the city, while at the same time renovating Chingwan-sa to ensure his mother's well-being. In general Buddhism was the faith of the masses. On the one hand the males of the court and the literati practised Neo-Confucianist ethics, while on the other hand, women and commoners believed in Buddhism. Buddhist art of the period accordingly incorporated many folk and shamanistic elements. Korean costumes appeared instead of Chinese ones, reflecting the influence of the prevailing genre painting movement in the eighteenth century. The secular world, moreover, became more important. It was in the Nectar Ritual paintings of the eighteenth century that this world first appeared, and the depiction of ordinary people in the background of Buddhist paintings was a major innovation of these years, showing that Buddhism had become the religion of the common people. It had also become reconciled with Korean Confucianism, with the introduction of Buddhist ancestral festivals and the assimilation in Korea of the Sutra of Filial Piety.[36] Late Choson Buddhist paintings are characterized by bright colours, predominantly red, green and blue. Groups of many figures became dominant, some outdoor taenghwa containing as many as two hundred figures. Faces, shoulders and arms were exaggerated and mouths became smaller with stylized spiral twirls to moustaches and beards. The nineteenth century saw a decline and simplification in Buddhist painting, reflecting the financial weakness of temples. Thick pigments, predominantly bright blue, were applied without discrimination and the compositions became stereotyped. Buddhist paintings became closer to folk paintings (see fig. 77).[37]

Paintings of Daoist immortals by artists such as Kim Myong-guk (1600–after 1662) and Kim Hong-do (1745–?1818) are evidence of the assimilation by Koreans of the Daoist painting tradition from China which was associated there with the Zhe school.[38]

Court painting

Although early Choson court painting is known to have existed, little is known of such painting up to the late Choson period, due to the lack of extant works. However, court painting in the eighteenth century reflected the confidence of the period, under kings Yongjo and Chongjo, in contrast to the insecurity of the two previous centuries. The distinction made in China between professional court artists and amateur painters was not as important in Korea. Korea had very few exceptional literati artists and they were not as influential as they were in China. Choson court paintings were usually composed collectively and were unsigned, although many of the artists involved were the best painters in the country, recruited through government examinations to the Bureau of Painting (Tohwawon), which had been established by the beginning of the dynasty. The Bureau was attached to the Ministry of Rites, reflecting its central role in producing works of art to portray and record important royal and state rituals. Unlike the central examination system, the talent-recruitment examination for the Bureau of Painting was not confined to the hereditary yangban aristocrats. Promotion tests consisted of copying old masters

64. Illustrated manuscript of the royal ritual record of the sixtieth anniversary of the consummation in 1749 of the marriage of Lady Hyegyong, wife of the murdered Crown Prince Sado and mother of King Chongjo, showing the polychrome court painting style. Ink and colours on Korean paper, dated 1809. Page ht: 47.5 cm; double page width: 57.5 cm.

from the palace collection, although sometimes Bureau painters were honoured with a ranked position outside the Bureau. This was so with Kim Hong-do. Scholar-official painters, who were not Bureau members, sometimes also participated in group painting projects for the court or state. Their names were usually recorded separately in recognition of their different status. Bureau painters belonged to the social group called chung'in or 'middle people'. Since their pay was rather low, Bureau painters often also undertook private commissions.

Korean court art was archaic in style, conventional and fairly repetitive, with a limited palette. Its function was to show the king's virtuous rule, through the depiction of rituals and ceremonies. During the Choson there was a proliferation of *uigwe* (records of rituals) and *uigwe-do* (illustrations of the records of rituals). These were stored in the Royal Library (Kyujanggak) and other branches of the Royal Archives established by King Chongjo. A fine example of such a painting can be seen in the British Library (fig. 64). Painted records of King Chongjo's visits to his father's relocated tomb and the newly constructed city of Hwasong (present-day Suwon) are also good examples of this type of work.[39] The five colours used in court painting (red, yellow, blue-green, black and white) are in contrast to the monochrome ink literati style and probably derive ultimately from the archaic Chinese theory of the five elements. Longevity motifs, deriving from Chinese Daoism, abound in Choson court paintings, such as the ten longevity symbols, or the sun, moon and five peaks theme. The latter were often portrayed in screen format, to be placed behind the throne (see fig. 80). The screen depicting the sun, moon and five peaks, when placed behind the throne, showed the king's intermediary position between heaven and earth.[40] Heavily influenced by ancient China, these paintings were intended to portray an ideal Confucian state as, by the eighteenth century, Korea regarded itself as the last bastion of true Confucian civilization. The archaic Chinese style led to the development of a Korean version of the painting of scholars' items, as seen in seventeenth-century Chinese paintings and prints. In late Choson Korea, screens painted in a dramatically simplified and schematic way with shelves full of books and writing equipment (*chaekkori* or 'books and things') provided symbols of Confucian culture (see fig. 81).

The use of the screen format for court painting derived from ancient China but its general use developed in Korea far beyond that of China. Although screen paintings are perhaps usually associated with Japan, in fact paintings of all subjects were produced in screen format in Choson Korea. The screen was ideally suited for use in Korean houses and served as a wind break as well as for decoration (see section on folk painting in chapter 5, pp. 149–55).[41]

Portrait painting

Most of the extant Choson period portraits date to the eighteenth and nineteenth centuries and are of scholar-officials, many of the portraits having been preserved carefully by their descendants (see fig. 62). Portrait painting was closely connected with the Confucian importance of family lineage and can be divided into six categories that depended on the social status of the subject: portraits of kings; meritorious subjects; elderly officials; literati; women; and portraits of Buddhist monks (see fig. 6), generally displayed in temples.[42] A large number of portraits were produced for the twenty-seven Choson kings. Taejo, the first king, had twenty-six portraits painted of himself, while Yongjo had a new portrait every ten years. The painter Kim Hong-do painted King Chongjo as crown prince and again in 1781 as king. He was therefore honoured with the title *oyong hwasa* or 'painter of the august countenance'.[43] Unfortunately many royal Choson portraits were destroyed during the Japanese invasions and more recently, during the 1950–53 Korean War. The Sungjongwon ilgi or Diary of the Royal Secretariat describes the complicated procedures followed when producing royal portraits. Divination was sometimes practised in order to find auspicious days for the work, which was often examined in progress by the king. Rough sketches were made before the portrait was painted in ink on silk. Then it was coloured, mounted and a title inscribed. This was followed by an enshrinement and citation of all the artists and supervising ministers. The painting of a royal portrait thus constituted a major state event, displaying the authority of the king.

There was a great increase in portrait painting of meritorious subjects or *kongsin* during the Choson. Sometimes as many as a hundred people were given this title at one time, as a result of distinguished service. It was a great honour for the whole family and succeeding generations. The portrait which inevitably accompanied the award of this title was usually carried out to a formula, with the subject dressed in his official robes, his rank badge on his chest and black silk hat on his head, seated with his hands folded. In the late Choson, this pose also became popular for portraits amongst aristocrats who had not received the meritorious subject status.

Many of the portraits of elderly officials which exist today are in the form of album leaves, although there are some hanging scrolls and even folding screens. These portraits are called *kiro-do* and were painted as a way of commemorating the subject, who would have been a virtuous character holding a respectable position, who had reached the age of sixty or seventy (see fig. 62).

The most common portraits were of the literati or sadaebu, usually executed as large paintings for ceremonial use. They are nonetheless generally more relaxed and individual in style. The subject sat cross-legged, wearing scholar's robes called *simui* or *hakchangui*, or on a chair wearing his official uniform. Self-portraits were also sometimes painted in the Choson: the literati painters Kim Si-sup (1435–93), Yun Tu-so (1668–1715) and Kang Se-hwang (1713–91) all painted self-portraits.

Paintings of queens were produced in the early Choson and enshrined together with those of kings in a hall for royal ancestral portraits. Confucian morals dictated that men and women should not meet, so it was impossible for a queen to sit for a male painter. The early Choson trend for having portraits of husbands and wives painted together seems to have died out after the mid-Choson.

In portrait painting it was considered very important not only to make the details accurate but also to capture the person's soul. It was commonly believed that the soul rested in the eyes and so, when a king's portrait was being executed, great care was taken to select an auspicious day for the painting of the eyes. In a well-known episode, Kang Se-hwang painted his self-portrait but was dissatisfied with it. Only when his friend Im Hui-su added a few brushstrokes along the lower edge of the cheekbones did Kang feel that his soul had been captured. However, although portraits aimed to show the physical characteristics and personality of the subject, they were also, to a great extent, idealized portrayals, designed to evoke reverence and respect. This reverence for portraits of their ancestors led Koreans either to bury them in a safe place or to carry them away when they fled from crises. Over one thousand Korean portrait paintings have survived.[44]

Plant and flower painting

The choice of bamboo painting as the first and most important subject for court painters reflected the taste of the scholar-officials in the Choson. Bamboo painting is usually divided into two styles: a conservative one, using outlines and wash; and a calligraphic one depending on individual brushstrokes. Although the earliest bamboo paintings in the conservative style date to the late sixteenth century, porcelain wares decorated with this style of painting dating to the second half of the fifteenth century suggest that bamboo painting was already popular then. In fact it probably flourished as early as the Koryo dynasty, as is evidenced by decoration on inlaid celadons and Buddhist paintings. Famous Choson dynasty bamboo painters in the calligraphic style are Yi Su-mun, active in the fifteenth century, and Yi Chong (1541–1624) (fig. 65), Yu Tok-chang (1694–1774) and Sin Wi

65. Left: Bamboo painting by Yi Chong (1541–1624). Bamboo painting was associated with integrity and highly regarded by Confucian scholars. Ink on silk, late 16th to early 17th century AD. 122.8 × 52.3 cm.

66. Right: Porcelain vase with underglaze iron-brown and cobalt blue decoration of grapevines, which were a favourite subject of Choson painters. Choson period, 17th–18th century AD. Ht: 39.7 cm.

(1769–1847).[45] As in China, bamboo was associated with austerity and integrity. It was also painted together with prunus or pine, as in China.

Grapevines, like bamboo, offer the painter scope to use calligraphic brushstrokes in depicting tendrils and fronds. Grape-painting also appeared in Korea as early as the Koryo and can be seen on celadons painted with grapevines. During the Choson grapes were a popular motif for decorating inlaid lacquer boxes and became popular amongst painters from the sixteenth century. Two famous grape painters of this time were Sin Saimdang, mother of the philosopher Yi Yul-gok, and Hwang Chip-jung (born 1533). Both painted in the boneless technique, depicting unformed grapes and connecting the grapes using short, horizontal lines. Yi Kye-ho (1574–after 1645), Hong Su-ju (1642–1704) and Yi In-mun (1745–1821) were later specialists in grape-painting, although the latter was more famous for his landscapes. There was an unusually close relationship between painting and porcelain decoration in the Choson (fig. 66), brought about by the practice of commissioning professional court painters to decorate porcelain wares destined for use by the court and officials. The result of this close cooperation can be seen in some very beautiful examples of porcelain decorated with grapes which are painted with elegance and subtlety.[46]

Landscape painting

The Choson period was one of great development in landscape painting in Korea. Landscape was the most popular subject amongst painters, despite its being ranked second in importance in the official test given by the Court to recruit academy painters. Of the subjects tested, the first was bamboo, the third was figure painting (people, animals and birds) and the fourth was flower painting.[47] This order reflected the traditional Chinese order of priority. It was under the influence of various Chinese schools of painting that landscape painting developed in the Choson. Korean artists first followed the Guo Xi monumental landscape tradition of the Northern Song. Later, however, elements of the Southern Song academy tradition and the Zhe school of professional artists of the early Ming also played a part. It is probably true to say that a 'Korean' school of landscape painting did not really emerge until the eighteenth century, when Chinese influences had been absorbed and transformed.[48]

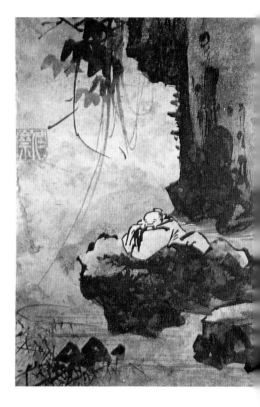

67. *A Scholar Contemplating the Water* by Kang Hui-an (1419–64), one of the three masters of the early Choson along with An Kyon and Choe Kyong. This painting of a scholar is closely related to the Ming Chinese Zhe school. Ink on paper, Choson period, 15th century AD. 23.4 × 15.7 cm.

The most important and influential landscape painter in the early Choson was the academy painter, An Kyon, who was active during King Sejong's reign in the fifteenth century under the patronage of Prince An-pyong (1418–53). The prince built up a large collection of Chinese paintings dating from the Tang to the Yuan, including seventeen by Guo Xi, who had a great influence on An Kyon. Unfortunately only one extant authenticated painting by An Kyon has survived, although others are attributed to him. In this work, called *A Dream Journey to the Peach Blossom Land,* An paints the dream of his patron, the prince. The style of this painting follows the Guo Xi tradition but the effect of monumentality is achieved by a combination and contrast of high distance and level distance and by a careful use of criss-crossing diagonal movements. These features were to become characteristic of later Korean landscape painting, as did the looseness and sketchiness of brushwork shown by An Kyon.[49]

In the sixteenth century, Korean painters show influence from the Ming Zhe school, modified in a typically Korean way. There was a strong tendency to reduce volume and space to flat planes with simply curved outlines and to sprinkle them with small form-elements.[50] The Korean treatment of space has been attributed to the influence of the Chinese Southern Song academy style, as exemplified by Ma Yuan. The early-sixteenth-century Korean academy painter Yi Sang-jwa is an example of a Korean painter who adhered faithfully to the one-corner composition of Ma Yuan. An example of an early Korean painter influenced by the Zhe school is the scholar-painter and contemporary of An Kyon, Kang Hui-an (1419–64). He was the deputy leader of the embassy to Ming China in 1455 and therefore must have seen many Zhe school paintings in Beijing. His famous painting, called *A Scholar Contemplating the Water* (fig. 67), is evidence of his debt to the

Zhe school in its composition, its way of depicting cliffs and rocks and the importance of the human figure. Its close resemblance to an illustration in the Chinese *Mustard Seed Garden Painting Manual* of 1679 is interesting as it presumably shows that an earlier Chinese painting must have been a model for both.[51]

Some painters of the middle Choson period adopted the literati manner deriving from the Ming Chinese Wu school of scholar-amateur painters, which had itself derived from the Four Masters of the Yuan. Although this school was associated with scholar-amateurs in China, this was not the case in Korea. It was the style of painting that was adopted, not the spiritual dimension that the painter wanted to express through the painting. In Korea this stylistic tradition is usually called Namjonghwa or Southern School. A professional or court painter could also be a Southern School painter in Korea, if he painted in that style.[52] The Wu or Southern school did not become really popular in Korea until the eighteenth century, when the Four Masters of the Yuan became very influential. Chong Son (1676–1759), one of Korea's most famous painters, was responsible for the dissemination of the Wu-Southern School style, as well as for the development of realistic landscape painting of actual places in Korea, known as *chin'gyong sansu*. With this innovation, Korean landscape painting really came of age. The combination of Southern School and 'real place' landscape can be seen in many of Chong's paintings (fig. 68).

68. *Complete View of the Diamond Mountains* by Chong Son (1676–1759). Chong Son painted real places around Seoul and in the famous Diamond Mountains, now in North Korea. Ink and colours on paper, Choson period, 1734. 130.7 × 94.1 cm.

Other eighteenth-century artists who were influenced by the Chinese Wu school are Sim Sa-jong (1707–66), Kang Se-hwang and Yi In-sang (1710–60). Kang Se-hwang also painted landscapes in imitation of Shen Zhou via the *Mustard Seed Garden Painting Manual* but he tried also to explore a new style. This can be seen in his album entitled *A Trip to Songdo*, where he sought to introduce the shading techniques of Western painting. He also used rows of dots, in the style of Mi Fu. An almost abstract design is formed, a graphic system based on planes and dots.[53]

Kim Hong-do's landscape paintings also show a radical development out of reliance on Chinese models. He chooses places from his own country, instead of idealized landscapes, and shows a strong penchant for geometric elements and for organizing the picture in a network of powerful, angular lines. The abstraction and stylization is highly exaggerated. Kim and Chong Son are both protagonists of what could be called the 'Korean graphic style' (see fig. 68).[54]

In the nineteenth century, the great poet, painter and calligrapher Kim Chong-hui (1786–1857; pen-name Chusa) and his followers carried on the Southern School style. The latest trends from Qing China were also absorbed. Kim Chong-hui introduced epigraphy and historiography of the Chinese classics from China as he was in close contact with Qing scholars and calligraphers. Many of his followers imitated his painting style, which combined a simple layout, an understated depiction of motifs using dry brushwork and a tendency to emphasize the spiritual. His disciple Ho Ryon and the versatile and eccentric painter Chang Sung-op (1843–97) led two lines of development in late Choson landscape painting.[55]

Genre painting

A growing interest in and concern for the lives of the common people during the second half of the eighteenth century was reflected in philosophy, literature and painting. In philosophy, it was expressed in the Sirhak or Practical Learning school of thought, while in literature, poetry by lower-grade officials of the chung'in and sang'in classes began to be published – a previously unheard-of phenomenon. There was a flourishing of novel writing in the Korean han'gul script. These novels usually concerned the corruption of yangban and the unfairness of the ban on marriage between the yangban and the lower classes or with the offspring of yangban and secondary wives. The living standards of some common people rose, to the extent that it was becoming more difficult to distinguish a man's class from the way he dressed. Nouveaux riches merchants were less bound by the yangbans' strict rules of conduct. This behaviour was depicted in the slightly erotic genre paintings of Sin Yun-bok (1758–?). He painted scenes of gentlemen and courtesans (*kisaeng*) at drinking parties or illicit rendezvous, as well as portraits of beautiful women, who must have been courtesans if they contravened Confucian morality and sat for him. Sin's predilection for these risqué subjects led to his dismissal from the Bureau of Painting.[56]

Kim Hong-do, on the other hand, concentrated on depicting the life of the common people. His most famous genre paintings are the twenty-five album leaves in the National Museum of Korea, representing everyday activities such as washing clothes, eating, tiling a house roof, and people such as wrestlers, entertainers, schoolboys, pedlars and farmers. The original paintings have been heavily retouched. Several copies of the album are in existence, including one in the British Museum, probably completed in the nineteenth century (fig. 69). Kim's paintings are characterized by the lack of any background and by the masterly arrangement of the figures in space, often in a circle. Another distinguishing feature of his work is the portrayal of round faces with large noses and horizontal, almond-shaped eyes.[57] Kim also painted gatherings of gentlemen (*ajip-to*) (fig. 70) and pictorial biographies (*pyongsaeng-do*) in which he included elements of landscape and buildings. He was one of the most versatile late Choson painters, mastering landscape, genre, religious, bird, flower and portrait painting. However, like a true artist, he had little regard for money and died in destitution.[58]

Other genre painters of this period were Yun Tu-so (1668–1715) and his son Yun Tok-hui and grandson Yun Yong, Cho Yong-sok (1686–1761), Kim Tu-ryang (1696–1763) and Kim Tuk-sin (1754–1822).[59] They depicted the changing nature of Choson society in the eighteenth century.

69. Above: *Ssirum* (Korean wrestling) after the original late-18th-century painting by Kim Hong-do. Kim's genre paintings show ordinary life in a humorous light. Here a sweet-seller, spectators and a pair of wrestlers are painted with simple strokes. Choson period, 19th century AD. 31 × 26 cm.

70. Right: Detail from *Gathering of Elders* by Kim Hong-do, dated 1804. White porcelain tableware can be seen on each individual tray-table and in the centre. Ink and light colours on silk.

姜白金姜白李白陳李李金林張林金金鄭尹張張白張馬李法金林金李李金金張林金李李金尹白李金李金馬金林陳金白白
弘應致弘宗敬範錫亨應爾履厦侯思樂賢宇養宗俊　　錫泆光南家章　學出侯光養師思宗品德　齊玩任協興濟發周良旻泳栴大挺祐祐
憙沫星烈倫碩禧押法坤源鳴僴玥誠玉連永嘉炯良禄蓋趺沼年實微珣奎儋慶良慶玉憲春正寓壽聖濟鳴珍嗷五温泳格榕張蓰宅

Sculpture

During the first half of the Choson, Buddhist sculpture showed some continuity from the Koryo, although displaying a certain naïvety. Few sculptures of great importance are known from the Choson, although many images continued to be made, mostly in bronze or wood. Common stylistic features are a squat and heavy shape, with thickly carved costumes. Votive wooden panels carved with many images in rows were particularly popular.[60]

Non-Buddhist sculptures consisted primarily of stone tomb figures of animals and officials which lined the entrances to important tombs, after the pattern of Chinese imperial tombs. The sculptural style, is, however, much less ornate and the figures are generally shorter than in the Chinese model. The statuary at the 'emperor-style' tomb of the last ruler, Sunjong, was carved by Chinese stonemasons and is consequently much more elaborate than that of either the earlier kings' tombs or his predecessor, Kojong.[61] Some non-royal tombs also featured stone tomb statuary, its elaborateness varying in accordance with the status and means of the family.

Lacquer

During the Choson period, lacquer was used predominantly on boxes and furniture for domestic use by the aristocracy, whereas in the Koryo it had been popular for Buddhist objects. Chests, low tables, clothes boxes, cosmetic cases, document boxes and sewing utensils were all decorated with lacquer and inlaid with mother-of-pearl, tortoise-shell and sometimes sharkskin. A considerable quantity of lacquer from the late Choson period remains but early Choson lacquer is rare.

The dating of early Choson lacquer is problematic and there is, at present, no clear chronology. A predominant feature of early Choson inlay is the use of scrolling vines or flowers, usually peonies or lotuses. In general early Choson inlaid lacquer does not use metal wire for the vine or flower scroll, but thin strips of shell. Several different types of flowers moreover grow from the same scroll. Very early fifteenth-century pieces frequently feature ogival panels and backgrounds densely filled, often in the form of circular dots. Leaves and petals are represented on the inlaid shells by a crackled pattern. By the seventeenth century the flowers and leaves are simpler and the flower or vine scroll becomes more regular and geometric, with the flowers being open rather than closed. Metal wire is again used and there is only one type of flower on each scroll.[62] On the basis of these features, the British Museum's box inlaid with peony scrolls can be dated to the

71. Lacquered wooden box with inlaid decoration of peony scrolls in mother-of-pearl. Choson period, 16th–17th century AD. Length: 39 cm.

sixteenth–seventeenth century (fig. 71). Lacquer pieces decorated with birds have been dated both to the very early Choson and to the sixteenth–seventeenth century.[63]

Three pieces of Choson inlaid lacquer in the Tokyo National Museum could be used as a basis for dating sixteenth-century Choson lacquer because they were commissioned by Ouichi Yoshitaka (1507–51). However, they are not typical because the shapes of two of the pieces, a writing desk and writing box, are Japanese, and the decoration is in a Chinese-influenced style. The third item in this set, a large box, is much more typically Korean.[64]

In the eighteenth century, inlaid flower scrolls became thicker and the flowers larger. Nineteenth-century lacquer was increasingly decorated with folk symbols of good luck and long life. Decorated objects inlaid with mother-of-pearl came to be associated with women and were used increasingly as cosmetic boxes, comb cases and sewing equipment. Some very high-quality boxes from this period feature lively decoration of large dragons using tortoise-shell and sharkskin to great dramatic effect combined with mother-of-pearl.

Painted ox-horn was also used in the Choson period to decorate boxes, sewing equipment, combs, pillow-ends and other small items. Some Korean scholars believe it is possible that this technique dates back to the Silla period in Korea, if a painted ox-horn ruler in the Shoso-in in Japan, closed in 756, is of Korean manufacture. However, this is a subject of some debate. The technique involves painting the thin, transparent slices of ox-horn on the reverse in bright colours mixed with glue and then sticking them on to the surface of wooden objects. Auspicious symbols were the main decorative motifs and the objects made were usually for the use of aristocratic women.[65]

Ceramics

During the Choson, ceramics were used for a variety of functions, including epitaph tablets, tomb furnishings, tablewares, ritual vessels and reliquaries. With the decline of Buddhism as a state religious cult, production of temple and other sacred vessels gave way to the manufacture of ceramics used for Confucian ritual. Chinese porcelain was imported and used by the kings and by aristocrats. This had a considerable effect on the development of people's taste and the Choson dynasty saw a progression from the widespread use of punchong wares at the beginning of the dynasty to the development of a native Korean porcelain in emulation of Chinese porcelain but with uniquely Korean shapes and designs.

Punchong wares

It is difficult to distinguish very late Koryo inlaid celadons of the late fourteenth century from early Choson inlaid punchong of the early fifteenth century (fig. 72). The late celadons became greyish-green in colour and the body became coarser. Both these features were also characteristic of punchong wares (*punchong sagi*), the name punchong being translated as 'powder green' or 'greyish-green'. Punchong was made throughout the first half of the Choson period, until the late sixteenth century. After the potters were abducted by the Japanese invaders at the end of the century, punchong died out and was replaced by porcelain. However, the demise of punchong had already started before the Japanese invasions and its total disappearance cannot be attributed solely to the capture of the potters. Its popularity decreased and it was gradually supplanted by white porcelain.

The terminology for the different types of punchong can be confusing, as Japanese as well as Korean terms are in general use. This is because the unpretentious punchong wares were highly prized by the Japanese for use as tea ceremony utensils from the sixteenth century onwards. Indeed, the Japanese invasions have been partly attributed to their desire to seize Korean potters for Japanese kilns and the term 'pottery wars' has been used by Japanese scholars to describe the invasions.[66] The main characteristic of punchong is the use of white slip to cover the fairly coarse grey stoneware clay body. Sometimes the slip was applied by dipping and sometimes by brushing. The patterns were applied using a variety of techniques, such as stamping, painting, inlay, incising or carving (sgraffiato). Finally a transparent, greyish-green glaze was applied and the piece was fired. The following are the main techniques with their English, Korean and Japanese terms. It is clear that the Japanese terms are less precise, many varieties of punchong being called Mishima, after the Japanese name for the Korean port used to export the wares to Japan.

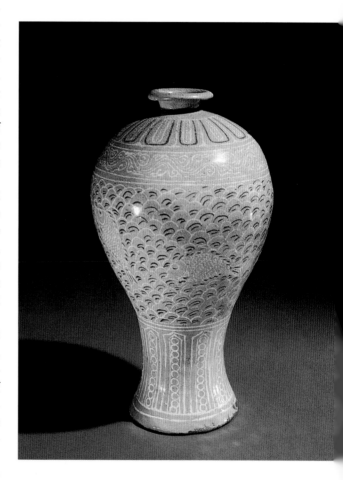

Inlaid wares (sanggam or Mishima): Incised designs are filled with white or black slip as in Koryo celadons. These can be subdivided into linear inlay (*son sanggam*) and planar inlay (*myon sanggam*). The latter is unique to punchong wares, making its appearance after 1420. It developed into reverse sgraffiato, where the background design is carved away.

Stamped wares (*inhwa* or Mishima): Repeated rows of stamped, regular patterns are applied, including the 'rope curtain' pattern or chrysanthemum florets. This technique reached a highpoint of popularity in the period between 1417 and 1468. Also included in this category are the stamped wares with inscriptions consisting of the names of government offices, production areas or of potters.

Sgraffiato wares (*pakji*; Japanese: *hori-mishima*): The design is incised and its background carved away to reveal the clay body. Sometimes iron pigment is applied to the revealed body to make it turn black in firing. Popular during the reign of King Sejong, both the technique and the designs show clear influence from Chinese Cizhou wares. Incised slip wares (*sonhwa, chohwa*; Japanese: *hori-mishima*) displayed incised linear decoration, without the background carved away.

Iron-painted wares (*cholhwa*; Japanese: *e-hakeme*): Slip is brushed on the entire surface and then designs are painted with a pigment containing iron, which fires black or dark brown. Lively fish and lotus designs are particularly popular, giving a spontaneous impression. This technique has been traditionally associated with Mt Kyeryong near Kongju, but is not limited to that area.

72. *Maebyong* vase with inlaid decoration of fish among waves. Inlaid *punchong* ware. Early Choson period, 15th century AD. Ht: 31.5 cm.

Brushed slip wares (*kwiyal*; Japanese: *hakeme*): The slip is applied with a coarse brush, leaving visible and decorative brushmarks. Produced all over the country in the latter half of the fifteenth and sixteenth centuries, often at the same kilns as white porcelain, these wares were probably intended for the common people as substitutes for the white porcelain used by the aristocracy.

Wares dipped in slip (*punjang, paekto*): Widely made in South Cholla province in the second half of the fifteenth and the sixteenth centuries, this plain white ware should not be confused with the white porcelain it was probably intended to imitate.

In general, the techniques that produced inlaid, stamped, sgraffiato and incised slip wares were predominant before 1470 and the remaining three after that date. The clay body was less pure and the glaze less evenly applied in the latter three techniques. Although punchong ware is often described as a popular, utilitarian ware, in practice it was used by the court and by aristocrats at the beginning of the Choson. For example, inlaid punchong vases were made for Princess Chongso (1412–24) and stamped punchong for Princes Wolsan and Onyong. Until 1420, white porcelain was rare, even at court, and punchong was used instead. The fact that inscriptions have been found on stamped punchong but not on slip-painted items may suggest that the latter were not used by the aristocracy, only by commoners.

Archaeological investigations have revealed punchong kiln sites dotted over the whole of Korea, particularly in the south. The kilns were climbing brick tunnels, situated on either a hillside or a man-made mound. Many excavated dated pieces can be used to establish a chronology of development.[67]

Porcelain

Although white porcelain had been made in the Koryo period at some of the kilns producing celadons (see section on Other wares in chapter 3, p. 106), its widespread production in Korea did not occur until the fifteenth century, when it developed rapidly. The *Sejong sillok* notes a census of kilns carried out in 1424–5 which shows the existence of 185 punchong kilns and 139 porcelain kilns at that time. The increase in production of porcelain during the reign of King Sejong can be partly attributed to the fact that it was needed to replace gold and silver, which was demanded as tribute by the Ming. In 1407 King Taejong had been forced to decree that ceramics and lacquer should be employed instead of gold and silver wares and by 1419 the use of gold and silver was prohibited at government functions. Even after the Ming removed gold and silver from the list of tribute in 1429, its use at the Korean court was not resumed.[68]

One of the important events in the development of porcelain in the early Choson was the establishment of the official government-controlled factory (*punwon*), probably inspired by the official Chinese kilns at Jingdezhen. The exact date of the establishment of the Punwon in Kwangju district, near Seoul (not Kwangju city in South Cholla province) is a subject of debate; it seems likely that it was in the second half of the fifteenth century, possibly in the late 1460s.[69] According to the *Sejong sillok*, the finest porcelain was made in four kilns, Kwangju, Koryong, Sangju and one other. Pure white, undecorated porcelain produced at this time was regarded as of high enough quality to be presented to the Ming emperor and was requested by the Ming as tribute. After the establishment of the Punwon at Kwangju, the white porcelain used at the Korean court was produced there exclusively.

73. Left: White porcelain
bottle vase, showing the
Confucian Korean
predilection for plain
white wares. Early Choson
period, 15th century AD.
Ht: 34 cm.

74. Right: Set of fourteen
porcelain epitaph tablets
decorated in underglaze
cobalt blue calligraphy
with details of the lineage
and achievements of
Kim Chun-gun (1814–47).
Choson period, c. 1849.
9 × 8 cm.

Other kilns produced the white porcelains which were used increasingly by aristocrats outside the court from the late fifteenth century onwards.

Korean and Japanese scholars have proposed various chronologies for Choson porcelain.[70] Chung Yang-mo divides the ceramic history of the dynasty into three periods: the early Choson (1392–1649), the mid-Choson (1651–1751) and the late Choson (1752–1910).[71] The early period is characterized by great influence from Chinese porcelain which was imported and used as models. Although the Korean preference was for plain

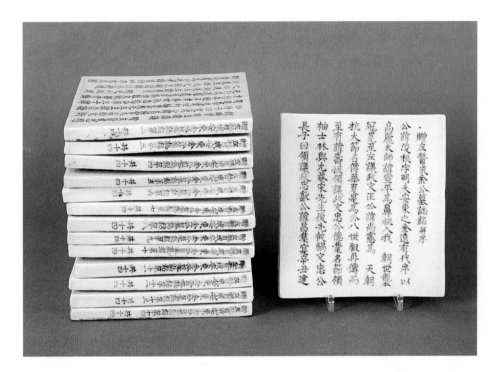

white wares, underglaze blue was also developed, at first using expensive cobalt imported from China. As early as the reign of King Sejo (1455–68), however, the discovery of a cobalt blue substitute (called Mohammedan blue after the Chinese term) was recorded at Miryangbu, Uisonghyon and Sungchonbu and that of iron-blue from Kangjinhyon. In 1469 it was recorded that potters 'tried the Mohammedan blue produced in Kangjinhyon and the result was satisfactory'.[72] The designs on early Choson blue and white often incorporate Chinese features such as bird and flower painting and floral lappets around the base and neck.

The plain white porcelain of this period is distinctively Korean, being creamier in colour than the bluish-white Chinese porcelain. Although vessel shapes were also influenced by China, for example pear-shaped vases (fig. 73), large lidded jars and stem-cups, some shapes were exclusively Korean, such as covered bowls. Inlaid decoration of lotus or foliage scroll designs in black slip was also produced on white porcelain in the early period and sometimes epitaph tablets were written with inlaid slip. Later in the Choson period, many of these tablets were produced, decorated in underglaze blue (fig. 74). Plain white porcelain was also used in the early Choson, in the same way as punchong ware, for placenta jars. (Great value was placed on placentas, perhaps because of their life-giving properties. The placentas of newborn children of high-ranking yangban and the royal family were often buried in small, sealed lidded jars within another, larger, jar).

Underglaze blue porcelain was at its peak of quality in the late fifteenth century, after which it went into a decline. The eighteenth century, however, saw a revival and the 'autumn grasses' design was particularly popular. The availablity of cobalt from China meant that many pieces of underglaze blue with a variety of designs could be produced, including writing utensils, wine and table vessels. Underglaze iron and underglaze copper-red decoration was used either alone or in combination (fig. 75; see also fig. 66).[73]

Up until the late Choson period the Punwon had been relocated every ten years to a new forest area in Kwangju district in order to ensure a good supply of firewood for the kilns. As the Punwon had moved around, the forest areas had been considerably reduced through the use of the slash and burn method of gathering firewood. However, in the early eighteenth century the Punwon was permanently located near present-day Kumsa-ri and Punwon-ri in Kwangju district near the Han river, and firewood was transported there by river.[74] From the late eighteenth to the early nineteenth century, many ceramics were made for use on the scholar's desk, such as water-droppers, brush-washers, brush- and paper-holders. These were usually decorated with underglaze cobalt blue, iron-brown or copper-red and their forms often imitated natural forms, such as fruit, animals, fish or mountains. Large storage jars decorated with dragons in underglaze blue, sometimes with details highlighted in red or brown, are also a feature of this period, as are vessels completely covered in underglaze blue or red or brown which has been brushed on with visible horizontal brushstrokes.

75. Porcelain vase decorated with a dragon painted in underglaze iron-brown. Choson period, 17th–18th century AD. Ht: 33.7 cm.

The fact that overglaze enamels were not developed in Korea, despite its close contacts with Qing China where these became prevalent, is probably largely because their bright colours did not appeal to Korean taste. In the Neo-Confucian Choson the preference was for plain, austere wares. There was also an increasing fashion in eighteenth-century Korea for 'Koreanization' in all aspects of cultural life, as epitomized by 'real landscape' and genre painting. As observed by Yi Kyu-gyong, a nineteenth-century Korean scholar: 'The greatest merit of white porcelain lies in its absolute purity. Any effort to embellish it would only undermine its beauty' (see fig. 73 and fig. 8).[75]

For further brief discussion of Choson ceramics, see Appendix 1.

Influence on Japanese ceramics

During the early Choson, ceramics were an important trade item between Korea and Japan, as the Japanese ceramics industry was less well-developed than that of Korea. Korea's punchong wares and white porcelains were greatly appreciated in Japan, where at that time few kilns were capable of making glazed ceramics. Punchong wares particularly appealed to adherents of the *wabicha* style of tea ceremony, who liked simplicity and humility above all. Korea's unpretentious punchong wares were well suited for use in that ceremony and were admired for their imperfections and roughness. Simple bowls which would have been used every day for eating rice in Korea thus came to be imported into Japan and were regarded as objects of great aesthetic beauty. Their value was reflected in the way they were preserved through generations, often being repaired with contemporary Japanese lacquer or gold leaf (fig. 76). Tea stains which penetrated the slip and caused discoloration were also highly prized as evidence of the bowl's age.

After Hideyoshi's invasions in the late sixteenth century and the consequent abduction of thousands of potters, colonies of Korean potters established themselves on Kyushu and started to produce the wares they had made in Korea. It is therefore difficult to tell whether pieces from this period were products of Japan or Korea, but in any case they were products of Korean potters. Koreans such as Yi Sam-pyong, Pal San, Son Kai and Li Kyong were instrumental in starting production at Karatsu, Takatori, Agano, Yatsushiro and Hagi, which were to become famous Japanese kilns. Yi Sam-pyong is further credited with the discovery in 1616 of porcelain clay in the Arita area. He built his kiln at Tengudani, thus starting the production of 'Japanese' porcelain. Yi, a native of Kongju county in South Chungchong province, is thought to have been an employee of the Punwon official factory at Kwangju and was therefore a potter of the highest ability, with advanced knowledge of kiln-building and glazing. Excavations at the Tengudani kilns have shown that the kilns used in the seventeenth century were Korean-style climbing kilns.

76. Stoneware punchong bowl with stamped slip decoration and later Japanese lacquer repairs. The Japanese had high regard for such wares, which were imported and used in the tea ceremony. They had considerable influence on subsequent Japanese ceramic development. Choson period, 15th century. Diameter: 16 cm.

Although there was little intermarriage between the Korean immigrants and the native Japanese, a gradual assimilation took place which resulted in distinctively Japanese interpretations of the original Korean ceramics being produced. Stamped and brushed slip decoration, for example, which were basic features of punchong wares, were adapted to Japanese taste, becoming more regular, geometric and decorative. Kyoto potters were particularly successful at applying punchong decorative techniques to shapes other than tea-bowls, and cylindrical-shaped Raku bowls decorated with stamped slip were first produced by the Korean potter who is known by his Japanese name of Chojiro.[76]

The fundamental role played by Korean potter-prisoners in the development of Japan's ceramic industry, both stoneware and porcelain, has been little appreciated in the West, despite the great popularity of the Japanese wares and the large numbers imported from the mid-seventeenth century onwards by the Dutch and the British.

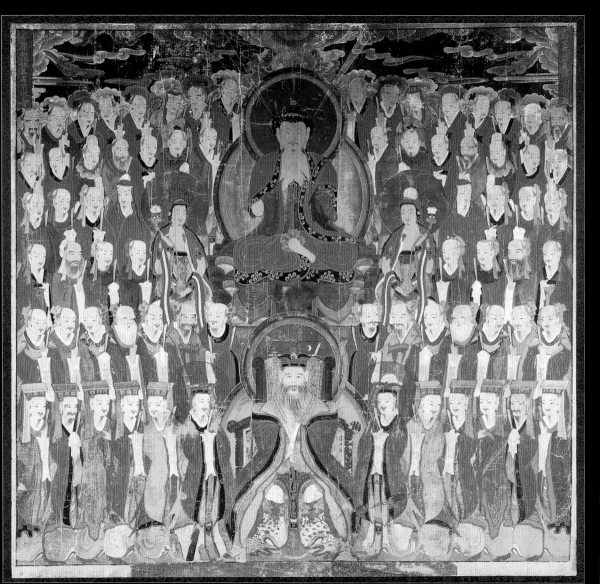

CHAPTER 5

Folk Art of the Late Choson

77. Painting showing Buddhist, Daoist and shaman iconography mixed together. It depicts the Tejaprabha Buddha (*Chisong kwangbul*) and the north pole star (*Pukkuk song*), surrounded by figures representing the nine planets and twenty-eight constellations. Mineral colours on coarse silk. Choson period, dated 1850–60. Ht: 95 cm.

F olk art in Korea is, of course, not limited to the late Choson period and continues to be produced and used in the present day. However, most of the existing examples of folk art date to that period. The question of what constitutes folk art is a complicated one but, for the purposes of this book, it will be treated from a fairly straightforward approach, concentrating on paintings and objects produced for use by ordinary people and associated with folk customs and folk beliefs. It has been said that Korean folk art is unique in that it is an art of all classes of people – the same themes, formats and styles being employed in paintings for the royal family, aristocrats, merchants and peasants. Those produced for the first group would have been painted by professional artists, while paintings for other sections of society were produced by itinerant village artisans using cheaper materials.[1]

Perhaps the most well-known and influential figure in the growth of the appreciation of Korean folk art in Korea and abroad during the latter half of the twentieth century is Zo Zayong (Cho Cha-yong), whose collection formed the basis of the former Emille Museum in Seoul. Zo was influenced by the ideas of Yanagi Soetsu and the Mingei or Folk Crafts movement in Japan in the early part of the century. Yanagi's somewhat patronizing views of Korean folk art were characterized by the expression 'hiai no bi' or 'beauty of sadness', reflecting Korea's unhappy history of invasions. He described truly beautiful crafts as those made from natural materials using traditional methods by unknown craftsmen and developed a particular empathy with Korean people and culture. Although particularly attracted to Korean white porcelain, Yanagi was also instrumental in the establishment of the Korean Folk Crafts Museum in 1924 and the Japan Folk Crafts Museum in 1936. Other protagonists in the Folk Crafts Movement were Hamada Shoji, Kawai Kanjiro, Shikiba Ryuzaburo and Bernard Leach.[2] Although Yanagi's views of Korean folk crafts were rather sentimental, he was instrumental in raising general awareness of their appeal.

Korean folk art collections in the West were mostly built up by the early travellers and diplomats who visited Korea during the late nineteenth century, in the period between the establishment of diplomatic relations with Western countries in the 1880s and colonization by Japan in 1910. In the United States the Bernadou collection at the Smithsonian and the Yu Kil-chun–Edward Morse collection at the Peabody Museum in Salem are perhaps the most important.[3] In Europe, the British Museum has a considerable collection in its Ethnography Department,[4] while the Ethnographic Museums in Leiden and Hamburg also have good collections. The accounts by Western travellers at this time provide an illuminating picture of life in late Choson dynasty Korea. The works of Isabella Bird Bishop, William Franklin Sands, Homer B. Hulbert, James Gale, Lilias Underwood and Henry Savage-Landor are particularly interesting.[5]

Folk religion

Folk art was closely associated with folk religion, annual folk festivals and ceremonies linked to important events in the life cycle, such as birth, marriage and death. Folk religion was a syncretic mix of native Korean shamanism, folk Buddhism and Daoism as well as certain aspects of Confucianism. All these were reflected in folk paintings (fig. 77).

Shamanism, the native Korean religion, has been defined by Zo Zayong as: 'The primitive religion believing in a heavenly spirit, spirits of sun, moon, stars, earth, mountains, water, rock, tree, ancestor, warriors and ghosts. It has faith in the magico-religious power of shamans who, in states of ecstasy, are capable of communicating with various spirits' (see fig. 78).[6] The origins of Korean shamanism have been traced back to the Neolithic period, and bronze star-shaped rattles dating to the third–second centuries BC may have been early shamanist ritual objects (see fig. 15). Silla gold crowns have also been seen as reflections of shamanist beliefs (see fig. 33), while the earliest textual reference to shaman paintings is in Yi Kyu-bo's *Tongguk Yi Sang-guk chip* (*Collected Works of Minister Yi of Korea*), dating to the Koryo period. There it is written that a shaman 'set up an altar in her house, with the walls of the room covered with many images of gods painted in tanch'ong, and sang and danced to the beat of a changgo [drum]'.[7] The Choson regime launched a systematic, official persecution of shamanism as a result of the reforms brought about by Neo-Confucians, driving shamanism underground and thus making it more accessible to women. Since becoming a shaman was one of the four professional roles officially permit-

78. Below: A modern shaman *kut* or exorcism ceremony. Since the Choson period most shamans have been women and the adherents to shamanism in modern times are also predominantly women, although there are male participants. Shaman paintings are in use on the wall.

79. Above: Sansin, the Mountain God, seated with his tiger and surrounded by long-life symbols such as deer and cranes. Ink and mineral colours on hemp and paper. Early 20th century. 137 × 113 cm.

ted to women, together with those of female physician, kisaeng and palace woman, shamanism offered women an alternative way of exerting some influence in a society where they had no authority, belonging in turn to their father, husband or son.[8] The general disapproval of shamanism expressed by the ruling class related in particular to its lack of propriety, the undignified dancing and music and the mixing of the sexes at rituals. In practice, however, shamans continued to work for the upper classes and at court right up to the end of the Choson dynasty. For example, Queen Min (1851–95) elevated her favourite shaman to the rank of princess.[9] Even Confucian scholars would offer prayers for success in passing state examinations at the shrine on Mt Inwang dedicated to Chilsong,

the Seven Star deity invoked by both shamanism and Daoism. In general, however, shamanism was mainly practised by the lower classes and by women.

Buddhism, in the Choson period, was also largely sponsored by women or by ordinary people, in face of the all-pervading influence of strict Koreanized Neo-Confucianism. Buddhist temples almost always included a small pavilion dedicated to Sansin, the Mountain God, who was not a Buddhist god at all (fig. 79). Indeed, Sansin is variously portrayed as a Confucian sage, a Daoist immortal, a Buddhist saint or as Tan'gun, the legendary founder of ancient Korea.[10] He is a good illustration of the syncretism at the heart of Korean folk religion.

Although Korea has no Daoist temples and Daoism is not well known there, many examples of overlap do in fact exist between popular Daoism and shamanism. For example, the Chinese God of Longevity known as Shou Lao is worshipped in Korea as the Southern Star spirit or Namguk song. His counterpart, the Northern Star spirit or Pukkuk song, controls the heavenly bodies and sometimes appears in folk Buddhist paintings in Korea (see fig. 77). The Jade Emperor or Okhwang sangjae is also worshipped both in Chinese Daoism and Korean shamanism, as are the Chilsong or Seven Star spirits.[11] Longevity and prosperity symbols associated with Daoism, such as peaches, turtles, cranes and sacred fungi, also appear frequently in Korean folk art (see fig. 79); in fact they often appear together as the ten symbols of long life or *sipchangsaeng*. Furthermore, the sun and moon paintings which appear on screens at court in Korea can be seen ultimately to have derived from Daoism (fig. 80).[12]

Confucianism had less impact on folk art in Korea, although there are examples of Confucian themes in folk painting, such as the eight characters portraying Confucian virtues (*munja-do*)(see fig. 82) and the 'books and things' or chaekkori screen paintings (see fig. 81). Shaman gods derived from Confucianism include the God of War (Guandi), a

80. Six-panel screen showing the sun, moon and five peaks, a theme with Daoist origins popular for both court and folk paintings. Late Choson period, 19th century. 90.5 × 270.5 cm.

deified general of the Chinese Han dynasty, often called 'the Chinese general' in Korea and particularly popular there after the Ming army had come to help the Koreans against the invading Japanese in 1592.[13] He is the most popular of five generals featuring in Korean shaman paintings (Obang Changgun).

Folk festivals and ceremonies

The most important occasions in the life cycle in traditional Korea were birth, one hundred days after birth, the first birthday, the coming-of-age ceremony, marriage, one's sixtieth birthday, and burial. Confucian values prized a baby son highly. On his first anniversary, a baby was dressed in special clothes and placed in front of a table on which were placed a variety of objects associated with future occupations. According to the object reached for by the baby, his future profession was indicated. If he reached for noodles, he was thought to be destined for a long life.

From the age of seven, girls and boys would be separated. The coming-of-age or 'capping' ceremony would be held for each sex at the age of about fifteen, when young men would have their plait tied up into a topknot and start to wear a horse-hair hat, and young girls would have their hair put in a plaited bun at the nape of the neck, fixed by a decorative hairpin.

Marriage occurred very early, often in the late teens, and was generally arranged by the parents and a go-between. Letters of intent were exchanged before the wedding, with details of the date and time of birth for fortune-telling purposes. On the wedding day, the bridegroom would go to the bride's house, taking a box of gifts and a letter confirming the marriage. It was at this point that a goose was presented by the bridegroom, as a symbol of fidelity. This later developed into the custom of giving wooden wedding ducks (see fig. 85). The groom would stay with the bride in her home for a few days before taking her back to his family home, where she would perform the ceremony of prostration before her in-laws.

The sixtieth birthday ceremony (*hwangap*) was important because it was rare for people to survive until that age in traditional Korea. It also marked the completion of a zodiac cycle of sixty years. A large banquet including chestnuts, dates and dried persimmons would be prepared by the children in thanksgiving for the long life of a parent. Each child would toast the parent and make a kneeling bow to him or her.

At funerals, the mourners would wear clothes of hemp and the funeral procession would follow a wooden funeral palanquin. Mourning was carried out for three years and a memorial ceremony would be held every year on the anniversary of the death.[14]

Confucian ceremonies to one's ancestors (*charye*) were also held at festival times during the year, particularly at lunar new year and at Chusok in the autumn. At lunar new year's day (*sollal*), children bowed to their elders and were given small amounts of money as gifts. Games such as *yut*, flying kites and spinning tops were traditionally played and soups such as *ttokguk* and *manduguk* consumed. Celebrated on the fifteenth day of the eighth lunar month, Chusok was a harvest festival day, when family members would gather from all over the country at their ancestral home. A memorial ceremony was traditionally held in the home during the morning and then again at the family grave site later in the day. In some regions, special rites such as the Kanggang Sullae circle dance were performed in the moonlight. Special Chusok foods included crescent-shaped stuffed rice cakes steamed in pine needles and fluffy rice cakes covered in bean paste, dates or chestnuts. Rice cakes are particularly associated with traditional festivals. The rice can be steamed, pounded, fried or made into dumplings. Pounded rice cakes were pressed into patterned moulds made of wood or porcelain and stuffings include beans, sesame, peas, honey, pine nuts, chestnuts and cinnamon. Other festival days were the Buddha's Birthday (eighth day of the fourth lunar month), when lotus-shaped paper lanterns were hung in temples and carried in street processions, and Tano Day (fifth day of the fifth lunar month), which was a traditional day of leisure after the spring planting. On Hansik (105th day after the winter solstice), food was offered at ancestors' graves. Cooking fires were not permitted, thus giving rise to the name 'hansik', meaning 'cold food'.

Folk painting

Korean folk painting had many diverse forms, both religious and secular, during the late Choson. It can be distinguished from the literati ink painting which was derived from China. Korean folk painting has been characterized by the terms directness, ruggedness, spontaneity, naïvety, strength, charm and vitality.[15]

Religious folk painting

It is customary in Korean Buddhist temples to find both Buddhist and shaman subjects depicted in the paintings displayed. Sometimes the shaman subjects are hung in a separate pavilion and sometimes the paintings themselves mix the different subjects. A seated Buddha might be surrounded, for example, by bodhisattvas and the four Buddhist guardian kings (*chonwang*) as well as by the Daoist God of Longevity and various shaman deities such as Taesin Halmoni or Chilsong (Seven Star spirit) (see fig. 77).

Korean Buddhist tradition was to repaint old paintings and temple buildings in order to enhance their beauty. The technique used was called tanchong, meaning 'red and blue', in reference to the predominant colours in this kind of painting. Monk-painters and teams of disciples painted designs on to stencils and small holes were pricked out around the outlines of the designs. The stencils were applied to the area to be decorated and coated with white powder, leaving an outline of the design. Each monk-painter was then responsible for applying one of the colours – up to ten – used to fill in the patterns. This folk tradition is still practised in the present day, its most famous representatives being the monks Manbong at Pongwon-sa in Seoul and Hyegak at Tongdo-sa near Pusan.[16]

Purely shaman paintings are used in shaman rituals or *kut* (see fig. 78). During the kut, the shaman claims divine status. She does not pray to the gods but becomes possessed by a god, uttering the words of the god within her to foretell the future. She will also indicate the name of the god by whom she is possessed by picking up one of the bowls on a table (each containing a different substance). Then she will jump up and dance violently. Shaman paintings are associated primarily with the northern and central regions of Korea, where charismatic or ecstatic shamanism prevails. They depict the deities which possess shamans during their *sinbyong* or ecstasy. The southern, hereditary *tang'ol* tradition has little use for them. In the south, shamans do not experience sinbyong and are not possessed by spirits.

Shaman paintings are either hung or pasted on a wall, or sometimes pegged on a line if the kut is held out of doors. They are also sometimes mounted on folding screens. It is thought that shaman paintings originated as expressions by the shamans themselves of their own religious experience. Artists and artisans were gradually commissioned to paint them and sometimes Buddhist monk-painters produced them. The latter show a distinct Buddhist influence, having a more balanced composition and painted in a more delicate fashion. The colours differ too, with much use of red in the Buddhist type, contrasting with a dominance of white, blue and yellow in the pure shaman type. The former are also often mounted as a rudimentary hanging scroll, with wooden cylinders attached to both ends.[17]

Shaman paintings are executed on silk, cotton and paper and vary in size, depending on whether they are images of one god or of a group of gods. The paintings often have a black outline underneath which can be re-used when the old image is peeled off and burned. They have a backing of several layers of paper with coarse silk or linen on the top. Mineral colours called *sokchae* are employed and the paintings are characterized by a lack of perspective and by bold exaggeration. The style is quite formulaic, with certain markers or attributes which can identify a certain god. The iconography of shaman paintings is a fixed and fairly limited one, subject to regional variations. The most commonly portrayed deity is Sansin, the Mountain God, usually depicted as an old man with a white beard seated beside a pine tree and accompanied by his messenger, the tiger (see fig. 79). Sometimes he is portrayed with a crown as the legendary Tan'gun. He is reputed to be able to bestow children. Sansin, together with Toksong (the Lonely Saint) and Chilsong (the Seven Star spirit), are often portrayed together in small free-standing shrines in Buddhist temples. Sansin also has his own shrines dotted all over the mountainous areas of the Korean countryside.

Some of the shaman gods depicted are clearly of Buddhist origin, such as the Five Guardians or Generals (Obang Changgun), who most probably derived from the four Heavenly Kings or chonwang, and the Sambul chesok or Three Buddhas, particularly common on shaman fans used by ecstatic shamans. Others such as Tan'gun, Yi Tae-jo and Guandi are historical or legendary figures. Other commonly depicted gods include the Dragon King (Yongwang) and the spirits of the sun and moon (Haenim and Talnim).[18]

Pujok or talisman pictures were placed on doors, storage chests, ceilings and walls to repel evil spirits. Very few of these have survived and they were never regarded as great art. They were usually renewed annually at the Tano festival and often featured animals such as the tiger, cockerel, dog and *haetae* or mythical lion.

Secular folk painting

Both the court and the yangban aristocracy as well as the common people patronized folk painting.

Folk painting produced for the court and the upper classes mostly took the form of screens. Some of these had a continuous composition over all the eight or so panels, while some had a different composition on each panel, all contributing to a central theme. Some screens were appropriate for specific rooms or for men or women. The screens were used as a protection against draughts in the cold winter climate and special screens were used for weddings, funerals and other such ceremonies. Poorer families would often borrow

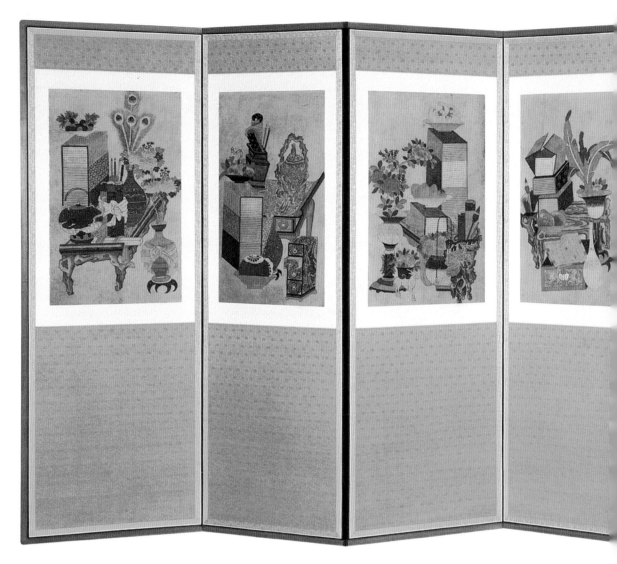

screens for special occasions. If compared with Chinese painting, the brushwork of Korean folk painting can appear crude or unsophisticated. However, its appeal lies in the boldness of the designs, the bright colours and the often humorous execution of conservative themes of prosperity, longevity and the repelling of evil.

Folk paintings used at court usually portrayed the sun, moon and five peaks (see fig. 80), the 'turtle ships' of Admiral Yi Sun-sin or the Guo Ziyi banquet. The first group has Daoist origins, the rocks and pines being symbols of longevity, while the five peaks symbolize the five mountains of Korea. The mountains rise from the waves just as the mythical peaks of the Daoist immortals' island of Penglai (Korean: Pongnae) arise from the eastern sea. Sun and moon screens in Korea have been seen as a sort of diagram of the universe, the sun symbolizing the king (yang) and the moon the queen (yin).[19] They were also apparently used in homes in the late nineteenth century.[20] The Guo Ziyi banquet theme, however, is purely Confucian, celebrating the Tang Chinese general Guo, who was regarded as a Confucian ideal and who enjoyed a happy retirement surrounded by his sons and grandsons.

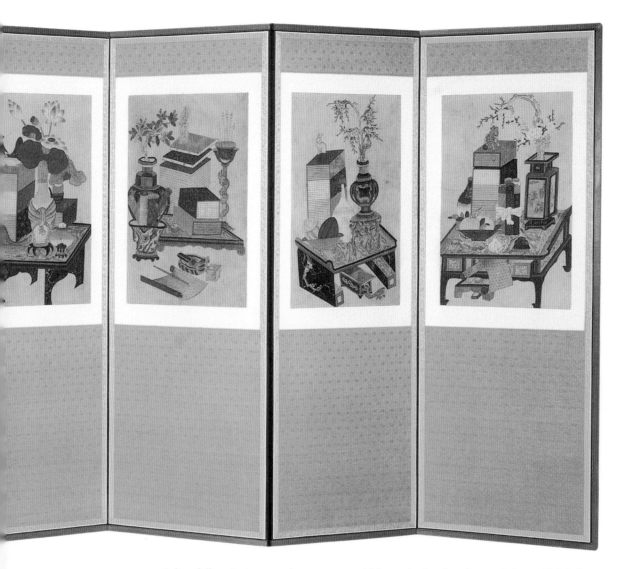

81. Eight-panel table-type *chaekkori* screen, showing books and objects associated with scholars. Ink and colours on paper. Late Choson period, 19th century. 50 × 140 cm.

Other folk paintings used at court would have depicted and recorded royal birthdays, processions, receiving of foreign ambassadors, Confucian ceremonies and historical events.[21] King Chongjo was particularly fond of chaekkori paintings of piles of books and scholars' objects. His interest may have been roused by the use of Western techniques of perspective, possibly under the influence of Jesuit painters in Beijing such as Giuseppe Castiglione.[22] Chaekkori is an example of a subject which occured both in court paintings and in folk paintings. There were three types of chaekkori: the first and most elegant type represented an actual bookcase, painted in a *trompe l'oeil* technique to look like a three-dimensional piece of furniture. The second type showed the scholars' objects strewn randomly over the painting in isolation. Both of these types have been called court-style chaekkori and were painted by named artists. The third type, known as table-type chaekkori, would have been used by less affluent people to enable them too to decorate their ordinary homes with depictions of Confucian scholarly objects (fig. 81). These paintings also included many auspicious fruit, animals and non-scholarly objects which had

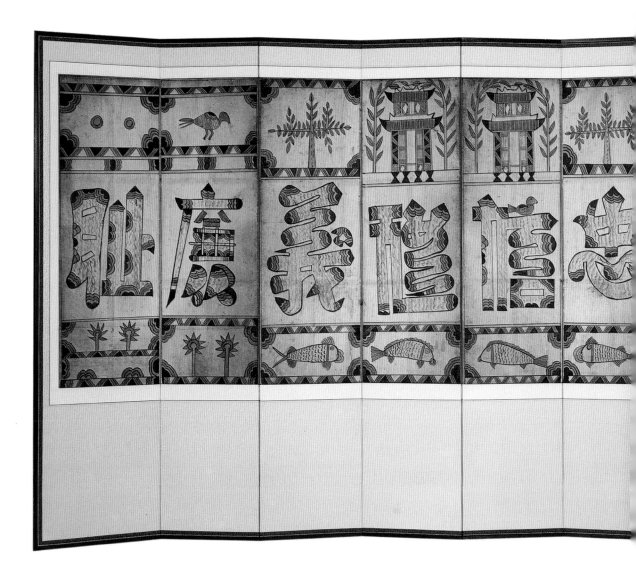

significance in the context of Korean folk beliefs, for example, many-seeded fruits such as melons and pomegranates, representing the wish for many children.[23]

Aristocrats also used folk paintings in their homes, despite the Confucian predilection for literati paintings. The themes used in the paintings were the same as those used by common people but the difference lay in the cost and quality of the materials used. In general, mineral colours were used, mixed with animal or fish glue. Court and yangban paintings often used silk while common people used paper or a coarse linen or hemp.

Common themes for yangban painted screens were the ten symbols of longevity, books and scholars' objects, hunting scenes and scenes of peaceful life.[24] Hunting screens have an interesting history, dating back to the Mongol conquest of Korea in the thirteenth century. Despite being associated with the hated occupiers, they enjoyed a vogue amongst military officers, extolling horsemanship and hunting. They usually portray the mounted horsemen wearing Mongol costume and riding amid a Mongolian steppe landscape.

82. Eight-panel *munja-do* screen painted with the eight Chinese characters for the traditional Confucian virtues, decorated with fish. Possibly from Cheju island. Ink and colours on paper. Late Choson period, 19th century. 50 × 180 cm.

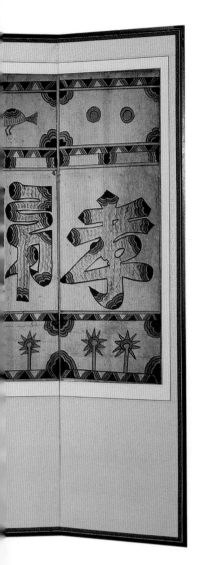

Other themes were used for folk paintings, by both yangban and commoners. Bird-and-flower painted screens usually consisted of pairs of various birds or animals such as deer, rabbits, fish or butterflies together with flowers. The pairs symbolize marital happiness and were therefore thought most appropriate for weddings or for a woman's bedroom. They were sometimes embroidered in bright colours with meticulous skill.

Peony screens had a certain sexual symbolism and were therefore associated with weddings and wedding nights, the peonies signifying the female and the garden rocks the male. Lotus screens often include fish or shellfish beneath the water of the lotus pond, some particularly elegant types having a continuous composition across all eight panels. Lotuses were symbols of purity in Buddhism and of fecundity in Daoism, because of their many seeds.

Fish screens contained many different layers of symbolism. Their auspiciousness lies in the fact that the Chinese character for fish is pronounced 'yu', the same as the character for superfluity or plenty. Because of the many eggs they produce, they are also symbols of fertility. Pairs of fish point to marital happiness, while carp are symbolic of successful scholars. Fish were also thought to be good guardians, since their eyes never shut. Fish screens were therefore regarded as appropriate for most rooms in a traditional house.

Grape screens were popular in the late Choson dynasty, although there seems no particular symbolism attached to them, apart perhaps from a certain exoticism emanating from the grapes' provenance in Central Asia. Grape-paintings overlapped into literati painting and were also used on porcelain (see fig. 66). When used on screens, they usually depicted one long vine extending over the different panels of the screen, painted in many shades of ink and featuring calligraphic curling tendrils.

People portrayed in folk paintings include the hundred children, a subject derived from China which symbolizes fecundity; also farming scenes and stories of filial piety. The agricultural scenes tend to show ordinary Korean people in Korean dress, while the second group, being mostly derived from Chinese stories, tend to feature figures wearing Chinese dress and in Chinese architectural settings. Daoist immortals are also a subject of Korean folk paintings and screens.

Calligraphy, very highly regarded by Confucian cultures, was associated in Korea with the Chinese literati painting tradition. However, calligraphy also appeared in Korean folk painting, despite the probable inability of many peasants to read the Chinese characters. Folk painting screens showing calligraphy include those with many different seal-script forms of the Chinese characters for long life and prosperity (Korean: *subok*). These are very decorative, as well as being thought auspicious, because of the many repetitions of the two characters. Other calligraphy screens, depicting the eight characters associated with Confucian virtues, are often decorated with pictures of animals, fish or birds (munja-do). The eight Confucian virtues are filial piety, brotherly love, loyalty, trust, propriety, duty, honour and humility. Fortunately, they fitted very well into the eight-panel screen format (fig. 82).[25]

Landscape folk paintings numbered among their most popular subjects the Eight Views of Xiao and Xiang (a Chinese theme) and the Diamond Mountains (Kumgangsan)

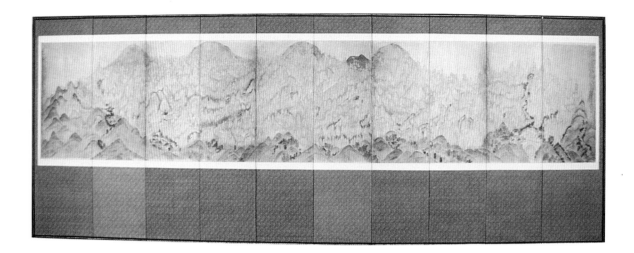

(fig. 83). The latter, being a truly Korean subject, was also a favourite theme of court painters such as Chong Son who took part in the 'real landscape' or 'true view landscape' movement of the eighteenth century (see fig. 68). Folk screens showing the Diamond Mountains usually depicted several famous sites or natural phenomena. Each site was often labelled on the painting with a small cartouche in red ink. The mountains' symbolism lies in the mixture of religious beliefs. In Buddhist terms, the name Kumgang refers to the Diamond Thunderbolt or vajra, which is suggested by the needle-like peaks of some of the mountains. In Daoism, they are thought of as the land of the Immortals; while in shamanism they are a focus for animism, many of the rocks resembling figures, such as animals, birds, mother-and-child, demons, dragons and so on. Diamond Mountain paintings were particularly associated with Tano Day, when the spirits were honoured and asked for assistance. Sometimes fans were painted with the Diamond Mountains and given on that day.[26] The Diamond Mountains, lying in what is now North Korea, have great significance for Korean people as a kind of national symbol.

Screens were not the only format for folk painting. Tigers and dragons were both regarded as protective and auspicious creatures in traditional Korea and featured in paintings. Tigers were held in particular awe and affection and appeared in many stories and legends from the Korean creation myth onwards. They were also present in Koguryo tomb paintings and as one of the guardian animals of the four directions, the tiger guarding the west. During the Choson period, tigers were thought to have powers of expelling evil spirits, and tiger paintings were therefore hung on gates of residences at the beginning of the Korean new year, to protect the family.[27] In many popular tiger paintings rabbits or magpies can be seen tormenting the tiger, which is portrayed in a humorous and unthreatening way. Sometimes the tiger has spots as well as stripes and is, in fact, half-tiger and half-leopard. In other paintings, groups or families of tigers are portrayed and sometimes a set of these paintings will form a screen. The tiger is also seen as the messenger of the Mountain Spirit (see fig. 79), as well as being one of the twelve zodiacal animals and appearing on military flags. Sometimes paintings of rocks are produced so that the rock resembles a tiger face or body. Other paintings concentrate on the skin of the tiger, demonstrating the idea that a tiger leaves its skin behind after its death, just as a man leaves his name and

83. Ten-panel Diamond Mountains screen, the famous sites marked in red characters. This mountain range has great religious significance and symbolism in Buddhism, Daoism and shamanism. Ink on paper. Choson period, 19th century. 123 × 597 cm.

fame behind. Tiger paintings usually portray a smiling tiger and much of the painting is highly stylized, the striped fur becoming almost like abstract patterns.[28]

Dragons were thought of as bringers of rain, as well as being one of the animals of the four directions, the dragon guarding the east. Dragons were supplicated for rain and for the resulting good harvests as well as being worshipped by fishermen and prayed to for successful catches. The Dragon King (Yongwang) is also one of the popular gods of Korean shamanism. During droughts, paintings portraying dragons surrounded by clouds were thrown into rivers and wells, in the belief or hope that they could bring rain. They were often painted in five colours and the faces and writhing bodies of the dragons were particularly ferocious. As in many tiger paintings, there was a high degree of stylization and simplification (see fig. 75).[29]

Sometimes tigers and dragons appeared in the same painting, either as door paintings, where they are showing a peaceful state of balance, or in paintings portraying a struggle between the two powerful creatures.[30]

Folk sculpture

Sculptures in stone and wood (fig. 84) were produced for use in association with tombs, temples and village rites. Stone figures varied, from the figures of civil and military officials and animals which stood in rows in front of royal and upper-class tombs, to more informal figures of husband and wife or of boy attendants. Particularly on Cheju island, stone figures of *harubang* – an old man or woman – were popular symbols of fertility and guarded against evil spirits. The stone figures of Cheju island are characterized by their simplified square bodies and circular heads with basic facial expressions.[31]

Stone changsung guardian posts, often phallic in shape, were used as symbols of fertility and prayed to by barren women seeking children. The oldest changsung date to AD 759

84. *Changsung*. These folk sculptures were traditionally situated at the entrances to villages in a guardian capacity.

and 1085 and are located in Porim and Tongdo Buddhist temples.[32] Stone changsung can be seen today strewn across the Korean countryside and possess a remarkable beauty. The faces are sometimes of military commanders or spirits and they are on occasion used as milestones or compasses by the roadside.

Other stone 'sculptures' are in fact natural phenomena – rocks which happen to resemble humans or animals or birds and have been invested with spiritual powers in the past, thought to be embodiments of the spirits inhabiting all natural formations. Many mountain areas in Korea include such rocks and the Diamond Mountains are regarded as particularly auspicious in this way, leading to many paintings of the varied natural features there.

Folk beliefs in Korea included belief in the efficacy of wooden changsung guardians placed at the entrances to villages and temples. Wooden changsung, sometimes called devil posts, consist of a length of tree trunk turned upside down and stuck in the ground, leaving the roots to serve as hair. Fierce, demon-like faces were carved under the hair and they

were originally brightly painted. Most surviving examples are now weathered and bare of paint. They stood in pairs, one male and one female, at the entrance to most rural villages. It was commonly believed that if one of these posts were removed, a man in the village would die. It is interesting that they were also used at the entrances to Buddhist temples even though they were of shaman origin (see fig. 84).[33]

Sottae are another sort of wooden sculpture, again usually placed at the entrance to a village for the repelling of evil spirits and the well-being of the villagers. These consisted of a tall wooden pole with one or two birds carved out of wood as if perched at the top of the pole. The most popular kinds of wood were pine or chestnut. Sottae were often used in

85. Carved wooden duck with painted decoration, for use at wedding ceremonies, wrapped in a wrapping cloth as a symbol of fidelity. Late Choson period, 19th century. Ht: 18.5 cm.

86. Wrapping cloth (*pojagi*), made of scraps of left-over material sewn together in a patchwork and used for wrapping gifts and covering food. Late 19th to early 20th century. 45 × 45 cm.

conjunction with changsung. Both had to be renewed every ten years or so. Both were focuses of village ceremonies at lunar new year or at Chusok; in some villages packages of food were hung on the changsung and chestnuts buried underneath it.[34]

Wooden sculptures of ducks (called *kirogi*) were a central feature of traditional Korean wedding ceremonies (fig. 85). They derived from the offering of a live goose by the bridegroom to the bride's mother, as a symbol of faithfulness. The bride's mother would then feed noodles to the goose, the noodles symbolizing long life and her approval of the marriage. Wooden ducks were used as replacements for the live goose. They were often beautifully carved and painted with bright colours, then wrapped in a *pojagi* or wrapping cloth (fig. 86).[35]

Masks

Masks were used in Korea for funerals, in shaman practices, to appease spirits and in masked dance-dramas.[36] The funeral masks, called *pangsangsi*, were made of wood or straw according to the status of the family and were used to lead funeral processions, in order to drive away evil spirits. A particularly large example in wood is preserved in the National Museum of Korea[37]

The oldest known Korean mask, made of black lacquered wood, dates from the Silla period (fifth–sixth century AD) and was excavated from Ho'u-chong in Kyongju in 1946. It was probably a guardian figure-type mask, used to repel evil spirits.[38] It has been suggested that folk masked dance-dramas may have derived from the masked plays staged at court during the Koryo, called *sandae chapkuk*. The question of the possible connections between these Koryo period masked plays and the better-known Japanese masked dramas is an interesting one, which awaits future research. There is no doubt that there is a connection between Japanese *gigaku* and Korean *ki'ak* masked drama of the earlier Paekche period. It is recorded in the *Nihon gi* that ki'ak was introduced into Japan in 612 by the Korean Mimaji.[39] Ki'ak was probably a vehicle for Buddhist evangelism, and the masks were said to have had Aryan features, suggesting transmission from India through Central Asia.[40]

However, by the Choson period, the village masked dance-dramas provided an acceptable way for the ordinary people to poke fun at the yangban aristocrats and the Buddhist church. Because their faces were hidden behind the masks, the people could act in a more daring way than would normally be expected in a hierarchical Confucian society. Masks used in these dance-dramas were usually made of wood, gourds or papier-mâché and the characters represented were standard for each dance-drama. Since the masks were quite fragile and were in heavy use, they had to be replaced at regular intervals. Many in fact were burned after use in a performance. There are therefore very few surviving masks of any antiquity, although one set of wooden masks from Hahoe village in North Kyongsang province is preserved in the National Museum of Korea and is thought to date to the Koryo period (fig. 87).

Most of the dance-drama masks represent human faces, but some represent deities and some are of real or imaginary animals. The yangban masks are very often deformed in some

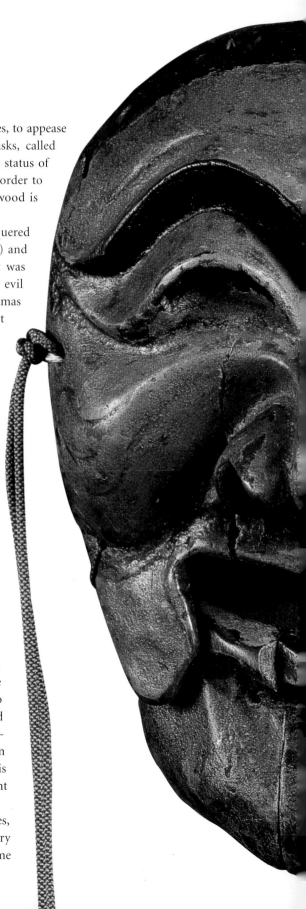

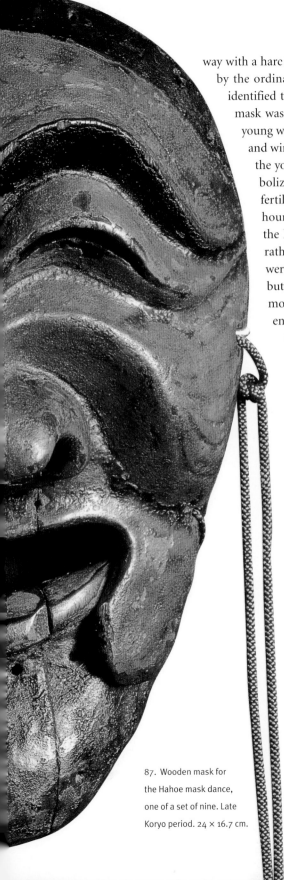

way with a harc lip, lop-sided mouth or a squint. This reflected the resentment by the ordinary people of the more privileged. The colours of the masks identified the age and sex of the characters. For example, an old person's mask was usually black, whereas that of a young man was red and of a young woman white. Traditionally in Korea black represented the north and winter, while red stood for the south and summer. The triumph of the young man over the old in the dance-dramas thus possibly symbolized the triumph of summer over winter, a relic of traditional fertility rites. Performances varied in length between three or four hours and a whole night. They were often performed at night, by the light of bonfires. For this reason, the details of the faces were rather exaggerated, so that they could be seen easily. Dance-dramas were held at different times in accordance with regional practices, but in general they were performed at festivals such as the first full moon, Buddha's Birthday, Tano Day and Chusok. Often the audience would end up participating enthusiastically in the finale, which would be accompanied by string, wind and percussion instruments.[41]

Among the best-known village dance-dramas is the one held at Hahoe. It is an example of a drama originally performed together with a shaman ritual or kut, for exorcising evil spirits. It was therefore called the Hahoe Pyolshin Kut and was traditionally performed every ten years at lunar new year or at times of particular misfortune. The practice died out in the 1920s but was revived in the 1970s. The dance-drama is now performed separately from the kut (although it was originally performed by villagers to entertain gods during the kut). The players were traditionally all male, as it would not have been appropriate for women to perform in public. The female parts were therefore played by men, sometimes in a very humorous fashion. The story is quite bawdy and the aristocrats of the village would therefore have regarded attendance at such a gathering as beneath their dignity. It involves nine characters: a bride, a scatter-brained meddler, a butcher (with a dancing ox), a grandmother, a coquette, a wayward Buddhist monk, a village fool, a nobleman and a scholar. During the performance the butcher extols the various aphrodisiac powers of ox testicles which are eventually purchased by the aristocrat after a fight over them with the scholar; the Buddhist monk seduces the coquette and the bride's marriage to the scholar is consumated. The masks, which are unusual because they have separate chins attached to the upper part with strings, are carved to show the singularities of each character in an exaggerated fashion, as caricatures. For example, the two-faced butcher's

87. Wooden mask for the Hahoe mask dance, one of a set of nine. Late Koryo period. 24 × 16.7 cm.

mask shows a grinning face when he looks up and a sinister face when he looks down, the village fool mask has no chin, the coquette's mask is heavily made-up, the grandmother's mask has a large mouth to show that she is perpetually hungry and perpetually complaining and both the aristocrat's and scholar's masks have dignified beards.[42]

Another well-known dance-drama, the Pongsan masked drama, originated in Hwanghae province in North Korea and also treats the themes of wayward monks, decadent aristocrats and conflict between an ugly wife and a seductive concubine. It also features a woolly lion with rattles for eyes which threatens to devour everyone, perhaps symbolizing the destruction of evil. The drama ends with the death of the ugly wife in a fit of jealous rage over her husband's affair with a concubine. The finale is a funeral rite carried out by a shaman, reflecting the probable original connection between the drama and a religious ceremony. Unlike the wooden Hahoe masks, the Pongsan masks are made of papier-mâché, painted in bright colours. The wind and percussion instruments accompanying the dance, the exuberant movements of the dancers and the colourful masks and costumes make the Pongsan mask-dance particularly dramatic. The Pongsan Mask Dance Preservation Society was formed in 1958 and there are monthly performances of this and other masked dance-dramas at the Seoul Nori Madang, an outdoor theatre for folk performing arts.[43]

Folk pottery

Domestic storage jars made of high-fired earthenware, called *onggi*, were remarked upon by Isabella Bird Bishop when she visited Korea between 1894 and 1897. She described the process of making them thus:

> At the village of Tomak-na-dali, where we tied up, they make the great purple-black jars and pots which are in universal use ... The potters pursue their trade in open sheds, digging up the clay close by. The stock-in-trade is a pit in which an uncouth potter's wheel revolves, the base of which is turned by the feet of a man who sits on the edge of the hole. A wooden spatula, a mason's wooden trowel, a curved stick, and a piece of rough rag are the tools, efficient for the purpose.[44]

These jars could be seen formerly in Korea on a terrace (*changdoktae*) outside each house, storing *kimchi*, soy bean paste, soy sauce, red pepper paste, grains, water, etc. (fig. 88). Kimchi, a kind of pickled cabbage, is one of Korea's best-known foods and was traditionally made during the *kimjang chol* or kimchi season in November. Cabbage was soaked in brine and then a mixture of radish, parsley, chives, ground red pepper, garlic, ginger, salted fish and oysters was laid between the leaves of the cabbage, which was then placed in large onggi.

Onggi pottery was also used to make chimneys, tiles or pipes and other receptacles for purposes such as brewing, storing anchovies or sprouting beans. The large storage jars had several different names, such as *tok*, *hangari* or *tanji*. Sometimes, as a sort of primitive refrigerator, they were buried in the ground in order to keep the pickled kimchi cold. A more prosaic use for onggi was as primitive lavatories, buried in the ground and emptied with a scoop, or as chamber pots (*yogang*).[45]

Typical onggi pots are decorated with a quick sweep of two thumbs, producing sketchy curved lines in the wet glaze (see fig. 88). Some show regional variations such as the

88. Right: Lidded storage jars (*onggi*) in use outside a traditional Korean building. Below: Large high-fired earthenware lidded storage jar (*onggi*) with paddled decoration inside and stylized plants outside, made by the potter's thumbs in the wet glaze. Late 19th to early 20th century. Ht: 97 cm.

stylized orchid found in Kyonggi and Chungchong provinces and the incised fish designs common on onggi produced out of black clay on Kanghwa island. Some onggi have wavy applied ridges like pie crusts around the wide part and some have two handles. The pots were made by the coil method, with beating tools to smooth the outsides and stamp patterns on the insides, in combination with a wheel. Kilns used included 'cannon' kilns, chamber kilns and beehive-shaped kilns.

Cooking vessels made of onggi pottery included rice-cake steamers, herbal medicine boilers and outdoor cooking stoves. Other specialist containers were wide cereal basins, spouted soy-sauce ewers, vinegar bottles, wine kettles and 'pure water bowls' for use in early morning household rituals. Sometimes onggi were also used to hold the household gods: Songju, the spirit of the ridgepole, Toju, the protector of the house site, and Chesok, the spirit of procreation. They were also a feature of shaman kut rituals, when the shaman would balance on a blade of a knife resting across the top of an onggi full of water.

It is interesting to note that many onggi potters in the late Choson period were Catholics. It seems that Catholic converts were forced to evade persecution by the Confucian authorities by escaping into remote mountainous regions. Pottery-making offered them the advantage of being able to move around undetected in the guise of onggi pedlars.[46]

Although onggi pottery is now rapidly disappearing and being replaced by metal and plastic containers, there is a growing appreciation of its beauty and history, leading to a revival of interest in its diverse forms.

Folk crafts

Many folk crafts used ordinary materials such as paper, wood or bamboo. Out of these were produced objects for everyday use which possessed a natural and unaffected appeal. One example of a craft producing beauty out of necessity was that of pojagi or wrapping cloths. These were squares of cloth, often patchwork ensembles using up household scraps of material. The results were beautiful masses of colour and pattern, used for covering food or wrapping presents (see fig. 86). Paper was also fashioned into useful and attractive crafts, such as boxes for ladies' sewing tools which were covered in brightly coloured papercuts in auspicious designs. A feature of folk crafts was the use of bright primary colours, in contrast to the yangban predilection for monochrome ink painting, white clothes and austere furnishings. Korean paper has long been valued in East Asia for its strength and texture and was used in the late Choson in a multitude of ways: for papering walls, floors and windows, for making kites, fans, lanterns, umbrellas, folk masks and rain hats as well as for fashioning paper flowers for special occasions. Even furniture was made by twisting paper into strands, weaving and lacquering it.[47]

Over thirty different kinds of wood were used for Korean furniture, the most popular being elm (zelkova), fruitwoods such as pear, gingko and persimmon, pine, paulownia and bamboo. Korean chests were functional as well as beautiful, being used to contain bedding, clothes, medicines and household goods such as rice. Very few contained drawers and the styles of furniture were extremely conservative. Hinges, locks and fittings made of brass or wrought iron were also developed into small works of art. Wood was also used for pillows, carpenter's lines, document boxes, bookshelves, small tables and paper-racks, moulds for rice cakes, game boards and pieces.

Bamboo crafts included scholars' brushpots and paper-holders, arrows and arrow-holders, furniture, fans and mats. Designs were sometimes burnt or scorched on to the surface of the bamboo objects with hot irons, using the traditional technique of pyrography. High-quality decorated mats made of sedge were particularly associated with Kanghwa island and often depicted the sipchangsaeng or ten auspicious symbols (fig. 89).

Metal crafts of the Choson primarily consisted of the intricate and beautiful hinges on traditional furniture as well as containers such as tobacco boxes made of iron inlaid in silver with auspicious patterns. Vessels for use at table were produced in sets in either brass or ceramic, while chopstick and spoon sets were made of brass or silver. Metal was also used to produce ornaments and accessories for ladies, particularly hairpins and the hanging ornaments called *norigae*, which would usually be worn on the chest, together with a knotted tassle called a *maedup*. Coloured enamels were used to decorate the ornaments, sometimes mistakenly called cloisonné enamels, although there is little evidence of any cloisons. The Korean enamels approximate rather to champlevé enamels, since the metal

89. Sedge mat, made on Kanghwa island and decorated with the traditional ten symbols of longevity (*sipchangsaeng*). Late Choson period, 19th century. Donated by E. Ogita after the Anglo-Japanese exhibition.

backgrounds seem to show evidence of having dips in them which are filled with the enamel. These enamels are characterized by bright colours and a thick consistency. They are used to fashion miniature birds, animals, butterflies, peaches and other objects thought to bring luck.

Mother-of-pearl and ox-horn crafts were more associated with aristocrats than the common people, being very expensive. Embroidery was predominantly carried out by aristocratic ladies in their homes, the common people having little time for such elegant pursuits.[48]

Traditional games

90. Drawing of girls in traditional costume playing on a seesaw, by Kisan (pen-name of Kim Chun-gun). Sets of these drawings of Korean customs were produced for foreigners after Korea became more open to Western visitors at the end of the 19th century. 20 × 12.5 cm.

Korean games can be divided into board games and outdoor games, although board games were also sometimes played sitting outside in a pavilion or on a verandah. Board games such as *paduk* and chess were played predominantly by men, while some of the outdoor games, such as seesaws and swings, were particularly enjoyed by young girls, confined to their family walled compounds. In fact it is said that these games, associated with Tano Day, were a way in which they could jump or swing up high in order to catch a glimpse of the world outside the walls (fig. 90).

The earliest evidence of dice-throwing games in Korea comes from the Unified Silla, in the form of a multi-sided wooden die which was excavated from Anap-chi lake. On it are written different forfeits, each one having to be performed according to which side was uppermost. This game was presumably associated with drinking parties, some of the forfeits being the writing of couplets or singing. Games such as backgammon (*ssangryuk*) and dominoes can be compared with similar versions played in other countries. In Korea, the backgammon pieces (called horses) were about 9 cm (3.5 in) high and often made of box-wood, either left natural or painted red. The board has high sides to prevent the pieces slipping off.

Paduk, played with counters made of stone on a wooden board, is also played in China, where it is called *weiqi*, and in Japan (*go*). However, the Korean paduk board differs from the Japanese in that it is a small hollow table as opposed to the Japanese solid block. Wires stretched across inside the Korean board make it resonate whenever a piece is laid on it (fig. 91). Korean chess (*changgi*) is a variant of Chinese chess (*xiangqi*), played broadly on the same principles and with the same pieces. Unlike Chinese chess, however, the Korean chessmen are octagonal, varying in size according to their value. One set of men have their names written in running script and one set in standard script, one set is coloured red and one green. Chess was traditionally regarded as a less scholarly game than paduk in Korea, played by provincials and common people.[49]

The promotion game (*songgyongdo*) was played on a chart with names of official positions written or printed on it. In the Korean version, moves were made according to the roll of a long, five-sided piece of wood with one to five notches on the sides. The official positions aimed for in playing the game rise up to the rank of minister of state, and there is even a goal called retirement. Since it was played in schools, perhaps it was intended as an

91. Wooden *paduk* board and pieces made of shell and stone. Played mainly by men, this game is also popular in China (where it is known as *weiqi*) and in Japan (known as *go*). Late Choson period, 18th–19th century. Width: 40 cm.

encouragement to pupils to achieve high rank, in a traditional society where official rank was all-important.[50]

The game of *yut*, played with four wooden blocks and a board, is associated with the lunar new year festival and was played by all members of the family and by all classes. The sticks have one flat side and one convex side, the flat side sometimes being lined with ivory in more expensive sets. Yut sets vary in length and thickness, the shorter ones being used by children and the longer ones being more elegant. They are thrown with one piece placed across the others and sometimes rebound from the roof. Pieces (which can be made of anything convenient) are called horses and are moved around the board, taking the opponent's pieces when they are landed upon, in the manner of other well-known board games. Yut sticks were also used for divination during the lunar new year period.[51]

More vigorous outdoor games and sports are associated with particular Korean festivals. Folk wrestling (*ssirum*), traditionally played on Tano Day and at Chusok for the prize of an ox, dates back in Korea to at least the Koguryo period, when it can be seen depicted on a tomb mural. Although, to the Western eye, it seems to have similarities with Japanese *sumo* wrestling, it is a native Korean sport, its name probably deriving from the Korean verb *ssiruda*, meaning to 'compete in strength'.[52] In Korean ssirum, each wrestler grasps the other's waistband with one hand and his leg with the other, the aim being to make one's opponent fall or touch the ground. Ssirum can also be seen depicted in eighteenth-century genre paintings (see fig. 69). Korean taekwondo has been called the world's oldest form of martial art, and differs from the Chinese and Japanese versions (kungfu and karate).[53] Other contests, such as tug-of-war and loop battles, usually took place between whole villages at festival times, while shuttlecock kicking and top-spinning were mainly played by children, the latter usually in winter on frozen ponds.[54]

Clothing and accessories

Fabrics used for traditional Korean dress (*hanbok*) include silk, cotton, ramie and hemp. Silk, used mainly by aristocrats, came in many different weights and weaves, some being opaque and some nearly transparent. Cotton and ramie also varied in thickness, the very fine varieties being used for summer wear. Korean costume was conservative, the basic forms being a full skirt (*chima*) and a short jacket (*chogori*) for women (see fig. 90) and trousers (*paji*) and jacket (*chogori*) for men. Men also wore a waistcoat, a long overcoat and a black horse-hair hat. Women's jackets were tied together by two sashes at the front, which became a decorative feature, with hanging ornaments or norigae suspended from them. Before the Choson period, hanging ornaments were suspended from the belt. Norigae were hung from decorative knots called maedup and were made of *paktong* (a kind of pewter), jade, coral or gold. They sometimes consisted of small knives (symbols of chastity), perfume or medicine boxes or needle cases (see also section on folk crafts, above).[55] Other accessories for women included earpicks, tweezers, hair-pins and combs, which they would have stored in cosmetic boxes consisting of several drawers and a folding mirror on the top. These were made of lacquered wood, sometimes inlaid with mother-of-pearl.

Men's accessories included a long beaded strap for the horse-hair hat and a woven silk cord worn around the chest. Fans were used by both men and women, aristocratic men's fans usually being of folding plain paper, sometimes decorated with calligraphy. Decorative fan accessories for men included carved open-work perfumers, compasses or wooden cylinders containing toothpicks or earpicks, which would have been attached from a knotted loop at the bottom of the fan. Rigid fans with a central handle were more often used by the common people. These were made of paper or woven bamboo and were often decorated with papercuts around the black lacquered wood handle. Sometimes they were made in the shape of lotus or paulownia leaves and the framework of the fans represented the ribs of the leaves in a naturalistic fashion.[56]

The weaving of fine horse-hair into a variety of shapes of hat for men was a highly specialized and difficult technique. Hats were worn both indoors and outdoors, the outdoor type having a wide brim and the indoor brimless type fitting under the outdoor one. A horse-hair headband was also worn around the forehead, to ensure that the hat did not slip off. The wide-brimmed hat perched on the top of the head and did not fit in the same way as a Western hat. A cone-shaped oiled paper hat was used to cover the horse-hair hat in times of rain. Hat boxes were made in a variety of woods, papier-mâché and lacquer.[57]

In the nineteenth century, spectacles came into use and can sometimes be seen depicted in chaekkori screens. Spectacle cases, made of sharkskin, lacquered wood, embroidered silk or woven paper, also developed into a craft form. Small drawstring purses (*chumoni*) were practical, as traditional Korean costumes had no pockets. Decorative purses were sometimes embroidered with auspicious symbols and became popular as gifts.

Western dress was officially adopted in 1900 by order of King Kojong. However, hanbok or traditional Korean costumes are still often worn for weddings and festivals.

荒峽三年夜秋風 第 寒情孤飛瀟湘 雁纵綠月中聲

癸亥秋仲 盤龍山人月田

CHAPTER 6

Twentieth Century

92. *Flying Cranes* by
Chang Wu-song (1912–),
one of the followers
of Kim Eun-ho. Ink
and colours on paper.
Ht: 90 cm.

During the first half of the twentieth century, Korea experienced an unhappy history: forcible colonization by Japan, forced enlistment of Korean men into the Japanese army and factories during the Second World War and forced transportation of many young Korean girls to be abused as 'comfort women' for Japanese soldiers all over Asia.[1] This was followed by the Korean War and the division of the country. Korea's suffering during this time is not generally known or acknowledged in the West.

The Japanese dominance over Korea was largely a result of their victory over China in the Sino-Japanese War of 1894–5 and their subsequent installation of a pro-Japanese government in Korea. In 1895 King Kojong was forced to proclaim the 'Guiding Principles for the Nation' in front of the tablets of his ancestors at the Royal Ancestral Shrine at Chongmyo and Queen Min, because of her links with Russia, was brutally assassinated by order of the Japanese Minister Miura Goro. This murder resulted, in the short term, in the installation of a pro-Russian government after King Kojong, in fear of his life, sought refuge in the Russian Legation in 1896. Then in 1897 King Kojong moved into the Toksu palace (conveniently close to the protection of the British, Russian and American legations) and proclaimed Korea an empire. However, by 1905 Japan had won recognition from all three of these countries of its paramount interests in Korea and had established a protectorate. Despite a mission to the Second Hague Peace Conference in 1907 by three envoys of King Kojong to plead the case for Korea's independence, this was followed in 1910 by Korea's colonization by Japan and King Kojong's forced relinquishing of the throne to his son Sunjong. Power now lay in the hands of the Japanese Resident-General, and protest was quelled by military force.[2]

The March First Movement of 1919 and the famous Declaration of Korea's Independence in Pagoda Park in Seoul were a result of clandestine independence movements established by Koreans in exile abroad and popular disturbances within Korea, protesting at the harshness of the Japanese rule. It forced the Japanese to adopt a policy of so-called 'enlightened administration', with supposed increased educational opportunities for Koreans, the establishment of Korean-owned daily newspapers such as the *Dong-a Ilbo* and the *Choson Ilbo* and other sops to the Koreans. There was a remarkable increase in the number of schools established, as well as a university. However, the ratio of Koreans to Japanese attending these schools was 1:26 and among those attending university it was about 1:100. The language used in schools and in officialdom was Japanese and from 1940 all Koreans had to take a Japanese name. Japan exploited cheap Korean labour and, having prospered out of the First World War, aimed to develop a profitable market in Korea for the investment of Japanese capital.[3]

Korea was swept up in the increased Japanese militarism of the 1930s, the subsequent invasion of China and Japan's role in the Second World War. Their sudden liberation from Japan in 1945 was unexpected and was followed by the occupation of the northern half of the country by Soviet troops and of the southern half by American troops. A temporary division line was drawn at the thirty-eighth parallel of latitude north. The first general election in Korea was carried out in May 1948 under United Nations supervision but it was only held in the south, as access to North Korea was frustrated by Soviet opposition. The one hundred seats in the National Assembly allocated to the northern provinces were therefore left unfilled. In June 1950 North Korea launched a surprise attack across the thirty-eighth parallel that escalated into the Korean War of 1950–53. United Nations troops from sixteen countries including the USA, Britain, France, Canada, Australia, the Philippines and Turkey fought together with the South Korean army against the North, which from October 1950 was supported by large numbers of Chinese troops. The war is formally still not over, but a temporary armistice agreement signed on 27 July 1953 remains in force. The huge losses of life and property caused by the Korean War reduced much of both halves of the country to ruins.[4]

The story of South Korea's postwar 'economic miracle' is a well-known and astounding one. However, it was accompanied by a very authoritarian style of government, heavily influenced by the military. Student protests were a regular feature, after the success of the 1960 student demonstration which brought down the government of President Syngman Rhee (1875–1965). A highpoint of Korea's postwar development and growing international importance was the highly successful Seoul Olympics of 1988. The slow but gradual development of democracy in South Korea culminated in the election as president in 1997 of the veteran opposition leader and ex-political prisoner Kim Dae-jung. Ironically this was accompanied by an economic downturn and resulting widespread unemployment. The prospects for unification with an extremely impoverished and politically volatile North Korea are at present uncertain.

Contacts with Western painting in the late Choson

Western painting techniques first became known in Korea in the eighteenth century, when Korean envoys to China came into contact with Jesuit missionaries in Beijing and brought back souvenirs of their visits, in the form of religious paintings and portraits by Western painters. Catholic painting clearly had a great effect on those Koreans who had the chance of seeing it adorning Beijing churches. Western perspective was a novelty and several Korean scholars commented on the realistic representation in Western paintings. These however were seen as aesthetically inferior, in contrast to traditional Korean painting which aimed to reflect the subject's inner spirit. Nude bodies, loose and unkempt long hair and rather untidy clothes, moreover, were puzzling to Koreans.[5]

However, by the end of the nineteenth century Korea was becoming more and more open to Western influence as foreigners arrived and settled there. Traditional Korean ink painting absorbed foreign influence and there are examples from this period of intriguing combinations of techniques. Foreign missionaries established Western-style schools, while buildings such as Myongdong cathedral (in the Gothic style) and the Stone Palace (Sokcho-jon) in the grounds of the Toksu palace (in the classical style), designed by Western architects, changed the appearance of Seoul.

Korea began to participate in international exhibitions, such as those in Chicago in 1893, Paris in 1900 and Hanoi in 1902. The Korean participants were amazed at the quality and variety of products from other countries. Perhaps as a result of this exposure to crafts and products abroad, the Korean government in 1900, on the recommendation of the French ambassador, Collin de Plancy, invited a French potter from Sèvres, called Remion, to advise on the establishment of a national school of crafts. Although nothing came of this plan, in 1908 the Hansong Studio was established, under a Japanese technical director, with the aim of promoting high-quality traditional crafts. In 1910, the Korean crafts displayed in the Korean Pavilion in the Anglo-Japanese exhibition in the White City in London were thought to be of sufficiently high quality to be donated to the British Museum (see figs 7 and 89).[6]

Foreign artists also visited Korea in this brief period of openness to the West, before the Japanese colonization of 1910. Female artists such as Constance Taylor and Elizabeth Keith produced paintings and prints of local people and places (see fig. 4), while the Dutchman Hubert Vos, arriving in Seoul in 1899, painted portraits of officials and even of King Kojong, as did the Frenchman Joseph de la Nexière around 1902. These artists did not stay long in Korea, but their Western oil technique was found intriguing enough to attract attention at the highest levels.[7]

Painting

Although a subject of much debate, it is generally agreed that the beginning of the Japanese colonial period in 1910 can be seen as the start of the modern period (*kundae*), as far as Korean art is concerned. This was when Western-style oil painting was introduced and grew in popularity. It was also the time when the first art school and first public art exhibition were established.

Art in the Japanese colonial period
The first art school, called the Institute for Calligraphy and Fine Arts (Sohwa Misulhoe Kangsupso), was founded in 1911 and was the first example of the use of the term 'fine art' (*misul*). Although initially established by the calligrapher Yun Young-ki, the three-year course was directed by two traditional ink painters, Cho Sok-chin (1853–1920) and Ahn Chung-sik (1861–1919). The latter's paintings had already absorbed some aspects of Western perspective. Early graduates of this Institute were Kim Eun-ho (1892–1978) (see fig. 92), Yi Sang-bom (1897–1972) and No Su-hyon (1899–1980), all three later to become renowned painters.

The first organized group of artists was the Society of Calligraphy and Painting (Sohwa Hyophoe), set up in 1918 mainly by teachers at the Institute and by Ko Hui-dong (1889–1965), Korea's first painter using the Western oil technique, who graduated from Tokyo School of Fine Arts in 1915. Ko's few surviving paintings show a mixture of a realistic rendering of form with an Impressionist-type palette. This was typical of the Japanized version of Western art that was taught in Tokyo and absorbed by the increasing number of Korean graduates who went there because it was much easier to get a visa for Japan than to go to the West to study. One of these, Kim Kwan-ho (born 1890), caused a stir in 1916 when his painting of two nude women won a prize in Japan. The painting of nudes was still regarded as shameful and embarrassing in Korea and photographs of this painting were banned from the newspapers. It is interesting to note that both Kim Kwan-ho and Ko Hui-dong abandoned Western-style painting, probably because of such difficulties.

The first annual art exhibition was the Hyopchon, which lasted from 1921 to 1936 and was established by the members of the Sohwa Hyophoe. All its members were Korean, some active nationalists. In contrast, the Sonchon or Choson Art Exhibition was established by the Japanese colonial government in 1922 and was increasingly a rival to the Hyopchon, lasting until 1944. Modelled on the Japanese official salon, Bunten, the Sonchon exhibition was originally divided into three sections: oriental (i.e. ink) painting, Western (i.e. oil) painting, and calligraphy and plant painting. The calligraphy section was later abolished and a sculpture section added, together with craft. Since entry was open to anyone who had lived in Korea for six months, many Japanese artists were eligible and all the judges, except for calligraphy, were Japanese. As a result, the Sonchon exhibition was seen as a tool for spreading Japanese influence in Korean painting.

INK PAINTING

As a reaction against the more traditional ink painting of Cho Sok-chin and Ahn Chung-sik, in 1923 a group of younger painters formed the Tongyon-sa association, which aimed to express a distinct Korean form of ink painting, rejecting the routine following of Chinese masters and the more colourful Japanese Nihonga style. Although this group, which included Yi Sang-bom, Pyon Kwan-sik (1899–1976), No Su-hyon and Yi Yong-wu (1904–52), did not last very long, it had a definite influence on the direction of Korean ink painting. In the same way as the Chin'gyong sansu or 'true view' landscape painters of the eighteenth century, these painters rejected ideal landscapes and instead concentrated on real places. However, they did not paint famous scenic spots such as the Diamond Mountains, but rather ordinary, humble, everyday countryside, perhaps following the example of the Impressionists. They also begin to adopt the Western practice of one-point perspective and to use titles indicating the time of day that the painting was executed (see fig. 95).[8]

The thick colour, fine brushstrokes and flat, decorative effect of Japanese Nihonga painting had a great mark on Korean animal and figure painting at this time. Kim Eun-ho was a Korean figure painter who studied in Japan in the 1920s and was influential in spreading the Nihonga style in Korea, particularly in the painting of women with flat, delicate colours.

The two schools of Yi Sang-bom and Kim Eun-ho became the mainstream of ink painting in the 1930s, with another, more conservative group centred on Huh Paik-ryon in the Honam region (the southwest corner of Korea). Kim Eun-ho's group, which organized an annual exhibition from 1936 to 1943, included such renowned painters, still living, as Kim Ki-chang and Chang Wu-song (born 1912) (fig. 92).

OIL PAINTING

Western painting techniques and schools largely came to Korea via Japan and were therefore already second-hand and Japanized. Japanese artists who had studied in Europe combined classicism and Impressionism or post-Impressionism. Korean painters such as Kim In-soong (born 1910) painted nudes with remarkable accuracy, while O Chi-ho (1905–82) painted in a completely impressionistic style, portraying clear and light colours of trees in blossom. Yi In-song (1912–50), whose works gained prizes in the Sonchon exhibition, painted in a more intimate, post-Impressionist manner, portraying Korean girls in a desolate landscape, symbolizing Korea's hopeless situation.

The success of Yi In-song's rather sentimental paintings led to an interest in folksy, pastoral scenes, as well as to an involvement by some artists in the Proletariat art movement, which used posters, cartoons and prints as a means of propaganda. Some artists who studied in Japan also became interested in new movements arriving there from Europe, such as Expressionism, abstract art and Fauvism. Korean artists in Tokyo in the mid-1930s were Kim Whan-gi (1913–74), Yu Yong-guk (born 1916) and Yi Kyu-sang. They participated in a small avant-garde group which experimented with geometric abstraction and exhibited in Seoul in 1941 (see fig. 100). Abstract art was, however, an unknown quantity to most Koreans at this time, even though it was at its height of popularity in Europe.

93. *Cows* by Yi Chung-sop (1916–56). For Yi, cows seem to have symbolized perseverance and toil, thus referring to Korea's unhappy situation. Oil painting on paper, 1953–4.

War period

With the development of Japanese militarism in the late 1930s, artistic freedoms were severely limited. An association of nationalistic Korean painters in Tokyo called the White Bull Association held several exhibitions before being forced to suspend its activities. The period from the Japanese invasion of China in 1937, through the Second World War until the end of the Korean War in 1953, was one of artistic chaos, although artists did continue to hold exhibitions in Pusan, where many Korean refugees were gathered. Some left-wing artists went to the north, while others were kidnapped by the Communists. The period immediately following the Korean War was also very difficult for artists, with materials scarce and foreign travel severely restricted. They were somewhat cut off from international artistic trends and did not really understand Modernism or abstract art. Some artists attempted to imitate Western ideas, while some wanted to get rid of foreign influence, particularly that of Japan. Two artists active during this period who stand out as creative individualists were Yi Chung-sop (1916–56) and Pak Su-gun (1914–65). Yi, a native of North Korea, studied in Japan in the 1930s and married the daughter of a Japanese businessman. During the Korean War he moved south with his family but he was so poor that his wife and children had to return to Japan. Yi's violent and distorted paintings express the sadness and anger at his forced separation from his family. Many feature family scenes, while others portray cows, symbolizing perseverance and unremitting labour – the situation both of Yi himself and of Korea as a nation (fig. 93). One painting entitled *Dancing Family* is clearly borrowed from Matisse's *La Dance*, while the colours and dynamic shapes of some of Yi's work have been compared to Van Gogh's. Although primarily an oil painter, many of his works were sketches done on postcards to his wife and on cigarette papers. He died of hepatitis at the age of forty in a state of some mental torment.[9]

94. *Seated Women* by
Pak Su-gun (1914–65).
Sometimes compared
with Millet, Pak uses
colour and texture
in a unique way.
Oil on canvas, 1958.
45.5 × 53.5 cm.

Pak Su-gun, in contrast, was a self-taught, more simple painter who produced humble and peaceful scenes from everday life, many featuring peasant women, usually modelled on his wife, grinding grain or washing clothes amongst traditional Korean houses and villages. Often compared to Millet, he developed his own thick painting surface built up on a hardboard base, the texture resembling the earthen walls of simple Korean cottages. The figures he painted in earthy browns, greys and creams were rather naïve, with square forms firmly delineated (fig. 94). The sparing use of colour gives greater prominence to his use of outline and to the unique texture of his work. Pak Su-gun is all the more remarkable for being totally outside any art group or movement and without any mentor. For this reason he has often been called a 'lonely artist' and remained largely unrecognized during his lifetime.[10]

Postwar period

INK PAINTING

The traditional ink painters Yi Sang-bom and Pyon Kwan-sik were the leading masters during the 1950s and 1960s, although Yi suffered at first from having been active and successful during the period of the Japanese occupation.[11] Yi's paintings of the four seasons, with his characteristic short brushstrokes and variation of ink tone, perfectly depicted morning mists and country scenes, far removed from the urban development around him (fig. 95). In contrast, Pyon was somewhat inconsistent and was sometimes criticized for being too free in expression. However, from a modern point of view his paintings were quite radically dynamic, making use of numerous dots and rough brushwork. His series of paintings of the Diamond Mountains, a traditionally favourite subject for ink painters, was notable for its use of unbalanced composition.

95. *In the Morning* by Yi Sang-bom (1897–1972). Ink and light colours on Korean paper, 1954. 69 × 273 cm.

Ink painters who experimented with abstract art and cubism were Park Nae-hyon (1921–79) and Yi Ung-no (1904–89). Park, a female painter educated in Japan, was influenced by cubism. Her painting *Street Shops* is a well-known example of an attempt to combine the traditional ink painting technique with the creation of flat planes using curves and diagonal lines. This painting won first prize in the National Art Exhibition in 1956. During the 1960s her paintings became more abstract, but remained balanced and ordered. She was married to the deaf painter Kim Ki-chang (Unbo) (born 1914), with whom she exhibited during the 1950s and 1960s both in Korea and abroad. In 1970 Kim

96. *Series II* by Kim Ki-chang. Kim, a deaf-mute, paints in a huge variety of styles, always in ink. 1989. 179.2 × 349.2 cm.

Ki-chang became the first Korean artist to have an exhibition at the Museum of Modern Art in New York. Although his early works were traditional in style, he moved towards abstractionism after the Korean War but kept to favourite lively subjects of fighting cocks, crabs and charging bulls. There is a certain innocence in Kim's paintings, which can be seen particularly in his later works. He also painted a *Life of Christ* depicting Christ in Korean dress, a painting which has become very well known in Korea. His later bold, unrestrained abstract works seem to express anger, which he has described as 'the agony of a man who can neither hear nor speak' (fig. 96). [12]

A group of ink painters from Seoul National University attempted to explore the abstract possibilities of ink painting in the 1960s and established a group called the Muklimhoe. This included Suh Se-ok (born 1927), Chong Tak-yong (born 1937), Min Kyong-kap (born 1933) and Chang Un-sang (1921–80). Led by Suh Se-ok, they experimented with different effects of brush and ink on various kinds of paper, trying to imbue their contemporary painting with the spirit of traditional ink painting and playing with the contrast of form and void (fig. 97). Song Yong-bang (born 1926), another member of this élite group, has explored calligraphic line and the spontaneous use of ink spreading on paper (fig. 98).

The Sumukhwa or Oriental Ink Movement of the 1980s was part of the general feeling

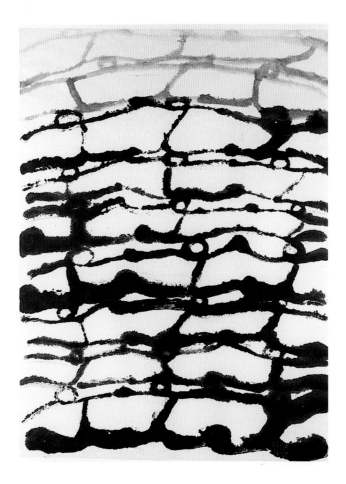

97. *People Dancing* by Suh Se-ok (1927–). Leader of the Muklimhoe, Suh experiments with the traditional ink technique. 1991. 162 × 130 cm.

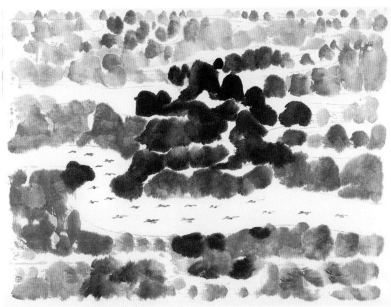

98. *Landscape* by Song Yong-bang (1926–). Ink and colours on Korean paper. Ht: 95 × 109 cm..

of trying to recover a national identity. Led by two professors at Hongik University in Seoul, Song Su-nam (born 1938) and Hong Sok-chang (born 1941), this group began to concentrate on subtle tonal variations of ink wash in an attempt to elicit an inner spirituality which was felt to be lost in a modern technological age (fig. 99).[13]

While these ink painters continue to explore the different possibilities of creating completely contemporary works using traditional techniques, artists such as Kwon Young-woo (born 1926) and Kim Choung-za (born 1929) also follow their individual paths of development of a truly Korean art, not imitating any Western movements or techniques.[14]

99. *Summer Trees* by Song Su-nam (1938–). Song is a leader of the Oriental Ink Movement, based at Hongik University, Seoul. Ink on paper, 1983. Ht: 65 cm.

OIL PAINTING

In the immediate postwar period, the focus for artists was the revived National Art Exhibition or Kukchon, which was held annually from 1953 until it was abandoned in 1979. This eventually became a source of discontent amongst the younger generation of artists as the jurors of the exhibition were older, more conservative artists and professors who tended to favour realistic works and to ignore abstract style. As a result, around 1957 several new groups of younger artists formed and modern art began to develop outside the Kukchon. New organizations included the Modern Art Association, the Creative Art Association and the New Plastic Group. These groups, largely composed of young men in their twenties and thirties who had experienced the horrors of war, generally felt that they could not express their frustration and anger through conventional painting methods. They held their own shows and in 1957 established an exhibition under a new organization called the

Contemporary Artists Association (Hyondae misulga hyophoe), led by Park Seo-bo (born 1931) and Kim Tschang-yeul (Kim Chang-yol; born 1929). This group soon became known as the Korean Informel, after the Art Informel in Europe or Abstract Expressionism in America of the 1940s and 1950s. The Korean Informel rejected geometric abstraction and painted relying only on personal intuition. Park Seo-bo's first attempts at splashing and dripping paint on the canvas were compared with Jackson Pollock, while Kim Tschang-yeul's work showed some affinity with Franz Kline and Pierre Soulage. Despite the derivative nature of Korean Informel, Park has always denied any connection with Western art movements and insisted that Informel was a native Korean development.

The Informel movement dominated the early 1960s in Korea and a younger generation including Yun Myong-ro (born 1936), Kim Bong-tae (born 1937) and Kim Chong-hak (born 1937) formed a subgroup called Actual and displayed their large canvases covered in thick brushstrokes of primary colours outside the Toksu palace on the day of the opening of the Kukchon exhibition in 1960. However, by the mid-1960s the Informel movement

100. *Rondo* by Kim Whan-gi (1913–74). Trained in Tokyo in the mid-1930s, Kim experimented with geometric abstraction after Western models. Oil on canvas, 1938. 61 × 72 cm.

had become somewhat less vibrant. New groups such as AV (Avant-garde) and Origin formed, producing rather mechanical works which were adaptions or imitations of various Western movements such as Hard Edge, Op Art, Neo-Dada and others. This reflected the increasing numbers of Korean artists who were going to France and North America to study. Korean artists also began to exhibit at international exhibitions such as the Sao Paolo Biennale and the Paris Biennale, while the first large-scale exhibition of Korean art treasures was sent to the USA and Europe.

As a result of this international exposure, some Korean artists in the 1970s began to establish themselves abroad: Lee U-fan (born 1936) in Tokyo, Kim Whan-gi and Paik Nam-june (born 1932) in the US, and Kim Tschang-yeul in Paris, where Nam Kwan (1911–90), Lee Se-duk (born 1921) and Pang Hae-ja (born 1937)[15] also settled in the postwar period. Kim Tschang-yeul's works often feature newspapers or Chinese characters combined with very realistic droplets of water.

Kim Whan-gi, perhaps Korea's most famous twentieth-century painter, was a pioneer of abstract painting in the 1930s (fig. 100), taught at Hongik University after the war and then left for Paris in 1956. In Paris he painted such traditionally Korean motifs as the moon, porcelain vases and cranes in paintings which were predominantly blue. These have been compared with works by Matisse or Braque. During his New York period, 1964–74, his work became bigger and more monumental, focusing on space, stars and the cosmos and featuring lines of dots repeated to make a line or plane. The paint he used was thinner, more like water-colour, and the brushes more slender. Kim was possibly influenced by the colour field paintings of artists such as Robert Motherwell, and these later works give an impression of infinite space.[16]

Another artist who painted traditional Korean motifs such as the moon, stars and birds was a friend of Kim Whan-gi, an individualist and innocent painter called Chang Uc-chin (born 1917). His eccentric and naïve paintings have been compared to those of Klee and Rousseau, but they portray a dream world which is completely unique to him. Like Pak Su-gun, Chang was an artist who cannot be labelled by any school or movement (fig. 101).[17]

Lee U-fan, although living and working in Japan, had a great effect on the development of modern art in Korea, particularly after the publication of his critical essays *In Search of an Encounter* in 1971. His philosophy studies and the influence of Kwak In-sik led him to emphasize extreme self-restraint and impermanence in his work, which ranges from oil paintings and woodblock prints to painting on ceramic (see fig. 110), sculptures and installations. His paintings often feature just one brushstroke.[18]

101. *Child Under a Tree* by Chang Uc-chin (1917–). Chang's paintings, characterized by their naïvety, have been compared to the work of Paul Klee. Oil on canvas, 1960. 41 × 32 cm.

The Monochrome movement dominated the 1970s, led by Park Seo-bo, Ha Chong-hyon (born 1935) and Yun Hyong-gun (born 1928). These artists rejected materialism, desiring a return to nature. Their rather severe paintings were characterized by a uniform surface and neutral monochrome colours (fig. 102). Park again rejected any connection with Western Minimalism, maintaining that his paintings were an attempt to empty himself and thus get closer to nature.[19] Others such as Suh Seung-won (born 1942),

102. *Burnt Umber* by Yun Hyong-gun (1928–). Oil on Korean paper, 1987. 63 × 94 cm.

Hang Jung-hee (born 1945) and Kwon Young-woo produced more individual works, Kwon celebrating the whiteness of traditional Korean paper, a focus also for the work of Chung Chang-sup (born 1927); Hang concentrated on colour and texture on canvas.

During the late 1970s the work of Pak Seng-kwang (1904–85) began to reflect the colours and patterns of traditional Korean folk art, shamanistic rituals and Buddhist temples. His 'shaman priestess' series, in a mixture of colour and ink, with thick and dynamic lines, represented a new step in the development of Korean art.

It was during the 1980s that the booming economy led some artists to protest against the unfair distribution of wealth between rich and poor and to start to express their views in a movement called Minjung misul or People's Art. They disliked Modernism and art for its own sake, calling for art to reflect social reality. They were, however, denounced as being left-wing and too idealistic. The political situation of a divided Korea, with a Communist regime so close, meant that such socialist tendencies were not tolerated for long in the

04/70   할 머 니 II

South. The Minjung movement was not limited to artists, but perhaps the best-known Minjung artist was O Yun (1946–85), who worked mainly in woodblock prints, producing images of exhausted factory girls and poor peasants (fig. 103) as well as folk scenes such as kimchi-making (see also section on Printmaking below).[20]

Sculpture

103. *Grandmother* by O Yun (1946–85). O was associated with the Minjung protest movement of the 1980s. Woodblock print, 1983. 51 × 36.6 cm.

Very few Korean sculptures remain from the period of Japanese administration up until 1945. Those that survive show a tendency to reflect the Japanese preoccupation with copying classical Western sculptors such as Rodin, Bourdelle and Maillol. However, Cho Kyu-bong's *Nude* shows a posture derived from Botticelli's *Birth of Venus*. Another sculptor of this period, Yun Hyo-chung (1917–67), in the 1940s produced works in wood of women in traditional Korean dress, while Kim Pok-jin (1901–40) made Buddhist sculptures for temples, in defiance of the tradition that Buddhist statues were usually made by artisans as opposed to artists trained in Western sculptural methods.[21]

In the postwar period many public monuments were erected with official sponsorship, as part of the rebuilding programme and in commemoration of war heroes or historical figures. This was not in truth a Korean custom at all, as great figures were traditionally commemorated in painted portraits. The monuments produced in the 1950s and 1960s in Korea were mostly the work of two men: Kim Hyong-seng and Yun Hyo-chung. As South Korea was under authoritarian rule and threatened by a Communist North Korea, the emphasis in these sculptures was, quite naturally, on patriotism, filial piety and other such solid virtues. Artistic creativity was not the main aim in sponsoring these statues and they were, to a certain extent, stereotypes. The statue of Admiral Yi Sun-sin by Kim Se-chung (1928–86) is perhaps the most famous of these public monuments. Erected in 1960 in Sejong-no, in the heart of central Seoul, it depicts one of Korea's most respected historical figures, a saviour of the nation who is portrayed in the same way as the military statues of the Choson dynasty that line the entrance to the royal tombs.

A more creative sculptor, Kyon Chin-kyu (1922–73), studied in Japan and produced a series of long-necked meditating figures of great spiritual awareness.[22] The late 1950s saw an increase in abstract sculptures by artists including Kim Chong-young (1915–82) and Song Young-su (1930–70), influenced by Brancusi, Arp and Hepworth. In the 1960s, more emotion came to be shown in the work of people such as Park Chong-bae (born 1935), whose prize-winning abstract metal sculpture, *Circle of History*, was exhibited in 1965. Sculptors such as Park, Choe Ki-won (born 1935) and Choe Man-rin (born 1935) could be seen as part of the Korean Informel movement of the 1960s, as they abandoned figurative work and attempted dramatic and aggressive works in iron, steel and concrete. The corroded or rusty surfaces seemed to reflect a pessimistic outlook.

In more recent times, the Olympic Sculpture Park Project of the 1980s brought together the work of many well-known sculptors from sixty-six different countries; these works are permanently exhibited at the site of the 1988 Seoul Olympics.[23] It was also at this time that the newly opened National Museum of Contemporary Art in Kwachon provided a venue for many outdoor sculptures by Korean artists such as Lee U-fan, Shin Sang-ho (born 1947), Lee Seung-taek (born 1929) and Kwak Duck-jun in the Open Air Sculpture Garden which surrounds it.[24]

Printmaking

Despite Korea's illustrious history in the field of printing from the Unified Silla period onwards, during the first half of the twentieth century there was little serious interest in printmaking. An exhibition of prints by William Blake was held in 1922 in Seoul, organized by a Japanese, while Korean magazines such as *Kabyok* and *Shinkajong* first used mass-produced prints for their covers in 1926 and 1934 respectively. Most artists regarded printmaking as a subsidiary hobby and there was no printmaking association. Choi Yong-lim (1916–85) was the first artist to produce serious prints, featuring folk stories and myths.

During the 1950s, after the Korean War, interest in woodblock printing grew and artists such as Pak Su-kun, Choi Yong-lim, Chong Kyu (1923–71), Choi Ji-won and Bae Woon-sung (1900–1978) produced serious works, very few of which survive. Some artists started to collect old woodblock prints and these, together with an increased interest in Western trends, had an influence on the development of woodblock printmaking in Korea during the decade. 1956 was the date of the first print exhibition by a Korean artist, Chong Kyu; in 1957 works by Yu Kang-yol (1920–76) were exhibited in Switzerland. Then in 1958 the Korean Woodblock Printing Association was established, the same year in which Lee Hang-song (born 1919) began to produce lithographs, using zinc plates instead of limestone and printing on *hanji* (traditional Korean paper).

At first, prints using linoleum, rubber and limestone, all introduced from the West, were characterized by interesting subject matter but poor technical quality. In the late 1950s silk-screen printing was introduced from the United States and proved very popular, particularly with Bae Ryung (born 1930) and Kang Hwan-sup (born 1927). Other influential figures in Korean printmaking at this time were Yun Myong-ro (born 1936; see fig. 105), Kim Chong-hak and Kim Bong-tae.

The 1960s were marked by the introduction of pop art and op art in Korea and a decline in abstractionism. Printmaking began to be taught in universities as an art rather than a craft and Korean printmakers began to take interest in the international printmaking exhibitions, such as those in Germany, Brazil and the US. Kim Bong-tae participated in the 1963 Paris Biennale, while Hwang Kyu-baik (born 1932) studied mezzotint in Paris at S.W. Hayter's Atelier 17 (fig. 104). After his return to the United States Hwang became relatively well-known, winning a prize at the Ljubljana Print Biennale in 1954 and later having a print used as the poster for the Sarajevo Winter Olympics of 1984. In 1963, the Korean Contemporary Printing Association was formed. It held an opening exhibition at Shinsegye Gallery and aimed to institute exchange exhibitions with Japan.

Printmakers during the 1970s either tended to produce fairly traditional woodblock prints or they were artists who used printmaking techniques but whose works are difficult to classify as printing and, rather, resemble paintings. After the *Dong-a Ilbo* daily organized the Seoul International Printing Biennale in 1970, there was a noticeable increase both in numbers of printmakers and in printing exhibitions. Silk-screen was the most popular technique and constituted the mainstream. Many artists went abroad to study and came back to teach in Korean universities and hold exhibitions at this time. Printmaking began to be seen as an independent art form rather than a subdivision of design. Rapid economic

104. *Saint Meditant* by Hwang Kyu-baik (1932–). Hwang studied at S.W. Hayter's Atelier 17 in Paris. Etching, 1969.

development and the expansion of art critics and art magazines during this period were also highly significant.

Although Western techniques have tended to overwhelm the Korean contemporary printing scene, woodblock printing is still flourishing and the Korean Modern Woodblock Printing Association has some 120 members. This may be due in part to the exciting work of O Yun, whose woodblock prints, featuring traditional Korean folk subjects as well as exhausted workers and hungry peasants, of greater political relevance, were part of the Minjung protest movement of the 1980s (see fig. 103). His figures are anonymous, full of strength and suffering. Although appearing simple, they were the result of hours of observation and sketches, on which he would write notes to himself saying: 'Be more simple, more succinct'. The angular lines and exaggerated features seem to capture the essence of the figure's life and movement. His subject matter has been compared with Kim Hong-do's genre paintings as has his habit of removing any extraneous elements from the background.[25]

During the 1980s there was a gradual removal of the distinctions between different art genres and an attempt at experimentation to try to transcend the technical restrictions of woodblock printing.[26] Ha Dong-chul (born 1942), one of the increasing number of Korean artists now active who trained in the United States, who for many years was the president of the Contemporary Printing Association, produces works featuring light

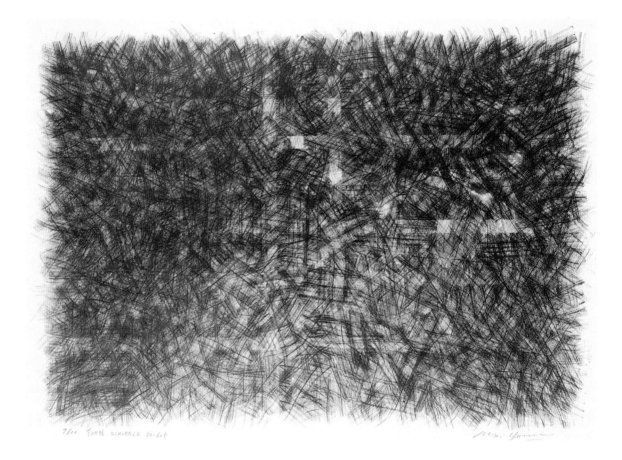

(fig.106). Sin Chang-sik (born 1959) is an artist who produced woodblock prints inspired by the 1988 Seoul Olympics. Reflecting the general feeling of national optimism at that time, they are full of light and colour, featuring subjects such as flames and torches. Older artists such as Yun Myong-ro have continued to produce more abstract, calligraphic prints (fig. 105) while more traditional woodblock printmaking is carried on by artists such as Kim Sang-yu (born 1926) and Kim Sang-ku (born 1945).

It is probably fair to say that in Korea printmaking is still undervalued as an art form. Artists tend to work primarily in oil or acrylic painting and still regard their print-making as a sideline, although there are exceptions to this rule. Serious art criticism of contemporary printmaking is lacking and there is relatively little documentary information about its recent history.[27]

105. *Scribble* by Yun Myong-ro (1936–), an influential figure in the development of Korean contemporary print-making. Lithograph, 1991. 53 × 76 cm.

106. *Light* by Ha Dong-chul. Trained in the USA, Ha is one of the leading figures in Korean contemporary print-making. Etching, 1989. 43.5 × 45 cm.

Ceramics

There is no doubt that Japanese appreciation of traditional Korean ceramics during the early part of the twentieth century had a distinct effect on the work of potters belonging to the Japanese Mingei or Folk Crafts movement, such as Hamada Shoji and Kawai Kanjiro and, through them, Western potters such as Bernard Leach and Lucie Rie (see fig. 8).[28] Japanese scholars such as Asakawa Noritaka and Asakawa Takumi, who lived for decades in Korea during this time, devoted their lives to the study of Choson period ceramics, collaborating with Yanagi in organizing the first Choson ceramics exhibition and publishing a classic textbook on the subject, *Richo no Toji*, in 1956. Paradoxically, Korean ceramics stagnated at this time, as the Japanese occupation resulted in a great deal of good kaolin-rich

Korean clay being exported to Japan for use there in the mass production of Japanese porcelain. Although in 1916 the largest Japanese porcelain company, the Nippon Koshitu Toki Kaisha, opened a branch factory in Pusan, Korea was gradually swamped with low-cost Japanese porcelain, resulting in the near collapse of the local industry.[29]

Despite a total boycott of Japanese goods in 1945 by the newly independent Korea, there was no resulting immediate renaissance of the Korean ceramic tradition. It was not until the country had started to recover from the Korean War that this gradually came about, and from around 1960 a contemporary ceramic movement started to develop.

107. Tall vessel with carved and incised decoration by Cho Chung-hyon (1940–). Cho's work recalls both Three Kingdoms tomb wares and later domestic storage jars (onggi). 1994. Ht: 60 cm.

Two groups of potters emerged. One was centred on Ichon, around the area in Kyonggi province to the southeast of Seoul where the Punwon official kilns had been sited in the Choson. The members of this grouping were in the main fairly traditional artisans who passed on their craft from generation to generation, from master-potter to apprentice. After the re-establishment of relations with Japan in the mid-1960s, they came into great demand from Japan. Perhaps the best known of them is Haegang, the studio name of Yu Kun-hyong (born 1894), who devoted his long life to the search for the re-creation of the traditional Koryo celadon and established the Haegang Research Institute and Museum in Ichon. He was successful in reproducing high-quality copies of traditional celadons.

The other group emerged in the universities where ceramics became established as a recognized subject in the art schools. Foremost among these are still Hongik, Seoul National and Ewha universities, which were also the first to establish ceramics departments in the late 1950s and early 1960s. The earliest teachers at these universities were Won Dae-jong (born 1920) at Hongik (a porcelain potter), Hwang Chung-ku (born 1919) at Ewha (a celadon potter) and Kwon Sun-hyung (born 1929) at Seoul National (a porcelain potter who specializes in glaze effects and also makes compositions of wall-tiles). An influential figure in the early development of contemporary Korean ceramics was Kim Che-won, director of the National Museum of Korea, which established the Korean Plastic Art Research Institute in 1955 with the help of the Rockefeller Foundation.[30]

As students graduated from these university departments and also studied abroad, new ideas began to emerge, combined with a new appreciation of Korea's great ceramic tradition. Some high-quality and innovative works were the result. Potters such as Kim Ik-kyung (born 1935), Shin Sang-ho (born 1947) and Cho Chung-hyon (born 1940) stand out as masters, nor should the eccentric and individualist works of Yun Kwang-cho (born 1946) be omitted.

Potters generally work in one tradition, however contemporary their products. The earthenware and onggi tradition is the chosen area of Cho Chung-hyon of Ewha University and Lee In-jin (born 1957) of Hongik. Cho's works recall the dramatic sculptural Silla funerary stands (fig. 107) and Lee's the onggi-ware storage jars. Both, however, have transformed the tradition and created completely original works. A potter basing his work on the early paddled pots of the 'Kimhae' tradition, Park Sun-gwan (born 1955) is remarkable for his adherence to traditional methods and tools.

Celadons lend themselves less to modernization than any of the other traditions and it is mostly in re-creating traditional shapes and motifs that the greatest success has been achieved in this area, by potters such as Haegang and Hwang Chung-ku. Some artists such as Kim Su-joung (born 1943) at Ewha have tried contemporary slants on celadons, but somehow the result is less than satisfactory, although sometimes elegant.

Potters working broadly in the punchong tradition include Shin Sang-ho (whose diverse skills have also been employed to produce celadons, porcelain and ceramic sculptures), Lee Jong-do (born 1953), Yun Kwang-cho and Hwang Chong-nye (born 1927). Shin uses carving, painting and stamping on his huge punchong-type works – traditional techniques but new shapes and sizes (fig. 108). Lee makes beautiful and classic wares, often with floral decoration, while Yun has progressed from throwing to slab-built asymmetrical vessels and sculptures, decorated in slip with simple geometric-shaped designs suggesting landscapes. His works manage to combine a sort of frenzied slapdash effect with that of calm meditation.

Perhaps the most exciting porcelain potter working at present in Korea is Kim Ik-kyung, who studied in New York between 1959 and 1961 and was inspired by the admiration of Western potters such as Bernard Leach to explore her own native ceramic tradition. Her plain white works are slab built and carved, based broadly on the shapes of Choson dynasty Confucian ritual wares, but they have developed beyond this to the creation of simple, strong statements of a timeless beauty

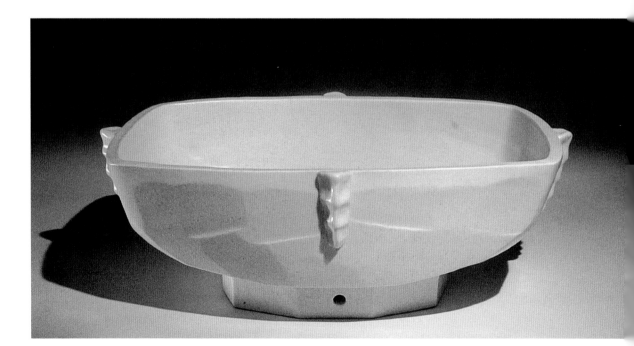

108. Left: Plate by Shin Sang-ho (1947–). Shin's work transforms the traditional inlay, painting and incising techniques used in Choson period punchong wares into contemporary works. 1994. Diameter: 58 cm.

110. Right: Porcelain plate made by Park Young-sook and painted in underglaze cobalt blue by Lee U-fan (1936–). Diameter: 30 cm.

109. Left: White porcelain dish by Kim Ik-kyung (1935–). Kim's work reflects the traditional Confucian ritual vessels of the Choson period. 1992. Length: 60 cm.

(fig. 109). Won Dae-jung's earlier work is thinner and more elegant, using traditional decorative techniques such as underglaze copper-red to great effect. Han Ick-hwan, also of the older generation, has produced masterpieces of traditional white porcelain. Park Young-sook's porcelain works feature beautiful underglaze iron-brown splashes and her very large dishes have developed into calm and elegant installations such as those based on the han'gul alphabet. She has also collaborated successfully with the painter Lee U-fan to produce a limited edition of tableware decorated by him in underglaze blue (fig. 110). Kim Kee-chul, an amateur potter, produces refined works in a traditional wood-fired kiln, based on natural flower and vegetable shapes, the most successful using unglazed porcelain clay.[31]

A general trend has been the gradual replacement of wood-fired kilns by gas and an increasing tendency towards slab-building and other techniques rather than throwing.[32] In recent years there has also been a growth in ceramic sculpture and in ceramic installations.[33] Ceramic artists such as Hwang Song-sil (born 1961), who studied in Finland, and Kim Jong-in (born 1957), who studied in England, as well as many others, have had some success in sculptural works, and ceramic installations such as Shin Sang-ho's horse heads show the direction that is being taken in this area. The retention of an awareness of Korea's long and illustrious ceramic tradition is proving more and more difficult, competing against an influx of Western ideas and trends.

Crafts

Some traditional Korean crafts are preserved under the Cultural Assets system, while more contemporary-style crafts are produced in many media by a variety of craftsmen, some of whom are professors at well-known universities such as Hongik and Seoul National (fig. 111).

The Cultural Assets system, which was officially initiated in 1962 with the passing of the

111. Square covered box of red lacquer inlaid with wood powder, mother-of-pearl and aluminium strips in a design of leaves and berries, by Kim Sung-soo. 1991. Ht: 27 cm.

Cultural Asset Preservation Act, was the result of a growing realization of the importance of preserving traditional ways in the face of the rapid modernization and industrialization which took place in Korea after the Korean War. In fact, by as early as 1916 a list of old buildings and properties which should be preserved had been compiled. By 1959 there were 44 wooden and 104 stone buildings on the list for South Korea. These designations are also in use in North Korea, which also appoints master craftsmen, calling them 'people's artists'. To a certain extent, the system used in South Korea is based on that already in operation in Japan. In Korea the system was set up to preserve folk arts and skills, whereas in Japan it is used to preserve fine arts as well. In Japan there is a fixed number of appointees and people are nominated for a lifetime's achievement rather than for a particular craft. Those in the folk crafts category do not receive a monthly stipend as they do in Korea.

The Cultural Assets system in Korea has four categories: Tangible Cultural Assets, Intangible Cultural Assets, Folk Cultural Properties, and Monuments. By the end of 1991, there were 2342 national and 2642 provincial Tangible Cultural Assets. These include buildings, ancient books, calligraphy, documents, pictures, sculpture and craftworks. The ninety-three Intangible Cultural Assets appointed by 1991 included music genres, dances, dramas, plays and rituals, food preparation, martial arts and manufactures. There were 224 Folk Cultural Properties, meaning public morals and customs relating to food, clothing, housing, religion, annual customs and so forth, which are regarded as 'indispensable to the understanding of changes and progress of national life'. The Monuments include ancient tombs and archaeological sites, kiln sites, palace sites, shell-mounds, scenic places, animals and plants 'of high scientific value'.

The term 'human cultural asset' originated from a series of newspaper articles on old arts and crafts written in the early 1960s for the daily *Hanguk Ilbo* by the late Ye Yong-hae. The Human Cultural Assets are the 'holders' (*poyuja*) of the Intangible Cultural Asset and, in general, they tend to be elderly people. Those under fifty are appointed as 'future holders' (*poyuja hubo*), while beneath them in the hierarchy are the four sub-categories of honour students, master students, students and ordinary students. In a system designed to ensure continuity, the holders at the top of the hierarchy are required to train and examine those below. In 1993, holders received a monthly wage of 600,000 *won*, with salaries decreasing down the scale to 50,000 *won* for students. The government office responsible for the implementation of this system as well as the co-ordination of publications, performances and exhibitions is the Munhwajae Kwalliguk, a branch of the Ministry of Culture.[34]

Crafts which are preserved under this system include beaten and inlaid metalwork, lacquer inlaid with mother-of-pearl, traditional ceramics, textile crafts such as embroidery, traditional Korean decorative knotting (maedup), painted ox-horn, bamboo crafts, furniture, horsehair hat-making, bows and arrows, masks and musical instruments. The annual competition at the Crafts Museum is an occasion for the discovery and recognition of new talent.[35]

In contrast to these traditional crafts, some artists are working in remarkable and innovative ways to produce contemporary works (see fig. 111), and there are now a considerable number of such art works collected by or exhibited at museums such as the National Contemporary Art Museum in Kwachon, the Hoam Museum and the Sonje Museum.

Developments in the 1990s

There has been a gradual blurring of the divisions between different media in the arts. For example, some artists bridge the division between Korean painting and Western painting: they might paint on Korean paper but use acrylic instead of or in combination with ink. Other artists, such as Yi Chong-sang (born 1938), started off in Korean painting and then developed in other directions, in his case into enamelled works. The contemporary art scene in Korea is diverse and the number of artists is burgeoning. With the beginnings of installation art and video art, the field has widened ever further during the 1990s. Paik Nam-june (born 1932), one of the early initiators and most successful proponents of video art in the world, is a Korean although resident abroad (fig. 112). Installation art has become more and more fashionable amongst the younger generation and has been featured abroad in the Korean section of the Venice Biennale as well as in numerous exhibitions within Korea. It is now sometimes difficult to identify any Korean elements at all in the works of the younger generation, who have adopted a truly global approach and whose works stand up to comparison with the most innovative artists worldwide.[36]

OVERLEAF

112. *The More, the Better*, pagoda-shaped video installation by Paik Nam-june (1932–) in the Ramp Core of the National Museum of Contemporary Art, opened in Seoul Grand Park in 1988, the year of the Seoul Olympics.

Chronology

DATES	CHINA	KOREA	JAPAN
5000	Neolithic cultures		Jomon period
1500		Neolithic period	
	Shang dynasty		
1000	Western Zhou	Bronze Age c. 1000 BC	
500	Eastern Zhou		
	Qin	Iron Age c. 400 BC	Yayoi period
BC 0 AD	Western Han		
	Eastern Han	Proto-Three Kingdoms 0–c. AD 300	
	Six dynasties	Three Kingdoms c. AD 300–AD 668 Silla Koguryo Paekche (Kaya)*	Kofun period
500			
	Sui dynasty		Asuka
	Tang dynasty	Unified Silla AD 668–935	Nara
	Five dynasties		Heian
1000			
	Song dynasty	Koryo dynasty AD 918–1392	
			Kamakura
	Yuan dynasty		Muromachi
1500	Ming dynasty		Momoyama
		Choson dynasty AD 1392–1910	Edo
	Qing dynasty		
1900			Meiji

*Traditional dates for the founding of the Three Kingdoms are:

Silla 57 BC
Koguryo 37 BC
Paekche 18 BC
Kaya AD 42
(see Chapter 2).

Glossary

Abhaya mudra Buddhist gesture of 'freedom from fear'

Ajip-to Paintings of gatherings of gentlemen

Amitabha Buddha, ruler of the Western Paradise

Anbang Inner room for women in a traditional house

Arhat Buddhist disciple

Armillary sphere Instrument which represents the heavens

Avalokitesvara Bodhisattva of compassion (Korean: Kwanum)

Avatamsaka sutra Garland sutra (Korean: Hwa'om)

Bhaisajyaguru Buddha of medicine or healing

Bodhi Tree-site of Buddha's enlightenment

Bodhisattva Enlightened being, a kind of Buddhist saint

Boneless Traditional ink-painting style

Bunten Japanese official Art Salon

Cakra The wheel of the Buddhist law

Chacha'ung Term for early Silla rulers

Chaekkori 'Books and things', a type of screen painting

Champlevé Enamelling technique of filling hollowed-out metal

Changdoktae Terrace outside a traditional Korean house

Changgi Korean chess (Chinese: xiangqi)

Changgo Traditional Korean drum

Changgyongho Long-necked vase from Three Kingdoms pottery

Changsung Wooden or stone carved guardian pole

Charye Confucian ritual ceremony to the ancestors

Chige A-frame, traditional wooden back-carrier

Chijang posal The bodhisattva Ksitigarbha

Chilsong Seven Star spirits

Chima Woman's traditional skirt

Chin'gol 'True bone', second rank in Silla hierarchy

Chin'gyong sansu 'Real place' or 'True view' landscape painting

Chisongmyo Dolmen

Chogori Traditional Korean jacket

Chogye Korean Buddhist sect formed in the Koryo

Chohwa punchong sagi Incised punchong wares

Cholhwa punchong sagi Iron-painted punchong wares

Chongbyong Kundika, Buddhist spouted water-sprinkler

Chongjagak T-shaped shrine building at a tomb

Chongsomdae Astronomical observatory in Silla capital

Chon'in 'Base people' or slaves

Chontae Buddhist sect (Chinese: Tiantai)

Chonwang Buddhist guardian kings of the four directions

Chopa-il Buddha's Birthday

Chulmun Comb-patterned Neolithic pottery

Chumoni Small drawstring purse

Chung'in 'Middle people', a social class

Chusok Harvest festival

Cizhou Northern Chinese stoneware (Song/Yuan)

Cloisonné Enamel technique of filling walled 'cloisons'

Deva Buddhist term meaning lord or god

Ding Northern Chinese white porcelain (Song)

Dolmen Ancient standing stone

Dou Chinese term for an ancient stem-cup shape

E-hakeme Japanese term for iron-painted punchong

Five elements Ancient Chinese philosophical theory

Four Masters of Yuan Four Chinese master painters of Yuan dynasty

Fucai/fuhong Chinese technique of painted tortoise-shell

Gaoli Chinese pronunciation of Koryo

Gigaku Japanese masked drama

Haenim Spirit of the sun

Haeso Standard script (Chinese: kaishu)

Haetae Mythical lion

Hakchangui Scholar's robes

Hakeme Japanese term for brushed slip punchong

Haliotis Kind of shell used in lacquer decoration

Hanbok Traditional Korean clothes

Hangari Large storage jar

Han'gul Korean script, invented in fifteenth century

Haniwa Japanese Kofun period pottery tomb figures

Hanji Traditional Korean mulberry-bark paper

Hansik 'Cold food' – traditional festival for ancestors

Harubang Stone folk figures of old men or women

Hori mishima Japanese term for incised/sgraffiato punchong

Hu Ancient Chinese vase with curved profile

Hunmin chong'um 'Proper Sounds to Instruct the People'

Hwabaek Council of aristocrats in the Silla

Hwangap Sixtieth birthday ceremony

Hwa'om Buddhist sect (Chinese: Huayan)

Hwa'omgyong Avatamsaka (Garland) sutra

Hwarang 'Flower Boys', Silla cult of noble youths

Hyondae misulga hyophoe Contemporary Artists Association (1957)

Hyopchon Annual Art Exhibition (1921–36)

Idu Ancient Korean writing system

Immortals Heavenly beings associated with Daoism

Ingan Munhwajae Intangible Cultural Asset

Inhwa punchong sagi Stamped punchong wares

Inwang Benevolent kings

Kanggang sullae Traditional circle dance by moonlight

Kayagum Korean zither

Ki'ak Early Korean masked drama

Kimhae Iron Age site and type of pottery (old term)

Kirin Unicorn

Kiro-do Portrait of an elderly worthy

Kirogi Wooden duck, folk carving used at weddings

Kisaeng Professional courtesan

Kobae Stem-cup from Three Kingdoms pottery

Kogok Curved jade ornaments on Silla gold jewellery

Ko'indol Korean word for dolmen

Kolpum 'Bone-rank' caste system in Silla

Kongsin 'Meritorious subject'

Koryo-sa Official history of the Koryo dynasty

Ksitigarbha Bodhisattva of mercy from hell

Kudara Kannon 'Paekche Kwanum' sculpture in Horyu-ji, Japan

Kuidong Type of Paekche pottery

Kukchon Annual National Art Exhibition (1953–79)

Kuksok 'National practice', Korean Neo-Confucianism

Kumgangsan The Diamond Mountains in North Korea

Kumsong 'City of Gold', Silla capital at Kyongju

Kun Korean measure of weight

Kundae Modern period

Kundika Buddhist water-sprinkler of Indian shape

Kurut pachim Tall pierced stands from Three Kingdoms pottery

Kut A shaman religious ceremony (exorcism)

Kuyonmun Type of Neolithic pottery with decorated rims

Kwaebul taenghwa Large outdoor Buddhist banner painting

Kwanum posal The bodhisattva Avalokitesvara

Kwiyal punchong sagi Brushed slip-decorated punchong wares

Kyo Buddhist textual school

Kyongjil Type of Iron Age stoneware pottery

Kyujanggak Royal Library

Lelang (Lolang) Chinese name for Nangnang

Lokapala Heavenly king, a Buddhist guardian

Longquan Southern Chinese celadon (Song/Ming)

Maebyong 'Plum blossom vase', actually a wine container

Maedup Traditional art of knotting silk threads

Mahasthamaprapta One of the bodhisattvas

Malgal Northern tribesmen of Tungusic origin

Mandorla Halo around a Buddhist sculpture

Manduguk Traditional dumpling soup

Manjusri Bodhisattva of knowledge and wisdom

Mantra Buddhist invocation, often meaningless

Maripkan Native Korean title for early Silla kings

Menhir Single standing stone

Mingei Japanese Folk Crafts Movement

Minjung misul People's Art Movement of the 1980s

Miruk Maitreya, Buddha of the future

Mishima Japanese term for some punchong wares

Misul Fine art

Mudang Shaman (female)

Muklimhoe Association of abstract ink painters

Munhwajae kwalliguk Cultural Assets Management Department

Munja-do Type of screen painting of Chinese characters

Mustard Seed Garden Chinese painting manual, printed in 1679

Myon sanggam Punchong ware with planar inlay

Naeyong-to Painting of the descending Amitabha

Namguksong Southern Star spirit

Namjonghwa Southern School of Choson-dynasty painting

Nangnang Han Chinese commandery near Pyongyang (Lelang)

Namin Southern faction in the Choson dynasty

Nihonga Japanese school of painting

Norigae Lady's pendant

Obang changgun The Five Generals portrayed in folk paintings

Ondol Traditional Korean underfloor heating system

Onggi High-fired earthenware domestic storage jars

Oyong hwasa 'Painter of the August Countenance'

Paduk Board game (Japanese: go, Chinese: weiqi)

Paekchung Festival for the souls of the dead

Paekto sagi Punchong ware dipped in slip

Paektu Holy mountain in Korea, on border with China

Paenggi Bronze Age pottery type of spinning-top shape

Paji Men's traditional trousers

Pakji punchong sagi Sgraffiato punchong wares

Paktong A white metal similar to pewter

Palgwan-hoe Buddhist festival for the dead

Panga sayusang Meditative pose (of seated Maitreya)

Pangsangsi Funeral mask

Piwon 'Secret Garden' in Changdok palace

Pojagi Traditional wrapping cloth for food and gifts

Pongae 'Lightning' pattern, Bronze Age pottery type

Pophwagyong Lotus sutra

Posal Bodhisattva, an enlightened being

Posang tangcho 'Precious visage' flower, a Buddhist motif

Pothi Form of book used in India

Poyuja 'Holder' of an Intangible Cultural Asset

Poyuja hubo Future 'Holder' of Intangible Cultural Asset

Pujok Talisman pictures, to repel evil spirits

Pukkuksong Northern Star spirit

Punchong sagi 'Powder green', type of Choson stoneware

Punjang sagi Punchong ware dipped in slip

Punwon Official Choson kiln from fifteenth century

Pure Land Buddhist sect

Pyongsaeng-to Pictorial biographies

Qingbai Bluish-white Southern Chinese porcelain

Repoussé Relief decoration hammered from reverse side

Rhyton Horn-shaped cup originating in Western Asia

Ru Very rare Northern Song Chinese celadon ware

Sadae 'Serving the great', i.e. the Ming

Sadaebu Scholar-bureaucrats

Sagyong Hand-written sutra manuscript

Sagyongwon Royal Sutra Scriptorium

Sakyamuni The historical Buddha, Prince Siddharta

Samantabhadra Bodhisattva

Samguk sagi History of the Three Kingdoms

Samguk yusa Memorabilia of the Three Kingdoms

Sancai Tang Chinese three-colour glazed pottery

Sanggam Inlay technique on celadons (see Appendix 1)

Sanggam punchong sagi Inlaid punchong wares

Sang'in Class of low-grade official

Sangjong yemun 'Detailed and Authentic Code of Ritual'

Sansin The Mountain god

Sarangbang Gentleman's study/reception room

Sarira Buddhist reliquary

Sejong sillok 'Veritable Record of King Sejong'

Sgraffiato Ceramic technique of carving away background

Simui Scholar's robes

Sinbyong Religious ecstasy (shaman)

Sinjung Tutelary deities

Sipchangsaeng Ten folk symbols of longevity

Sirhak 'Practical learning'

Sohak 'Western learning' (Catholicism)

Sohwa Hyophoe Society of Calligraphy and Painting (1918)

Sohwa Misulhoe Kangsupso Institute for Calligraphy and Fine Arts (1911)

Sokchae Mineral colours

Sollal Lunar new year's day

Son Buddhist sect (Chinese: Chan, Japanese: Zen)

Sonbi Traditional scholar

Sonchon Choson Annual Art Exhibition (1922–1944)

Songgol 'Sacred bone', top rank of Silla hierarchy

Sonhwa punchong sagi Incised-slip decorated punchong wares

Son sanggam Linear inlay technique of punchong

Sottae Wooden bird(s) on a pole guarding a village

Sowon Confucian private academy

Ssangryuk Korean backgammon

Ssirum Korean wrestling

Subok Prosperity and long life

Sueki Japanese high-fired stoneware

Sumo Traditional Japanese wrestling

Sumukhwa Oriental Ink Movement (1980s)

Sunggyongdo Traditional promotion game

Sutra Buddhist scripture, sermon of the Buddha

Taekwondo Korean martial art

Taenghwa Buddhist banner painting or hanging scroll

Talnim Spirit of the moon

Tanchong Type of polychrome painting

Tangol Southern hereditary shaman tradition

Tan'gun Legendary founder of Korea in 2333 BC

Tanji Large storage jar

Tano Day A traditional spring festival

Ten Longevity Symbols Folk motifs of long life (Sipchangsaeng)

Thangka Tibetan equivalent of taenghwa

Tohwawon Bureau of Painting

Tok Large storage jar

Toksong The Lonely Saint (shaman god)

Tongyonsa Association of Korean-style ink painters(1923)

Tripitaka Koreana Entire Buddhist scriptures on woodblock

Trompe l'oeil Western technique of painting perspective

Ttokguk Traditional soup

Uigwe-to Illustrated records of rituals

Umso System of protected official appointments

Vairocana Buddha popular in the Unified Silla

Vajra Thunderbolt symbolizing indestructability

Wabicha Japanese style of tea ceremony

Wajil 'Tile ware', type of Iron Age proto-stoneware

Wang Chinese/Korean term for king

Wa/Wae Early Japanese/Korean name for western Japan

Wu Ming Chinese scholar/amateur painting school

Yangban The upper classes (literally: two classes)

Yang'in Commoners

Yondung-hoe Buddhist festival of the lotus lanterns

Yongwang The Dragon King (shaman god)

Yonjil Type of Iron Age earthenware pottery

Yue Celadon ware from southern China

Yunggimun Type of Neolithic pottery with raised designs

Yut Traditional game (similar to spillikins)

Zelkova Korean elm

Zhe Ming Chinese school of professional painters

Collections of Korean art

The following list is not meant to be exhaustive, merely a guide to some
of the major Korean collections for those interested to seek them out.

Korea

NATIONAL MUSEUMS IN SEOUL,
CHONGJU, KIMHAE,
KONGJU, KWANGJU, KYONGJU,
PUYO AND TAEGU

HORIM MUSEUM, SEOUL

KANSONG MUSEUM, SEOUL

NATIONAL FOLK MUSEUM,
SEOUL

HOAM MUSEUM, YONGIN

NATIONAL MUSEUM OF
CONTEMPORARY ART, KWACHON

UNIVERSITY MUSEUMS: SEOUL
NATIONAL UNIVERSITY, EWHA
WOMEN'S UNIVERSITY, YONSEI
UNIVERSITY, KORYO UNIVERSITY,
ALL IN SEOUL

Europe

BRITISH MUSEUM, LONDON

VICTORIA AND ALBERT MUSEUM,
LONDON

ASHMOLEAN MUSEUM, OXFORD

FITZWILLIAM MUSEUM,
CAMBRIDGE
(GOMPERTZ COLLECTION)

MUSÉE GUIMET, PARIS

MUSÉE ROYAL DE MARIEMONT,
BRUSSELS

MUSEUM OF FAR EASTERN ART,
COLOGNE

NATIONAL MUSEUM OF
DENMARK, COPENHAGEN

RIJKSMUSEUM, AMSTERDAM

North America

FREER GALLERY,
WASHINGTON, DC

BROOKLYN MUSEUM, NEW YORK

METROPOLITAN MUSEUM,
NEW YORK

ASIAN ART MUSEUM,
SAN FRANCISCO

BOSTON MUSEUM OF FINE ARTS

LOS ANGELES COUNTY
MUSEUM OF ART

PORTLAND ART MUSEUM,
OREGON

SACKLER GALLERY,
HARVARD UNIVERSITY
(HENDERSON COLLECTION)

SEATTLE MUSEUM

ROYAL ONTARIO MUSEUM,
TORONTO

Japan

IDEMITSU MUSEUM, TOKYO

MINGEIKAN, TOKYO

NEZU MUSEUM, TOKYO

SEIKADO FOUNDATION, TOKYO

TOKYO NATIONAL MUSEUM

KYOTO NATIONAL MUSEUM

NARA NATIONAL MUSEUM

YAMATO BUNKAKAN, NARA

MUSEUM OF ORIENTAL
CERAMICS, OSAKA

TOKUGAWA MUSEUM, NAGOYA

ILLUSTRATION REFERENCES
Except where otherwise noted, illustrations
have been provided by the British Museum
Photographic Service (BM), © The British
Museum; registration numbers begin with
departmental initials.

FRONTISPIECE: Ministry of Culture, Seoul
CONTENTS: Mark de Fraeye
1 Ministry of Culture, Seoul
2 BM OA 1996.6-18.02
3 British Library OIOC 1047.b.4
4 BM P&D 1932.5-14.37, purchased through
the Contemporary Art Society
5 BM JA
6 BM OA 1936.10-9.0121
7 London Borough of Hammersmith &
Fulham Archives
8 Photo Lord Snowdon, BM OA 1999.3-2.1,
Hahn Purchase Fund
9 BM JA 1924.7-14.05
10 National Museum of Korea
11 National Museum of Korea
12 Professor Martina Deuchler
13 Kim Gwon-gu
14 Kim Gwon-gu
15 After Lee Chung-kyu, 1996. 'The bronze
dagger culture of Liaoning Province and
the Korean peninsula', Korea Journal,
36/4:24
16 BM OA 1945.10-17.223, Oscar Raphael
Bequest
17 National Museum of Korea
18 National Museum of Korea
19 After Lee Chung-kyu, 1996. 'The bronze
dagger culture of Liaoning Province and
the Korean peninsula', Korea Journal,
36/4:20
20 National Museum of Korea
21 National Research Institute of Cultural
Properties, Seoul
22 Ministry of Culture, Seoul
23 Samsung Foundation of Culture, Korea
24 Ministry of Education, Science, Sports
and Culture, Tokyo
25 Samsung Foundation of Culture, Seoul
26 Ministry of Education, Science, Sports
and Culture, Tokyo
27 BM JA OA+8
28 National Museum of Korea
29 National Museum of Korea
30 National Museum of Korea
31 BM OA+583, Sir A.W. Franks Bequest,
ex-Gowland collection
32 National Museum of Korea
33 National Museum of Korea
34 National Research Institute of Cultural
Properties, Seoul
35 National Museum of Korea
36 National Research Institute of Cultural
Properties, Seoul
37 BM OA 1992.6-15.24, donated by Dr
A.G. Poulsen-Hansen
38 Jane Portal
39 Ministry of Culture, Seoul
40 Shaanxi Provincial Cultural Relics
Bureau, China
41 Ministry of Culture, Seoul
42 Ministry of Culture, Seoul
43 National Museum of Korea
44 BM OA 1983.10-8.01
45 Tokyo National Museum
46 National Research Institute of Cultural
Properties, Seoul
47 Lent by Dr Hahn Kwang-ho, CBE
48 BM OA 1945.11-10.1, donated by Lady
Invernairn
49 BM OA 1974.10-31.1; BM OA 1936.10-
12.198
50 Boston Museum of Fine Arts, MA
51 BM OA 1966.12-21.1
52 BM OA 1978.5-22.1, donated by Mr and
Mrs I. Clark; Lent by the late Sir John and
Lady Figgess
53 BM OA 1931.6-18.1, donated by the
Misses Alexander
54 BM OA 1938.5-24.763

55 BM OA 1911.6-7.16, donated by George
Eumorfopoulos
56 OA BM 1936.10-12.202
57 National Museum of Korea
58 After fig. 46, Horace H. Underwood,
1934. Korean Boats and Ships. Seoul
59 British Library Maps c.17.f.14
60 Ministry of Culture, Seoul
61 Ministry of Culture, Seoul
62 BM OA 1996.3-29.01
63 BM OA 1920.3-17.1
64 British Library OIOC Or.7458
65 Hoam Museum, Yongin
66 Ashmolean Museum, Oxford, donated by
Mr and Mrs K.R. Malcolm in memory of
their son, John Malcolm
67 National Museum of Korea
68 Hoam Museum, Yongin
69 BM OA 1961.5-13.04
70 Yi Dong-ju Collection
71 BM OA 1979.12-19.1
72 BM OA 1936.10-12.129
73 National Museum of Korea
74 BM OA 1997.7-21.1-14, Hahn Purchase
Fund
75 Manchester City Art Gallery
76 BM JA 1947.12-17.17
77 BM OA 1996.10-3.01
78 National Research Institute of Cultural
Properties, Seoul
79 BM OA 1990.11-13.02
80 Hoam Museum, Yongin
81 BM OA 1994.4-14.01
82 BM OA 1991.7-18.01
83 Hoam Museum, Yongin
84 National Research Institute of Cultural
Properties, Seoul
85 BM OA 1991.12-20.1
86 BM OA 1991.12-23.4
87 National Museum of Korea
88 National Research Institute of Cultural
Properties, Seoul; BM OA 1990.11-14.9
89 BM Ethno 1910
90 BM OA+0482
91 BM OA 1996.10-1.1
92 BM OA 1995.10-12.02, donated by the
artist
93 Hoam Museum, Yongin
94 Hoam Museum, Yongin
95 National Museum of Contemporary Art,
Kwachon
96 National Museum of Contemporary Art,
Kwachon
97 BM OA 1991.11-23.01, donated by the
artist
98 BM OA 1991.12-30.01
99 BM OA 1995.10-12.08
100 Hoam Museum, Yongin
101 Hoam Museum, Yongin
102 BM OA 1991.12-17.041
103 BM OA 1997.11-7.02
104 BM OA 1998.6-10.02, acquired in 1969
by BM P&D
105 BM OA 1991.12-23.04
106 BM OA 1991.12-17.06
107 BM OA 1995.10-11.1
108 BM OA 1995.10-11.8
109 BM OA 1992.10-10.1
110 BM OA 1996.6-19.4, donated by Park
Young-sook
111 BM OA 1994.5-25.3
112 National Museum of Contemporary
Art, Kwachon

APPENDIX 1
1 BM SR
2 BM SR
3 BM SR
4 BM SR

APPENDIX 2
1 BM C&M 1884.5-11.1189, Tamba
collection
2 BM C&M 1986.11-41.1
3 BM C&M 1985.2-23.9; BM C&M 1991.4-
17.2
4 BM Ethno As.1920.6

Notes

Introduction

1. Lautensach 1988, p.82

2. See Kim-Renaud (ed.) 1992

3. See chapter 2 (section on Silla metalware, with particular reference to gold crowns) and chapter 5 (section on folk religions)

4. See chapter 5 (section on folk religions)

5. Lautensach, op.cit., p.39

6. Lautensach, op.cit., p.42

7. Ledyard 1971, p.218

8. Ledyard, op.cit., p.216

9. Lautensach, op.cit., p.48

10. Lautensach, op.cit., p.44

11. Gale 1898; Hulbert 1906; Allen 1908; Underwood 1908

12. Carles 1883; Aston 1885

13. Bishop 1898/1985

14. Sands n.d.

15. Sands, op.cit., pp.135–6

16. Carles 1883, p.12

17. Hulbert 1906, p.295

18. Bushell 1899, p.333

19. See Peter Kornicki's chapter on Aston in Cortazzi and Daniels (eds) 1991

20. Gowland 1895, p.323

21. Sayers 1987, p.48

22. Steinberg 1968, pp.14–15

23. See Portal 1995 and 1996

24. Sayers 1987, p.53. See also Kikuchi 1994

25. See Leach 1978

26. See Portal 1999

27. See Portal 1992; Henderson 1983; Hornby 1988

28. See Barnes 1996 for an account of the development of archaeology in Korea

29. See San Francisco 1979; Whitfield (ed.) 1984. See also McKillop 1992; Smith (ed.) 1998

30. Kim Won-yong 1979, pp.21–2

31. See, for example, Okazaki Takashi 1993 in *Cambridge History of Japan*, vol.1, pp.268–316; Gompertz 1980

32. Pak 1998(b), p.50

33. Seckel 1977, pp.52–61

34. Gompertz 1963, p.2

35. See Pak 1977,1982,1987/8, 1988 and 1995 (in bibliography for chapter 3)

36. See Jungmann 1995

Chapter One

1. See Sohn 1970 and 1974; Yi 1978 and 1982; Kim Won-yong 1986, pp.25–9; Nelson 1993; Barnes 1993.

2. See Andersson 1934

3. Barnes, op.cit., p.50

4. Kwon 1990; Nelson, op.cit., p.43

5. Kim, op.cit., p.28; Nelson, op.cit., p.30

6. Kim, loc.cit.; Nelson, op.cit., p.30 and p.41; Bae 1997, p.31. It is interesting to note that the Chon'gok-ri site was first discovered in 1978 by an American serviceman, G.Bowen.

7. All palaeolithic dates used here are taken from the National Museum of Korea's 1996 chronology.

8. Nelson 1993, p.43; Yi 1983

9. Yi 1983, p.27

10. Lee 1984 and 1992; Nelson, op.cit., pp.47–8

11. Nelson, op.cit., pp.49–51; Sohn 1974.

12. Sohn, op.cit.; Barnes, op.cit., p.63; Nelson, op.cit., pp.38–9

13. Kim Won-yong 1986, p.29; Nelson, op.cit., pp.53–4

14. Im 1995, pp.31–4

15. Im 1996, pp.5–6

16. See Im 1996; Nelson (ed.) 1995

17. Im, op.cit., pp.9–12

18. See Nelson 1993, pp.58–9; Barnes 1993, p.69

19. See Nelson, op.cit., p.100

20. Nelson, op.cit., pp.99–101; Barnes, op.cit., pp.78–9

21. Nelson, op.cit., p.72

22. Nelson, op.cit., pp.70–2

23. Kim and Ahn 1993, p.25; Nelson 1993, p.69

24. Nelson, op.cit., pp.73–4

25. Im 1996, p.7

26. National Museum of Korea 1993, p.22; Nelson 1993, p.88

27. Nelson, op.cit., p.78

28. Im, op.cit., p.6; Barnes, op.cit., p.71; Nelson, op.cit., p.97

29. Kim Won-yong 1986, pp.32–3; Nelson 1993, pp.79–80; Barnes 1993, p.78; Han Young-hee 1997, pp.30–31

30. Nelson, op.cit., pp.97,110

31. Nelson, op.cit., p.72 and pp.106–7; Kim Won-yong 1986, p.34

32. Kim Won-yong, loc.cit.

33. Im 1995, p.35

34. Im, op.cit., pp.36–8

35. Choi Mong-lyong 1984, pp.24 and 31; Nelson 1992, p.183; Barnes 1990

36. Nelson 1993, pp.159–161; Kim Won-yong 1986, p.35; Choi Mong-lyong 1984, pp.23–34

37. See Lee Chung-kyu 1996

38. Choi Mong-lyong, op.cit., pp.25–6; Nelson, op.cit., pp.147–50

39. Choi Mong-lyong, op.cit., p.28; Nelson, op.cit., pp.150–52; Kim Won-yong, op.cit., pp.165–9

40. Choi Mong-lyong, loc.cit.

41. See Lee Ki-baik 1984, p.12

42. Barnes 1993, pp.162–3; Shin 1997, pp.35–6

43. Kim Won-yong, op.cit., pp.35–41; Nelson 1993, pp.138–46; Barnes, op.cit., pp.160–167

44. Sasse 1996, p.78; Ahn and Kim 1993, p.363

45. Sasse, op.cit., pp.82–3, 89

46. Lee Chung-kyu 1996, pp.17–19

47. Lee Chung-kyu, op.cit., pp.22–5; Barnes 1993, pp.162–4; Nelson 1993, pp.132–5

48. Kim Won-yong 1963

49. Barnes, op.cit., p.164

50. Nelson, op.cit., p.138

51. Lee Chung-kyu 1996, p.20

52. Nelson, op.cit., pp.116–7

53. Lee, loc.cit.

54. Nelson 1993, p.123

55. Kim Won-yong 1986, p.138

56. Denes 1995, pp.85–93

57. Choi Sung-rak 1996, pp.28–31

58. Barnes 1993, pp.208–9

59. Michaelson 1992, pp.60–65

60. Barnes, op.cit., pp.209–14; Nelson 1993, pp.168–9 and 186–190; Umehara Sueji 1926.

61. Choi Sung-rak 1996, p.33; Barnes 1992, p.206

62. Barnes 1992, pp.197–206; Barnes 1993, p.217

63. Pak 1996, pp.39–54

Chapter Two

1. Translated by Ha and Mintz 1972

2. See *Asahi Shimbun* 1992, exhibition catalogue, *Kaya – Ancient Kingdoms of Korea*

3. See Okazaki Takashi in Brown (ed.) 1993; Hong Wontack 1994

4. Nelson 1993, pp.207–8; Kim Won-yong 1986, p.389; Barnes 1990, pp.126–31

5. Nelson op.cit., p.210

6. Lee Ki-baik 1984, pp.38–40

7. Barnes 1993, p.224; Nelson, op.cit., pp.211–3

8. Kim Won-yong 1966 (reprinted 1986), pp.390 and 397

9. Kim Won-yong, op.cit., pp.390–5

10. Kim Won-yong, op.cit., pp.395–6; Mason 1993, pp.31–2

11. Nelson 1993, pp.211,216

12. Whitfield (ed.)1984, pp.52–3; Nelson, op.cit., pp.216,219

13. Lee Ki-baik 1984, pp.36–7 and 41–4.

14. Nelson, op.cit., p.231

15. Kim Won-yong 1986, pp.223–6; Whitfield (ed.)1984, pp.61–4

16. Shin 1986, p.329

17. Whitfield, op.cit., p.54

18. Shin, loc.cit.

19. Kim and Ahn 1993, pp.81–5; Covell 1984, pp.57–9

20. Whitfield, op.cit., pp.61–4

21. National Museum of Korea 1994, exhibition leaflet; Cho 1994

22. Hong 1994, pp.251–4

23. Whitfield (ed.)1984, pp.57–8

24. Kim Won-yong 1986, pp.231–7

25. Whitfield, op.cit., p.55

26. See Ledyard 1975; Kirkland 1981; Okazaki 1993

27. Nelson 1993, pp.237–8; Ledyard, op.cit.; Kirkland, op.cit.; Okazaki, op.cit.; Barnes 1993, p.245; Barnes 1994, p.109

28. Barnes 1994, p.121

29. Nelson 1993, pp.238–43

30. Kim Won-yong 1986, p.189

31. Nelson, loc.cit.

32. Tite, Barnes and Doherty 1992, p.68

33. Barnes 1992, p.199

34. Barnes 1993, p.232

35. Nelson 1991, p.104

36. Lee Ki-baik 1984, p.66

37. Nelson 1993, pp.247–9

38. Nelson 1991, pp.101–7

39. Whitfield (ed.)1984, pp.90–91

40. See Lee (ed.) 1993–6, vol.1, p.32–3

41. Whitfield, op.cit., p.86; Nelson 1993, p.250

42. Pak 1988; Bailey 1994

43. Nelson, op.cit., p.252

44. Whitfield, op.cit., p.97

45. See Kim Won-yong 1985(a); Han Byong-sam 1983

46. Kim Won-yong, op.cit., p.32

47. Kim-Paik 1994

48. Kim-Paik, op.cit.

49. See Whitfield (ed.)1984, p.77

50. Lee Nan-young 1989; Kim Won-yong 1968

51. See Kim-Lee 1986, pp.93–7; McCallum 1982 and 1995; Best 1992

52. See, for example, Hong 1994, pp.255–8

53. Hong, op.cit., p.265

54. See Kim Won-yong 1986, pp.257–62; Barnes 1993, pp.244–5; Hong 1994, pp.15–20; Ledyard 1975; Okazaki Takashi 1993; Covell 1984, pp.12–25

55. Lee Ki-baik 1984, pp.66–71

56. Lee Ki-baik, op.cit., pp.76–85

57. Jeon 1974, p.33

58. Kim-Lee 1986, p.99

59. Lee Ki-baik 1984, p.86

60. Lee Nan-young 1989, pp.86–8; Whitfield (ed.) 1984, p.134; Jeon 1974, p.238; Kim and Ahn 1993, pp.166–8

61. Kang 1991, pp.26–9, 30–5, 40–44; Whitfield, op.cit., pp.115–7; Swart 1991

62. Lee Insook 1994, pp.73–81; Kwon 1991, p.7

63. Lee Nan-young 1989

64. Reischauer 1955, p.276

65. See Choi 1996; Lee Nan-young 1991

66. Kwon 1991

Chapter Three

1. See Lee Ki-baik 1984, pp.124–8

2. Lee, op.cit., p.128

3. Lee, op.cit., p.129

4. Deuchler 1992, p.29

5. Lee Ki-baik 1984, p.134

6. Lee, op.cit., pp.139–46

7. Lee, op.cit., pp.148–9

8. Gompertz 1963, p.25

9. Lee Ki-baik 1984, p.158

10. Deuchler 1993, p.57

11. Deuchler, op.cit., p.66

12. Deuchler, op.cit., p.69

13. Lee Ki-baik 1984, p.119

14. Deuchler forthcoming, pp.5–6

15. Lee, op.cit., p.132

16. Lee, op.cit., pp.123–4

17. Grayson 1989, p.114

18. Lee Ki-baik 1984, p.134

19. Lee, op.cit., p.154

20. Lee, op.cit., p.131

21. Loc. cit.

22. Jeon 1974, p.172

23. Jeon, op.cit., pp.265–6. See also the astronomical painted screen in the Whipple Museum, Cambridge, UK

24. Jeon, op.cit., p.173

25. Jeon, op.cit., pp.174–5

26. Lee Ki-baik 1984, p.170

27. See Kim and Ahn 1993, p.470

28. Kim and Ahn, op.cit., pp.258–9 and p.472; Till 1989, pp.27–33

29. Choi Sun-u 1983, pp.7–8; Maeng 1964, p.17

30. See McKillop 1992, p.94

31. Lee Ki-baik 1984, pp.168–9; Kim and Ahn 1993, pp.244–7

32. Lee Ki-baik, op.cit., pp.135–6; Kim and Ahn, op.cit., pp.248–51

33. Chung Young-ho 1994, pp.227–8; Chin 1995, pp.265–6

34. Chung Young-ho, loc.cit.; Kim and Ahn, op.cit., p.251 and p.491

35. Kim and Ahn, op.cit., p.255 and p.494; Chung Myong-ho 1994, p.247

36. Pak 1987(a), p.357. I am indebted to Professor Pak for most of the information included in this section

37. Pak, loc.cit.

38. Pak, op.cit., p.358

39. Pak, op.cit., p.360

40. Pak, loc.cit.

41. Pak, op.cit., p.363

42. Pak, op.cit., pp.356–8

43. Mun 1994, p.48. See also an anecdotal account in Covell 1978 and 1979

44. Choi Sun-u 1983, p.7; Maeng 1964, p.17

45. See Pak 1987(b), pp.519–21, for a discussion of this question and other interpretations of the Amitabha configuration

46. Ahn 1986, pp.48–50

47. Pak 1977, p.98 and 1995, p.159

48. Pak 1995, p.157

49. Mun 1994, p.52

50. Pak 1987(b), pp.526–7

51. Pak, op.cit., pp.524–5 and p.527

52. Whitfield (ed.) 1984, p.184

53. See Ahn 1994, p.43; Choi Sun-u 1983, pp.6–7

54. Ahn 1993, pp.184–8

55. Kim-Lee 1986, p.100; Kim Won-yong 1986, p.337

56. Kim-Lee, op.cit., p.101

57. Kim-Lee, loc.cit.; Grayson 1989, p.112

58. See Rhie 1987, 1988 and 1992

59. Kim-Lee, loc.cit.

60. See Paludan 1991

61. Kessler 1993, pp.107–9. It has been suggested that these Liao masks reflect shamanist beliefs of the Khitan

62. Kim Won-yong 1986, pp.340–1; Kim and Ahn 1993, pp.225–6

63. Jeon 1974, pp.238–9

64. See Lee Nan-young 1995 for a discussion of Koryo metalworking techniques

65. Kim Won-yong 1986, pp.365–6; Kim and Ahn 1993, pp.235–6

66. See, for example, Whitfield (ed.) 1984, p.133

67. Choi Eung-chon 1988, pp.40–41

68. See Kim Won-yong 1986, p.369; McKillop 1992, p.104

69. Lee Nan-young 1992, pp.155–68

70. Kim and Ahn, op.cit., p.240

71. See Lee Nan-young, op.cit., pp.117–37

72. Gompertz 1960–62, p.8

73. See *Tae Koryo Kukbo chon* 1995, pp.211–13

74. Op.cit., p.261

75. Figgess 1977, p.93; Gray 1967–8, p.133

76. Kim Won-yong 1986, p.369

77. Watt 1991, p.307

78. Watt, op.cit., p.304

79. Kim Won-yong 1986, p.371

80. Pak 1998, pp.411–5. Professor Pak suggests that these boxes may have been for incense rather than for ladies' cosmetics.

81. Kim Won-yong, op.cit., p.371; Watt 1991, p.306

82. Watt, loc.cit.

83. Kim Won-yong, op.cit., p.370

84. Gompertz 1960–2, p.7

85. Gompertz, op.cit., p.17; Mowry 1986, p.24

86. Feng 1986, pp.49–53

87. Gompertz, op.cit., p.12

88. Wood 1994, p.60

89. Medley 1975, pp.2–3 and 1977, pp.80–6

90. Gompertz, op.cit., p.12

91. See Appendix 1 for composition of inlay material

92. For a technical analysis of Koryo inlays, see Vandiver 1991

93. For Changsha wares see Lam 1990, pp.115–34. The Burrell Collection in Glasgow also has an underglaze copper-red celadon bowl but the quality is not quite as fine as the British Museum's example.

94. For example, Nomori 1944; Koyama 1961

95. See Kang 1989, pp.148–62 for an overview. Also Choi Sun-u 1983; Chung Yang-mo 1986 and 1991; Yun 1993; Kim Jae-yeol 1994; Koh 1999.

96. Chung 1986, p.264 and 1991, pp.245–9

97. See Koh 1999, pp.51–69. The excavation work of Kim Jae-yeol and Choi Kun at these two sites provides new evidence about the wide footrims (*haemurigup*) associated with China. Kim Jae-yeol assigns a date of the early ninth century to the oldest layer at So-ri.

98. Choi Sun-u 1983, p.6

99. Kang 1989, pp.185–6

100. Kim Jae-yeol 1994, pp.114–15; Gompertz 1963, pp.26–8

101. Gompertz 1960–2, pp.9–10

102. Gompertz 1963, pp.55–8

103. Yun forthcoming

104. Chung Yang-mo 1986, p.264

105. Whitfield (ed.) 1984, pp.135–6

106. Wood 1994, p.52

107. Gompertz 1963, p.65

108. Chung Yang-mo 1986, p.264

109. Itoh and Mino 1991, p.74

110. Itoh and Mino, op.cit., p.63

111. Gompertz 1960–62, p.11

Chapter Four

1. Lee Ki-baik 1984, p.189

2. See Kim-Renaud (ed.) 1992

3. Lee, op.cit., p.191

4. Lee, op.cit., p.192

5. Underwood 1934/1979

6. Lee, op.cit., pp.209–13

7. Lee, op.cit., pp.215–17

8. See Kim Hong-nam (ed.) 1993

9. For an illuminating account and interpretation of this incident, see Kim-Haboush 1995 (the memoirs of Lady Hyegyong, Chongjo's mother and Sado's wife)

10. Lee Ki-baik 1984, pp.262–6

11. Grayson 1989, p.152

12. Grayson, op.cit., pp.153–4

13. Lee, op.cit., pp.204–7

14. Lee, op.cit., pp.217–8

15. See Deuchler 1992, pp.287–93

16. Lee, op.cit., pp.232–9; Grayson, op.cit., pp.164–72; Kim-Haboush 1995, pp.23–32

17. Lee Ki-baik 1984, pp.239–40

18. Ramsey 1992, pp.43–50

19. Jeon 1974, pp.175–84

20. Yi and Jeon 1992, pp.97–101; Jeon 1974, pp.46–9 and pp.108–12

21. Jeon, op.cit., pp.52–64

22. McCune 1983, pp.22–3; Jeon, op.cit., pp.280–97 and pp.306–15

23. Lee, op.cit., pp.241–2; Jeon, op.cit., pp.301–4

24. Till 1992, pp.4–11

25. A surviving tanchong artist is the Buddhist monk Lee Man-bong who works at Pongwon temple in Seoul

26. See Adams 1982; Bartholomew 1993

27. Kang Woo-bang 1993, pp.84–6

28. Kim Hong-nam 1991, pp.29–31

29. Kim Hong-nam 1994, pp.32–5

30. Sorensen 1989, p.9; Kim Hong-nam 1991, pp.24–5

31. Kim Hong-nam, op.cit., pp.31–3

32. Adams 1974, pp.36–41; Kim Hong-nam, op.cit., p.38

33. See Ahn 1976

34. See for example the triad *Sakyamuni Buddha and Attendant Bodhisattvas* in the Burke Collection, New York, illustrated in Kim Hong-nam 1991

35. Kim Hong-nam 1991, pp.37–40

36. Kang Woo-bang 1993, pp.79–98

37. Kim Hong-nam, op.cit., pp.44–6

38. See Jungmann 1990, pp.22–9

39. Kim Hong-nam 1994, pp.28–37

40. For more information about the significance of these screens, see Yi Song-mi 1996/7, pp.13–24

41. Kim Hong-nam 1993, pp.46–55; Kim-Haboush 1993, pp.14–21

42. Cho 1992, p.34. Most of the information included here about portrait painting is derived from Cho Sun-mie's works

43. Kim-Paik 1982, pp.126–7

44. Cho, op.cit., pp.34–41; Ahn 1979, pp.40–42

45. Kim-Paik 1992, pp.21–4; Yi Song-mi 1998, pp.61–8

46. Kim-Paik, op.cit., pp.24–5; Yi Song-mi 1996, pp.315–7 and pp.323–5

47. Ahn 1987, p.4

48. For different accounts of the development of Korean landscape painting in the Choson, see Seckel 1979; Whitfield (ed.) 1984; Ahn 1987, 1988 and 1994

49. Seckel 1979, pp.70–71. See Ahn 1974 for a discussion of the Guo Xi tradition and its effect on Korean landscape painting. Also Ahn 1987. The extant painting by An Kyon is now in Japan at Tenri University Library, near Kyoto

50. Seckel, loc.cit.

51. Ahn 1987, p.12; Kim-Paik 1983, p.373

52. See Ahn 1992, p.26

53. Seckel 1979, p.72; Ahn 1992, pp.28–9; Whitfield (ed.) 1984, p.186

54. Seckel, loc.cit.

55. Ahn, op.cit., pp.31–3

56. Kim-Paik 1982, pp.168–74

57. Kim-Paik 1983, pp.43–4

58. Yi Tong-ju 1973, p.64; Kim-Paik 1982, p.118

59. Huh 1992, pp.23–4

60. Kim-Lee 1986, pp.101–2; Ahn and Kim 1993, pp.323–4

61. For a description of the layout of Choson royal tombs, see Bacon 1957, pp.1–40; Adams 1974

62. Watt 1992, pp.308–10; Kawada and Takashi 1986

63. Garner 1979, pp.175–77; Lee Nan-hee 1993, p.97

64. Watt, op.cit., p.310

65. Choi Sun-u 1985, pp.123–4

66. Mino 1991, p.32

67. See Yun forthcoming, pp.2–8; Kang Kyong-suk 1989, pp.265–340; Chung Yang-mo

1991(a), pp.328–61; Kim Young-won 1992; Whitfield (ed.) 1984, pp.155–7

68. Kim Young-won 1992, p.211

69. Kim, op.cit., p.214; Yun forthcoming, p.11

70. See Kang Kyong-suk 1989, pp.356–63

71. Chung Yang-mo 1991(a), pp.121–76 and 1991(b), pp.46–9

72. Yun forthcoming, p.18

73. Itoh 1999, pp.299–300

74. Yun forthcoming, p.10; Chung Yang-mo 1991(b), pp.46–9

75. Chung, loc.cit.

76. See Cort 1984, pp.18–29; Yun 1991, pp.50–55; De Ment 1981, pp.20–7

Chapter Five

1. Moes 1983, p.20

2. Kikuchi 1994, pp.23–7

3. See National Museum of Korea, exhibition catalogue 1994.

4. Some of the British Museum's ethnographic collection was donated by the Japanese colonial administrator E.Ogita, after the Japan-British Exhibition of 1910 at the White City, London, at which there was a Korean Pavilion. See Portal 1995(a)

5. See Bishop 1897/1985; Sands n.d.; Hulbert 1906; Underwood 1904; Gale 1898; Savage-Landor 1895

6. Zo 1983

7. Kim Tae-gon 1988, p.11

8. Kim-Harvey 1979, pp.3–4

9. Kim-Harvey, loc.cit.

10. Paik-Kim 1998, p.10

11. Moes 1983, p.129; Zo 1983, pp.101–5

12. Moes, op.cit., p.25; Yi Song-mi 1996/7, pp.17–19

13. Walraven 1991/2, pp.21–44; Moes, op.cit., p.128

14. Adams 1989, pp.100–103

15. Moes, op.cit., p.13

16. Paik-Kim 1998, pp.12–13

17. Portal 1995(b); Kim Tae-gon 1988; Kendall 1985

18. Portal, op.cit.; Moes 1983; Kim tae-gon, op.cit.

19. Moes, op.cit., p.25

20. Yi Song-mi 1996/7, p.23

21. Moes, op.cit., pp.24–7; Paik-Kim 1998, pp.13–16

22. Black and Wagner 1998, pp.24–7

23. Black and Wagner, loc.cit.

24. See Moes, loc.cit.; Kim Ho-yon 1979

25. Moes 1983, pp.109–11; Paik-Kim 1998, pp.58–9

26. Moes, op.cit., pp.106–9

27. Paik-Kim, op.cit., p.62

28. Zo 1974

29. Kim-Paik, op.cit., p.60

30. Zo, op.cit., p.152

31. Kim Hong-nam 1997, p.65

32. Rhie 1988, pp.122–3

33. Moes 1983, p.113

34. Rhie, loc.cit.

35. See Adams 1989, p.101; Sayers 1988, p.28

36. Chan 1977, pp.57–8

37. Shim Yi-sok 1993

38. Yi Tu-hyon 1989, pp.15–16; 1995, pl.1

39. Aston 1924/1972, p.144

40. Chan 1977, p.59

41. Shim U-song 1994; Shim Yi-sok 1993; Yi Tu-hyon 1989

42. See Kim-Hogarth 1990; Kim Sung-kyun 1998; Shim Yi-sok 1993

43. Lee Kyong-hee 1993, pp.89–95

44. Bishop 1897/1985, p.85

45. Sayers 1987, pp.55–89

46. Sayers, op.cit., pp.36–47

47. Adams 1989, pp.121–2

48. See Huh 1988

49. Culin 1895/1991, pp.79–100

50. Culin, op.cit., pp.77–8

51. Culin, op.cit., pp.66–76

52. See Choe 1986, p.17

53. See Kim Kyong-ji 1986

54. Adams 1989, pp.134–5; Culin 1895/1991, pp.36–43

55. Yi Song-mi 1992, pp.12–15

56. Yonsei University Museum 1995

57. Adams 1989, p.110

Chapter Six

1. Howard (ed.) 1995

2. Lee Ki-baik 1984, pp.288–95

3. Lee Ki-baik, op.cit., pp.346–54

4. Lee Ki-baik, op.cit., pp.373–81

5. Much of the information in this section of this chapter has been taken from Kim Young-na 1994; O Kwang-su 1979; Lee Ku-yol 1984

6. Portal 1995, pp.47–50

7. Kim Young-na, op.cit., p.151

8. Lee Ku-yol, op.cit., pp.45–69

9. Hoffman 1988, pp.23–32

10. O Kwang-su 1986, pp.70–73

11. Yi Kyong-song 1965, pp.26–8

12. Anon 1987, pp.48–53

13. Kim Young-na 1994, p.194; O Kwang-su 1975(b), pp.56–60 and 1979, pp.257–9; Lee Ku-yol 1984, pp.195–206; Song 1991; Hong 1994

14. See Kim Choung-za 1994; *Kwon* 1990

15. See Nam 1969; Biggs 1992, pp.50–63

16. O Kwang-su 1975(a), pp.60–63

17. Yi Kyong-song 1987

18. Kim In-hwan 1994; Biggs, op.cit.

19. See Biggs 1992; O Kwang-su 1979, pp.229–34

20. See Cho Hung-youn 1987; You 1987

21. Most of the information on contemporary sculpture is taken from Kim Young-na 1994 and her unpublished work, as well as from Choi Tae-man 1995

22. See Choi Tae-man, op.cit., pp.120–23

23. Kim Young-na 1994, pp.199–200

24. See National Museum of Contemporary Art 1993(a)

25. You 1987, p.44

26. Yun 1993, p.81

27. Most of the information in this printmaking section is taken from Yun 1993; from the National Museum of Contemporary Art catalogue 1993(a); and from Kim, Yun, Suh and Ha 1991

28. See Leach 1940, for example

29. Van Gucht 1996, pp.34–5; Sayers 1987

30. For an overview of the development of contemporary ceramics in Korea, see National Museum of Contemporary Art 1994(a)

31. Most of these potters' works are illustrated and discussed in Van Gucht 1996

32. Cho Chung-hyon 1994, pp.146–9

33. See, for example, catalogue of the Korean Ceramic Art Association's Italian exhibition 1997, which features many young ceramic sculpture artists

34. Howard 1989 and 1994; Howard unpublished; Yim and Im 1996

35. See Yi Chong-sok 1974; Crafts Museum annual competition catalogues

36. See, for example, National Gallery of Victoria, Australia, 1998

References and Further Reading

The following references and suggestions for further reading are arranged by chapter, offering a range of material relevant to each chapter. For this reason, works in English, Korean and occasionally Japanese have been placed together.

Periodicals

KOREAN

Hanguk kogohakpo (Journal of the Society of Korean Archaeological Studies)

Hanguk sanggosa hakpo (Journal of the Ancient History Society)

Kogohak (Archaeology)

Kogohakchi (Journal of the Korean Institute of Archaeology and Art History)

Kogohakpo (Journal of the Korean Archaeological Society)

Misulsa yongu (Journal of the Art History Association)

Misul charyo (National Museum of Korea Journal)

WESTERN

Ars Orientalis, University of Michigan, USA

Artibus Asiae, Ascona (Switzerland)

Arts Asiatiques, Musée Guimet, Paris

Arts of Asia, Hong Kong

Culture Coréene, published by the Centre Culturel Coréen, Paris

Korea Journal, published by UNESCO, Seoul

Korea Observer, published by the Institute of Korean Studies, Seoul

Korean Culture, published by the Korean Cultural Center, Los Angeles, CA

The Korean Repository, Seoul 1892–8

Korean Studies, University of Hawaii, Center for Korean Studies, HI

Koreana, published by the Korea Foundation, Seoul

Oriental Art, London

Orientations, Hong Kong

Papers of the British Association of Korean Studies (BAKS)

Transactions of the Oriental Ceramic Society (TOCS), London

Transactions of the Korea Branch Royal Asiatic Society (TKBRAS), Seoul

General

Books on Korea, Korean art in general and in museum collections, and books quoted in the introduction.

Ahn, Hwi-joon, 1980. *Hanguk hoehwasa*. Seoul

Allen, Horace M., 1908, repr.1975. *Things Korean: A Collection of Sketches and Anecdotes Missionary and Diplomatic.* Seoul

Asian Art Museum of San Francisco, 1979. *Five Thousand Years of Korean Art*, exh. cat. San Francisco, CA

Aston, W.G., 1885. *A Journey from Soul to Songdo in Aug 1884.* Commercial Reports by HM Consul-General in Korea 1882–3. London

Bailey, Lisa, and Liz Wilkinson, 1997. 'Korean art in the Victoria and Albert Museum', *Korean Culture*, 18/1: 4–11

Barnes, Gina, 1996. 'Archaeology' in 'Korea', *Macmillan Dictionary of Art*, vol.18: 381–2. London

Bean, Susan, and Frederic Sharf, 1997. *The Korean Collection of the Peabody Essex Museum.* Salem, MA

Bennett, Terry, and Martin Uden, 1997. *Korea Caught in Time.* Reading, UK

Bishop, Isabella Bird, 1897, repr.1985. *Korea and Her Neighbours.* London

Bushell, Stephen, 1899, repr. 1981. *Oriental Ceramic Art.* London

Cambon, Pierre, 1994. 'Il y a 100 ans: la Corée au Musée Guimet', *Culture Coréene*, 38 (November 1994)

Carles, W.R., 1883. *Report by Mr Carles on a Journey in two of the Central Provinces of Corea in Oct 1883.* Commercial Reports by HM Consul-General in Korea. London

Choi, Sun-u, 1979. *Five Thousand Years of Korean Art.* Seoul

Chung, Hyung-min, 1988. 'Quiet assertion: Korean art at the Metropolitan Museum of Art, New York', *Orientations* (January 1988): 16–27

Cortazzi, Hugh, and Gordon Daniels, 1991. *Britain and Japan 1859–1991.* London

De Fraeye, Mark, and Frits Vos, 1995. *Korea, Scenic Beauty and Religious Landmarks.* Freiburg (Germany)

Eckhardt, Andreas, 1929. *Geschichte der Koreanische Kunst.* Leipzig

Figgess, John, 1985. 'Korean Art in the United Kingdom: Part 1, The Collections of London and Oxford', *Korean Culture*, 6/2 (June): 5–16

Gale, James, 1898, repr. 1973. *Korean Sketches.* London

Gompertz, G.St.G.M., 1963. *Korean Celadon and Other Wares of the Koryo Period.* London

Gompertz, G.St.G.M., 1980. 'The importance of Korean art', *Oriental Art*, 26/2 (Summer): 209–18

Gowland, William, 1895. 'The dolmens and other antiquities of Korea', *Journal of the Anthropological Institute*, 24 (1895)

Griffis, W.E., 1882. *Corea: The Hermit Nation.* New York

Hamel, Hendrik, trans. Br Jean-Paul Buys of Taizé, 1994. *Hamel's Journal and a Description of the Kingdom of Korea 1653–1666.* Seoul

Han, Byong-sam *et al.*, 1984. *Chonichi Koryu Nisennen* (Two Thousand Years of Korean-Japanese Exchange), exh. cat. Seoul

Hanguk misul chonjip (Complete fine arts of Korea), 1978. 15 vols. Seoul

Hanguk ui mi (Arts of Korea), 1984. 24 vols. Seoul

Harris, Victor, 1996. 'The Gowland Collection in the British Museum'. *Apollo*, 143/409 (March): 3–8

Henderson, Gregory, 1983. 'Korean art in Western collections: 6 and 7, The collection of the Gregory Hendersons', *Korean Culture*, 4/3: 5–15 and 4/4: 28–37

Ho-Am Museum, 1996. *Masterpieces of the Ho-Am Art Museum*. Seoul.

Hoare, J.E., 1997. *Korea*, World Biographical Series 204. Oxford

Hornby, Joan, 1988. 'The Korean collection at the National Museum of Denmark', *Korean Culture*, 9/4: 14–22

Hulbert, Homer B., 1906. *The Passing of Korea*. New York

Jungmann, Burglind, 1995. 'Confusing traditions: Elements of the Korean An Kyon school in early Japanese Nanga landscsape painting', *Artibus Asiae*, 55: 303–17

Keith, Elizabeth, and Elspet Robertson-Scott, 1946. *Old Korea: the Land of the Morning Calm*. London

Kikuchi, Yuko, 1994. 'Yanagi Soetsu and Korean crafts within the Mingei Movement', BAKS Papers, 5: 23–38

Kim, Che-won and Kim Won-yong, 1966. *The Arts of Korea*. London

Kim, Che-won, and Kim-Lee Lena, 1974. *Art of Korea*. Tokyo, New York and San Francisco

Kim, Hong-nam 1985. 'Korean art in Western collections:10, The Metropolitan Museum of Art', *Korean Culture*, 6/1: 4–16

Kim, Won-yong, 1977. 'Some aspects of the interrelation of Korean, Chinese and Japanese art', *Korea Journal* (November), 17: 11

Kim, Won-yong, 1979. 'Philosophies and styles in Korean art – a prelude to the study of Korean art', *Korea Journal*, 19: 4 (April)

Kim, Won-yong, 1986. *Art and Archaeology of Ancient Korea*. Seoul

Kim, Won-yong, and Ahn Hwi-joon, 1993. *Hanguk misulsa* (History of Korean art). Seoul

Kim-Paik, Kumja, 1991. 'The new Korean gallery at the Asian Art Museum of San Francisco', *Korean Culture*, 12/4: 18–25, 40–41

Kim-Renaud, Young-key, 1992. *King Sejong the Great, the Light of 15th Century Korea*. Washington, DC

Korea Foundation, 1989–95. *Korean Relics in the United States, Western Europe and Japan*, 5 vols. Seoul

Korea Foundation, 1994–6. *Korean Cultural Heritage,* vol. 1: *Fine Arts,* vol. 2: *Thought and Religion.* Seoul

Lautensach, Hermann, 1945. *Korea: A Geography Based on the Author's Travels and Literature*. Trans. and rev. by K. and E. Dege, 1988. Berlin and Heidelberg

Leach, Bernard, 1978. *Beyond East and West: Memoirs, Portraits and Essays.* London

Ledyard, Gari, 1971. *The Dutch Come to Korea*. Seoul

Lee, Junghee, 1998. *Azaleas and Golden Bells: Korean Art in the Collection of the Portland Art Museum and in Portland Private Collections.* Portland, OR

Lee, Peter H. (ed.), 1993–6. *Sourcebook of Korean Civilization*, 2 vols. New York

Lee-Kalisch, Jeonghee, and Roger Goepper, 1999. *Korea: Die Alten Königreiche*, exh.cat., Kultur Stiftung Ruhr, Essen

Macmillan Dictionary of Art, 1996. 'Korea', vol. 18: 245–385

McCune, Evelyn, 1962. *The Arts of Korea.* Vermont and Tokyo

McKillop, Beth, 1992. *Korean Art and Design*. Victoria and Albert Museum. London

Miles, Richard, 1991. *Elizabeth Keith: The Printed Works*. Pacific Asia Museum, Pasadena, CA

Moes, Robert J., 1987. *Korean Art from the Brooklyn Museum Collection*. New York

Mowry, Robert, 1982. 'Korean Art in Western Collections: The Asia Society', *Korean Culture*, 3/1: 3–9

Nelson, Sarah, 1993. *The Archaeology of Korea*. Cambridge, UK

Pak, Youngsook, 1984. *Koreanische Tage: Korean Art 5th–19th Centuries from European Museums and Collections.* Museum Altes Rathaus, Ingelheim am Rhein

Pak, Youngsook, 1989. 'Western research on Korean art history' in *Cahiers d'Etudes Coréenes*, 5: 219–29. Paris

Pak, Youngsook, 1998(a). 'The Korean collection in the Metropolitan Museum of Art' in Judith Smith (ed.), *Arts of Korea*, pp.402–50. New York

Pak, Youngsook, 1998(b). 'The art of Korea at the Metropolitan Museum of Art', *Orientations* (September): 50–60

Portal, Jane, 1992. 'The Korean Collection of Dr A.G. Poulsen-Hansen', *Orientations* (December): 51–6

Portal, Jane, 1995. 'The origins of the British Museum's Korean Collection' in TKBRAS, 70: 37–52

Portal, Jane, 1995–6. 'Korean ceramics in the British Museum: A century of collecting' in TOCS, 60: 47–59

Portal, Jane, 1997. 'Arts of Korea in the British Museum', *Arts of Asia*, 27/4: 96–105

Portal, Jane, 1998. 'Koryo dynasty art in the British Museum', *Orientations* (September 1998): 69–75

Portal, Jane, 1999. 'A Korean porcelain jar from the Bernard Leach Collection', *Apollo* (November 1999)

Pratt, Keith, and Richard Rutt, with additional material by James Hoare, 1999. *Korea: A Historical and Cultural Dictionary*. Richmond, Surrey, UK

Sands, William Franklin, n.d., repr. 1975, 1990. *Undiplomatic Memories: The Far East 1896–1904*. London

Savage-Landor, A.H., 1895. *Corea or Cho-sen: The Land of the Morning Calm*. London

Sayers, Robert, 1987. 'The Korean onggi potter', *Smithsonian Folklife Studies*, 5. Washington, DC

Seckel, Dietrich, 1977. 'Some characteristics of Korean art', *Oriental Art*, 23/1: 52–61

Smith, Judith (ed.), 1998. *Arts of Korea*, exh. cat. Metropolitan Museum of Art, New York

Smith, Stanley, 1917. 'Korean arts and crafts', *The Korea Magazine*: 485–563

Steinberg, David I., 1968. 'The National Museum of the Republic of Korea' in TKBRAS, 44

Underwood, Lilias, 1904, repub. 1977. *Fifteen Years Among the Top-knots*. New York

Van Alphen, J., 1993. *Korea Keramiek*. Antwerp and Leiden

Whitfield, Roderick (ed.), 1984. *Treasures from Korea*, exh. cat., British Museum. London

Whitfield, Roderick, and Pak Youngsook (eds), 1986. *Korean Art Treasures*. Seoul

Wylie, Hugh, and Koh Wonyoung, 1999. *Korea: A Timeless Beauty*, exh. cat. Royal Ontario Museum, Ontario

Yokohama Museum of Art, 1996. *Eyes Toward Asia*, exh. cat. Yokohama

Yonemura, Ann, 1983. 'Korean art in the Freer Gallery', *Korean Culture*, 4/2: 5–15

CHAPTER 1

PREHISTORIC PERIOD

An, Deog-im, 1993. 'The excavation of Songgungni shell middens on Anmyon Island, Korea' in BAKS Papers, 4: 177–196

Andersson, J.G., 1934. *Children of the Yellow Earth: Studies in Prehistoric China*. London

Arimitsu, K., 1966. 'An objective view of Japanese archaeological works in Korea' in TKBRAS, 42: 75–9

Bae, Ki-dong, 1989. 'The significance of the Chongokni stone industry in the tradition of the Palaeolithic culture in East Asia'. Ph.D. dissertation, University of California, Berkeley, CA

Bae, Ki-dong, 1997. 'Chongok-ri Palaeolithic site', *Koreana*, 11/1

Barnes, Gina L., 1990. *Hoabinhian, Jomon, Yayoi, Early Korean States*. Oxford

Barnes, Gina L., 1992. 'The development of stoneware technology in Southern Korea' in C. Melvin Aikens and Song Nai Rhee (eds), *Pacific North-East Asia in Prehistory*, pp.197–206. Washington, DC

Barnes, Gina L., 1993. *China, Korea and Japan: The Rise of Civilization in East Asia*. London

Choi, Chong-gyu, 1982. 'Aperçu sur les fouilles faites à Choyang-dong et leur signification', *Revue de Corée*, 14/2: 40–62

Choi, Mong-lyong, 1984. 'Bronze Age in Korea', *Korea Journal*, 24/9

Choi, Mong-lyong *et al.*, 1992. *Han'guk sonsa kogohaksa (yongu hyonhyang gwa chonmang)*. Seoul

Choi, Sung-rak, 1996. 'The Iron Age culture in Southern Korea and its Chinese connection', *Korea Journal*, 36/4: 28–38

Choo, Youn-sik, 1994. 'Objects, sinkers, nets, behavior and subsistence' in BAKS Papers, 5: 131–86

Denes, Laurence, 1995. 'Les sépultures en grandes jarres du bassin du Yongsan-gang', *Arts Asiatiques* 50 (1995): 85–93

Falkenhausen, Lothar von, 1990. 'The State of Yan and its northeastern connections'. Paper delivered at Society for American Archaeology Meetings, Las Vegas, NV

Han, Byong-sam, 1974. 'Neolithic culture of Korea', *Korea Journal*, 14/4: 12–17

Han, Byong-sam, 1977. 'Important prehistoric sites', *Korea Journal*, 17/4: 14–17

Han, Byong-sam (ed.), 1984. *Han'guk kogohak jido* (Archaeological Maps of Korea). Seoul

Han, Young-hee, 1997. 'Amsa-dong prehistoric dwelling site', *Koreana*, 11/1

Han'guk Munhwachae Poho Chaedan, 1993. *Munhwa yuchok palgul tolok*. Seoul

Han'guk Yoksa Minsok Hakhwae, 1997. *Han'guk ui amgakhwa*. Seoul

Im, Hyo-jae, 1984. 'Korean Neolithic chronology: a tentative model', *Korea Journal*, 24/9: 11–17

Im, Hyo-jae, 1992. *Han'guk kodae munhwa ui hurum*. Seoul

Im, Hyo-jae, 1995. 'The new archaeological data concerned with the cultural relationship between Korea and Japan in the Neolithic Age', *Korea Journal*, 35/3: 31–39

Im, Hyo-jae, 1996. 'The Korean Neolithic Age and its cultural relationship to Northeast China', *Korea Journal*, 36/4: 5–16

Kang, Bong-won, 1993. 'Social structure in a Megalithic tomb society in Korea' in BAKS Papers, 4: 197–215

Kim, Jeong-hak, 1963. 'The origin of the Korean nation', *Korea Journal*, 3/7: 29–31

Kim, Jeong-hak, 1978, trans. Richard and Kazue Pearson. *The Prehistory of Korea*. Honolulu, HI

Kim, Jung-bae, 1974. 'Bronze Age culture in Korea', *Korea Journal*, 14/4: 18–24

Kim, Won-yong, 1963. 'Bronze mirrors from Shih-erh t'ai ying-tzu, Liaoning', *Artibus Asiae*, 26/3–4: 207–214

Kim, Won-yong, 1977. 'Prehistoric art', *Korea Journal*, 17/4: 7–13

Kim, Won-yong, 1982. 'Discoveries of rice in prehistoric sites in Korea', *Journal of Asian Studies*, 41/3: 513–8

Kim, Won-yong, 1986. *Art and Archaeology of Ancient Korea*. Seoul

Kim, Won-yong and Ahn Hwi-joon, 1993. *Han'guk misulsa*. Seoul

Lee, Chung-kyu, 1996. 'The bronze dagger culture of Liaoning Province and the Korean peninsula', *Korea Journal*, 36/4: 17–27

Lee, Ki-baik (trans. Edward E. Wagner with Edward J. Shultz), 1984. *A New History of Korea*. Cambridge, MA

Lee, Yung-jo: *see* Yi, Yung-jo

Lim, Byong-tae, 1996. *Han'guk chongtonggi munhwa ui yongu*. Seoul

Michaelson, Carol, 1992. 'Mass production and the development of the lacquer industry during the Han dynasty', *Orientations* (November): 60–65

National Museum of Korea, 1992. *Han'guk ui chongtonggi munhwa* (The bronze culture in Korea), exh. cat. Seoul

National Museum of Korea, 1993. *Han'guk ui son/wonsa togi* (Pre- and proto-historic pottery of Korea), exh. cat. Seoul

Nelson, Sarah M., 1990. 'The Neolithic of northeastern China and Korea', *Antiquity*, 64: 234–48

Nelson, Sarah M., 1992. 'Mumun'togi and megalithic monuments' in BAKS Papers, 3: 183–94

Nelson, Sarah M., 1993. *The Archaeology of Korea.* Cambridge, UK

Nelson, Sarah M., 1995. *The Archaeology of North-east China beyond the Great Wall.* London and New York

Nelson, Sarah M., 1996. 'Protohistoric burial patterns in Korea', *Korea Journal*, 36/2: 26–32

Okazaki, Takashi, 1993. 'Japan and the continent' in Delmer M. Brown (ed.), *The Cambridge History of Japan*, vol. 1: *Ancient Japan*, pp.268–316. Cambridge, UK

Paek, Hong-ki, 1994. *Tongbuk'a pyongji togi ui yon'gu.* Seoul

Pak, Yang-jin, 1996. 'Archaeological evidence of Puyo society in Northeast China', *Korea Journal*, 36/4: 39–50

Pearson, Richard, 1982. 'The archaeological background to Korean prehistoric art', *Korean Culture*, 3/4: 18–29

Riotto, Maurizio, 1995. 'Jar-burials in Korea and their possible social implications', *Korea Journal*, 35/3: 40–53

Sasse, Werner, 1996. 'Prehistoric rock art in Korea: Pangudae', *Korea Journal*, 36/2: 75–91

Shin, Kwang-seop, 1997. 'Songguk-ri prehistoric site', *Koreana*, 11/1

Sohn, Pow-key, 1970. 'Prehistoric culture', *Korea Journal*, 10/10: 4–24

Sohn, Pow-key, 1974. 'Palaeolithic culture of Korea', *Korea Journal*, 14/4: 4–11

Taylor, Sarah, 1989. 'The introduction and development of iron production in Korea: a survey', *World Archaeology*, 20/3: 422–33

Tite, M., G. Barnes, and C. Doherty, 1992. 'Stoneware identification among protohistoric potteries of South Korea' in Proceedings of the Shanghai Conference on Science and Technology of Ancient Ceramics 2: 64–9. SRSSTAC, Shanghai

Umehara, Sueji, 1954–6. 'Two remarkable Lo-lang tombs of wooden construction excavated in Pyongyang, Korea' in Archives of the Chinese Art Society of America 8: 10–21, 10: 18–29

Watson, William, 1971. *Cultural Frontiers in Ancient East Asia.* Edinburgh

Yi, Yung-jo, 1978. 'A new interpretation of the prehistoric and historic chronology of Korean archaeology', *Korea Journal*, 18/6: 33–8

Yi, Yung-jo, 1982. 'Palaeolithic and mesolithic cultures in Korea: an overview', *Korea Journal*, 22/3: 39–46

Yi, Yung-jo, 1983. 'Progress report on the Palaeolithic culture of Turubong No.2 cave at Ch'ongwon', *Korea Journal*, 23/8: 22–33

Yi, Yung-jo, 1994. 'Micro-blade core in Korea with special reference to the tool-making techniques of Suyanggae'. Institute of Prehistory, Chungbuk National University, Korea

Yi, Yung-jo, 1996. 'Suyanggae yuchok ui hugi kusokki sidae munhwa' in papers from the First International Symposium on Suyanggae and her Neighbours, pp.1–24. Chungbuk University Museum, Korea

Yi, Yung-jo, with Yun Yong-hyun, 1992. 'Tanged points and micro-blade cores from Suyanggae site, Korea'. Paper for International Symposium on Micro-blade Industry in Northern Eurasia and Northern North America, Sapporo University, Japan

Yun, Mu-byong, 1991. *Han'guk chongtonggi munhwa yon'gu.* Seoul

CHAPTER 2

THREE KINGDOMS AND UNIFIED SILLA PERIOD

Adams, Edward, 1979. *Kyongju Guide: Cultural Spirit of Silla in Korea.* Seoul

Adams, Edward, 1986. *Korea's Pottery Heritage I.* Seoul

Asahi Shimbun, 1992. *Kaya: Ancient Kingdom of Korea*, exh. cat., Tokyo National Museum. Tokyo

Aston, W.G., 1924, repr. 1972. *Nihongi: Chronicles of Japan from the Earliest Times to AD 697.* Tokyo

Bailey, Lisa K., 1994. 'Crowning glory: headdresses of the Three Kingdoms period' in BAKS Papers, 5: 83–103

Barnes, Gina L., 1992. 'The development of stoneware technology in Southern Korea' in C. Melvin Aikens and Song Nai Rhee (eds), *Pacific North-East Asia in Prehistory*, pp.197–206. Washington, DC

Barnes, Gina L., 1993. *China, Korea and Japan: The Rise of Civilization in East Asia.* London

Barnes, Gina L., 1994. 'Discoveries of iron armour on the Korean peninsula' in BAKS Papers, 5: 105–130

Best, Jonathan W., 1982. 'Diplomatic and cultural contacts between Paekche and China', *Harvard Journal of Asiatic Studies*, 42/2: 443–501

Best, Jonathan W., 1992. 'Imagery, iconography and belief in early Korean Buddhism', *Korean Culture*, 13/3 (Fall): 23–34

Best, Jonathan W., 1996. 'Redating the earliest Silla-related entries in the "Paekche annals" of the Samguk Sagi', *Hanguk sanggosa hakpo*, 21: 147–71

Best, Jonathan W., 1998. 'Profile of the Korean past' in Judith Smith (ed.), *Arts of Korea.* pp.14–38. New York

Brown, Delmer M. (ed.), 1993. The *Cambridge History of Japan*, vol. 1: *Ancient Japan.* Cambridge, UK

Bush, Susan, 1989. 'Some parallels between Chinese and Korean ornamental motifs in the late 5th and early 6th centuries', *Archives of Asian Art*, 34: 60–78

Chi, Kon-gil, 1995. *Kyongju Namsan*, cat., Kyongju National Museum, Kyongju

Chin, Hong-sop, 1984. *Hanguk ui pulsang.* Seoul

Cho, Yong-jong, 1994. 'Chungguk Posan hyangroe kwanhan kocha', *Misul charyo*, 53, 54

Choi, Che-sok, 1996. *Chongch'angwon (Shoso-in) sojangpum gwa Tong'il Silla.* Seoul

Chon, Kwan-u, 1974. 'A new interpretation of the problems of Mimana', *Korea Journal*, 14/2: 9–23 and 14/4: 31–43

Covell, Jon Carter, and Alan Covell, 1984. *Korean Impact on Japanese Culture.* Seoul and Elizabeth, NJ

Cunningham, Michael R., 1995. 'Notes on early Japanese and Korean ceramics', *Orientations* (September): 91–6

Gowland, W., 1895. 'Notes on the dolmens and other antiquities of Korea', *Journal of the Anthropological Institute*, 24: 316–31

Grayson, James H., 1977. 'Mimana: a problem in Korean historiography', *Korea Journal*, 17/8: 65–6

Ha, Tae-hung, and Grafton K. Mintz (trans.) 1972. *Samguk Yusa: Legends and History of the Three Kingdoms of Ancient Korea*. Seoul

Han, Byong-sam, 1983. *Hanguk ui mi: Togi*. Seoul

Han, Byong-sam, 1991. *The Mysterious Ancient Kingdom: Kaya*. exh. cat., National Museum of Korea, Seoul

Harris, Victor, 1996. 'The Gowland Collection in the British Museum: archaeology in nineteenth century Japan', *Apollo*, 143/409: 3–8

Hayashi, Ryoichi (trans. Robert Ricketts), 1975. *The Silk Road and the Shoso-in*. New York and Tokyo

Henderson, Gregory, 1969. *Korean Ceramics: An Art's Variety*. Division of Art Gallery, Ohio State University

Hong, Wontack, 1994. *Paekche of Korea and the Origin of Yamato Japan*. Seoul

Hong, Yun-gi, 1996. *Hanguk'in yi mandun Ilbon kukbo*. Seoul

Hwang, Su-young, 1983. *Hanguk ui mi: Pulsang*. Seoul

Jeon, Sang-woon, 1974. *'Science and Technology' in Korea: Traditional Instruments and Techniques*. Cambridge, MA

Kang Duk-hee, 1983. 'Gold crowns of Shibarghan in Afghanistan and of the Three Kingdoms period of Korea', *Korea Journal*, 26: 35–8

Kang, Woo-bang, 1991. *The Art of Sarira Reliquary*, exh. cat., National Museum of Korea

Kang, Woo-bang, 1995. *Hanguk pulgyo chogak ui hurum*. Seoul

Kidder, J.E. Jr, 1985. 'The archaeology of the early horse-riders in Japan' in *Transactions of the Asiatic Society of Japan*, 3rd series/20: 89–123

Kim, Dal-su, 1995. *Ilbon sok ui Hanguk munhwa yuchokul chajaso*. Seoul

Kim, Hong-nam, 1991. 'China's earliest datable white stonewares from the tomb of King Muryong (d.AD523)', *Oriental Art*, 37/1 (Spring)

Kim, Won-yong, 1966, repr. 1986. 'Wall-paintings of Koguryo tombs', *Korea Journal*, 6/4: 21–3

Kim, Won-yong, 1968, repr. 1986. 'Clay figurines of old Silla', *Korea Journal* 8/4

Kim, Won-yong, 1974. 'On the possible Silla envoy depicted on the wall painting of the tomb of Li Hsien, Tang dynasty', *Kogo misul*, 123/4: 17–25

Kim, Won-yong, 1985(a). *Silla togi*. Seoul

Kim, Won-yong, 1985(b), repr. 1986. 'A cylindrical pottery stand from Seoul: a possible relationship with Japanese Ento-Haniwa' in Papers in Commemoration of the 77th birthday of Professor T. Mikami. Tokyo

Kim, Won-yong, 1986. *Art and Archaeology of Ancient Korea*. Seoul

Kim, Won-yong, 1991. 'Ancient Korean envoys on a wall-painting in Samarkand' in *Korean Culture and the Silk Roads*, pp.183–5. UNESCO, Seoul

Kim, Won-yong, and Richard Pearson, 1977, repr. 1986. 'Three royal tombs: new discoveries in Korean archaeology', *Archaeology*, 30/5: 302–13

Kim, Won-yong, Okazaki Takashi, and Han Byong-sam, 1979. *Sekai toji zenshu* (Catalogue of the world's ceramics), 2nd edn, vol. 17: *Korean Prehistoric and Ancient Periods*. Tokyo

Kim, Won-yong, and Ahn Hwi-joon, 1993. *Hanguk misulsa*. Seoul

Kim-Lee, Lena, 1986. 'Buddhist sculpture' in Roderick Whitfield and Pak Youngsook (eds), *Korean Art Treasures*. Seoul

Kim-Lee, Lena, 1993. *Hanguk kodae pulgyo chogaksa yongu*. Seoul

Kim-Lee, Lena, 1998. 'Tradition and transformation in Korean Buddhist sculpture' in Judith Smith (ed.), *Arts of Korea*, pp.250–93. New York

Kim-Paik, Kumja, 1994. 'Bold and whimsical forms: Korean ceramics of the Three Kingdoms period in the collection of the Asian Art Museum of San Francisco', *Orientations* (February 1994)

Kirkland, R.J., 1981. 'The "Horseriders" in Korea: a critical evaluation of a historical theory', *Korean Studies* 5: 109–28

Kwon, Young-pil, 1991. 'Ancient Korean art and Central Asia: Non Buddhist art prior to the tenth century', *Korea Journal* (Summer 1991): 5–20

Kwon, Young-pil, 1997. *Silku Rodu misul: Chung-ang Asia eso Han'guk kkaji* (The Art of Silkroad: From Central Asia to Korea), with English summary. Seoul

Ledyard, Gari, 1975. 'Galloping along with the horse-riders: looking for the founders of Japan', *Journal of Japanese Studies* (Spring 1975)

Lee, Hee-soo, 1991. 'Early Korea-Arabic maritime relations based on Muslim sources', *Korea Journal* (Summer 1991): 21–33

Lee, In-sook, 1993(a). *Hanguk ui kodae yuri*. Seoul

Lee, In-sook, 1993(b). 'The Silk Road and ancient Korean glass', *Korean Culture*, 14/4: 4–13

Lee, In-sook, 1994. 'Ancient glass trade in Korea' in BAKS Papers, 5: 65–82

Lee, Junghee, 1992. 'The evolution of Koguryo tomb murals', *Korean Culture*, 13/2: 12–17 and 40–44

Lee, Ki-baik (trans. Edward E. Wagner with Edward J. Shultz), 1984. *A New History of Korea*. Cambridge, MA

Lee, Nan-young, 1989. *Silla ui toyong*, Kyongju National Museum

Lee, Nan-young, 1991. *Kyongju wa Silku Rodu*, Kyongu National Museum

Lee, Peter H. (ed.), 1993–6. *Sourcebook of Korean Civilization*, 2 vols. New York

Lu Sixian and Chan Tangdong, 1984. 'Gold ornaments of the northern ancient nomadic tribe excavated from Da Mao Qi, Inner Mongolia', *Wenwu*, 1984/1

McCallum, Donald F., 1982. 'Korean influence on early Japanese Buddhist sculpture', *Korean Culture*, 3/1: 22–9

McCallum, Donald F., 1995. 'The Buddhist triad in Three Kingdoms sculpture', *Korean Culture*, 16/4

Mason, Penelope, 1993. *A History of Japanese Art*. New York

Munhwajae kwalliguk, 1974(a). *Muryong Wangnung*. Seoul

Munhwajae kwalliguk, 1974(b). *Ch'onma-ch'ong palgul chosa pogoso*. Seoul

Munhwajae kwalliguk, 1975/6. *Kwangju Hwangnam-dong 98 ho kobun palgul yak pogo*. Seoul

National Museum of Korea, 1980. *Anap-chi Pond*, special exhibition of artefacts excavated from Anap-chi Pond. Seoul

National Museum of Korea, 1994. *Pongnae-san incense burner*, special exhibition. Seoul

Nelson, Sarah M., 1991. 'The statuses of women in Ko-Silla: evidence from archaeology and historic documents', *Korea Journal*, 31/2: 101–7

Nelson, Sarah M., 1993. *The Archaeology of Korea*. Cambridge, UK

Okazaki, Takashi 1993. 'Japan and the continent' in Delmer M. Brown (ed.), *The Cambridge History of Japan*, vol. 1: *Ancient Japan*, pp.268–316. Cambridge, UK

Pak, Youngsook, 1984. 'Internationalism in Korean art', *Orientations*, 15/1

Pak, Youngsook, 1988. 'The origins of Silla metalwork', *Orientations* (September 1988): 44–53

Reischauer, Edwin O., 1955. *Ennin's Travels in T'ang China*. New York

Rhie, Marilyn M., 1984. 'The Korean Buddhist image: embodiment of the transcendent', *Korean Culture*, 5/1

Shin, Yong-hoon, 1986. 'Architecture' in Roderick Whitfield and Pak Youngsook (eds), *Korean Art Treasures*. Seoul

Swart, Paula, 1991. 'Korean reliquaries: votive objects of Buddhism', *Korean Culture*, 12/4

Till, Barry, 1990. 'Korean burial figurines: a mortuary custom adopted from China', *Korean Culture*, 11/3

Tite, M.S., Gina L. Barnes, and C. Doherty, 1992. 'Stoneware identification among protohistoric potteries of South Korea' in Proceedings of the Shanghai Conference on Science and Technology of Ancient Ceramics 2: 64–9. SRSSTAC, Shanghai

Tokyo National Museum, 1993. *Korean and Other Asian Ceramics Excavated in Japan*, exh. cat.

Umehara, Sueji, 1952. 'Newly discovered tombs with wall-paintings of the Kao-kou-li dynasty', Archives of the Chinese Art Society of America, 6: 8–9

Whitfield, Roderick (ed.) 1984. *Treasures from Korea*, exh. cat., British Museum. London

CHAPTER 3

KORYO PERIOD

Ahn, Hwi-joon, 1986. 'Korean painting: a brief history' in Roderick Whitfield and Pak Youngsook (eds), *Korean Art Treasures*, pp.31–90. Seoul

Ahn, Hwi-joon, 1993. 'Koryo pulhwa ui hwihwasa uiui' in *Koryo Yongwonhan mi* (Exhibition of Koryo Buddhist painting), Seoul

Ahn, Hwi-joon, 1994. 'Korean painting: influences and traditions' in *Korean Cultural Heritage*, vol. 1: *Fine Arts*. Seoul

Chin, Hong-sop, 1995. *Hanguk ui sok misul*. Seoul

Choi, Eung-chon, 1988. 'Korean Buddhist metal art', *Orientations* (September 1988): 34–43

Choi, Sun-u, 1983. 'Koryo ceramic art and woodwork', *Korea Journal*, 4/10: 4–13

Choi, Sun-u, *et al.* 1978. *Sekai toji zenshu* (Catalogue of the world's ceramics), 2nd edn, vol. 18: *Koryo Dynasty*. Tokyo

Choi-Bae, Soon-taek, 1984. *Seladon-Keramik der Koryo-Dynastie 918–1392*. Cologne

Chung, Myong-ho, 1994. *Hanguk sokteng yangsik*. Seoul

Chung, Yang-mo, 1986. 'Korean pottery and porcelain' in Roderick Whitfield and Pak Youngsook (eds), *Korean Art Treasures*, pp.263–324. Seoul

Chung, Yang-mo, 1991. *Hanguk ui tojagi*. Seoul

Chung, Young-ho, 1994. 'Pagodas: symbols of the Buddha' in *Korean Cultural Heritage*, vol. 1: *Fine Arts*, pp.222–9. Seoul

Covell, Jon Carter, 1978. 'Korea's "unknown legacy" from the Koryo period', *Korea Journal*, 18/12

Covell, Jon Carter, 1979. 'A "vendetta" over a Koryo period "Willow Kuanyin"', *Korea Journal*, 19/1

Deuchler, Martina, 1992. *The Confucian Transformation of Korea*. Cambridge, MA

Deuchler, Martina, forthcoming. 'Connoisseurs and artisans: a social view of Korean culture' in *Catalogue of the Gompertz Collection of Korean Ceramics in the Fitzwilliam Museum*. Cambridge, UK

Feng, Xianming, 1986. 'Koryo celadons excavated in China', *Orientations* (May 1986): 49–53

Figgess, John, 1977. 'Mother of pearl inlaid lacquer of the Koryo dynasty', *Oriental Art*, 23 (Spring 1977): 87–95

Fontein, Jan, 1956. 'Notes on Korean lacquer' in *Bulletin van vereeniging van vrienden der Aziatische Kunst*, 3rd series, 6 (September)

Garner, Harry, 1979. *Chinese Lacquer*. London

Gompertz, G.St.G. M., 1960–2. 'Hsu Ching's visit to Korea in 1123' in TOCS. London

Gompertz, G.St.G.M., 1963. *Korean Celadon and Other Wares of the Koryo Period*. London

Gompertz, G.St.G.M., 1979. 'Korean inlaid lacquer of the Koryo period' in TOCS, pp.1–31. London

Gray, Basil, 1967–8. 'Korean inlaid lacquer of the thirteenth century', *British Museum Quarterly*, 32: 132–7

Grayson, James, 1989. *Korea: A Religious History*. Oxford

Griffing, Robert P., 1968. *The Art of the Korean Potter*. New York

Griffing, Robert P., 1977. 'Some Koryo celadons in the collection of the Honolulu Academy of Arts', *Oriental Art*, 23: 68–79

Hangst, Kurt, 1984. 'Results of mineralogical examination of Koryo period celadon shards' in Choi-Bae Soon-taek, *Seladon-Keramik der Koryo-Dynastie 918–1392*. Cologne

Hwang, Soo-young, 1964. 'Koryo metalwork', *Korea Journal*, 4/10: 18–20

Itoh, Ikutaro, and Mino, Yutaka, 1991. *The Radiance of Jade and the Clarity of Water: Korean Ceramics from the Ataka Collection*, exh. cat. New York

Itoh, Ikutaro, 1992. 'Koreanisation in Koryo celadon', *Orientations* (December 1992): 46–50

Jeon, Sang-woon, 1974. '*Science and Technology' in Korea: Traditional Instruments and Techniques*. Cambridge, MA

Kang, Kyong-suk, 1989. *Hanguk tojasa*. Seoul

Kessler, Adam T., 1993. *Empires Beyond the Great Wall: The Heritage of Genghis Khan*. Natural History Museum, Los Angeles

Kim, Jae-yeol, 1994. 'Jade green: Koryo celadon' in *Korean Cultural Heritage*, vol. 1: *Fine Arts*. Seoul

Kim, Won-yong, 1986. *Art and Archaeology of Ancient Korea*. Seoul

Kim, Won-yong, and Ahn, Hwi-oon, 1993. *Hanguk misulsa*. Seoul

Kim-Lee, Lena, 1986. 'Buddhist sculpture' in Roderick Whitfield and Pak Youngsook (eds), *Korean Art Treasures*. Seoul

Kim-Lee, Lena, 1989. *Hanguk kodae pulgyo chogaksa yongu*. Seoul

Koh Choo, Carolyn, 1999. 'A comparative scientific study of the earliest kiln sites of Koryo celadon', *Archaeometry*, 41: 51–69

Koyama, Fujio, 1978. *Sekai toji zenshu* (Catalogue of the world's ceramics), 2nd edn, vol. 13: *Koryo Dynasty*. Tokyo

Lam, Timothy See-yiu, 1990. *Tang Ceramic: Changsha Kilns*. Hong Kong

Lee, Ki-baik (trans. Edward W. Wagner with Edward J. Shultz, 1984. *A New History of Korea*. Cambridge, MA

Lee, Nan-young, 1983. *Hanguk ui tonggyong*. Seoul

Lee, Nan-young, 1992. *Hanguk kodae kumsok kongye yongu*. Seoul

Lee, Nan-young, 1995. 'Koryo sidae ui kumsok kongye' in *Tae Koryo kukbo chon*, pp.268–76. Seoul

Lee, Yu-kuan, 1972. *Oriental Lacquer Art*. New York and Tokyo

McKillop, Beth, 1992. *Korean Art and Design*, Victoria and Albert Museum. London

Maeng, In-jae, 1964. 'Koryo paintings' *Korea Journal*, 4/10: 14–17

Masako, Shono, 1982. 'The Koryo sutra box with scroll ornament inlaid in mother of pearl' in *Lacquer-work in Asia and Beyond*, Colloquies on Art and Archaeology in Asia, 11. London

Medley, Margaret, 1975. *Korean and Chinese Ceramics*. Fitzwilliam Museum, Cambridge, UK

Medley, Margaret, 1977. 'Korea, China and Liao in Koryo ceramics', *Oriental Art*, 23: 80–6

Mowry, Robert D., 1986. 'Koryo celadons', *Orientations* (May 1986): 24–39

Mun, Myong-dae, 1991. *Koryo pulhwa*. Seoul

Mun, Myong-dae, 1994. 'Koryo Buddhist painting: a mirror of religious values and aristocratic tastes' in *Korean Cultural Heritage*, vol. 1: *Fine Arts*. Seoul

Nara National Museum, 1996. *Buddhist Images of East Asia*, exh. cat.

National Folklore Museum, 1989. *Hanguk chilgi yichonnyon* (2000 years of Korean lacquer), exh. cat. Seoul

Nomori, Ken, 1994. *Korai toji no kenkyu*. Tokyo

Okada, Jo, 1978. *Toyo shitsugei-shi no kenkyu*. Tokyo

Pak, Youngsook, 1977. 'Ksitigarbha as supreme lord of the underworld', *Oriental Art*, 23/1

Pak, Youngsook, 1982. 'Object of the month: illuminated manuscript of the Amitabha Sutra', *Orientations* (December 1982): 46–8

Pak, Youngsook, 1987(a). 'Illuminated Buddhist manuscripts in Korea', *Oriental Art*, 33/4

Pak, Youngsook, 1987(b). 'Amitabha triad: a Koryo painting in the Brooklyn Museum' in *Festschrift for Professor Kim Won-yong on his Retirement*. Seoul

Pak, Youngsook, 1995. 'The role of legend in Koryo iconography (1): The Ksitigarbha triad in Engakuji' in K.R. van Kooij and

H.van der Veere (eds), *Function and Meaning in Buddhist Art*. Groningen

Pak, Youngsook, 1998. 'The Korean art collection at the Metropolitan Museum' in Judith Smith (ed.), *Arts of Korea*, pp.402–50. New York

Paludan, Ann, 1991. *The Chinese Spirit Road: The Classical Tradition of Stone Tomb Statuary*. New Haven, CT and London

Portal, Jane, 1997. 'Korean celadons of the Koryo dynasty' in Freestone and Gaimster (eds), *Pottery in the Making*, pp.98–103. London

Rawson, Jessica, 1984, repr. 1990. *Chinese Ornament: The Lotus and the Dragon*. London

Rhie, Marilyn M., 1987. 'Early Koryo Buddhist sculpture' in *Korean Culture*, Pt 1 (Fall 1987), Pt 2 (Summer 1988), Pt 3 (Summer 1992)

Seckel, Dietrich, 1977. 'Some characteristics of Korean art', *Oriental Art*, 23: 52–61

Tae Koryo kukbo chon, 1995. Exh. cat., Hoam Gallery. Seoul

Till, Barry, 1989. 'The mausoleum of Koryo King Kongmin', *Korean Culture* (Summer 1989)

Vandiver, Pamela B., 1991. 'The technology of Korean celadons' in I. Itoh and Y. Mino (eds), *The Radiance of Jade and the Clarity of Water: Korean Ceramics from the Ataka Collection*, exh. cat. New York

Watt, James J.C.Y., 1991. *East Asian Lacquer: The Florence and Herbert Irving Collection*. New York

Whitfield, Roderick (ed.), 1984. *Treasures from Korea*, exh. cat., British Museum. London

Wood, Nigel, 1994. 'Parallels between Yue wares and Koryo celadons' in BAKS Papers, 5: pp.39–64

Yoshino, Tomio, 1954. 'Korai no raden ki', *Bijutsu kenkyu*, 175 (May 1954)

Yun, Yong-yi, 1993. *Hanguk tojasa yongu*. Seoul

Yun, Yong-yi, forthcoming. *Catalogue of the Gompertz Collection in the Fitzwilliam Museum*. Cambridge, UK

CHAPTER 4

CHOSON PERIOD

Adams, Edward B., 1974 and 1977. *Through Gates of Seoul: Trails and Tales of the Yi Dynasty*, 2nd edn.,2 vols. Seoul

Adams, Edward B., 1982. *Palaces of Seoul: Yi Dynasty Palaces in Korea's Capital City*. 2nd edn. Seoul

Ahn, Hwi-joon, 1974. 'Korean landscape painting in the early Yi period: the Kuo Hsi tradition', Ph.D. dissertation, Harvard University

Ahn, Hwi-joon, 1975. 'Two Korean landscape paintings of the first half of the 16th century', *Korea Journal*, 15/2: 31–41

Ahn, Hwi-joon, 1979. 'Portraiture of Korea', *Korea Journal*, 19/12: 39–42

Ahn, Hwi-joon, 1980(a). *Han'guk hoehwa sa* (A history of Korean painting). Seoul

Ahn, Hwi-joon, 1980(b). 'An Kyon and *A Dream Visit to the Peach Blossom Land*', *Oriental Art*, 26/1: 59–71

Ahn, Hwi-joon, 1987. 'Korean landscape painting of the early and middle Choson period', *Korea Journal* (March 1987): 4–17

Ahn, Hwi-joon, 1988. *Han'guk hoehwa ui chont'ong*. Seoul

Ahn, Hwi-joon, 1992. 'A scholar's art: painting in the tradition of the Chinese Southern School', *Koreana*, 6/3: 26–33

Ahn, Hwi-joon, 1994. 'Traditional Korean painting' in Young Ick Lew (ed.), *Korean Art Tradition*, pp.83–147. Seoul

Ahn, Hwi-joon, 1998. 'The origin and development of landscape painting in Korea' in Judith Smith (ed.), *Arts of Korea*, pp.294–329. New York

Ann-Baron, Ok-sung, 1981. *La peinture des lettrés en Corée au XVIIIe siecle*. Paris

Bacon, Wilbur, 1957. 'Tombs of the Yi dynasty kings and queens' in TKBRAS 33: 1–40

Bartholomew, Peter, 1993. 'Choson dynasty royal compounds: windows to a lost culture' in TKBRAS 68: 11–44

Becker, Sister Johanna, 1998. *Karatsu Ware: Tradition of Diversity*. Tokyo

Cho, Sun-mie, 1983. *Hanguk ui chosanghwa*. Seoul

Cho, Sun-mie, 1992. 'Korea's portrait paintings', *Koreana*, 6/3: 34–41

Choi, Sun-u, 1985. 'Lacquer ware and ornaments' in *Traditional Korean Art*. Seoul

Choi-Bae, Soon-taek, 1982. 'Kalligraphie und Kunsttheorie des Kim Chonghui (1786–1857)'. Inaug. dissertation, University of Cologne

Chung, Sae-hyang, 1996. 'Kim Hong-do's village school: conjectures on some possible artistic antecedents', *Orientations*, 27/8: 83–8

Chung, Yang-mo, 1991(a). *Hanguk ui tojagi*. Seoul

Chung, Yang-mo, 1991(b). 'The merit lay in absolute purity; white porcelain of the Choson dynasty', *Koreana*, 5/3: 46–9

Cort, Louise, 1984. 'Korean influences on Japanese ceramics', *Orientations* (May 1984): 18–29

De Ment, Terri, 1981. 'The pirating of a ceramic tradition', *Korean Culture*, 2/3: 20–27

Deuchler, Martina, 1992. *The Confucian Transformation of Korea*. Cambridge, MA

Ewha Women's University Museum, 1994. *Kwangju Punwonri yo chonghwa paekja*, exh. cat.

Garner, Harry, 1979. *Chinese Lacquer*. London

Gompertz, G.St.G.M., 1968. *Korean Pottery and Porcelain of the Yi Period*. London

Grayson, James, 1989. *Korea: A Religious History*. Oxford

Hanguk Munwon, 1995. *Munhwa yusan: Wangnung*. Seoul

Ho-am Art Gallery 1993. *Punchong sagi myongpumchon* (Masterpieces of punchong ware), exh. cat. Seoul

Huh, Young-hwan, 1992. 'Choson era landscape and genre painting', *Koreana*, 6/3: 20–25

Itoh, Ikutaro and Mino, Yutaka, 1991. *The Radiance of Jade and the Clarity of Water; Korean Ceramics from the Ataka Collection*, exh. cat. New York

Itoh, Ikutaro, 1999. *Color of Elegance, Form of Simplicity: The Beauty of Korean*

Ceramics from the Rhee Byung-chang Collection, exh. cat., Museum of Oriental Ceramics, Osaka

Jeon, Sang-woon, 1974. *'Science and Technology' in Korea: Traditional Instruments and Techniques*. Cambridge, MA

Jungmann, Burglind, 1988. 'Korean landscape painting under the influence of the Chinese Zhe School'. Ph.D. dissertation, University of Heidelberg

Jungmann, Burglind, 1990. 'Immortals and eccentrics in Choson dynasty painting', *Korean Culture* (Summer 1990): 22–31

Jungmann, Burglind, 1995. 'Confusing traditions: elements of the Korean An Kyon School in early Japanese Nanga landscape painting', *Artibus Asiae*, 55: 303–17

Jungmann, Burglind, 1998. 'Ike Taiga's letter to Kim Yusong and his approach to Korean landscape painting' in *Review of Korean Studies I*, pp.180–95. Songnam

Kang, Kyong-suk, 1986. *Punchong sagi yongu*. Seoul

Kang, Kyong-suk, 1989. *Hanguk tojasa*. Seoul

Kang, Woo-bang, 1993. 'Ritual and art during the eighteenth century' in Kim Hong-nam (ed.), *Korean Arts of the Eighteenth Century: Splendor and Simplicity*, pp.79–98. New York

Kawada, S., and T. Takashi, 1986. *Korai richo no raden*. Tokyo

Kim, Hong-nam, 1991. *The Story of a Painting: A Korean Buddhist Treasure from the Mary and Jackson Burke Foundation*. New York

Kim, Hong-nam (ed.), 1993. *Korean Arts of the Eighteenth Century; Splendor and Simplicity*. New York

Kim, Hong-nam, 1994. 'Tragedy and art at the eighteenth century Choson court', *Orientations*, February 1994: 28–37

Kim, Hong-nam, 1998. 'An Kyon and the Eight Views tradition' in Judith Smith (ed.), *Arts of Korea*, pp.366–401. New York

Kim, Won-yong, and Ahn, Hwi-joon, 1993. *Hanguk misulsa*. Seoul

Kim, Young-won, 1992. 'A study of Choson ceramics of the 15th–16th centuries'(in Korean with English abstract). Ph.D. dissertation, Seoul National University

Kim-Haboush, JaHyun, 1988. *A Heritage of Kings: One Man's Monarchy in the Confucian World*. New York

Kim-Haboush, JaHyun, 1995. *The Memoirs of Lady Hyegyong; The Autobiographical Writings of a Crown Princess of Eighteenth Century Korea*. Berkeley, CA

Kim-Lee, Lena, 1986. 'Buddhist sculpture' in Roderick Whitfield and Pak Young-sook (eds), *Korean Art Treasures*, pp.93–102. Seoul

Kim-Paik, Kumja, 1982. 'Kim Hong-do (1745–before 1818): a late Yi dynasty painter', Ph.D. dissertation, Stanford University

Kim-Paik, Kumja, 1983/4. 'Two stylistic trends in mid 15th century Korean painting', *Oriental Art*, 29/4 (Winter): 368–76

Kim-Paik, Kumja, 1986. 'A Yi dynasty court painter Kim Hongdo (1745–before 1818): seen through the Tanwon Yumuk and his landscape paintings', *Oriental Art*, 32/1 (Spring): 34–48

Kim-Paik, Kumja, 1990–1. 'The introduction of the Southern School painting tradition to Korea', *Oriental Art*, 36/4: 186–97

Kim-Paik, Kumja, 1992(a). 'Chong Son, his life and career', *Artibus Asiae*, 52: 329–43

Kim-Paik, Kumja, 1992(b). 'Bamboo and grapes in Choson dynasty painting and porcelain decoration', *Korean Culture* (Summer 1992): 18–25

Kim-Renaud, Young-Key (ed.), 1992. *King Sejong the Great: The Light of 15th Century Korea*. Washington, DC

Koyama, Fujio, *et al.*, 1956. *Sekai toji zenshu* (Catalogue of the world's ceramics), 1st edn, vol.14: *Yi Dynasty*. Tokyo

Kwon, Young-pil. 1985. 'Die Entstehung der "koreanischen" Bambusmalerei aus der Mitte der Yi-Dynastie (1392–1910)', inaug. dissertation, University of Cologne

Kwon, Young-pil (ed.), 1996. *The Fragrance of Ink: Korean Literati Paintings of the Choson Dynasty from Korea University Museum*, exh. cat. Seoul

Lee, Ki-baik (trans. Edward W. Wagner with Edward J.Schulz), 1984. *A New History of Korea*. Cambridge, MA

Lee, Nan-hee, 1993. 'A study of mother of pearl inlaid lacquer in the Choson period' (in Korean, with English abstract), M.A. dissertation, Ewha Women's University Graduate School

Lee, Won-bok, 1997. 'Artistic achievment in the paintings of Hyewon, Sin Yun-bok', *Misulsa yongu*, 11: 97–127

Lim, Chun, 1964. 'Yi architecture as synthetic art', *Korea Journal*, 4/3: 22–9

McCune, Shannon, 1975. 'Some Korean maps' in TKBRAS 50: 70–102

McCune, Shannon, 1983. 'Korean maps of the Yi dynasty', *Korean Culture*, 4/3

Mino, Yutaka, 1991. 'Koryo and Choson dynasty ceramics' in I. Itoh and Y. Mino (eds), *The Radiance of Jade and the Clarity of Water: Korean Ceramics from the Ataka Collection*, pp.27–34

National Folklore Museum, 1989. *Hanguk chilgi yichonnyon* (2000 years of Korean lacquer), exh. cat. Seoul

National Museum of Korea, 1986. *Choson sidae tongsinsa* (Korean envoys to Japan in the Choson dynasty), exh. cat. Seoul

Pak, Un-sun, 1994. 'Kumgangsando yongu' (in Korean with English abstract), Ph.D. dissertation, Hongik University, Seoul

Pak, Un-sun, 1997. *Kumgangsando yongu*. Seoul

Ramsey, S. Robert, 1992. 'The Korean alphabet' in Kim-Renaud Young-key (ed.), *King Sejong the Great: The Light of 15th century Korea*, pp.41–50. Washington, DC

Seckel, Dietrich, 1979. 'Some characteristics of Korean art II: preliminary remarks on Yi dynasty painting', *Oriental Art*, 25/1: 62–73

Shin, Young-hoon, 1989. *Han'ok ui chohyong*. Seoul

Sorensen, Hendrik Hjort, 1989. *The Iconography of Korean Buddhist Painting*. Leiden

Till, Barry, 1992. 'Stone sculptures at Korea's "emperor-style" tombs', *Korean Culture*, 13/2: 4–11

Underwood, H.H., 1934, repr. 1979. *Korean Boats and Ships*. Seoul

Watt, James J.Y., 1992. *East Asian Lacquer: The Florence and Herbert Irving Collection*. New York

Whitfield, Roderick, 1984. 'Painting' in R. Whitfield (ed.), *Treasures from Korea*, pp.182–7, exh. cat., British Museum. London

Yi, Song-mi, 1996. 'Bird and flower painting' and 'Literati ink painting' in *Macmillan Dictionary of Art*, vol. 18: 315–7 and 323–5. London

Yi, Song-mi, 1996/7. 'The screen of the five peaks of the Choson dynasty', *Oriental Art*, 42/4: 13–24

Yi, Song-mi, 1998(a). 'Artistic tradition and the depiction of reality' in Judith Smith (ed.), *Arts of Korea*, pp.330–65. New York

Yi, Song-mi, 1998(b). 'Yi Chong: the foremost bamboo painter of the Choson dynasty', *Orientations*, 29/8: 61–8

Yi, Tae-jin, and Jeon, Sang-woon, 1992. 'Science, technology and agriculture in 15th century Korea' in Kim-Renaud Young-key (ed.), *King Sejong the Great: The Light of 15th Century Korea*, pp.95–102. Washington, DC

Yi, Tong-ju, 1973. 'Tanwon Kim Hong-do: his life and works', *Korea Journal*, 13/8: 59–64

Yi, Tong-ju, 1982. *Han'guk hoehwa sosa*, 2nd edn. Seoul

Yi, Tong-ju, 1995. *Uri Nara ui Yet Kurim*. Seoul

Yoshida, Hiroshi, 1996. *The World of Bright Beauty of the Neighbouring Land* (Richo kaiga/Yi dynasty paintings), exh. cat. (in Japanese), Yamato Bunkakan, Nara

Yu, Joon-yong, 1976. 'Chong Son (1676–1759), ein koreanischer Landschaftsmaler aus der Yi-Dynastie', Inaug. dissertation, University of Cologne

Yun, Yong-i, 1991. 'Koreans shaped base for Japan's pottery: origin of Satsuma and Arita wares', *Koreana*, 5/3: 50–55

Yun, Yong-i, 1993. *Han'guk tojasa yongu*. Seoul

Yun, Yong-i, forthcoming. *Catalogue of the Gompertz Collection in the Fitzwilliam Museum.* Cambridge, UK

CHAPTER 5

FOLK ART OF THE LATE CHOSON

Adams, Edward B., 1989. *Korean Folk Art and Craft.* Seoul

Ahn, Hwi-jun, 1998. 'Uri minhwa ui yihae' in *Auspicious Dreams: Decorative Paintings of Korea*, pp.150–55. Ho-am Museum, Seoul

Aston, W.G., 1924, repr. 1972. *Nihongi: Chronicles of Japan from the Earliest Times to* AD *697.* Tokyo

Bishop, Isabella Bird, 1897, repr. 1985. *Korea and Her Neighbours.* London

Black, Kay, 1981. 'Religious aspects of folk painting', *Korean Culture*, 2/2: 2–9

Black, Kay, and E. Wagner, 1993. 'Ch'aekkori paintings: a Korean jigsaw puzzle', *Archives of Asian Art*, 46: 63–75

Black, Kay, and E. Wagner, 1998. 'Court style ch'aekkori' in Paik-Kim, Kumja (ed.), *Hopes and Aspirations: Decorative Paintings of Korea*, pp.21–30, Asian Art Museum of San Francisco

Chan, Amemiya, 1977. 'Origins of Korean mask dance drama', *Korea Journal*, 17/1: 57–64

Choe, Sang-su, 1986. 'Korean style wrestling: ssirum', *Korea Journal*, 26/8: 15–19

Culin, Stewart, 1895, repr. 1991. *Korean Games.* New York

Gale, James, 1898, repr. 1973. *Korean Sketches.* London

Ho-am Art Museum, 1983. *Minhwa kolchak chon*, exh. cat. Seoul

Ho-am Art Museum, 1998. *Auspicious Dreams: Decorative Paintings of Korea*, exh. cat, Seoul

Howard, Keith, 1989. *Bands, Songs and Shamanistic Rituals.* Seoul

Huh, Dong-hwa, 1988. *Crafts of the Inner Court*, exh. cat. Museum of Korean Embroidery, Seoul

Huh, Dong-hwa, and Sheila Middleton, 1990. *Traditional Korean Wrapping Cloths*, exh. cat. Fitzwilliam Museum, Cambridge, UK

Hulbert, Homer B., 1906, repr. 1969. *The Passing of Korea.* Seoul

Kendall, Laurel, 1985. *Shamans, Housewives, and Other Restless Spirits: Women in Korean Ritual Life.* Honolulu, HI

Kikuchi, Yuko, 1994. 'Yanagi Soetsu and Korean crafts within the Mingei Movement', in BAKS Papers, 5: 23–38

Kim, Chol-sun, 1991. *Han'guk minhwa non'go.* Seoul

Kim, Ho-yon, 1979. 'Analytic classification of Korean folk painting', *Korea Journal*, 19/1: 12–20

Kim, Hong-nam, 1997. *The Power of Old Korean Stone Sculptures.* Seoul

Kim, Kyong-ji, 1986. 'T'aekwondo: its brief history', in *Korea Journal*, 26/8: 20–25

Kim, Sung-kyun, 1998. *Winding River Village.* Private publication

Kim, Tae-gon, 1988. *Han'guk mushindo.* Seoul

Kim, Tae-gon, trans. Chang Soo-kyung, 1998. *Korean Shamanism: Muism.* Seoul

Kim-Harvey, Young-sook, 1979. *Six Korean Women: The Socialization of Shamans.* St Paul, MN

Kim-Hogarth, Hyung-kee, 1990. 'The Hahoe mask dance', *Arirang* (Spring 1990): 6–13

Knödal, Susanne, 1998. *Heilrituale und Handys. Schamaninnen in Korea.* Hamburg

Lee, Doo-hyun, 1968. 'Korean masks and mask-dance dramas', *Korea Journal*, 8/3: 4–10

Lee, Kyong-hee, 1993. 'Dynamic symbolism of Pongsan mask dance' in *Korean Culture: Legacies and Lore*, pp.89–95. Seoul

Lee, O-young, 1994. *Korea In Its Creations.* Seoul

Minsok Hak'hwi, 1996. *Minsok nori wa minjung uisik.* Seoul

Moes, Robert, 1983. *Auspicious Spirits: Korean Folk Paintings and Related Objects.* New York

National Folk Museum, 1988. *Tigers in Korean Folk Art*, exh. cat. Seoul

National Folk Museum, 1994. *Chungbuk chibang changsung sottae sin'ang.* Research Report of the National Folk Museum, vol. 15

National Folk Museum, 1995. *Han'guk ui chongyi munhwa*, exh. cat. Seoul

National Museum of Korea, 1994. *Korean Collection from the Peabody Essex Museum*, exh. cat. Seoul

National Museum of Kwangju, 1985. *A Survey of Boksu Culture in Korea*, exh. cat. Kwangju

Onyang Folk Museum, 1980. *Han'guk ui minsok*, cat. of collection, Seoul

Paik-Kim, Kumja, 1998. *Hopes and Aspirations: Decorative Paintings of Korea*, exh. cat., Asian Art Museum, San Francisco

Paik-Kim, Kumja, and Huh, Dong-hwa, 1995. *Profusion of Colour: Korean Costumes and Wrapping Cloths of the Choson Dynasty*, exh. cat., Asian Art Museum, San Francisco

Pak, Yong-suk, 1972. 'The thought embodied in Korean folk painting', *Korea Journal*, 12/7: 51–6

Portal, Jane 1995(a). 'The origins of the British Museum's Korean Collection' in TKBRAS, 70: 37–52

Portal, Jane, 1995(b). 'Korean shaman paintings', *Oriental Art* (Spring 1995): 2–9

Rhie, Jong-chul, 1988. *Changsung: Village Guardian God of Korea.* Seoul

Sands, William Franklin, n.d., repr. 1975, 1990. *Undiplomatic Memories: The Far East 1896–1904.* London

Savage-Landor, A.H. 1895. *Corea or Chosen: the Land of the Morning Calm.* London

Sayers, Robert, with Ralph Rinzler, 1987. *The Korean Onggi Potter.* Washington, DC

Sayers, Robert, 1988. *Sun and Moon: Traditional Arts of Yi Dynasty Korea*, exh. cat., San Francisco Craft and Folk Art Museum

Shim, U-song, 1994. *Tal.* Seoul

Shim, Yi-sok, 1993. *Han'guk ui namutal.* Seoul

Suk, Joo-sun, 1985. *Clothes of Joson Dynasty: The Suk Joo-sun Memorial Museum of Korean Folk Arts,* Dankook University. Seoul

Till, Barry, 1998. *The Land of Morning Calm: Arts and Folkcrafts of Korea.* Victoria, BC, Canada

Underwood, Lilias H., 1904, repub. 1977. *Fifteen Years among the Top-knots.* New York

Walraven, B., 1991–2. 'Confucians and shamans', *Cahiers d'Extrême Asie,* 6: 21–44

Yi, Song-mi, 1992. *Korean Costumes and Textiles,* exh. cat., IBM Gallery, New York

Yi, Song-mi, 1996/7. 'The screens of the five peaks of the Choson dynasty', *Oriental Art,* 42/4: 13–24

Yi, Tu-hyon, 1989. *Han'guk ui ka'myon-guk.* Seoul

Yi, Tu-hyon, 1995. *Han'guk ka'myon-guk.* Seoul

Yonsei University Museum, 1995. *Han'guk ui puchae,* exh. cat. Seoul

Yun, Yol-su, 1994. *Han'guk ui mushindo.* Seoul

Yun, Yol-su, 1995. *Minhwa yiyagi.* Seoul

Zo, Za-yong, 1974. *Art of the Korean Tiger,* Emille Museum, Seoul

Zo, Za-yong, 1982. *Guardians of Happiness: Shamanistic Tradition in Korean Folk Painting,* Emileh Museum, Seoul

Zo, Za-yong, 1983. 'Symbolism in Korean folk painting' in *Traditional Korean Painting,* pp.96–120, UNESCO, Seoul

CHAPTER 6

TWENTIETH CENTURY

Adams, Clive, 1992. *Flow From the Far East: Recent Korean Art Scene,* exh. cat., Barbican Centre, London

API, 1989. *Unbo, Kim Ki-chang.* Seoul

Biggs, Lewis, 1992. *Working With Nature: Contemporary Art from Korea,* exh. cat. Tate Gallery, Liverpool

Cho, Chung-hyon, 1994. 'The past, the present and the future of Korean contemporary ceramic art' in *National Contemporary Art Museum.* Seoul

Cho, Hung-youn, 1987. 'The characteristics of Korean *Minjung* culture', *Korea Journal,* 27/11: 4–18

Choi, Kong-ho, 1996. *Han'guk hyondae kongyesa ui yihae.* Seoul

Choi, Tae-man, 1995. *Han'guk chogak ui onul.* Seoul

Chong, Chung-hwan, 1970. 'Preservation of Cultural Properties', *Korea Journal,* 10/1: 10–12

Chong-ang Ilbo, 1994. *The Faces of Contemporary Art 40 years,* exh. cat. Seoul

Choson Ilbo Misulgwan, 1991. *Shin Sang-ho punchong sagichon.* Seoul

Dong Ah Gallery, 1995. *Sangho Shin, Dreams and Heads,* exh. cat. Seoul

Ewha Woman's University, 1991. *20 Korean Modern Painters,* special exh. Seoul

Fouser, Robert, 1997. 'Looking for Chaemi: Nam June Paik and Korean modernist aesthetics', *Korean Culture,* 18/2: 14–25

Han'guk Munhwachae Poho Chaedan, 1994. *Han'guk ui chontong kongye* (Traditional handicraft of Korea). Seoul

Ho-am Art Museum 1995. *Chang Ucchin,* exh. cat. Yongin

Hoffman, Frank 1988. 'Yi Chung-sop's life and art', *Korean Culture,* 9/4: 23–32

Hong, Sok-chang, 1994. *Hong Sok-chang,* exh. cat., Museum of Chinese Art, Beijing

Howard, Keith, 1989. 'Namdotul norae: ritual and the Korean Intangible Cultural Asset System', *Journal of Ritual Studies,* 3/2: 203–16

Howard, Keith, 1994. 'The Korean kayagum: the making of a zither' in BAKS Papers, 5: 1–22

Howard, Keith (ed.), 1995. *The Stories of the Korean Comfort Women.* London

Howard, Keith, unpublished. *The Cultural Asset System.* London

Hyundae Gallery, 1994. *Whanki Lithograph.* Seoul

Jinro, 1995. *Jinro International Ceramic Art,* exh. cat., Hongik University Ceramic Research Institute, Seoul

Kang, Tae-hi, 1997. 'Korean minimalism and Lee Ufan', *Misulsa yongu,* 11: 153–171

Kim, Bong-tae, Yun Myung-ro, Suh Seung-won, and Ha Dong-chul, 1991. *Han'guk hyondae panhwa* (Korean contemporary prints). Seoul

Kim, Choung-za, 1994. *Choung-za Kim.* Seoul

Kim, In-hwan, 1994. 'The artistic world of Lee Ufan', *Koreana,* 8/4: 58–63

Kim, Young-na, 1994. 'Modern Korean painting and sculpture' in Young Ick Lew (ed.), *Korean Art Tradition,* pp.151–200. Seoul

Kongpyong Art Centre, 1993. *Lee Chong-do, Lee In-chin, Lee Kang-hyo: Three Potters,* exh.cat. Seoul

Korea-Britain Centennial Committee, 1983. *Korean Ceramics Today,* exh. cat., South Bank Arts Centre Exhibition. London

Korean Culture and Arts Foundation, Art Centre, 1989. *Kwon Soon Hyung: 14th Ceramic Show.* Seoul

Korean Overseas Information Service, 1984. *Koreanische Tuschmalerei: Erforschung der Tradition* (Contemporary Korean ink paintings), exh. cat.

Korean Overseas Information Service/Korea Foundation, 1991. *Keramik* (Contemporary Korean ceramics in Sweden, Germany and France), exh. cat.

Kwon Young-woo, 1990, exh. cat., Hoam Gallery. Seoul

Leach, Bernard, 1940. *A Potter's Book.* London

Lee, Ki-baik (trans. Edward W. Wagner with Edward J. Shulz), 1984. *A New History of Korea.* Cambridge, MA

Lee, Ku-yol, 1984. *Kundae Han'gukhwa ui hurum.* Seoul

Lee, Kyung-hee, 1989. *The Reproduction of Koryo Celadon.* Taegu

Lee, Kyung-sung, see Yi, Kyong-song

Lee, Yil, 1986(a). 'Modernism in Korean fine arts', *Korea Journal,* 26/1: 12–19

Lee, Yil, 1986(b). 'The influence of French art on Korean art', *Korea Journal*, 26/6: 44–50

Lim, Moo-keun, 1994. 'Korean contemporary ceramic art from the 1950s to the present' in *National Contemporary Art Museum*, 1994(a). Seoul

Musée Cernuschi, 1978. *Peintures Coréenes contemporaines de style traditionnel*. Paris

Musée Cernuschi, 1980. *Un Peintre officiel Coréen, Chang Woo-soung*. Paris

Musée Cernuschi, 1992. *Tradition et modernité, 20 céramistes Coréens contemporains*. Paris

Nam, Kwan 1969. 'My artistic apprenticeship in Paris', *Korea Journal*, Pt 1 (9/6: 27–34), Pt 2 (9/7: 25–32), Pt 3 (9/8: 31–6)

National Gallery of Victoria, Australia, 1998. *Slowness of Speed* (Korean installation art by seven young artists), exh. cat.

National Museum of Contemporary Art, 1992. *Namjune Paik: Videotime, Videospace*. Seoul

National Museum of Contemporary Art, 1993(a). General introductory catalogue. Seoul

National Museum of Contemporary Art, 1993(b). *Forty Years of Contemporary Korean Printmaking*, exh. cat. Seoul

National Museum of Contemporary Art, 1994(a). *Thirty Years of Korean Contemporary Ceramic Art*, exh. cat. Seoul

National Museum of Contemporary Art, 1994(b). *Lee Ufan*, exh. cat. Seoul

O, Kwang-su, 1971. 'Yi Chung-sop: the man and his art', *Korea Journal*, 11/1: 42–6

O, Kwang-su, 1975(a). 'Artistic career of Kim Hwan-gi', *Korea Journal*, 15/3: 60–63

O, Kwang-su, 1975(b). 'Song Su-nam and his world of art', *Korea Journal*, 15/10: 56–60

O, Kwang-su, 1979. *Han'guk hyondae misulsa*. Seoul

O, Kwang-su, 1986. 'Art of Pak Su-gun', *Korea Journal*, 26/2: 70–3

O Yun Kinyom Saophwi, 1996. *O Yun: tongnae saram, saesang saram*. Seoul

Office of Cultural Properties, 1995. *The Preservation and Transmission System for the Intangible Cultural Properties of the Republic of Korea*. Seoul

Portal, Jane, 1995. 'The origins of the British Museum's Korean Collection' in TKBRAS, 70: 47–50

Sasse, Werner, 1991. '*Minjung* theology and culture' in BAKS Papers, 1: 29–41

Sayers, Robert, 1987. *The Korean Onggi Potter*. Washington, DC

Seoul Gallery, 1986. *Shin Sang-ho: Ceramic Exhibition*. Seoul

Shin, Sang-ho, 1994. 'Traditional pottery: retrospect and prospects' in *National Contemporary Art Museum*. Seoul

Song, Su-nam, 1991. *Mok, pohyon kwa sanghyong*. Seoul

Sun Gallery, 1991. *Yoon Kwang-cho: Ceramics*, exh. cat. Seoul

To Gallery, 1988. *Three Punchong Potters Today*, exh. cat. Seoul

Tokyo Gallery, 1983. *Kim Yikyung*, exh. cat. Tokyo

Van Gucht, Bie, 1996. *Nature et religion dans la céramique Coréene contemporaine*, Musée Royal de Mariemont, Brussels

Wells, Kenneth M. (ed.), 1995. *South Korea's Minjung Movement: The Culture and Politics of Dissidence*. Honolulu, HI

Won, Tong-sok, 1986. 'Development and characteristics of modern Korean painting', *Korea Journal*, 26/1: 20–27

Yi, Chong-sok, 1974. 'Contemporary folk crafts of Korea', *Korea Journal*, 14/1: 55–8

Yi, Kyong-song, 1965. 'Yi Sang-bom, his life and art', *Korea Journal*, 5/3: 26–8

Yi, Kyong-song, 1978. 'Ceramist Miss Hwang Chong-nye', *Korea Journal*, 18/10: 47–8

Yi, Kyong-song, 1987. 'Chang Uc-chin and a return to nature', *Koreana*, 1/2: 30–36

Yi Suk-ja, 1989. *Han'guk hyondae tongyanghwa yongu*. Seoul

Yim, Dawn-hee, and Im, Jang-hyuk, 1996. *Preservation and Transmission of Korean Intangible Cultural Properties (ICP)*. Seoul

You, Hong-june, 1987. 'Life and art of O Yun: plebeian motif in ethnic style', *Korea Journal*, 27/1: 37–45

Yu, Chun-sang, 1986. 'Forty years of fine arts in Korea: 1945–85', *Korea Journal*, 26/1: 4–11

Yu, Keun-jun, 1971. 'Ceramicist Kwon Soon-hyung', *Korea Journal*, 11/7: 28–33

Yu, Keun-jun, 1973. 'Modern epoch in Korean art', *Korea Journal*, 13/8: 21–6

Yu, Kun-hyong, 1984. *Koryo Celadon: The Autobiography of Haegang, Yoo Keun-hyeong*. Seoul

Yun, Myung-ro, 1993. 'Formation and development of Korea's contemporary woodblock printing', *Koreana*, 7/2: 79–81

APPENDIX 1

Technology and Sources of Korean Celadon

By Michael Hughes and Louise Joyner

Introduction

This appendix examines two main aspects of Korean celadon: firstly, the technology of Korean ceramics – how they were made, and how scientific analysis has exposed the potter's skill in producing such fine ceramics. Among points for consideration are the types of clay used; how the potters achieved the remarkable celadon glazes; how the innovative use of inlaying, a difficult and painstaking technique, was employed to enhance Koryo celadons; and the special types of kilns developed for firing the pottery. It looks secondly at the question of origins – can we identify where a particular ceramic ware was made using scientific methods? This appendix explores how trace element analysis applied to Koryo celadons has shown that it is possible to distinguish by this means between celadons produced in different centres in Korea and has allowed a start to the attribution of individual pieces in the Museum's collections to the kiln district where they were made. Trace element analysis has also demonstrated the similarities and differences in clay composition between Koryo celadons and the earlier Yue wares produced in south China, with which Koryo celadons have general affinities.

While the scope of this appendix includes Korean ceramics of the eleventh to fifteenth centuries, the Koryo celadons of the eleventh to twelfth centuries were the zenith of production, and most scientific work has concentrated on them. There seem so far to have been no scientific studies of the very earliest celadons, of the ninth to early tenth century, but as this was probably a period of experimentation, especially with glaze formulations, it would well be worthy of scientific study. By the time of the Koryo celadons, a well-characterized stable glaze formulation equivalent to that used on Chinese Yue wares had been adopted, a

tradition which remained, remarkably, exceedingly consistent over succeeding centuries.

The ceramics of the Choson dynasty which succeeded the Koryo period are known particularly for *punchong* ('powder green') wares, the standard pottery thrown in the fifteenth and sixteenth centuries, in the first half of the Choson period. In the main these wares were thicker and heavier than those of the Koryo, and the types of inlaying were more geared to mass production, and so used stamped and rolled decoration. These wares were succeeded by plain white porcelain, for daily uses as well as ceremonial. In the fifteenth century, one variety of white porcelain was inlaid with black in incised lines. Underglaze painting in brown iron oxide, which was present in the Koryo period, continued. Underglaze cobalt blue porcelain was produced from the fifteenth century onwards, though its production was always vulnerable to disruption of the supplies of cobalt, which had to be imported.

Technology

Clays

From an early period the key ceramic types in Korea were stonewares, a high-fired pottery with a dense, impermeable fabric, often grey in colour and covered by a glaze. During firing, some of the body material fuses to form a glassy phase (vitrification) which links together the still-crystalline original fabric into a very hard product, though without reaching complete melting where the pot collapses under its own weight as the body fuses. Stonewares had been made in China from an early date, with a significant difference in clay mineralogy between those produced in northern China and those manufactured in the south of the country. Northern Ding wares were made from natural stoneware clays which are high-firing, rich in alumina and low in flux elements. A typical analysis of Ding body composition, as shown in table 1, has alumina contents in excess of 25 per cent. In contrast, the stoneware materials of southern China, including those of northern Zhejiang province where Yue wares were made, are quartz-rich and flux-rich lower-firing materials derived from weathered igneous rocks, and their alumina contents are nearer 17 per cent. Geologically, the igneous rocks which underlie southern China continue under the East China and Yellow seas and continue as the landscape of Korea, some 300–400 miles to the northeast. Hence the same type of raw materials available to potters in southern China for making Yue wares are also present in the Korean peninsula, and the Koryo celadons were made from a weathered igneous rock material with similar chemical composition to that of Yue wares (see table 1). These materials are rich in quartz (hence the high silica content in table 1), contain also some clay, but are particularly rich in fine-grained mica (sericite) which not only, like clay, imparts plasticity to the body, but also acts as a flux or fusing element because of its high potassium content. (The higher potassium levels in the Yue wares and Koryo celadon analyses of table 1 may be contrasted with that of the northern Chinese Ding wares.) From a technical point of view, since these materials fuse at a lower temperature than the high-alumina, low-flux stoneware clays of northern China, the maximum kiln temperature required to successfully fire them would be lower, and therefore save on fuel. The celadon clays fire to a grey colour due to their iron oxide content.

An unglazed, high-fired dark grey stoneware was produced which was the pottery in ordinary use, whereas the celadons were used in court circles and in Buddhist temples. The underglaze iron oxide, *cholhoe chonga*, was derived from Chinese Cizhou wares.

Glazes

The glazes of Koryo celadons are lime-alkali glazes, made by fluxing with lime in the form of wood ash, which also contains a proportion of alkali. Such stoneware glazes can be made to contain both lime and alkali in proportions which produce a balance of

Table 1: Major element composition of the bodies of Koryo celadons and Yue and Ding wares (mean and one standard deviation) from published data

	Sadang-ri[1]	Yuchon-ri[2]	Yue[3]	Ding[4]
	Koryo	*Koryo*		
silica	73.5±1.9	73.8±1.2	76.3	63.8
alumina	18.2±1.4	18.7±1.02	16.8	29.7
iron oxide	2.60±0.66	2.30±0.27	2.50	0.82
magnesium oxide	0.47±0.18	0.33±0.08	0.6	0.92
calcium oxide	0.43±0.17	0.32±0.10	0.35	2.1
sodium oxide	0.56±0.20	0.52±0.10	0.93	0.28
potassium oxide	3.10±0.43	3.37±0.29	2.80	1.7
titanium oxide	0.98±0.09	1.07±0.33	0.93	0.68

All results are in weight per cent.

1. Sadang-ri: data averaged from Choo 1995:Table 2, Group no. I3-I6
2. Yuchon-ri: data averaged from Choo 1995:Table 2, Group no. III
3. Yue: data from Wood 1994
4. Ding: data from Pollard and Hatcher 1994: Table 6

oxides close to a technically perfect recipe (about two parts lime to one part alkali), i.e. the glazes are stable and glassy.[1] Small changes in the minor oxides or iron, titanium, manganese and phosphorus will give the full range of celadon colours found on East Asian pottery. Such proportions will give good stoneware glazes above about 1200° centigrade. It is the effect of titanium on iron which controls the range of colours from light blue to olive green in celadon glazes. It seems that the yellowish tint of titanium combines with the blue of reduced iron to produce a green celadon glaze. The perception of colour varies somewhat in differing descriptions of the colours. It has been suggested that the lower levels of titanium oxide and iron and higher potassium oxide in the body fabric and glazes of Koryo celadons compared to Yue wares indicated that the Koryo potters used porcelain-stones rather than body-clays in their celadon glaze recipes.[2] Porcelain-stones share these composition features. Analysis of a rock collected at one of the main celadon production sites at Sadang-ri (see map 5, p.222) showed that the rock consisted of a volcanic ash, known as tuff, as did many of the porcelain-stones of the Jingdezhen type of southern China.[3] However, analyses of typical Koryo celadon glazes suggest that mixtures of porcelain-stone with about 30–50 per cent of wood ash were the most typical glaze recipes used by these potters. This proportion in the mixture will provide a material that will fuse at the lowest possible temperature (*c.*1170° centigrade – the eutectic or minimum) for mixtures of the two materials, and is therefore close to an 'ideal' composition.

Chinese glazes from the period of the Eastern Han onwards show a general decrease in the percentage of lime (calcium oxide). Koryo celadons most closely resemble the lime contents of the earliest formulations of the Eastern Han to Five Dynasties period (AD 25–960), rather than those of the Song period (AD 960–1279). Yue wares were produced in Zhejiang province during the ninth–tenth centuries, and were widely exported. It has long been recognized that the Yue wares were a founding influence on Koryo celadons (see section on Yue wares, below). In their glaze colours, however, Yue wares are greener, while Koryo celadons tend more towards a very pale green with a greyish tint. Chinese green and white glazes commonly contain a white layer of the mineral anorthite which formed during firing between the body and the glaze. In the Koryo celadons, however, this anorthite layer is rare, and its absence renders the celadon glaze greyer in colour than that on Chinese equivalent stonewares, as the grey body colour shows through the semi-transparent glaze layer.[4] Anorthite forms only slowly in glazes once the maximum temperature has been reached, and its absence in Koryo celadons may be attributable to a short firing-cycle for the Korean kilns, a consequence of the kiln design. A short kiln, compared to Chinese dragon-kilns, allowed faster firing and cooling rates, which made the Korean glazes less likely to develop anorthite crystals in the early stages of cooling. Such a kiln permitted a relatively rapid rise in temperature to the maximum, followed by only a brief dwell at that temperature before more rapid cooling than for Chinese stonewares.

Developments in glaze technology in the Choson period followed from changes in the type of production, to producing on a larger scale for more widespread consumption. Stamped and impressed designs on the punchong wares permitted more rapid production as against the laborious techniques of carved and inlaid wares. The glaze thickness also decreased to around half that on the Koryo celadons, and there was more limited attention to the preparation of glaze materials – they were not ground as finely – so glazes are more variable in composition. Analysis confirms that Choson glazes are similar to Koryo in composition, but with greater variability in the concentrations of many elements.[5] At the same time, black inlay was no longer used and white inlay was rapidly applied by slip painting into rolled or stamped decoration.

Inlays

Towards the middle of the twelfth century, in the Koryo period, an important innovation took place in decoration, the use of inlay on celadon, known as *sanggam*. The designs were incised into the leather-hard clay of the vessel, and then the inlay painted or spread into the incised design before being fired. Finally the whole vessel was dipped in glaze and fired a second time. The materials used for the inlays have not, however, been properly identified until recently, and in the past were often called 'slip inlay', that is, a thick suspension of fine clay in water.[6]

Typical examples of white and black inlays on Koryo celadons and Choson punchong ware have been examined in the scanning electron microscope (SEM) at the British Museum's Department of Scientific Research to determine the materials used. Figure 1 shows a cross-section at increasing magnifications through a sherd of Koryo celadon. The white inlay is visible as a darker rectangular area, carefully cut into the body and underlying the glaze layer. The minerals filling the inlay are clearly different in shape and size to the body fabric. The white inlay has a granular appearance in the SEM and is composed of three mineral phases. The predominant phase is one that resembles a stack of 'books' (figure 1, bottom right). Elemental analysis indicates that these were originally the clay mineral kaolinite, which on firing altered to mullite (identified by X-ray diffraction analysis).[7] Other minerals identified in the white inlay include quartz (the dark grains in figure 1, bottom left), and alkali feldspar (the light grains, same figure). This combination of

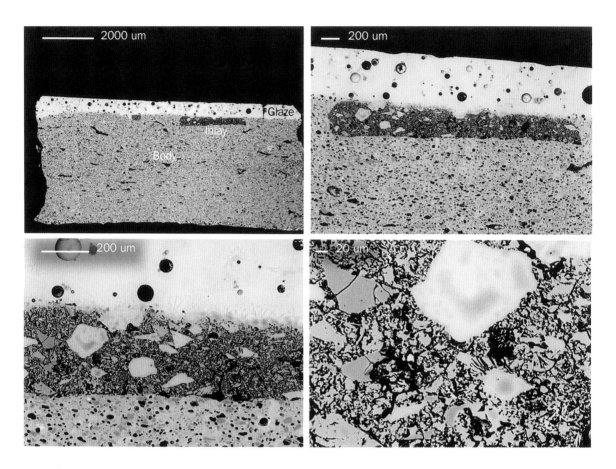

Figure 1. White inlays on Koryo celadons

Top left: SEM photomicrograph of the white inlay in a cross-section of a Koryo celadon sherd, K40. In this back-scattered electron image, which enhances the contrast between areas of different chemical composition, the inlay appears dark coloured. Note the sharp angular incision into the body which is filled with the inlay, with the glaze applied as a continuous layer over the body and inlay. *Top right*: Detail of the white inlay showing the sharp contact with the body. The granular nature of this inlay can be discerned. *Bottom left*: Detail of the white inlay showing its granular nature. *Bottom right*: The granular white inlay is composed of stacks of 'books' of mullite altered from kaolinite (medium grey), quartz (darker grains) and alkali feldspar (lighter grains).

minerals indicates that these white inlays were made of an impure kaolinitic clay containing quartz and feldspar.

Two different types of black inlay have been identified in the SEM with different compositions and textures; one lath-rich and the other granular. There are, however, some black inlays that show both types of texture suggesting that they may both have developed from the same raw material. The *lath-rich black inlay* has lathlike crystals of calcic plagioclase feldspar and occasional quartz grains set in a glassy matrix (see figure 2, left pair). The quartz grains are relicts from the original raw materials, having a rounded appearance produced through reaction with the glassy melt. The most striking feature is the abundant plagioclase laths, which appear to have crystallized out of the melt produced during the firing process. The black coloration is due to clusters of minute (ca. 2 μm) euhedral grains of iron-rich black spinels of variable

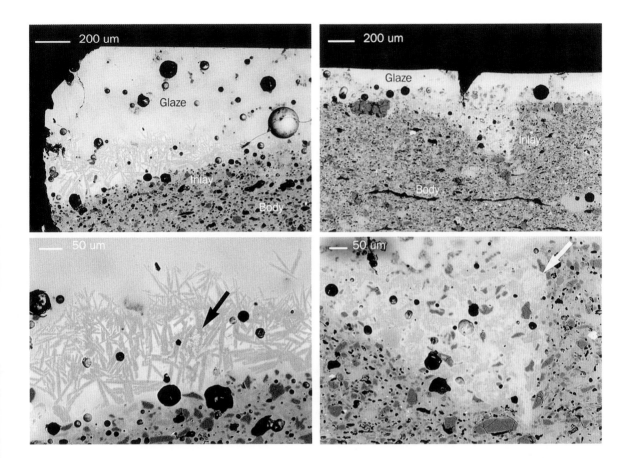

Figure 2. Black inlays on Koryo celadons

Top left: SEM back-scattered electron image of the lath-rich black inlay (light colour) in a cross-section of a Koryo celadon sherd, K40. The incision is filled with the lath-rich black inlay, with the glaze applied as a continuous layer over the body and inlay. *Bottom left*: Detail of the lath-rich black inlay showing the lathlike crystals of calcic plagioclase feldspar and occasional quartz grains (dark grains) set in a glassy matrix (light area). The black colouration is due to clusters of minute (ca. 2 μm) euhedral grains of iron-rich spinels of variable composition, distributed sporadically throughout the inlay (a black arrow indicates one such cluster). *Top right*: SEM back-scattered electron image of the granular black inlay (light colour) in a Koryo celadon, K41. The incision into the body is filled with the granular black inlay, with the glaze layer over the body and inlay. *Bottom right*: Detail of the granular black inlay showing quartz grains (dark) and the grains rich in aluminosilicates (medium grey) set in a less extensive glassy matrix (light area). The black colouration is due to minute (ca. 2 μm) euhedral grains of iron-rich spinels of variable composition which occur in clusters, distributed sporadically throughout the inlay (a white arrow indicates one such cluster).

composition, sporadically distributed throughout the inlay (in the centre of figure 2, lower left). These spinels appear to have formed during firing.

The *granular black inlay* is composed of grains rich in aluminosilicates (possibly originally a mixture of kaolinitic and ferruginous illitic clays), together with grains of quartz in a less extensive glassy matrix (see figure 2, right). The quartz grains often have a rounded appearance like the aluminosilicates, having diffuse margins with the glassy matrix suggesting they have been partially melted. The iron compounds in the inlay probably acted as a flux. Minute (ca. 2 μm) euhedral grains of iron-rich spinels of rather variable composition occur in clusters distributed sporadically throughout the inlay, and appear to have been precipitated from the melt around nucleation centres (see figure 2, lower right). As in the *lath-rich inlays*, these clusters of spinel give the inlay its black coloration.

The *lath-rich inlay* contains more calcium than the

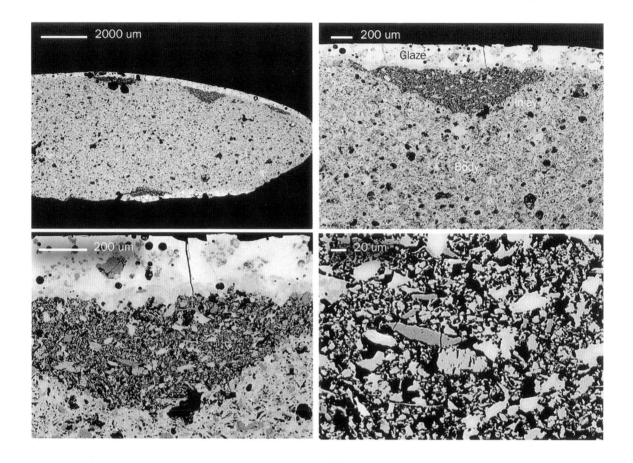

Figure 3. White inlay on punchong

Top left: SEM back-scattered electron image of white inlays (dark colour) in a cross-section of a Choson punchong ware, K95. Note the more rounded and shallower incision into the body which is filled with the white inlay. This contrasts with the sharper incision made for the white inlays in the Koryo celadons, reflecting a difference in the application of the inlay. While the Koryo celadons are incised, the Choson punchong wares are stamped or impressed with the white inlay. Again, the glaze is applied as a continuous layer over the body and inlay. *Top right*: Detail of the white inlay showing the sharp but more rounded contact with the body. The granular texture of this inlay can be discerned. *Bottom left*: Detail of the white inlay showing its granular nature. The Choson punchong ware white inlays are less compacted than those in the Koryo celadons having a more open porous texture. *Bottom right*: The granular white inlay is composed of stacks of 'books' of mullite, altered from kaolinite (medium grey), quartz (darker grains) and alkali feldspar (lighter grains).

granular black inlay (8–10 wt per cent calcium oxide compared with 1–2 wt per cent), indicating that the chemistry of the two black inlay types are different. The higher calcium content of the *lath-rich inlay* could be due to the incorporation of about 50 per cent glazing mixture.[8] However, it seems quite likely that the amalgamation of glazing mixture into the inlay was incidental and may have occurred during firing. Certainly 'seepage' of glaze into the inlay can sometimes be seen around the edges of granular black inlays in some samples, with the crystallization of calcic plagioclase laths around the margins. This interpretation, that the high calcium content of the *lath-rich inlays* is fortuitous, is perhaps supported also by the observations on the *granular black inlays*. The low calcium content (1–2 wt per cent calcium oxide) of these inlays shows that they could not have been produced by adding ilmenite and magnetite to the glaze mixture (around 15 wt per cent calcium oxide). Rather, they appear to have been formed using ferruginous clay(s), and it may be that these granular inlays reflect more closely the composition of the raw material used which would have been the same for all of the black inlays.

The inlay techniques on Choson ceramics developed into slip-painting, such that the range of techniques widened to include true inlay; slipped and incised; stamped and filled; slipped and painted with iron oxide; and slipped and left plain. An example of a white inlay on a punchong ceramic of this period has been analysed in the SEM (figure 3). The mineral grains are less densely packed together in the punchong inlay, which is not sharply cut as in the Koryo celadon but appears as a shallow impression in the surface of the body. The minerals present in the inlay, and their chemistry, indicate the selection again of an impure kaolinitic clay. Punchong wares with their inlaid designs had declined by about 1592–8, giving way to white porcelain favoured by the upper classes.

Underglaze iron decoration

The other type of decoration, found on later Koryo celadons of the fourteenth–fifteenth centuries, used an underglaze iron, made from an iron-rich slip painted onto the body, which was then covered with glaze and fired. The oxidized firings used for these pots gave a more yellowish or amber tint to the glaze, from the presence of oxidized iron, which may have been deliberately intended to yield a more harmonious appearance with an amber glaze and dark-brown slip, as against a well-reduced greenish-blue celadon with underglaze black slip, presenting a rather stark colour contrast.[9]

Kilns

About 270 kilns of the period have been located in Korea, of which 240 were in Cholla province in the south. The dense concentration of kilns in this area reflects the favourable geographical situation of ample supplies of clay and wood for fuel, as well as easy transport by sea to the Koryo capital at Kaesong. Many kilns were built on the lower slopes of the hills near the coast. The construction of Korean kilns of the Koryo period was based on Chinese kiln constructions of the 'hill-climbing type' from the late Tang and Five Dynasties periods, which required sloping ground. The long 'dragon' kiln developed in south China in the Warring States period (485–321 BC) and consisted of a short tunnel built up a low slope. The physical effect of a long, almost horizontal kiln is to force the hot combustion gases into a horizontal path, which slows the flame-speed by comparison with an updraft kiln. This slower flame-speed transfers heat more effectively to the wares, and allows higher kiln temperatures to be achieved. By allowing air into the kiln below the stoking-hole in current use, the incoming air required by the burning fuel was preheated as it passed over the cooling wares which had just been fired, further raising the efficiency of the process. A careful optimization of the firing was achieved, whereby the maximum temperature was reached with the minimum fuel and heat conserved or exchanged with the incoming air required for firing. A very fuel-efficient firing resulted. About forty kilns have been located at Sadang-ri on the lower reaches of the Yongmun river, spanning the tenth to the fourteenth centuries, but mainly dating to the twelfth and thirteenth centuries. Kiln no.7 at Sadang-ri, for example, was an official kiln producing celadon vessels for royal demand.[10] The typical slope of such kilns can be judged from another excavated at Sadang-ri, at Tangjon, built on a natural slope, rising at an angle of 5–6° towards the back. (This is considerably less than the 25°-slope used by modern Korean potters who still fire in such kilns.[11]) It had a sandy floor, with a number of chambers, each with two or three openings. Besides those at Sadang-ri, the most important kilns were those of Yuchon-ri in Puan district (see map 5, p.222), where some forty-five kilns were located.

The usual form of kiln for the celadons was constructed on a slope to exploit the rising heat of the fire, and was 5–17 m (16–55 ft) in length and about one metre (3.2 ft) in width.[12] The kiln interior was divided into several chambers by partition walls; the form is reminiscent of a split bamboo cane, by which it is often named. Kiln supports and saggars formed part of the internal furniture of the kilns. Some kilns did not have internal inbuilt divisions, but at intervals, walls of saggars were piled across the kiln width and plastered into place to subdivide the space. In present-day

Map 5.

Map showing the location of the principal celadon kiln sites of the Koryo period in Korea, including those from which reference samples have been analysed by neutron activation analysis.

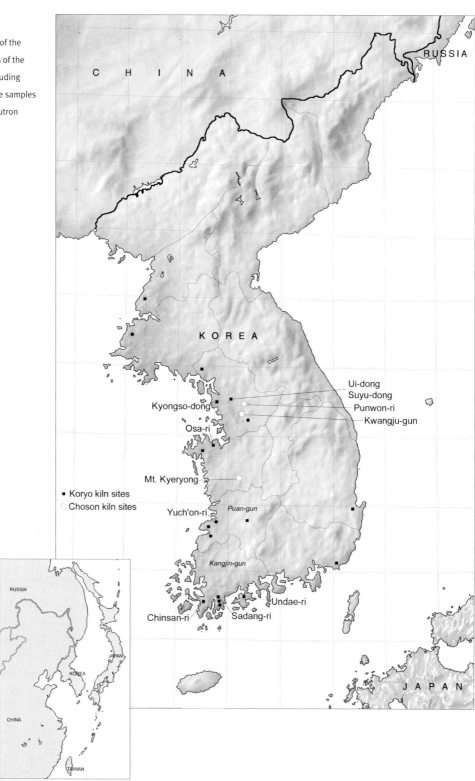

Ui-dong
Suyu-dong
Punwon-ri
Kwangju-gun

Kyongso-dong

Osa-ri

Mt. Kyeryong

■ Koryo kiln sites
○ Choson kiln sites

Yuch'on-ri

Puan-gun

Kangjin-gun

Undae-ri

Chinsan-ri

Sadang-ri

CHINA

KOREA

RUSSIA

JAPAN

RUSSIA

JAPAN

KOREA

CHINA

TAIWAN

Korea, potters construct similar kilns, with stoking holes in the top of the kiln located at intervals up its length for charging the interior with fuel.[13] The fire is started in the fire-mouth at the bottom, and gradually works its way up the slope, the incline driving the hot combustion gases upwards, heating the next part of the chamber. The system of firing is thus very efficient, with the heat of combustion lower down beginning to heat pots further up, as the zone of highest heat travels up the kiln. The holes on the top of the chamber are for adding fuel as the fire progresses. The effect of stoking with fuel is to raise one short section of kiln to temperature, and the stoking then proceeds to the next pair of holes.

The Choson period annals record 139 porcelain kilns and 185 for the production of stoneware.[14] Punchong was clearly manufactured in quantity, for use at all levels in society. Excavated punchong kilns were shown to be tunnel-like climbing kilns built of brick and sited on hillsides or man-made mounds.

In modern Korean kilns, temperatures of 1250° centigrade are obtained, though the temperature rise and fall is relatively rapid.

Origins

One of the first questions which people ask about an object in a museum collection is 'where did it come from?' In the case of Korean pottery, this becomes a question of how to attribute a celadon piece to its place of manufacture.[15] Most pieces of modern pottery, both mass-produced and those made by a studio potter, have identification marks printed or stamped into them. By contrast, very few, if any, Korean celadons bear any marks which betray their place of manufacture. Moreover, in the absence of contemporary detailed written records of exactly which styles or forms of pottery were produced where, it is not possible to use documentary evidence to suggest a place of production for a celadon piece. We are therefore left with the paradox that while large numbers of Korean celadon pieces survive in private and public collections, and numerous kiln sites are known in Korea, we cannot tie any particular piece with a high degree of certainty to its place of production.

Study of the subject has nonetheless led to a number of broad outlines emerging that the principal kiln sites for Koryo celadons were located in southwest Korea, in two main areas: the Puan area of North Cholla province and the Kangjin area in South Cholla province (see map 5, opposite). Historical studies suggest that these probably produced the bulk of the celadons now known. From there, the celadons were transported by ship to the Koryo capital at Kaesong, now just in North Korea, north of Seoul. There they were used by the royal family, aristocrats and in the all-powerful Buddhist church.

However, this still does not answer the question whether a particular celadon piece can be attributed to a specific production centre. At this point scientific methods of investigation can be exploited to provide an alternative method of solving the puzzle: if differing compositions of clay were used at different production centres, such variations could perhaps be detected by chemical analysis. At first sight, however, chemical analysis has only shown so far that the body compositions of celadons from the two major production centres are very similar for the major element constituents, because the local clays used at the two different centres are very similar in mineralogy and their methods of formation. The traditional view that the technology of production of Koryo celadons developed from the earlier Chinese Yue wares has led to research which compared the body and glaze compositions of these two groups.[16] It has become clear from this that Koryo celadons are difficult to distinguish by major-element body composition from Yue wares manufactured several hundred miles away across the South China Sea, although there are some differences in glaze composition and the body analyses show slight differences in silica, alumina and soda. The reason for the similarity lies in a sweep of geological deposits of the Upper Jurassic period which covers both southern China and much of the Korean peninsula with similar stoneware clays.

Provenance studies

At this point, the approaches encouraged by provenance studies – the aim of which is to find the source or 'provenance' of pottery – can be brought into play.

A considerable amount of research into world pottery has taken place in recent years in provenance studies, driven by the success of the method in providing answers to questions of origin.[17] In particular, the more detailed kind of chemical analysis, commonly called trace element analysis, can be applied, i.e. looking for those chemical elements which are present in the natural clay but at concentrations so small (usually in the parts per million range) as to have no effect on the physical or firing properties of the clay, and therefore not recognizable by the potter. The trace elements do, however, provide a sort of chemical 'fingerprint' of the original clay precisely because their pattern is not usually affected by anything the potter does. The trace element pattern in the finished pot thus reflects that of the original clays as dug from the ground, and all pottery manufactured from the same clay will have the same pattern. Even if it is not known exactly which clay bed was used at a particular manufactory, typical examples of the products, e.g. small broken fragments (sherds) found at the site of an ancient kiln, can be analysed and the local 'fingerprint' determined. Such trace element analysis has been carried out regularly for ancient pottery for at least forty years, and its origins go back much further to the end of the nineteenth century.[18]

The successful outcome of provenance projects usually depends on a number of factors: being able to formulate the question in scientific terms (e.g. 'is there a chemical difference in composition between pottery from sites A and B?'); having a good reference collection of pottery of known origin; using an analysis technique able to measure accurately the concentration of a range of chemical elements; there being significant differences in composition between the sources of the pottery that analysis can recognise; using a statistical procedure to interpret the results that inspires confidence and can compare in detail the analysis of test pieces against the reference pieces of known origin. Differences of opinion may exist between scholars over the place of manufacture, or sometimes only a small fragment of a whole piece may be available, and the fragment may have little or no design upon it. In addition, when fragments of celadons are dug up on excavations in other countries,

there is no way of linking the excavated pieces with known kilns. In all these cases, scientific investigation usually has something to offer. Numerous studies have shown that clay from one locality, if not always of a single composition, has at least a reasonably uniform and limited compositional range, whereas clays from different locations (towns, countries, continents) have different chemical compositions because they reflect differences in the underlying geology.

NEUTRON ACTIVATION ANALYSIS[19]

Neutron activation analysis is one of the most sensitive methods for chemical analysis ever developed, and has proved very popular for provenance studies in archaeology. It excels in sensitivity, accuracy and the wide range of elements which can be measured in a single sample. For the celadons in the British Museum's collections, we in the Museum team needed to sample the body fabric, which is, however, extremely hard in substance. After trying various methods we eventually obtained samples from the complete vessels in the Museum's collections, using small diamond-embedded abrasive wheels. These were fitted into a small, low-voltage power drill, the abrasive wheel was slowly rotated and held against an area usually on the base of the vessels where the sampling would not be visible when the objects are on display. Small amounts of the body fabric were abraded away as fine powder, which was collected for analysis. We also had a collection of sherds of celadons found in Korea at known kiln-sites. We took samples for analysis from these by cutting off a thin slice from an edge and grinding the slice into powder in a small mortar.[20]

Batches of about sixty samples for analysis, each sealed in a small pure silica tube, were irradiated with neutrons in a nuclear reactor together with six samples of a standard clay of already known chemical composition.[21] The elements in the small sample of clay become radioactive, and we are able to detect with our counting equipment the radioactivity of more than twenty-five of these elements and from these measurements work out the concentrations of those elements in each sample.

We were able to sample more than fifty of the celadons in the collections, mostly using abrasion with

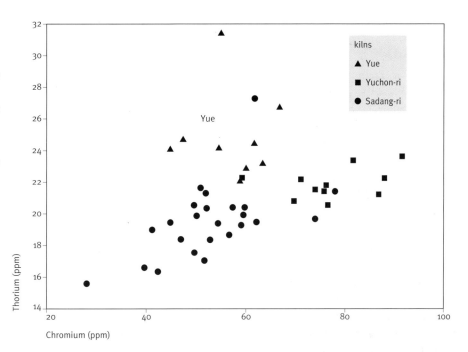

Figure 4. Scatter plot of the concentrations of the trace elements chromium and thorium in the reference sherds from the Korean celadon kilns at Sadang-ri and Yuchon-ri, and a representative selection of Chinese Yue wares. This shows that there are differences in the concentrations of the element chromium between the sherds from the two Korean kilns, and between the Korean kilns and Chinese Yue wares for another trace element, thorium.

the diamond burr on the footring of each object. Almost without exception the vessels are complete; some had been repaired with gold in the traditional manner, but even these could not safely (or aesthetically) be disassembled before sampling. We also obtained analyses on more than sixty samples of reference sherds from eight known kilns whose location in Korea is shown on map 5 (p.222), against which to compare the celadons in the collections. The samples were all of celadons with the well-known green-blue glaze except for the sherds from Kyongso-dong, which were of yellowish-green. Both plain, incised and inlaid sherds were included among the samples. No significant difference in body composition were noted among the three decorative types.

RESULTS

With few exceptions, the analyses all showed that the clays used had relatively low contents of iron (less than 2 per cent), as would be expected for stoneware clays which fire at high temperatures. The trace elements, however, did show differences between the products of different kiln sites. For example, figure 4 shows a scatter plot for the pair of trace elements chromium and thorium, where higher levels of chromium can be

observed in the Yuchon-ri celadons compared to those from Sadang-ri, with two exceptions. Other transition metals such as cobalt and zinc show the same pattern. Figure 4 also shows that apart from two Korean samples, the Yue wares have higher proportions of thorium relative to chromium than either of the Korean kiln sites.

We have used computer programs for statistics to try to match up the celadons to the reference kiln groups.[22] This is essentially an attempt to find two chemical 'fingerprints' for kiln and celadon which match for as many elements as possible. Since it was believed that the most important production centres for celadons were at Yuchon-ri and Sadang-ri, we first compared the analyses of the test pieces by discriminant analysis with the kiln material from these two places. It was possible to assign many of the pieces to these two kiln sites, as they corresponded in trace element composition to the analyses of the sherds from these kilns. When all the statistical tests had been run, out of the total of fifty-two test pieces only eleven pieces could not be assigned to a kiln group: a very satisfactory success rate.

When we examined how the assignments of the celadons in the collections decorated by different means had turned out, we found that there seemed to be no systematic differences in composition between the test pieces with different decorative techniques (plain, moulded and inlaid) assigned to the same kiln, and examples of all three decorative styles are attributed to both of the major kiln sites at Yuchon-ri and Sadang-ri. There are two bowls decorated with parrots in the Museum's collection and both are assigned to production at Sadang-ri; three kundikas and two mae-byong were also assigned there, but none to Yuchon-ri.

The three ceramics with underglaze iron were all associated by analysis with reference kiln sherds from the site at Chinsan-ri. This assignment accords very well with the discovery in 1980 of a large-scale kiln producing great quantities of underglaze iron ceramics at this site.[23] The three pieces of this type of ware in the collections appear therefore to be examples of the product of this kiln.

The three unglazed pieces in the collections, together with an early kundika in yellowish-green glaze all had compositions which placed them within the range of the reference ceramics from the kiln at Kyongso-dong, which also had a yellowish-green glaze. The association of all three unglazed pieces with a common origin seems quite significant.

From the results of the assignment of the celadons in the Museum's collections based on trace element analysis, the majority show the trace element pattern of the Sadang-ri kilns in the extreme south of Korea; a smaller proportion are assigned to the Yuchon-ri kilns in North Cholla provionce; underglaze iron objects are assigned to the kilns at Chinsan-ri in South Cholla province; and unglazed pieces to Kyongso-dong in the Seoul region.

Yue wares

Chinese Yue wares, traditionally viewed as the precursors of Korean celadons, are green-glazed stoneware celadons made in southeast China in northern Zhejiang province over a long period from the fourth to the eleventh centuries, with procedures and raw material resources consistently maintained over this time.[24] Unlike Ding and other northern Chinese stonewares, which were made from secondary clays rich in alumina, the bodies of southern Chinese Yue wares and Korean celadons are rich in quartz.

Body analyses of Yue wares for the major elements have been published by a number of authors, who have shown that they have very similar major element patterns to Korean celadons (see table 1).[25] Although Yue wares can be distinguished visually from the later Korean counterpart, we tested whether the trace element patterns of the Yue wares were distinct, given their similarity in major elements. Nine typical Yue ware sherds were analysed by neutron activation analysis and the results showed only a relatively small spread in concentrations of the major and trace elements, but there are clear chemical distinctions between them and the celadons (see figure 4).[26] The Yue wares have significantly higher concentrations of the rare earth elements, and of thorium and uranium, while the concentrations of chromium and cobalt are lower than in many of the Korean celadons. Given the enormous distance separating the clay resources of the Chinese mainland (Yue) and the Korean peninsula (celadons), it was not surprising that the raw materials can be distinguished by their trace element patterns. Perhaps it is more surprising that they are not more different. Such differences do not seem to have been noted before in the literature, although neutron activation analyses of Yue wares have been published.

Notes

1. Wood 1978, p.46; Wood 1999 gives a detailed account of Chinese glazes

2. Wood 1994, p.52; Wood 1999, p.38

3. Wood 1994, p.53

4. Vandiver 1991, p.156

5. Vandiver, Cort and Handwerker 1989; Newman 1991

6. Some recent scientific work has identified the white inlays as crushed quartz with minor amounts of clay and glass, and the black inlays as glaze materials with crystalline inclusions of quartz, anorthite and ilmenite, with magnetite as the principal colorant (Vandiver, Cort and Handwerker 1989; Vandiver 1991). Another study concluded that the white inlays were of mullite, and the black inlays of iron oxide (Hangst 1984)

7. This is consistent with Hangst's identification of mullite in the white inlays

8. As suggested by Vandiver, Cort and Handwerker 1989; Vandiver 1991

9. Wood 1994, p.56

10. Nomori 1944, p.159, quoted in Choi-Bae 1984, p.30

11. Rhodes 1968, p.34

12. Choi-Bae 1984

13. Rhodes, op.cit., pp.26–9: figs.28, 30–32

14. Whitfield (ed.) 1984, p.156

15. A more technical and detailed account of the provenance study on celadons has been published in Hughes, Matthews and Portal 1999

16. Wood 1994

17. M.J.Hughes, 1991. 'Tracing to source'. In S.Bowman (ed.), *Science and the Past*, pp.99–116. London

18. Harbottle 1976 refers to the analysis of Greek Athenian pottery for the Boston Museum of Fine Art in 1895

19. For a recent review of the general applications of this technique see Susan J.Parry, 1991. *Activation Spectrometry in Chemical Analysis*. Chichester

20. Such sampling introduced no measurable levels of contamination for the elements sought by analysis. However, this method was unsuited to complete objects

21. The reactor is at the Centre for Analytical Research in the Environment (CARE), Ascot, part of Imperial College, University of London. For a fuller description of the method of analysis used at the British Museum, see Hughes, Cowell and Hook 1991

22. We used discriminant analysis to assign the test pieces to some production centres, and then principal components and cluster analysis to make assignments for further pieces where the kiln samples were too few for discriminant analysis. These methods have been described by Shennan 1997, Baxter 1994 and Wishart 1988

23. Itoh 1991, pp.62–3

24. Medley 1980, pp.94–7; Vainker 1991, pp.68–72

25. Pollard and Hatcher 1986; Wood 1994; Wood, Freestone and Stapleton 1995

26. Nine elements have a coefficient of variation of c.±7%, a further ten c.±10%, which indicates a very consistent clay composition

References

Barnes, G., 1992. 'The development of stoneware technology in Southern Korea'. In C.M. Aikens and Song Nai Rhee (eds), *Pacific North-East Asia in Prehistory*, 197–208. Washington, DC

Baxter, M. 1994. *Exploratory Multivariate Statistics in Archaeology*. Edinburgh

Choi-Bae, Soontaek, 1984. 'Location and construction of the kilns in the Koryo period'. In Soontaek Choi-Bae (ed.), *Celadon Wares of the Koryo Period, 918–1392*, 30–37. Cologne

Choo, C.K. Koh, 1992. 'A preliminary study of traditional Korean celadons and their modern developments'. In P.B. Vandiver, J.R. Druzik, G.S. Wheeler and I.C. Freestone (eds), *Materials Issues in Art and Archaeology III*. Materials Research Society Symposium Proceedings, 267:633–8. Pittsburgh PA

Choo, C.K. Koh, 1995. 'A scientific study of traditional Korean celadons and their modern developments'. *Archaeometry*, 37/1:53–81

Gompertz, G.St.G.M., 1963. *Korean Celadon and Other Wares of the Koryo Period*. London

Gompertz, G.St.G.M., 1964. *Korean Celadon*. New York

Hangst, K, 1984. 'Results of mineralogical examination of the Koryo period celadon sherds'. In Soontaek Choi-Bae (ed.), *Celadon Wares of the Koryo Period, 918–1392*, 233–41. Cologne

Harbottle, G., 1976. 'Activation analysis in archaeology'. In G.W.A. Newton (ed.), *Radiochemistry* 3: 33–72. The Chemical Society, London

Hughes, M.J., M.R.Cowell and D.R. Hook, 1991. 'Neutron activation analysis procedure at the British Museum Research Laboratory'. In M.J. Hughes, M.R. Cowell and D.R. Hook (eds), *Neutron Activation and Plasma Emission Spectrometric Analysis in Archaeology*. British Museum Occasional Paper 82:29–46. London

Hughes, M.J., K.J. Matthews and J. Portal, 1999. 'Provenance studies of Korean celadons of the Koryo period by neutron activation analysis'. *Archaeometry*, 41/2: 287–310

Itoh, I., 1991. 'The ceramics'. In *The Radiance of Jade and the Clarity of Water: Korean Ceramics from the Ataka Collection*, exh. cat., Art Institute of Chicago:37–150. New York

Lee, C., O.C. Kwun, N.B. Kim, and I.C. Lee, 1985. 'Neutron activation analysis of Korean clays and pottery'. *Bulletin of the Korean Chemical Society*, 6/4:241–6

Lee Chul, Kang Hyung Tae and Kim Seungwon, 1988. 'Characterization of Korean porcelain sherds by neutron activation analysis'. *Bulletin of the Korean Chemical Society*, 9/4:223–31

Medley, M., 1980. *The Chinese Potter*, 2nd edn. Oxford.

Newman, R., 1991. 'A compositional and microstructural study of Korean celadon glazes of the eleventh to fifteenth centuries'. In P.B. Vandiver, J. Druzik and G.S. Wheeler (eds), *Materials Issues in Art and Archaeology II*. Materials Research Society Symposium Proceedings, 185:423–34. Pittsburgh PA

Nomori, K., 1944. *Korai toji no kenkyu* (Studies on Koryo Ceramics). Tokyo

Pollard, A.M. and H. Hatcher, 1986. 'The chemical analysis of oriental ceramic body compositions: Part 2 – Greenwares'. *Journal of Archaeological Science*, 13:261–287

Pollard, A.M. and H. Hatcher, 1994. 'The chemical analysis of oriental ceramic body compositions: Part 1 – Wares from North China'. *Archaeometry*, 36/1:41–62

Portal, J., 1997. 'Korean celadons of the Koryo dynasty'. In I.C. Freestone and D.R. Gaimster (eds), *Pottery in the Making: World Ceramic Traditions*, 98–103. London

Rhodes, D., 1968. *Kilns: Design, Construction and Operation*. London

Shennan, S., 1997. *Quantifying Archaeology*, 2nd edn. Edinburgh

Tite, M.S., G.L. Barnes and C. Doherty, 1992. 'Stoneware identification among prehistoric potteries of South Korea'. In Li Jiazhi and Chen Xianqin (eds), *Science and Technology of Ancient Ceramics 2 (ISAC 92)*, 64–9. Shanghai Research Society of Science and Technology of Ancient Ceramics

Vainker, S.J., 1991. *Chinese Pottery and Porcelain: From Prehistory to the Present*. London

Vandiver, P.B, 1991. 'The technology of Korean celadons'. In *The Radiance of Jade and the Clarity of Water: Korean Ceramics from the Ataka Collection*, exh. cat., Art Institute of Chicago:151–8. New York

Vandiver, P.B., L. Cort and C. Handwerker, 1989. 'Variations in the practice of ceramic technology in different cultures: a comparison of Korean and Chinese celadon glazes'. In M.D. Notis (ed.), *Cross-craft and Cross-cultural Interactions in Ceramics*. Ceramics and Civilization series, 4:347–88. American Ceramic Society, Columbus OH

Whitfield, R. (ed.), 1984. *Treasures from Korea: Art Through 5000 Years*, exh. cat., British Museum. London

Wishart, D., 1987. *Clustan User Manual*, 4th edn. University of St Andrews

Wood, N., 1978. *Oriental Glazes: Their Chemistry, Origins and Re-creation*. London

Wood, N., 1994. 'Technological parallels between Chinese Yue wares and Korean celadons'. *BAKS Papers,* 5:39–64

Wood, N., 1999. *Chinese Glazes*. London

Wood, N., I. Freestone and C. Stapleton, 1995. 'Some technological parallels between Chinese Yue wares and Korean Koryo celadons'. In P. Vincenzini (ed.), *The Ceramics Cultural Heritage*, 175–82. Faenza

APPENDIX 2

Korean Money

By Helen Wang

The earliest metal money found in Korea was imported Chinese knife money of the Warring States period (475–221 BC), found in the provinces of Pyong'an and Cholla, and thought to have been taken there by Chinese settlers. When the Chinese Han dynasty occupied northern Korea in 108 BC it introduced its *wuzhu* (Korean: *oshuchon*, i.e. 'five-grain') coins as the official currency. Large quantities of oshuchon have been found in tombs in the Nangnang (Lelang) region. The Koguryo and Silla kingdoms which emerged in the first centuries AD in Korea continued to use oshuchon, and did not issue new coins.

Koryo period (AD 918–1392)

Korea's first coins were issued in 996 by the kingdom of Koryo. They were copper and iron imitations of Chinese Tang-dynasty coins. The front of the coin copied the Chinese inscription *Qianyuan zhongbao*, 'heavy coin of the Qianyuan period' (Korean: *Konwon*

chungbo), and two characters, *dongguo*, meaning 'Eastern kingdom' (Korean: *Tongkuk*), referring to Koryo, were added to the back.

The first Korean coins with original inscriptions were copper coins issued by the Koryo king, Sukjong, in 1097 and 1102 (see fig. 1). The inscriptions were arranged in the same way as on contemporary Chinese Song-dynasty coins, and followed the same terminology as on Chinese coins: *tongbao*, 'circulating treasure' (Korean: *tongbo*) and *zhongbao*, 'heavy treasure' (Korean: *chungbo*). A variety of scripts was used: clerical, regular, seal and cursive scripts. The inscriptions stated that the coins were issues of Koryo:

Tongguk tongbo	'Coin of the Eastern Kingdom'
Tongguk chungbo	'Heavy coin of the Eastern Kingdom'
Haedong tongbo	'Coin of the Land East of the Sea'
Haedong chungbo	'Heavy coin of the Land East of the Sea'
Samhan tongbo	'Coin of the Three Hans', i.e. Korea
Samhan chungbo	'Heavy coin of the Three Hans', i.e. Korea

Examples of these coins have been found in Koryo tombs in Kaesong and on Kanghwa island. No further coins were made in Korea until the fifteenth century, but Chinese coins continued to be imported and provided Korea with a currency. The Sinan shipwreck found off the western coast of South Korea in 1976 contained 26,775 kg (58,905 lb) of Chinese coins, mostly dating from the Song dynasty.

Silver vases (Korean: *unbyong*) are thought to have been issued as money from 1101. Made in the shape of the territory of Koryo and incised with official seals,

Figure 1. Bronze Haedong tongbo coin, 1097–1105.

they were used for high-value transactions for over two hundred years. In 1282 a law was promulgated, fixing the exchange value of rice at 2700–3400 litres (713–898 US gal) of rice for one silver vase. In 1287 King Chungyol permitted the use of broken pieces of silver instead of heavy silver vases, and gradually the vases went out of use. Unfortunately no silver vases have survived.

In the 1390s the dwindling supply of copper and silver led the way for the preparation of Korea's first paper money. The government department which managed cotton and linen was abolished and a new government office, the Chasom Chohwago, was established and instructed to print mulberry-paper money. However, these early notes were never issued; by 1392, the Koryo dynasty was over, the Chasom Chohwago was closed down, and its printed paper money and engraving blocks were all burnt.

Choson period (1392–1910)

The first money of the Choson period was paper money, printed on mulberry paper, and known as *chohwa*. It was issued in 1401 by the Sasomso, a mint and office in charge of the hemp-cloth tax. It was not successful: in 1402 King Taejong decreed it could be used alongside hemp cloth as a means of payment, but in 1403 he suspended circulation of paper money. New mulberry-paper money was issued in 1410, this time with the reign period of the Chinese Yongle (Korean: Yongnak) emperor (1403–24) printed on it. The main function of the new notes was to pay taxes, but again they were not widely used, and had to be withdrawn in 1425. None of the early paper money has survived.

In 1423 King Sejong issued new coins with the inscription *Choson tongbo* ('coin of Choson'), written in the regular script style found on Chinese Ming-dynasty coins. The Sasomso was given responsibility for issuing the Choson tongbo coins. At first the coins circulated alongside paper money, with a theoretical exchange rate of one paper money note = one coin = 1.8 litres (63 fl oz) of rice. However, in practice, three coins were needed to purchase 1.8 litres of rice. The Choson tongbo coinage was not considered successful.

'Arrow money' or *Chon pe* was introduced in 1464 to serve both as currency and as weapons in time of emergency. In the shape of a willow leaf with a fixed arrowhead and about 5.5 cm (2.14 in) long, 'arrow money' had a four-character inscription, reading *Palbang tongbo* ('Coin of the Eight Directions'). The exchange rate was one piece of arrow money to three paper notes.

In 1625 new coins were made, again using the Choson tongbo inscription of 1423, but with a different style of calligraphy. Eight years later the government decided to issue coins with a new inscription, using Japanese copper received as tribute. The Sangpyongchong (Food Supply Stabilization Office) was given responsibility for producing the new coins, and the inscription they bore, *Sangpyong tongbo* ('coin of stabilization'), referred to the name of the office. The Sangpyong tongbo soon became the national currency, and were Korea's most popular coins, remaining in circulation until 1890. Their success led to the opening of mints at another twenty-four government offices. To identify the office of issue, the different mints added one or two Chinese characters on the back of the coins.

The weight and size of Sangpyong tongbo coins varied during the two and a half centuries (1633–1890) of their circulation. In 1679 double-weight brass Sangpyong tongbo coins were issued, with the character for the numeral 'two' placed below the hole on the reverse. In 1742 standard-size Sangpyong tongbo coins were produced again. Ten years later the Military Training Command, the Special Army Unit and the Court Guard Military Unit issued reduced-size Sangpyong tongbo coins, in order to ease the copper shortage. The 1752 coins had a single character below the hole on the reverse: the character for metal, wood, water, fire or earth, or a character from the Chinese text known as the *Thousand Character Classic*.

In 1866 the regent Taewongun ordered the Court Guard Military Unit to make bronze token coins. These large coins had the usual Sangpyong tongbo inscription on the obverse, and the reverse inscription indicated that they were worth one hundred standard-size coins, hence their name, *Tangbaekchon* ('worth 100 coins'). Although nominally carrying this value, the Tangbaekchon contained only five or six times as much metal as a single Sangpyong tongbo coin. As a result, the value of money in circulation decreased and prices rose so high that the Tangbaekchon had to be withdrawn from circulation.

In order to economize on coin production, the Korean government decided to legalize the use of Chinese coins, which had been smuggled into Korea in the 1860s. The government itself began to import Chinese coins, and allowed their use at par with Sangpyong tongbo coins. As Chinese coins had only one-third the intrinsic metal value of Korean coins, this was a way of raising revenue for a few years, until the ban on imported Chinese coins was re-implemented in 1874.

Modernization

In 1882 the Korean government, under King Kojong, began to reform Korea's coinage system. The first new coins were cast in silver in three denominations, one, two and three *chon*, and were marked with a blue enamel circle in the centre of the coin. The new coins no longer had a square hole in the centre, as on earlier 'cash' coins, but nonetheless retained a four-character inscription on the front of the coin, reading *Taedong*, meaning 'Great east', and the denomination. The Taedong silver coins circulated alongside the Sangpyong tongbo coins, but instead of stabilizing the domestic economy, as the Korean government had hoped, the superior Taedong coins flowed out of Korea or were hoarded. They were made from silver imported from China, and as the price of Chinese silver rose, production of Taedong coins became increasingly expensive and was brought to a halt in 1883.

In that year Korea and Japan signed an agreement on commercial regulations and customs duties. The Dai Ichi Ginko (First National Bank of Japan) opened at the Korean ports of Pusan and Inchon as an authorized agency dealing with customs duties. To simplify the collection of such duties, in 1884 the Bank issued customs drafts similar to modern bank drafts. These were a convenient way of making payments and were adopted for use in commercial transactions.

In 1884 a machine-minting section was set up at the central mint in Seoul. Machinery was imported from Germany and personnel were hired first from Germany and later from Japan. In 1888 new silver and bronze coins were struck at the mint, with a dragon design copied from Japanese contemporary coins. This issue was not popular in Korea. In 1892 a new Government mint (Chonhwan'guk) was established in the port of Inchon, with equipment and expertise from Japan. New issues of coins, with modified designs, were struck at the Inchon mint. The denomination for this coinage was revised with each new issue (in 1888, 1000 *mun* = 1 *warn*; in 1892, 100 *fun* = 1 *yang* and 500 fun = 1 *whan*), until the system settled in 1907 with 100 chon = 1 *won*. The 1907 issue was intended to parallel the Japanese currency system, where 100 *sen* = 1 *yen*.

At the same time as the Inchon mint was established in 1892, a new Money Exchange Office was opened to exchange old coins for new. This office also printed Treasury Department (Hojo) paper money in four denominations: fifty, twenty, ten and five yang of silver. These notes were never issued: in 1893 competition among rich Japanese for the minting rights at the Inchon mint prompted the Korean government, with help from China, to liquidate the loan owed to Japan and recover the minting rights for Korea. However, lack of funds and operational technology soon brought production to a standstill.

In 1894 the Korean government issued new regulations governing the issuance of Western-style money to establish a modern monetary system. The new money was to be used to pay taxes, salaries and wages, and was generally intended to replace the old money. Foreign money would remain valid in Korea until there were sufficient new coins in circulation, as long as it was equal to the Korean money in quality, weight and value. The silver standard was adopted, and large quantities of Japanese and Mexican silver coins flowed into Korea, where they became the main means of settling trade accounts.

When Japan adopted the gold standard in 1897, Japanese silver coins lost their value as legal tender. The Dai Ichi Ginko issued new coins stamped with the character for 'silver' for exchange with the old silver coins. Suspicious of the Japanese, the Koreans invited the Russian financial advisor, Eugeny Alexeyev, to check the circulation of the new Japanese coins. In 1898 Russia established the Russo-Korean Bank at its Legation in Seoul, and new designs were developed for coins and paper money, but before they could be issued, Alexeyev was summoned back to Russia and the Russo-Korean Bank was closed down. Japanese silver yen coins became the standard currency in Korea, despite the Currency Act of 1901 which sought to ban them from circulation.

Japan's adoption of the gold standard in 1897 also brought problems for the Dai Ichi Ginko, which handled Korean customs duties. As the Korean customs houses were still obliged to receive payment in silver coin, in 1902 the Japanese Financial Department allowed the Dai Ichi Ginko the sole right to issue unregistered drafts payable at sight. New notes were printed at the Printing Bureau of the Japanese Financial Department, and were issued in Korea at the Pusan, Mokpo, Seoul and Inchon branches of the Bank. These notes were successful at Pusan and Mokpo, but unpopular at Seoul and Inchon.

In 1902 the pro-Russian party in Korea developed a campaign to exclude the Dai Ichi Ginko money, and the Korean government banned the use of Dai Ichi Ginko notes at the ports. But the Dai Ichi Ginko had prepared sufficient reserve gold to redeem the notes on demand that the credit of the bank notes actually rose, and, contrary to the intentions of the Korean government, circulation of the notes increased everywhere except Seoul and Chinnampo. In 1903 the Korean government eventually lifted the ban on the notes, on condition that reports on the issue of Dai Ichi Ginko notes be submitted to them twice a year.

Twentieth century

The early twentieth century saw the increasing influence of Japan in Korean affairs, culminating in 1910 with the abdication of the last Choson king, bringing Korea under direct Japanese rule. Japanese coinage soon replaced the Korean coinage.

In 1904 Korea signed an agreement with Japan, and Megata, the former Director of the Taxation Bureau of the Japanese Financial Department, became Financial Advisor in Korea. Megata proposed reform of the monetary system, recommending that the Korean government should abolish the Government mint, which since 1900 had issued excessive quantities of cupro-nickel coins, should allow the Osaka mint in Japan to mint new coins; and should establish a Central Bank in Korea. The Korean government agreed, and as there was no central bank in Korea at the time, entrusted the Dai Ichi Ginko to carry out the financial and monetary changes. The Dai Ichi Ginko notes were declared legal tender, and the old cupro-nickel coins were collected in.

Korea's first central bank, the Bank of Korea, was opened on 10 November 1909. Everything that had previously been handled by the Dai Ichi Ginko (paper money, issuing rights, Treasury accounts, money adjustment, etc.) was handed over to the Bank of Korea. The Bank requested that the Printing Office of the Financial Department of Japan print its notes, but as this was not possible, it was decided that previously unissued Dai Ichi Ginko notes should be put into circulation temporarily as Bank of Korea notes. New designs and denominations were determined with the approval of the Bank of Korea, but had to be changed in 1910, when Japan annexed Korea.

In 1910 the Bank of Korea was reorganized into the Central Bank of Chosen and 29 March 1911 was renamed as the Bank of Chosen. Previous issues of Dai Ichi Ginko notes were now regarded as issues of the Bank of Chosen. The Bank's influence reached as far as Japanese annexed territory. From 1917 it took over affairs previously handled by the Yokohama Specie Bank, such as gold-note issue, National Treasury receipts and payments in Manchuria. Bank of Chosen notes circulated in the railway zones of Kwantung and Southern Manchuria, and as Japanese military aggression advanced in East Asia, the notes circulated as far afield as Manchuria, China, Siberia and Mongolia. In 1914 and 1915 the Bank of Chosen issued its own yen notes. The old notes were gradually withdrawn from circulation and had completely disappeared by 1921. A second series of Bank of Chosen notes was issued in 1935.

At the end of the Second World War in 1945, allied

Figure 2. 10,000-won note of the Bank of Korea (South Korea), 1983. The obverse of the note (seen here) portrays King Sejong the Great (reigned 1418–50) of the early Choson, with the water clock invented during his reign.

forces occupied Korea to accept the Japanese surrender, and following the Potsdam Conference later that year Korea was divided into northern and southern zones at the 38th parallel. South Korea established the Republic of Korea in August 1948. The following month North Korea set up the Democratic People's Republic of Korea. Coinage did not recommence in either the north or the south for another eleven years, although paper money remained in circulation. A new central bank, the Bank of Korea, opened in South Korea on 12 June 1950. It evolved out of the Bank of Chosen, and all previous issues of paper money were now regarded as Bank of Korea notes. American military notes were also issued in South Korea, where the US government backed Syngman Rhee.

The Korean War broke out on 25 June 1950 after the armed forces of communist North Korea attacked in the south. Under Western, notably US, pressure, the UN condemned the invasion and called for military assistance to South Korea. The North Korean army engaged in economic warfare, issuing Bank of Chosen notes in the territories it gained in South Korea and

forcing the Bank of Korea, which had moved to Taegu, to issue new 1000-won and 100-won notes to exchange for the old notes. In 1951 the Printing Office of the Japanese Government transferred the printing plates for paper money to the Government Printing Agency of Korea, in Pusan. New 1000- and 5000-won notes were issued in 1952.

A second currency reform was planned in 1953 to secure a safe foundation for finance, money circulation and industrial activities after the Korean armistice. New notes were issued between 1953 and 1959, and the Republic of Korea's first coins, in denominations of ten, fifty and one hundred *hwan*, were issued in 1959. The coins used designs featuring Korean historical subjects, such as the ironclad ships of Admiral Yi of the sixteenth century.

The third currency reform took place in June 1962, its objectives being to supply funds for economic and industrial development and to control inflation. The old hwan were banned and the new won were issued as legal tender, with a nomimal value of one-tenth of the old hwan. Old bank notes and bills of payment were ordered to be deposited with banking organizations by 17 June 1962. The following day all descriptions of hwan were changed to won and reduced in value at the ratio of 10:1, and all banknote deposits were frozen. New banknotes, printed by Thomas de la Rue in

Figure 3. Left: 50-chon coin of North Korea, 1978. Right: 100-won coin of South Korea, 1978.

England, were imported into Korea. Old notes and coins remained in circulation, though at one-tenth of their face value, until there were sufficient new ones to replace them. Hwan coins were eventually disqualified as legal tender in 1975. New intaglio printing machines were installed at the Government Printing Agency in the 1960s, and since then Korean notes have been printed in Korea. In 1966 the Bank of Korea took over responsibility for issuing coins, and made new 1-, 5- and 10-won coins.

Rapid economic development in the 1970s brought a demand for high denomination money: 5000-won notes were issued in 1972 and 10,000-won notes in 1973 (see fig. 2 for such a note issued in 1983). These were the first Korean notes to have watermarks to protect against counterfeiting. Newly designed middle denomination notes of 500 won and 1000 won were issued in 1973 and 1975 respectively. Higher denomination coins were also introduced: 1970 saw a 100-won coin, depicting King Sejong (reigned 1418–50) and 1982 a new 500-won coin, depicting a flying crane. Since the 1970s there have also been many commemorative issues in many denominations, including the 50,000-won gold coin struck to celebrate the Seoul Olympics of 1988.

North Korea issued its first coins in 1959. These were made from aluminium, and had the national wreath and star emblem on the back. They were modelled on the coins of neighbouring China, which during the Korean War had proved to be a close ally. In 1987 new 1-won and 5-won coins were issued with designs featuring the birthplace of North Korea's long-time leader, Kim Il Sung (1912–94), the Pyongyang Arch of Triumph and the Juche Tower. Since then North Korea has produced many commemorative issues in many denominations.

Coins issued in 1978 by North and South Korea are illustrated at fig. 3.

Korean coin-shaped charms

The practice of using coin-shaped charms (*pyolchon* or *pyolton*, 'special money') was borrowed from China, and from the late eighteenth to the early twentieth centuries distinctive coin-shaped charms, finely made with delicate high-relief or open-work, were produced in Korea, probably in the capital, Seoul. Reports by late nineteenth-century Western travellers in Korea indicate that it was then fashionable for women to wear coin-shaped charms attached to purses and waist-sashes. Most charms were made of brass, with a smaller number made of bronze and silver, occasion-

Figure 4. Korean chatelaine, for holding traditional keys. The coins are used as decoration, symbolizing wealth. Chatelaines were usually painted with bright enamels and decorated with textile banners and tassels.

ally coloured with red, green or blue enamel. Although round charms tended to predominate, other shapes were not uncommon. Some pieces were officially made to commemorate royal events, such as weddings and the construction of castles; others were simply designed to bring good luck. Chatelaines (*kaegumpae*), comprising large groups of coin-shaped charms, were often made for wedding gifts (fig. 4). The inscriptions and designs are usually highly symbolic, with many inscriptions referring to the traditional 'five blessings of life' (*obok*): longevity, wealth, health, virtue and natural death. The five blessings were also represented by pictorial elements: for example, the crane, deer, tortoise and pine-tree all symbolize longevity; the carp symbolizes success through endeavour; and the dragon and phoenix together symbolize a perfect marriage.

The Korean Collection in the Department of Coins and Medals, British Museum

The Department holds over 2300 Korean 'cash' coins, mainly purchased in the early 1880s, from the three important private collections of Hosea Ballou Morse (1855–1934), Customs Commissioner in China (acquired 1883); Christopher Gardner (1842–1914), HM Consul at Yichang in China (acquired 1883); and Kutsuki Masatsuna (also known as Kuchiki Ryukyo, 1750–1802), lord of Tamba in Japan (acquired 1884).

The number of Korean coins dating to the 1880s and after is much smaller, and mainly consists of pieces presented to the Museum by named individuals. The most recent coins are largely selected from the anonymous donation-boxes around the Museum.

There is also a small collection of Korean paper money: one Dai Ichi Ginko note; ten Bank of Chosen notes; twelve pre-1980 Bank of Korea notes; twelve

Bank of Korea notes from the 1980s and 1990s; and one North Korean bond of 1950. A further seven Bank of Korea notes, 1950–62, are part of the Chartered Institute of Bankers Loan, housed in the Department.

In addition to the strictly numismatic material, there are 175 Korean coin-shaped charms, six medals and six badges.

A small number of pieces are on display in the HSBC Money Gallery and the new Korean Gallery. All other pieces may be seen by appointment in the Department of Coins and Medals.

Further Reading

Bank of Korea, 1971. *Hanguk hwape chonsa* (Korean monetary history). Seoul

Bank of Korea, 1982. *Hanguk-ui hwape* (Korean money). Seoul

Kim, S., 1986. *Hanguk hwape kakyok tokgam* (A collection of Korean banknotes and coins). Seoul

Mandel, E.J., 1972. *Cast Coinage of Korea*. Racine, WI

Ramsden, H.A., 1910. *Corean Coin Charms and Amulets*. Yokohama

Starr, F., 1917. 'Corean charms and amulets, a supplement' in TKBRAS, 8: 42–79

Index

Page numbers in italics
refer to illustrations.